Queer Forster

Worlds of Desire:

The Chicago Series

on Sexuality, Gender,

and Culture

Edited by Gilbert Herdt

Edited by

Robert K. Martin and

George Piggford

Queer Forster

The University of Chicago Press

Chicago & London

For biographical notes on the volume editors and contributors, see pages 291–92.

The University of Chicago Press, Chicago 60637
The University of Chicago Press, Ltd., London
© 1997 by The University of Chicago
All rights reserved. Published 1997
Printed in the United States of America
06 05 04 03 02 01 00 99 98 97 1 2 3 4 5

ISBN: 0-226-50801-3 (cloth)
ISBN: 0-226-50802-1 (paper)

The title page illustration is a detail from Paul Cadmus's *What I Believe* (see p. xiv). Chapters 1, 5, and 6 contain unpublished material by E. M. Forster from the Forster Archive, King's College, Cambridge, © The Provost and Scholars of King's College, Cambridge. Chapters 4 and 10 were previously published; for details, see pages 87 and 215.

Library of Congress Cataloging-in-Publication Data

Queer Forster / edited by Robert K. Martin and George Piggford.
        p.   cm. — (Worlds of desire : the Chicago series on
    sexuality, gender, and culture)
        Includes bibliographical references and index.
        ISBN 0-226-50801-3 (cloth : alk. paper). —
        ISBN 0-226-50802-1 (pbk. : alk. paper)
        1. Forster, E. M. (Edward Morgan), 1879–1970—Criticism
    and interpretation.   2. Homosexuality and literature—England—
    History—20th century.   3. Gay men's writings, English—History
    and criticism.   4. Sexual orientation in literature.   5. Gay men in
    literature.   6. Desire in literature.   7. Sex in literature. I. Martin,
    Robert K., 1941–   .   II. Piggford, George.   III. Series: Worlds of
    desire.
    PR6011.058Z8335   1997
    823′.912—dc21   97-9960
                                                                 CIP

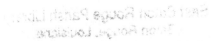

To our mothers

Contents

Preface

This book grew out of a connection that began at the 1992 New York MLA. There, over pasta and white wine, we discussed possibilities for future collaborations. *Queer Forster* represents the first substantial product of an intellectual interaction that never ceases to provoke, disturb, and challenge. We feel certain that it is but the first of many such undertakings.

Collaboration is not, of course, simply a matter of agreeing, and we have tried in putting together this volume, and especially in writing its introduction, to listen to each other's voice and to speak across gaps of experience and temperament. We have often operated with the technique we call "gremlinizing," in which each one reads the other's work with a critical eye, suggesting alterations, entering into disagreement, and testing the solidity of argument.

This technique is not meant to produce a single, unified voice or perspective. Rather, we intend the introduction of this volume to be at the very least bivocal, allowing certain conflicts or disagreements to emerge. Although we think it will remain possible to hear occasionally one voice or the other, we hope that both will be heard as traces, or that our two voices will become audible palimpsestically. We ourselves cannot always recall who first wrote any given sentence, so much has each come to be part of a tightly woven fabric. In a very real sense we each owe our greatest acknowledgment to the other. We literally could not have done it alone.

At the same time, we wish to express our gratitude to several sources of support and encouragement. In particular, we would like to thank the Social Sciences and Humanities Research Council of

Canada for material assistance. A three-year grant to Judith Scherer Herz and ourselves made possible research in Cambridge and contributed in a significant way to the preparation of this collection.

In England we benefited from the remarkable resources of the Modern Archive Centre, King's College, Cambridge. Archivist Jacqueline Cox and her assistant Elizabeth Stratton guided us deftly through the challenges of textual editing, and Jacqueline Cox in particular shared with us her close familiarity with the Forster papers. Both of them contributed to making our work a pleasure. We are also grateful to the Provost and Scholars of King's College, the Society of Authors, and Dr. Donald Parry for graciously allowing us to include unpublished Forster material in this collection.

Closer to home, we appreciate warm support throughout all stages of the editorial process offered by the talented staff of the University of Chicago Press, especially its senior editor Doug Mitchell. The readers for the Press, Richard Dellamora and Christopher Looby, offered invaluable suggestions for revisions.

The Département d'études anglaises at the Université de Montréal has offered continuing financial support. We are particularly indebted to the Chair's secretary, Michelle Braun, whose friendly demeanor and unflagging energy have made the realization of this project possible.

Above all, we thank our contributors, every one of whom has offered us new insights into Forster's texts and who have collectively made working on this project a delight.

Montreal, December 1996.
R. K. M. and G. P.

Abbreviations: Works by Forster

AE	*Albergo Emepedocle and Other Writings*
AH	*Abinger Harvest*
AN	*Aspects of the Novel*
AS	*Arctic Summer and Other Fiction*
CB	*Commonplace Book*
CT	*Collected Tales of E. M. Forster*
GLD	*Goldsworthy Lowes Dickinson*
HD	*The Hill of Devi and Other Indian Writings*
HE	*Howards End*
LJ	*The Longest Journey*
LTC	*The Life to Come and Other Stories*
M	*Maurice*
MT	*Marianne Thornton: A Domestic Biography*
PI	*A Passage to India*
RV	*A Room with a View*
SL	*Selected Letters of E. M. Forster*
TCD	*Two Cheers for Democracy*
WAFT	*Where Angels Fear to Tread*

Note on the Editions of Forster's Texts: We have used, wherever possible, the Abinger Edition of the works of E. M. Forster (published in the United Kingdom by Edward Arnold and in the United States by Holmes and Meier). At the time this book went to press, the publication of the Abinger Edition, suspended for a number of years, had recently been resumed by André Deutsch. Titles not available in the Abinger Edition are cited from the first American edition, excepting *Aspects of the Novel,* which is cited from the first British edition.

Queer Forster

Paul Cadmus, *What I Believe.*
Reproduced by permission of the D. C. Moore Gallery, New York.

1

Introduction: Queer, Forster?

Robert K. Martin and George Piggford

The title of this collection may at first appear to be something of an oxymoron. How can the editors of this volume, you may well ask, attach such an epithet to an author who is so clearly gay? Aren't these editors just trying to be trendy? Although we do not deny the trendiness of the term "queer," it is our hope to scrutinize it carefully both in this introduction, and, in more oblique ways, through the arguments presented in the twelve essays that follow it. The contributors to this volume have all been asked to use the notoriously slippery term "queer" with care and precision. But the ambiguity of the title is intentional. We intend "Queer Forster" to signify, in a range from the query "Queer? Forster?" through the assertion "Queer: Forster" and the conflation "Queer/Forster," something of a celebration: "Queer Forster!" We are, of course, aware of the nearly insurmountable difficulties in any attempt to communicate intention; thus, this range is in no way meant to exhaust the possibilities of meaning of our title.

In this introduction, we have attempted to explore the theoretical implications of juxtaposing "queer" with "Forster," which we hope will provide insights into both the current state of queer theory and the current state of Forster criticism. We do not accept wholeheartedly the arguments and assumptions either of queer theory or of previous Forster studies, but both of these bodies of work provide a basis for the readings explored in this volume. In the spirit of the best of queer criticism, we have sought to capture a polyphony of voices that can inform each other without imposing domination or closure.

1. "WHAT I BELIEVE"

E. M. Forster's "What I Believe," an essay from 1938, begins by acknowledging, just before the beginning of the Second World War, the inadequacy of liberalism. As he writes, "Tolerance, good temper and sympathy are no longer enough in a world which is rent by religious and racial persecution, in a world where ignorance rules . . ." (TCD 81). They are not enough, but they are all we have, at least for the moment. Liberalism is "crumbling" (TCD 89), but the individual remains, as a possible citizen of the republic of Love, which alone might receive three cheers (as contrasted to the two cheers which he accords democracy). The American painter Paul Cadmus, known for his nudes and for his deliberate violations of patriotism and prudery, began corresponding with Forster at around the same time that he was working on his painting "To E. M. Forster" (reproduced in Kirstein 76). This painting depicts a dressed woman reading, with a nude man sprawled beside her, and a lighthouse (echoing the Alexandrian lighthouses which lend their names to Forster's *Pharos and Pharillon*) in the background. This small work, with its emphasis on sexual difference and hope (Forster amusingly speculated that the figures were his fictional creations Margaret Schlegel and Stephen Wonham [Kirstein 80]), was followed by a large painting to which Cadmus gave the name of Forster's essay—"What I Believe" (see illustration opposite p. 1)[1]—for Forster was for him "a great influence [and] a mentor" (qtd. in Kirstein 77).

Forster presides over the left-hand side of Cadmus's "What I Believe" with his hands open in a position indicating the good sense of his credo. Draped across his chest is a sashlike yellow ribbon inscribed "Love, the Beloved Republic." In front of him is a male couple including the painter himself surrounded by his friends. The figures, all nude, around Forster and Cadmus suggest heterosexual and homosexual couplings and at least one bisexual trio. A general impression of sexual fluidity might be associated with the figures. In addition, the people who populate the left-hand side of the panel are engaged in various activities: reading (Forster's "What I Believe," of course), painting, embracing, piping (Pan-like), lounging, and building. At the extreme left of the painting three men are beginning to construct a modest house. The various activities on this side are affectionate and casual, not heroic. The opposite side of the panel is surmounted by a crumbing fortress that contrasts sharply with the domesticity and modest scale of the partially built house. Volleys of missiles are sent out from the fortress, which is presided over by a "fuhrer-like mannequin" (Kirstein 80). The bodies on the right are deformed and ugly, with exaggerated physical attributes; physical appearance records spiritual value for Cadmus. This side is a warning of what might happen "If dictators took over" (qtd in Kirstein 77), as Cadmus has explained—even the grave digger covers his face at this vision of horror that seems to owe much to Bosch-like depictions of the damned. Much of the painting's appeal comes from its celebration of the nude—predominantly male—body, as well as from its remarkable translation of the ideas of Forster, with its evocation of a lost Arcadia and its hope for a restored universal culture rendered in the lighthouse, whose beam Forster almost "touches" with his left hand. Rising from the lighthouse, the clouds seem to form a question mark, leaving open the ability of society to realize Forster's utopic vision after the cataclysm of the Second World War.

Cadmus's painting reminds us of the presentation of love throughout his work, in forms running from the lustful to the ideal. For example, the famous "The Fleet's In" from 1934 (reproduced in Kirstein 25), which appalled the Navy, shows a variety of forms of desire—not merely the streetwalkers, but the embraces between sailors themselves, and the figure of the red-tied homosexual man offering a cigarette to a sailor on the left side of the canvas. Cadmus saw in such figures a sense of freedom from inhibition that was also important to Forster's work as a grounding for a utopian vision of resistance to evil. As in many of Forster's posthumous stories, for Cadmus desire is universal, promiscuous, and real. Cadmus's work crosses the boundaries between body and soul, offering a Whitman-like restored body. Cadmus's translation of Forster's essay provides an indication of a felt need for a continuing liberalism against the threat of fascism: it is a liberalism that joins together difference, even while preserving particularity. Cadmus's paintings capture a world in which love in all its forms still retains a power to contest and perhaps even defeat tyranny.

We call attention to these paintings as a way of turning to Forster's liberal humanist project and its fortunes. It may be worth remembering that Cadmus himself has resisted the use of the term "gay" to describe his work, rejecting a term seen by queer theory as at once minoritizing and sanitizing. Instead he sees his work as "queer," by which he intends an older meaning, one nevertheless echoed in current reappropriations of the term (23).

Like Cadmus, Forster can be understood as a queer artist, as one who seeks to disrupt the economy of the normal. Although he was capable of being ironic about his mythological fictions when he ascribed them to Rickie Elliot in *The Longest Journey,* Forster placed the mythological "Story of a Panic" (1904), his first published fiction, at the head of his first collection of short stories. This story presents, in an account of cultural disorientation and sexual awakening that would recur throughout Forster's fiction, the seduction of a young English gentleman, Eustace, by a poor Italian fisher-boy, Gennaro, an incarnation of the god Pan. Early in the story, a group of English tourists experience a moment of unaccountable panic in a wood. Eustace, a member of the party, reacts much differently from the others to this experience. The moment of their panic is an epiphanic moment for Eustace, whose personality is transformed by it. He becomes wild and energetic, in stark contrast to his former enervated self. He also becomes open to the advances of Gennaro, who encourages him, Pan-like, in resisting the polite manners of the English. With Gennaro's help, Eustace disappears from their world forever; he is last seen "jumping over the parapet" (CT 37) of a garden wall. Eustace's fellow English travelers can only be mystified by his transformation and disappearance.

Cloaking this tale of sexual awakening in the well-known and domesticated myth of Pan allowed Forster to draw upon a world of desires otherwise unmentionable in an Edwardian context and to work against a sentimental generalization. The encounter with an erotic other, at once threatening and appealing, remains a constant throughout Forster's work. "The Story of a Panic" describes, or, more accurately, fails to describe, a moment that can only be recalled in terms of horror—despite Eustace's epiphany the English narrator sees only "blank, expressionless fear" (CT 11), a "brutal overmastering physical fear" (CT 12) that will echo in the Marabar Caves of *A Passage to India.*

One of the "queerest" elements of Forster's work is his insistence on the peculiarities of passion, a force that constantly works to undermine any move to a reassuring "gayness." Forster's sense of a constantly baffling eros that can strike at any moment, touching anyone, and that is not gentle and loving but powerful and disruptive prevents any easy binaristic demarcation between the "straight" Forster and the "gay" Forster. Judith Scherer Herz has observed that the surface of a "straight" novel, such as *The Longest Journey* (straight, that is, as published prior to Forster's "outing" by the posthumous publication of the "gay" novel and stories), parts to reveal a homosexual subtext (Herz, "Double" 259–63). Such a formulation may now seem a bit tame, its binaries too neatly fixed, but Herz's understanding is fundamental to seeing Forster as a queer writer of fictions that repeatedly seek to run amok, or, to use Forster's later colonial metaphor, to go native in response to a subversive call of the flesh.

"The Story of a Panic" points to two connotations of the Pan reference. On the one hand, there is the double meaning of panic (or "Pan-ic"): Eustace's apparent fear, which becomes his triumphant loss of identity in his metamorphosis, and the more conventional form felt by the proper English for whom decorum, like identity, must be maintained at any price. On the other hand, Pan points to the pan-sexuality that Eustace adopts, discovering polymorphous pleasure that can communicate at least the suggestion of bestiality, becoming in a series of transformations worthy of Woolf's *Orlando* a dog, a bat, a bird, a cloud. Forster's fiction opens out in this way, extending the possibilities of desire to disrupt. It is not a question, therefore, of asking if "The Story of a Panic" is a "gay" story—it is a story of sexual awakening and the recognition of difference, including a challenge to the boundary between the human and the animal.[2]

Anyone holding to the traditional view of Forster as sexually naive, earnest, and lacking in the playfulness that marks postmodern culture would do well to turn to "My Own Centenary" (1927), a fantasy that Forster wrote about himself, as if in *The Times* of 2027. This sketch indicates that Forster has no illusions about any easy realization of the fantastic dreams that often mark his fictions. The Turtons and Burtons of *A Passage to India* may seem like foolish remnants of a lost colonialism, but in "Centenary" Lady Turton (her rank now advanced) is to unveil the statue of Forster in Kensington Gardens (next, no doubt, to the famous statue of Peter Pan). The intention of the sculptor was "to represent him [Forster] as pursuing an ideal. Since, however, the Gardens are largely frequented by the young and their immediate supervisors, it was felt that something more whimsical would be in place, and a butterfly was substituted" (AH 62). Presumably thinking of Peter Pan and his creator J. M. Barrie, and pointing discreetly to his own dissident sexuality, Forster, in the voice of *The Times,* mischievously signals the national hero's "love of little children" (AH 62). Forster also suggests that Lady Turton, back in England, has lost her pomposity—characterizing her as "the energetic Vice-President" of the "Imperial Daisy Chain" (AH 62). Forster's text argues delightfully against heroic celebration and its assurances, revelling instead in inconsistency and an omnipresent sexuality. Above all, Forster views with horror the capacity of a culture for assimilation of difference and resistance. Seeing "Forster" as "what is best and most permanent in ourselves" (AH 63) (as the fanciful 2027 *Times* claims) is a humorous self-congratulation by which Forster depicts the misrepresentation of his own career in the context of a larger social project of silencing difference. Foster saw the possibility of his own assimilation with characteristic irony and resisted it.

If Forster seems gay because of his supposed naive idealism, his constant undercutting of such idealism should indicate that he is far too slippery to be contained within any simple category. We hope to offer a view of a Queer Forster, not to propose a new taxonomy and certainly not to proclaim a national hero, even of a Queer Nation, but to point to a spirit of contradiction, a queer way of being that resists all verities and that is aware of its own implication in the very values it seeks to explode. A Queer Forster who remains elusive, sharp-witted, and multifarious.

2. GAY TO QUEER

One Hundred Years of Homosexuality—the provocative title of David Halperin's book calls attention to the fact that, in Halperin's words, echoing and modifying Foucault's famous account of the invention of the homosexual as identity out of the sodomite as actor, "Before 1892 there was no homosexuality, only sexual inversion" (15). But if it announces a date for the invention of the homosexual, may it not also announce a date for his or her demise? Must we now add to our list of "posts"— postmodern, poststructural, postcolonial, postfeminist—posthomosexual? Are we now living *after* homosexuality? Can lesbians and gays exist after the death of the subject?[3]

The development of "queer" as a category to replace "lesbian and gay" is indeed a product of the 1990s, and its results are still under evaluation. Striking in any case is the speed with which it has been adopted, even if many observers would still doubt the extent of commitment to the new term. Could one, as more cynical observers might suggest, simply go through one's old computer files with a "Search and Replace" function, substituting "queer" wherever "gay" occurs? Of course, the relationship between lesbian and gay studies and queer theory is much more complicated than this question suggests. However, numerous scholars associated with the politics of gay liberation sometimes wish that such a simple hypertextual operation could move toward settling the seemingly never-ending debates generated by queer theory. Certainly, the distinction between the two approaches is based most interestingly not on matters of sexuality but on questions of identity and its problematization. While the theory of sexuality and desire in the 1990s has become almost uncontestedly queer, the studies have remained largely lesbian and gay, in part because lesbian and gay studies never elaborated a theory and identified instead an object of attention, while queer theory has no readily identifiable textual object of study.

The reappropriation of "queer" is fairly easy to date: most people would agree in assigning its origins to Teresa de Lauretis and her 1991 issue of *differences* on queer theory. De Lauretis gives several reasons for adopting the term, one of them a dissatisfaction, widespread among lesbians, with the term "gay" and its successors, "gay and lesbian," or even "lesbian and gay." These terms amount, even when the order is reversed, to a kind of parenthetical add-on that can do service by testifying to an inclusiveness and above all to a symmetry that do not exist. It is easy enough to see that the putatively gender-neutral "gay" was rejected as implying men only or predominantly, only to have "gay and lesbian" still imply the centrality of "gay." One must wonder, though, if "queer" will not follow the same route: after all, what inclusive term can there be that is not the product of a system of gender asymmetry? One of the premises of this study, however, is that there is a value in utilizing the term "queer" strategically, particularly in order to produce readings of the texts of an author such as Forster, traditionally identified as gay, in order to find and analyze the aporias often invisible to earlier gay readings. We are not yet ready to proclaim the advent of the age of the postqueer, although like many postmodern terms, "queer" seems to signify its demise even at its first articulation.

De Lauretis also argues against the origins of "gay and lesbian" in a model of marginality, which in the United States amounts to an ethnic or racial model. Queer theorists agree in refusing to be a voice of a marginalized other that seeks to move from the margin to the center of the page; they also join in refusing to see themselves speaking for what she calls "just another, optional 'life style'" (iii) in the context of a disabling American pluralism. Although many proponents of queer theory reject what they see as an elision of difference in lesbian and gay studies and liberation movements, they risk replicating it with a utopian vision of subversive popular culture and a harmonious world of Derridean "différence." Lee Edelman has recently attempted to counter this strain in queer theory, stating, in effect, "We Ain't Family." He asks, "Why, after all, should a movement intent on social, intellectual, and political intervention—intent, therefore, on instructing hegemonic culture in the necessity of a different understanding of difference—continue to conjure for itself the dominant dream of a common language?" ("Queer" 345). Edelman's query is meant to critique a certain form of utopian queer theory that has developed since the publication of de Lauretis's issue of *differences*.

But how can queer theory engage in a project of generalization and universalization and at the same time keep from lulling itself into the dream of a common language? If we are to believe Michael Warner, queer "rejects a minoritizing logic of toleration or simple political interest-representation in favor of a more thorough resistance to regimes of the normal" (xxvi); rather than ask to be seen as normal, the queer theorist revels in "abnormality." For Eve Kosofsky Sedgwick, queer self-understanding derives from an experience of stigmatization. This experience is limited to queers, although judging from an essay such as Sedgwick's "Queer and Now," we are *all* potentially queer. For her, "one of the things that queer can refer to [is] the open mesh of possibilities, gaps, overlaps, dissonances and resonances, lapses and excesses of meaning when the constituent elements of *anyone's* gender, of *anyone's* sexuality aren't made (or *can't be* made) to signify monolithically [first two emphases ours]" (*Tendencies* 8). Although it is easy to recognize the virtual omnipresence of stigmatization, one might ask whether one really wants to base one's sense of self on an experience of hostility. One would hasten to add that there may be homosexuals for whom stigmatization is not, or is not recognized as, a fundamental and defining experience, but the response would be just as quick—they may be homosexuals, but they are not queer.

For Sedgwick, the sense of stigmatization is "embrace[d]" by queer theory, whereas it was "repudiat[ed]" (*Tendencies* 157, n.8) by lesbian and gay studies. And at least in many accounts, the sense of stigma must be linked to a sense of empowerment, hence the queer adoration of the diva. In their "Divinity" performance piece, Michael Moon and Sedgwick—herself no mean diva—identify a powerful "interface between abjection and defiance" (*Tendencies* 218). Queer insists upon its anger without acknowledging the anger animating gay liberation politics. For anyone who lived through the gay liberation of the 1960s and 1970s, it is sometimes difficult to recognize the caricature of it critiqued by some queer theorists, whose notion of gay liberation is based on a far more assimilationist model of the 1980s.

At the same time, however, the insights of queer theory into the instability and provisionality of the homosexual subject provide a useful rethinking of the assumptions behind the gay political action of the 1960s and 1970s. Gay liberation politics celebrated the new-found rights of the ostensibly stable subject imposed upon it by a heteronormative society. According to queer theory, the oppositional model that underpinned gay politics served to reproduce a binary that disadvantaged and isolated the homosexual subject by situating it as the other of an always heterosexual self. Simultaneously, however, in a Foucaultian reversal of discourse the gay model created a new militant identity, which served in many ways as the precursor of queer militancy.

It is important in any reading of the paradigm shift from "gay" to "queer" to emphasize two of the defining features of queer, in contrast to gay: its preoccupations with discourse and with performativity. These aspects of queer theory have been most usefully articulated by Judith Butler. It becomes clear when reading a text such as Butler's *Bodies that Matter* that where gay studies focused on the relationship between lived historical experience and text,[4] queer theory is interested in the intersections between various kinds of discourses. Butler's queer theory is heavily indebted to Derridean poststructuralism and tends to view history as a function of textuality, using "citationality" as a catchword (see Butler 12–16). For Butler, "the historicity of discourse implies the way in which history is constitutive of discourse itself. It is not simply that discourses are located *in* histories, but that they have their own constitutive historical character" (282). In earlier gay criticism, history was assumed to be a category separate from discourse, but Butler's concept of historicity suggests that critics have access to discourse only and that history is a function of discourse. Queer theory is interested not in the body qua body, but in reading the "body" in ways that make interpretable its constituent possibilities, gaps, overlaps, dissonances, resonances, etc.

This emphasis closely relates the discursive to what Butler identifies as the performative: "If the power of discourse to produce that which it names is linked with the question of performativity, then the performative is one of the domains in which power acts *as* discourse" (225). The performative, through citational repetition in discourse, produces—or materializes—the "body" as a category that asserts an illusory naturalness. Traditional accounts of the body have asserted its importance as a privileged site on which one reads the gendered and the sexual. In gay criticism, the relationship between the body and its sexual identity could be viewed as uncomplicated and even self-evident and thereby take as its task the discovery of a presumed "true" self concealed by convention or repression. By examining the body as the product of repetitive discursive practices, Butler undermines its presumed unity and troubles the relationship between the discourses of biology and of psychology. Butler's emphasis on the abjected subject points to a fundamentally Kristevan psychoanalytic model, in contrast to Sedgwick's more social model of stigmatization. For Butler, the focus of queer theory becomes an attack on the unified subject and the epistemology of the hermetic body because that subject and its body have been produced through the operations of heteronormative power structures. Such structures seek to marginalize those whose desires run counter to supposed "natural"—but actually naturalized—impulses. By exposing the constructedness of the body, Butler attempts to undermine the forces which regulate it.

This study, although it does not accept the arguments and conclusions of queer theorists unreservedly, does, like them, seek to examine the theoretical and critical forces that produce the illusion of a stable category—the author—in ways that privilege the normative over the disruptive. By reading Forster as a synecdoche for just such a struggle over meaning, we hope to examine the impact of queer theory on a "gay" author. How might we read Forster differently in light of queer theory? What is the effect of a reading process that challenges stable categories on an author who has been seen as, among other things, a gay hero? While it is important to acknowledge the idealism of much gay criticism of the 1970s in the construction of a positive and heroic Forster, at the same time it is prudent to guard against a simple inversion of that figure by a process of debunking and exposing. We hope therefore to read the critical construction of Forster genealogically in the Nietzschean sense, to examine closely the links in the "sign chain" which have produced "E. M. Forster" in the literary institution.[5] Finally, we aim to challenge various understandings of Forster that are unaware of their positionality in a history of readings of Forster and desire.

3. A QUEER LIFE?

Although much poststructuralist theory has celebrated the death of the author, the two French theorists most directly concerned with the articulation of the author's demise devote considerable attention to both biography and autobiography. Both Roland Barthes and Michel Foucault are also, not coincidentally, the two most influential French theorists of sexuality. Even though we recognize that an author's life is an *account* of a life, and hence always already textualized, we are inspired by the example of Barthes's own autobiography, which asks to be read as a novel. Following Barthes's lead, we aim in this section to find in the narratives of Forster's life moments that, if textual, are nonetheless crucial for an understanding of sexuality and desire in his writing.

Edward Morgan Forster was born in 1879 into a middle-class English family. His father, a scion of the liberal, evangelical Clapham Sect, died when Forster was an infant. He was brought up mainly by his mother and a number of aunts. His overprotective mother remained a strong influence on him until her death in 1945. The other significant maternal figure in Forster's childhood was his great-aunt Marianne Thornton, who upon her death left him a legacy that enabled him to enjoy a moderate income and to attend Cambridge University. Forster, surrounded in his youth almost exclusively by women, was from a very early age sexually attracted to a succession of garden boys in his family's employ. The most intense of these relationships was with a boy named Ansell (who would lend his name to two very different characters in Forster's fiction): the transgressive nature of their friendship must have been clear to Forster when his mother suddenly and without explanation dismissed the boy of whom young Morgan was so fond. The fact that Forster's mother planned an April 1895 holiday in Normandy for the young Morgan and herself also suggests the hasty actions of a mother anxious about her son's improper desires. They crossed the channel just days after the scandal of the first Wilde trial had burst onto the headlines of the British papers, as Nicola Beauman has pointed out (69–70).

After Forster's repressive home life under the watchful eyes of his mother, and after miserable years at preparatory and public school where he was bullied and ostracized by many of the other boys, Cambridge, which Forster attended from 1897–1901, came as a revelation for him. He was elected to the Apostles, a secret society that included many "minorities" (as Forster called homosexuals) and that fostered free and explicit discussion of controversial topics, including sexuality. Until the end of his life, Forster remained loyal to many of his fellow Apostles, a number of whom became closely associated with the Bloomsbury Group. Cambridge, too, played an important continuing role, providing him with a permanent home beginning in 1946.

At Cambridge Forster became involved in a romantic friendship with a fellow undergraduate, Hugh Meredith, the model for Clive Durham in *Maurice*. Although the two men were very close, the physical element of the relationship was confined to passionate kisses. Forster believed during this period that his sexual identity, his status as what he termed a "minority" (qtd. in Furbank, *Life* 1:111) was an essential aspect of his personality even though he had not yet consummated his desire for other men. Long before his first "full physical" sexual experience, which occurred on an Alexandrian beach in 1916 (Furbank, *Life* 2:35), Forster notes in a diary entry dated 1904 that he had better "make copy out of" his "minority" status, then writes, "I too have sweet waters though I shall never drink them. So I can understand the draughts of others, though they will not understand my abstinence" (qtd. in Heine xxxix).[6] The lack of actual sexual relations does not reflect a lack of passionate desire on Forster's part. For example, his later attraction to Indian men was prompted by a long romantic friendship with Syed Ross Masood, whom Forster met in 1906. Although later in life Forster realized his desires with various partners, all of whom were male, his writing suggests that sexual activity is irrelevant to his status as a "minority."

It would seem difficult to apply the universalizing discourse of queer theory to a self-proclaimed minority, but in accounts of Forster's life and in his own writings one can find numerous examples of queer desire. Forster was aware of the constructedness of his own sexual identity at the same time that he accepted fairly uncritically the biologizing and naturalizing assertions of sexologists such as Havelock Ellis. Understandably rife with sexual inhibitions in the aftermath of the Wilde trials, Forster was in the prewar period hesitant to explore physically his sexual desires. Therefore, his understanding of sexuality came mainly from books. A reading list dated 1907 suggests a variety of sexual discourses influenced Forster's understanding of homosexuality: "Sturge Moore, A. E. Housman, Symonds, Pater, Shakespeare, Beddoes, Walt Whitman, E. Carpenter, Samuel Butler, Fitzgerald, Marlowe" (qtd. in Furbank, *Life* 1:159; see also Martin, "Edward" 45, n. 8). His understanding of desire most likely developed from his reading of such disparate texts, whose accounts of illicit desire provide both overlapping and competing notions of what Forster called "minority." Forster was keenly aware, therefore, of the plurality of ways of discussing desires with which he believed he had some affinity.

Forster's sexual desires can be queered or complicated by emphasizing his desire for men of other classes and of other ethnicities and races and by examining Forster's sadomasochistic tendencies. These irregular desires are inscribed in the early novels and short stories. In his first published novel, *Where Angels Fear to Tread,* the object of desire for three middle-class English characters—Lilia Herriton, Caroline Abbott, and Philip Herriton—is an Italian dentist's son, Gino. Gino's relationships with Lilia and Philip are both sexually charged and intermittently violent. Even an ostensibly "heterosexual" text such as *A Room with a View* sees sexuality as a potentially destabilizing force that undermines class and convention. Forster wrote his first five novels as, in effect, a "virgin" who had never proceeded beyond kisses and hugs. Forster had encountered sexuality mainly through texts, whose views of desire contributed to the complex treatment of sexual relations in Forster's prewar fiction.

Forster's first important sexual relationship was with an Alexandrian tram conductor, Mohammed el Adl. Forster spent World War I as a Red Cross official in Alexandria; for him, as for other homosexual men of his generation, the perceived "Orient" provided a space for alternate sexualities, thereby continuing Forster's attraction to the "South" as expressed in the Italian novels but with the added complications of race and colonialism. The Greek poet Constantine Cavafy became Forster's intellectual guide to the multiple nationalities of the city and to the poetic celebration of male beauty. Forster was attached to el Adl and his memory for the rest of his life; Forster's idealization of their relationship is evident from his correspondence and from the unpublished Cavafy-like poems "To See a Sinadino Again" (1924) and "That the Mere Glimpse" (1920s), which ends "Of course I have other men; /But it is only you I love."

Although Forster had first visited India as a tourist in 1912–13, his experiences in Alexandria in many ways prepared him for a second trip to India to accept a temporary position as the private secretary to the Maharajah of Dewas State Senior in 1921–22. His position in a native court made his implication in the colonial project inescapably clear, even as he employed his satirical wit at the expense of the colonial establishment in a number of letters home and eventually in *A Passage to India*. As a white Briton, Forster could not establish the kind of democratic relations he sought, or claimed he sought: he was inevitably implicated in colonial power and guilt. An important testament to these conflicting impulses may be found in his "Kanaya" manuscript, an omitted chapter from his Indian memoir *The Hill of Devi*. In it, he describes a sexual relationship that developed between him and his Indian barber at the Maharajah's court. Forster had apparently not realized the social difficulties of such a relationship for both him and the barber. When the barber, Kanaya, attempted to blackmail Forster, Forster was forced to acknowledge the mere "carnality" (HD 323) of the relationship and to recognize his own "desire to inflict pain" (HD 324). Such an account both testifies to Forster's inevitable complicity in the erotics of power and invites a new and less moralistic (a queerer?) reading of Forster's work that can take account of a sadomasochism that has frequently been silenced or condemned. Forster's well-known avowal, "I want to love a strong young man of the lower classes and be loved by him and even hurt by him. That is my ticket" (Beauman 302), has been read in terms of class but rarely explored in terms of the eroticism of pain.[7]

Forster's most significant relationship, which began in 1930 and lasted until Forster's death, was with a working-class Englishman, Bob Buckingham. Forster quickly grew very attached to Buckingham, a London policeman, who came to know well Forster's circle of literary, homosexual friends, a number of whom (Christopher Isherwood, J. R. Ackerley) also had working class partners. The relationship was complicated by Buckingham's marriage in 1932, but after a few painful months Forster, Buckingham, and his new wife May settled into a situation of "domestic intimacy" (Beauman 351), a queer triangle with Bob at its apex. The Buckinghams' son was even named Morgan in honor of Forster, his godfather, while Buckingham frequently accompanied Forster on his travels. May Buckingham and Forster developed a close friendship of mutual trust and affection. Relationships such as Forster's with the Buckinghams, whatever the role played by physical sex, indicate a range of sexual and emotional possibilities—at least for the men—that can be seen as part of a queer identity but would have been mysterious to earlier gay critics drawing on a model of exclusive homosexuality. In this way, the Buckingham ménage puts into question essentialist, binarized paradigms of sexual identity. Not surprisingly, when Forster suffered the last of his strokes in his rooms at Cambridge (in 1970), he was brought to the Buckinghams' home, where he died; his ashes were strewn on May's rose bushes.

Forster's recent sympathetic critics have on occasion overlooked the complications of his sexual relationships, perhaps fearing that their revelation might harm Forster's reputation. The homophobic response to the publication of *Maurice,* which came close to eliminating Forster from the canon of British modernism, indicates that they were not completely wrong in their fears. Although Forster's early critics did not have access to these putatively incriminating texts, which Forster showed only to a small number of close friends, there were many textual hints in the published works that pointed the way to the exploration of such questions. Prior to Forster's death in 1970, critics who often benefited from Forster's assistance in their research were understandably unwilling to write in a way that might have seemed to betray his confidence. Furthermore, until 1967 homosexuality was criminalized in British law, a fact that rendered frank discussion of that aspect of Forster's work virtually impossible.

4. FORSTER'S "BENT" AND THE EARLY CRITICS

As queer theory has taught us, homophobia may precede homosexuality, much as anti-Semitism can exist without Jews. This apparent reversal of chronological order, difficult to grasp in a gay model that rests upon identities, makes sense in a more generalized, queer idea of alterity and abjection. In the homophobic regime, one need not prove a charge of homosexuality but merely suggest a defining difference—and if possible link that difference with sexuality and gender.

Thus, it is in studies of E. M. Forster that, long before his death, he could be attacked in a veiled homophobic manner, while more favorably inclined critics felt compelled to be silent. One of the most striking examples of such an attack can be found in F. R. Leavis's 1938 review of Rose Macaulay's *The Writings of E. M. Forster*. Leavis knows, of course, that Forster is homosexual, but propriety (and the libel laws) prohibits his saying so. He also knows, or seems to believe that he knows, that Forster's work is diminished by his sexuality—that although Foster shows a "real and very fine distinction," this distinction is "oddly limited." We might understand this "odd" limitation (we insist on Leavis's pregnant word) if we had "biographical information" (34); although we want to avoid "prying" (34), we may look at the milieu, namely the scorned Bloomsbury Group, whose sexuality made D. H. Lawrence, Leavis's measure of man, think with repulsion of dung beetles. For Leavis, Forster's problem is being caught between Jane Austen and Lawrence (a queer site?), from which it is but the slightest *glissando* to being caught between sexes.

That this is indeed the tenor of Leavis's remarks may be seen clearly in his next paragraphs and their insistent use of two terms—"bent" and "spinsterly" (35). Let us begin with the second of these, as the more obvious. Forster has, according to Leavis, "a characteristic spinsterly touch" and "a rather spinsterly poise" (35). Quite how one might measure this *écriture de vielle fille* is not certain, but the implication at least is that Leavis is speaking of matters of style. That pretense is soon abandoned, however, as Leavis shifts to "a *curious* spinsterish *inadequacy* in the immediate presentation of love [emphases ours]" (35). The "curious . . . inadequacy" is in fact directly the product of the spinster, male or female, a sexlessness that Leavis argues is at odds with a belief in "emotional vitality" (35). One of the proofs of this inadequacy is that "serious love between the sexes doesn't come in" to *Where Angels Fear to Tread,* a telling phrase that amounts to a tautology, since in the world of Leavis all "serious" love is perforce "between the sexes" (35).

Leavis's other key word is "bent," and in using it he comes closer to displaying his hand, and his homophobia. The word is used four times in two paragraphs. Leavis begins by discussing a "bent of interest" (35), in which the mythological world of Pan and the passionate world of Italy are joined. The phrase is slightly unusual, but it does point to an interesting continuity in Forster's work. In the following sentence, however, we are back at the beginning of Leavis's argument, for Forster now displays "a bent that plays an essential part in the novelist's peculiar distinction" (35). If Leavis does not define the precise terms of the "bent," it is because he does not need to, since a man who writes in a "spinsterly" manner can also easily be said to be bent, as well as to have a bent. Leavis can assume that many of his readers will catch the significance of the term, while for others it will remain coded and hence invisible, even while its work is being done. Forster displays "what may be called for the moment the Lawrencian bent" (35), and that bent comes, in an interestingly contradictory manner, from being at once too much *like* Lawrence (presumably in the depiction of passion and violence between men) and too much *unlike* Lawrence, that is, too much like Jane Austen, the paradigmatic spinster.

In this world, which speaks volumes about Forster's fictional silence after *A Passage to India,* gender is largely a matter of size, which means importance. Forster's writing is "only too unmistakably minor," an insignificance that is displayed when he is measured against "a master [Henry James] whose depiction of human behavior is not marginal and whose knowledge of passion is profound" (36). James is "complex," while Forster is stigmatized as a writer of "surprising immaturity" (36). It is not that there is no justification for such comments. As we have already noted, Forster did write of sexual relations that he had not experienced, but that does not, of course, suggest that they had not been desired or imagined. Leavis's attack on Forster, accompanied by a repeated claim of admiration, suggests the context in which Forster would be read until the 1960s, as a largely forgotten minor writer of charming stories and fictions that are oddly cut off from the human (read heterosexual).

Only a few years after Leavis, in 1943, Lionel Trilling published *E. M. Forster,* an important study that in part answers Leavis by dealing with Forster as a serious thinker, insisting on "the cogency of his mind" (3). Trilling places Forster in a liberal tradition, but slightly askew to that tradition. Liberalism, as defined by Trilling, is based on a good/ bad binary that requires oppositional thinking. Forster's playfulness and willingness to critique institutions, as well as his characteristic ironic mode, make him resist such simplistic assumptions: he will "play the old intellectual game of antagonistic principles," but "only to mock it" (9). What this means in concrete terms is that Forster can create a symbolic man like Gino in *Angels* to embody the "pagan spirit," but he never loses sight of Gino's other characteristics, that he is "coarse, dull, vain," etc. (9). While Trilling does not comment directly on homosexuality, he is aware of Gino's "passionate nature" that can "overwhelm the reason" (53) of the text's male protagonist Philip, who is attracted both to Gino's physical beauty and to his cruelty.

Although Trilling establishes Forster's American reputation for the following decades, and although he usefully demonstrates the contradictory spirit in Forster that generally prevents him from being sententious, he too is subject to a kind of liberal utopianism that will come to haunt Forster's reputation and obscure his ironies. Trilling's concluding sentence to his chapter on *A Passage to India,* "Forster's book is not about India alone; it is about all of human life" (121), would echo through later academic criticism and become responsible for a number of well-meaning generalizations that dangerously obscure the very precision of Forster's observations and the sophisticated political analysis that underlies them and that totally efface any nuanced treatment of sexuality.

Trilling has no hesitation in proclaiming *Howards End* as Forster's masterpiece, but Wilfred Stone, writing in 1966, sees it as a failure— Forster "has become the partisan of much that is sick and corrupt" (*Cave* 266). Stone's is an important study that anticipates the best of later Forster criticism, but it is also limited in its perspective, in large part by a hostile vocabulary that hints at illness and sterility. Judging Forster harshly, particularly in *Howards End,* Stone sees a promise of "decadence and brutality," with, instead of connection, only "a lonely and circular futility." These outbursts seem to have been prompted by the novel's conclusion: for Stone Forster "does not want sex, but only the heir" (*Cave* 266). Forster's critique of heterosexuality is thus transformed by Stone into a charge of sterility, by the logic that an absence of heterosexuality means no sexuality and that love can only be expressed sexually.

Elsewhere in *The Cave and the Mountain* Stone is more measured. He is one of the first critics actually to describe some of Forster's characters in terms of homosexuality (Frederick Crews in *The Perils of Humanism* simply raises the question as a possible explanation of Beebe in *A Room with a View* [see Crews 85, n. 7]). Stone finds *Room* the only novel in which "the problem of continuance . . . is met in a straightforward sexual way" (232)—despite the homoerotic scenes, the plot of *Room* remains heterosexual. In the other novels, Philip (in *Angels*) displays a "weak and unfocussed homosexuality" (182), while Rickie *(Longest Journey)* shows "latent homosexuality" (193). Most important is Stone's association of homosexuality with Forster's liberalism. He comes as close to acknowledging the roots of Forster's politics in his sexuality as he can when writing about a living author. Astutely drawing on Forster's 1938 review of a Wilde biography, Stone claims that Forster's sense of an alteration in public opinion since the Wilde trial indicates a concern "far more important to Forster" (354) than his cautious comments on changes in social attitudes suggest. As Stone puts it, Forster "has always sympathized with this alienated minority [homosexuals]," and "his liberalism [hatred of racism and militarism] is inseparable from these facts" (354). In other words, Forster's sense of his own stigmatization provides metonymically for an identification with other oppressions; what we might now call his queerness can in this way become the occasion for a political awareness of the need to envision a utopia of différance. Stone could not have gone further when he was writing in 1965 with Forster's assistance.

5. CRITICISM SINCE 1970

Forster's death in 1970 and the subsequent publication of *Maurice* and *The Life to Come* opened the floodgates for critical studies incorporating his sexual themes.[8] In the context of the overwhelmingly homophobic response to the publication of these texts (see Gardner 433–74), many gay critics felt compelled to write positive assessments of Forster's work and to argue for the validity of his homosexual themes. Forster's death coincided with the gay liberation movement, which sought a language of freedom that it believed it could find in Forster's work. Claude Summers's comprehensive and thorough study of Forster, entitled *E. M. Forster,* although published in 1983, may stand as a representative of much gay-affirmative criticism of the 1970s. Forster is, first of all, "an incisive interpreter of the human heart" (1)—not, it should be noted, of a heart of a particular class or nationality or sexual practice, but of all that is "human." Such universalizing, which has its origin in a desire to put in context the marginalization of gay men, characterizes the work throughout. *Angels* is "a serious study of salvation" (27), while *The Longest Journey* is defined "as nothing less than a search for meaning in life" (53). Taking issue with hostile readings of *Maurice,* Summers argues that the novel is "not an expression of wish-fulfilling fantasy but rather . . . a realistic depiction . . . of his hero's gradual awakening to—and ultimate salvation by—the holiness of direct desire" (143). It is easy to understand Summers's resistance to the term "fantasy," although friendly critics such as Kathleen Grant find it appropriate (see Grant 191–203), but it seems a mistake to insist on the novel's realism (the realistic is always tenuous in Forster) and an even greater mistake to fall into the language of romantic religion. Although Forster invests the conclusion of *Maurice* with much more than his usual tempered optimism, it is clear why later queer critics would be troubled by the transcendentalizing and romanticizing that all too often accompanied the first wave of gay studies.

As Robert Martin has shown in his "Edward Carpenter and the Double Structure of *Maurice*" (1983), the novel's debate over sexual identity is a conflict between two discourses of the homosexual, both located in a particular time and place. These two discourses are identified with two important late nineteenth-century sexual theorists, John Addington Symonds and Edward Carpenter. The first of these is associated with an elitist idealism[9] and the second with radical socialism and feminism. Thus, for Martin the novel is not, as it was often taken to be, a plea for homosexuality, but rather a dramatized conflict between competing models of same-sex desire. Martin's approach attempts to counter a view that sees *Maurice* as radically different from Forster's other—putatively heterosexual—fictions. In another important essay, "The Double Nature of Forster's Fiction" (1978), Herz, by tracing the existence of what she terms a "homosexual subtext" in Forster's early novels, makes it impossible for critics to praise the virtues of the ostensibly straight novels while demeaning *Maurice* and the posthumous short fiction. For Herz, there are not two Forsters, but only one, whose voice is modulated by the conditions of discourse. Summers takes a similar position, arguing that "the division of Forster's canon into homosexual and heterosexual works is . . . insidious" (*Forster* 141).

Alongside the gay-positive readings of Summers, Martin, and Herz, there developed in the 1970s and 1980s a body of hostile commentary, particularly focused on the publication of *Maurice* and *The Life to Come*. Perhaps the most hostile work is Jeffrey Meyers's *Homosexuality and Literature 1890–1930* (1977), which covers *A Room with a View* as well as the two posthumous volumes. Meyers maintains some of the clichés about Forster; for instance, he echoes Leavis and goes him one further by seeing a "spinsterish and effete quality" (96) in the novels. Meyers's section on *Maurice* begins with a homophobic joke, as he refers to "a different kind of pastoral penetration" (99). It is downhill from there on. The representation of love is "hysterical" ("lyrical" might do as a less charged term), "there are no interesting characters" (100–101), the bad drains in Clive's *mother's* house are an "anal symbol" (100), Maurice is attracted to a lower-class lover "with whom sex replaces shit" (104), and so on. The stories are just as bad in Meyers's view—they are "puerile, pathetic, sentimental, and thoroughly unimaginative" (108), "trivial and . . . indecent" (113), since they are unable to "transcend the purely personal" and be "transfigured into a literary masterpiece" (113).

For Barbara Rosecrance, "Forster cannot overcome his ambivalence about the homosexual condition," produced by the "fact" that homosexuals can "never achieve . . . wholeness" (153). Despite the frankness of that admission of prejudice (although "wholeness" is exactly the kind of category rejected by queer theory), Rosecrance couches her argument in aesthetic terms. Whereas the other heterosexual novels show "depth" and "complexity," *Maurice* is "univocal" (152). Even if one grants some truth to that, Rosecrance's readings of the novel do not inspire confidence. For her, Alec Scudder "is an opportunist who exploits the class system for his advantage" (152), while Clive shows "wisdom and moral ascendancy over the grosser Maurice" (165) by refusing to consummate his relationship with Maurice. Rosecrance seems to have been inspired partly by Cynthia Ozick, who greeted *Maurice* with an essay that argues that the novel is a "*fairy* tale [emphasis ours; pun no doubt intended]" (82), a term which she borrowed for her subtitle when she reprinted the essay. Further, providing no evidence, she argues that Forster thinks that homosexuality is "wrong: naturally wrong" (84).

These attacks from cultural conservatives were matched by those from the left. British gay activists Andrew Hodges and David Hutter published a pamphlet entitled "With Downcast Gays" accusing Forster of "homosexual self-oppression" and naming him "Closet Queen of the Century" (20). According to Hodges and Hutter, Forster "betrayed other gay people by posing as a heterosexual and thus identifying with our oppressors" (21). They make no distinction between "posing as a heterosexual" and what might be thought of as the open secret that Forster's sexuality had become by the 1960s. Neither do they explain Forster's unwillingness to "out" himself after the decriminalization of homosexuality in 1967 in relation to Forster's state of health by this time: the public attention it would have drawn to Forster might literally have been fatal for a man who had already suffered a number of strokes. Forster did display a sense of solidarity with future gay or queer readers, at least, by preparing *Maurice* and *The Life to Come* for publication and by preserving his diaries and papers for the future. As in the cases of his defense of Radclyffe Hall's *The Well of Loneliness* and D. H. Lawrence's

Lady Chatterley's Lover, Forster preferred an argument about the right to publish and read to a (dubious) claim that makes any positive treatment of homosexuality a good book. The writers attribute Forster's reluctance to "come out" to his unwillingness to endanger what they term his "privileged status," as he "relaxed into the undemanding security of a life fellowship at King's College" (19). Their close association of Forster with Cambridge—even though he only went there to live in his late 60s as an honorary fellow—is part of a class-biased reading of Forster that places him firmly in a privileged literary elite symbolized by Cambridge itself. Association with the University does suggest male privilege, but it also might be linked with homosexual betrayal of the nation, as in the Burgess/MacLean spy scandal of the 1950s.

Forster's suspicion of nationalism takes on a new pertinence in the light of postcolonial studies. The concern with postcolonialism in the 1970s and after has made *A Passage to India* a privileged text, with Forster portrayed variously as a colonial exploiter and as a staunch opponent of British imperial rule. For Benita Parry, *Passage* is the "epitaph" to "liberal-humanism" ("Epitaph" 140), but it is also for her "a humanist's repudiation of "symbolic concord" ("Epitaph" 139). In a later essay she holds that *Passage's* "realis[m] . . . act[s] to legitimate the authorised categories of the English bourgeois world" ("Politics" 28–29). Despite the view that Forster employs a realism that is necessarily politically conservative, other critics have questioned Forster's commitment to a realism that is frequently interrupted. For example, Gillian Beer argues that *Passage* is "a book *about* gaps, fissures, absences, and exclusions" (45), the very qualities that realism is supposed to avoid.

Although some feminist readers have seen the putative attempted rape as a sign of misogyny, recent *Passage* criticism, such as Brenda Silver's, has seen Aziz, for example, as a product of both feminization and colonization. Sara Suleri locates *Passage* "on the cusp between colonial and postcolonial narrative" (144). Her view is close to Mary Louise Pratt's depiction of the "anticonquest" text that seeks to undercut but finds it cannot speak except from its privileged position at once outside and within. Pratt sees in the anticonquest genre a strategy that could be employed by European bourgeois subjects to "secure their innocence in the same moment as they assert European hegemony" (7). Other critics have argued less sympathetically, in Tony Davies's terms, that "the bond between the widower Aziz and the bachelor Fielding is grounded in a 'homosocial' solidarity" ("Introduction" 17). Such a view allows for a reading that locates male-male desire at the core of the novel but makes that desire dependent upon the subordination of women. For Davies, the friendship plot diverts attention from the novel's political themes, substituting a romantic politics in which interracial affection is posited as capable of eliminating injustice and brutality. Parminder Bakshi locates the novel in "the tradition of homosexual Orientalism" (32). For her, India is not a nation or even a place so much as an Other to England, serving to reflect back on an English need for, among other things, a freer sexuality. Thus one can assert that Forster's disruptive attitude toward the Empire cannot be replicated in the Indian context: he must always speak as a colonizer. His self-perceived homosexual identity nuances, but probably cannot eliminate, his relationship to dominant structures of power, however much he might imagine a subversive role for male friendship across racial lines.

Recent critics, influenced both by postcolonial analyses and by the poststructuralism of queer theory, read against the grain in order to bring into focus a text's contradictions, exceptions, inconsistencies. In the case of Forster, this desire to reveal the gaps in the text coincides with a rejection of an idealized portrait of Forster the liberal. Forster may *seem* to praise a classless sexuality, but a second look may reveal a different Forster, less ideal, more the product of his culture and its blindnesses. As Christopher Lane puts it in *The Ruling Passion,* "Forster's short stories are suffused by sexual indeterminacy and colonial ambivalence, not class harmony and inter-racial romance" (146). For Joseph Bristow in *Effeminate England,* Forster's contestation of "imperialist masculinity . . . is exceptionally conflicted" (56). Such readings usefully recall the emphasis too often placed on Forster's idealism and the omissions it requires. At the same time, Forster seems to us to be less naive about his own inconsistencies—his queerness—than has been suggested in these readings. Forster usually escapes from any threat of pomposity through a consistent use of irony that can be directed against himself as well as against others. As seen, for example, in an essay such as "My Wood" (AH 22–26)—with its recognition that Forster is caught up in a system of capitalist appropriation even in moments of apparent idealism—the Forsterian ironic mode is in many ways a self-critical mode.

6. QUEER FORSTER

The essays gathered in this volume, taken as a group, constitute a narrative that spirals incrementally toward a revised understanding of Forster's fictions. The collection moves generally from antecedents (Edward Carpenter and Henry James) to contexts (Bloomsbury and Cambridge) to texts, considering works from Forster's earliest undergraduate writing to stories written over a half-century later. In light of this range, we have organized the essays in roughly chronological order, although we are not unaware of the difficulties of establishing an order for the Forster canon. *A Room with a View,* after all, was the first novel Forster began, though he published two novels before completing it. More important for our purposes, *Maurice,* not published until 1971, was written in 1913–14. As Richard Dellamora has argued in his "Textual Politics/Sexual Politics," one's reading of the novel will be quite different depending upon the historical context one imagines for it, whether it be the date of composition or the date of publication. Similarly, a number of homoerotic stories were composed at dates from just after the turn of the century to the late 1950s, although they were not published until the early 1970s.[10] In general, our collection proceeds from readings of Forster's earliest writing through his World War I era fiction, whatever its date of publication, to his later colonial texts. Thus, unlike many studies of Forster, this volume does not end with *Maurice,* but moves from that text to "The Other Boat" and *A Passage to India. Queer Forster* is rounded out with something of an epilogue, Martin's meditation on the possibility of what he calls "queer begetting" throughout Forster's career.

Although we begin with antecedents, they are not to be understood as source studies that establish a single, unidirectional pattern of influence. Certainly, a great many possible models for Forster's work have been cited—Jane Austen, George Meredith, Samuel Butler, to name a few— but we are interested in somewhat more tentative filiations. Gregory Bredbeck draws upon a figure, Edward Carpenter, well-known to Forster critics for his influence on *Maurice,* in an essay that reexamines Carpenter's "India" as part of an interrogation of sexual identity. Examining a more canonical figure of English literature, Henry James, Eric Haralson explores the continuing tensions produced over mutual anxieties of carnality. Both Bredbeck and Haralson employ a dynamic model of literary relations that is embedded in culture.

James and Carpenter reflect the literary landscape of Forster's youth. As an undergraduate at Cambridge, Forster formed connections that would lead him into associations with individuals who have collectively come to be labeled "Bloomsbury"—Lytton Strachey, Leonard Woolf, John Maynard Keynes, Clive Bell, and Virginia Woolf and Vanessa Bell through their brother Thoby Stephen. Christopher Reed shows how this group has been unfairly attacked by certain feminist scholars who have alleged that it was dominated by gay men, representatives of an oppressive patriarchy. He takes issue with this view by revealing the homophobia that all too often underlies it. George Piggford interrogates readings of British modernism that downplay the importance of Bloomsbury and characterize its members as the decadent dregs of an exhausted civilization. His essay asserts that the biographical writings of Strachey, Woolf, and Forster employ a common camp, parodic mode. Piggford argues for a recovery of that mode as a way of remapping—and queering—the terrain of modernism. Joseph Bristow focuses on the relationship between Forster and Woolf and their contrasting views of Cambridge. He argues that Forster retained a deep allegiance to many of the values he had encountered as an undergraduate, along with a sense of male privilege. He uses close readings of *The Longest Journey* and a number of Forster's other early writings to substantiate his sense of Forster's loyalty to his homosexual brothers.

Forster's idealism, once seen as the source of his importance, has recently been viewed as compromised in the light of poststructural readings.[11] Judith Scherer Herz locates the demarcation between the real and the ideal in formal terms. For her, the operatic is what emerges when the realist frame cannot hold; it is the explosion of a queer lyric voice out of narrative. Her reading of *The Longest Journey* demonstrates the persistent power of opera as performance and as interruption. For Debrah Raschke, the ideal in Forster is not a momentary excess but a condition of existence in the Western philosophical tradition. Drawing on her reading of feminist philosopher Luce Irigaray, Raschke shows that Clive's rejection of Maurice in the novel of that name represents the critique of a Platonic idealism that is hostile to the body. Christopher Lane argues in his essay against a tradition of Forster criticism that has taken for granted that Forster's idealist assertions are consistent with the texts of his fictions. Debunking that Forster, Lane's paper calls attention to moments of betrayal in Forster's posthumously published fiction that are at odds with the idealistic humanism outlined in Forster's "What I Believe." Lane calls attention to what he sees as an absence of the erotic in Forster's utopian vision and cites autobiographical texts including "Kanaya" as examples of Forster's complicity in power relations such as British colonialism.

Colonizer or anticolonialist? The question often seems as unanswerable as one asking "What really happened in the Caves?" The intersections of sexuality and colonialism lie behind Tamera Dorland's essay on "The Other Boat." Although the story was written after *A Passage to India*, we have included Dorland's essay before the two studies of that novel since the story records a passage from Europe to India, via, tellingly, Egypt, the site of Forster's first sexual encounters. Therefore, it provides a bridge between Forster's European fictions and *A Passage to India*. Dorland's essay calls attention to the liminal space of the ship crossing from West to East via the Suez Canal. It is in this space that what Dorland perceives as the powerful voice of maternal law in Forster's fiction begins to lose its authority, opening up a space of uncertainty and illegibility at the same time that it enables an exploration of the connections between sexuality, race, and violence. Similar connections lie at the heart of Charu Malik's essay, which examines in detail the figure of the punkah wallah in *A Passage to India*. Her reading sees the punkah wallah as a disruptive force that signals the political role of Aziz's trial for rape in a colonial system of control. The novel's search for an interracial male friendship cannot quite be realized; however, in Malik's reading the basis for such a new ordering of relations is provided in the novel's challenge to categories of the masculine and the oriental. Yonatan Touval argues for an identification of the colonized oriental subject and the feminine. Colonial India becomes in Touval's reading a "queer nation" that is indecipherably *différant*. For him, the colonial regime attempts to impose a regularity and sexual conformity that are at odds with an Indian erotic tradition; Forster's novel in effect records a failed attempt to read India.

The final essay in the collection begins by observing a frequently reiterated pattern in Forster's fiction in which the texts conclude with the constitution of an alternate family—often a same-sex couple with a child. Martin argues that this scene represents Forster's attempt to locate a possibility for continuation without the necessity of physical begetting. These culminating moments are for Martin not simply idealized representations, for they often reflect a physical struggle between men that clearly carries erotic force. Martin's essay includes a reading of "Little Imber," Forster's last substantial fiction.

As is clear from this brief survey, the essays gathered in this volume represent a variety of critical perspectives that can explicitly or implicitly interrogate each other. For example, although there are a number of essays written from a feminist perspective, they do not all agree in their evaluation of Forster's position in feminist debates. Whereas Bristow's essay has been influenced by a model of reading Cambridge and Bloomsbury as homosexual, misogynist, and patriarchal and as inimical to the feminist project of Virginia Woolf, both Reed and Piggford see Woolf as sharing with Forster in a Bloomsbury project that seeks to develop an antipatriarchal language and form. Raschke's essay, too, engages with feminism, in her case Irigaray's rereading of Western metaphysics; her essay assumes that the patriarchal order preexists social practice and is embedded in consciousness rather than in institutions. A similar difference between two postcolonial readings may be found by comparing Malik's and Touval's essays. Malik's essay asserts that *A Passage to India* points toward a future union between East and West, whereas Touval's essay rejects any such connection as an impossibility. Most important, the essays in this volume take very different stands toward queer theory. They all utilize the insights of prominent queer theorists to a greater or a lesser degree. But a number of our contributors imply, at least, an uneasiness with the basic tenets of queer theory as we have outlined them here. Whatever our various commitments to queer theory, no one writing now is likely to want to perpetuate the myth of a sage gay E. M. Forster for all occasions.

Queer Forster? This book invites an exploration of that question with an open mind and with a renewed sense of the multiplicity and diversity of desire.

Notes

1. Cadmus's painting is also reproduced in color in Kirstein 79, and in Dellamora, "Textual" 160.

2. The "queerness" of "The Story of a Panic" was obvious to at least one early reader. In 1904 Charles Sayle, Assistant Librarian at the University Library, Cambridge, interpreted the story for John Maynard Keynes: " 'Oh dear,' Sayle exclaimed . . . , 'oh dear, oh dear, is this young King's'; and he explained to Keynes what the story was really about. Having . . . how should he put it . . . having had an unnatural act performed upon him by a waiter at the hotel, Eustace commits bestiality with a goat, then when he has told the waiter how nice it all has been, they try it on with each other again. 'While alive to the power of the writing, to its colour, its beauty, its Hellenic grace,' fluted Sayle, 'I am still amazed . . . I am horrified . . . and *longing* to meet the author.' " (Furbank 1:114; all ellipses except the first are Furbank's). Responses such as Sayle's indicate there were readers—at least in certain circles—capable of penetrating the "open secret" of Forster's stories (see Joseph Bristow, in this volume, and LJ 302–03 for further discussions of Sayle's reading).

3. We do not mean to conflate the psychological/medical category "homosexual" with the social/political categories "lesbian and gay." We recognize, however, that lesbians and gays are the product of a counterdiscourse in which pathologizing enabled a sense of identity and community. The liberation movements of the 1960s and 1970s permitted the emergence of a politically charged lesbian and gay studies, although they often did so by accepting an essentialist model of identity that would in turn be challenged by social construction theories in the light of Foucault, particularly his *History of Sexuality*.

4. See, for example, Stephen Adams, *The Homosexual as Hero in Contemporary Fiction;* Robert K. Martin, *The Homosexual Tradition in American Poetry;* Claude Summers, *Gay Fictions.*

5. At the same time, popular film adaptations of five (out of six) Forster novels have played an important part in the construction of a romantic "Forster film" that can mute the political and sexual tensions of Forster's texts. Three Merchant Ivory productions—*A Room with a View* (1986), *Maurice* (1987), and *Howards End* (1992)—have found many enthusiastic viewers. While the visibility of producer Ismail Merchant and director James Ivory as an artistic couple and collaborative team has undoubtedly encouraged similar projects and brought widespread attention to Forster's texts—most importantly *Maurice,* through their brave and touching adaptation—their success has been purchased at no small price. For many viewers the films are too complicit in an aestheticism that seems enamored of English upper class life. These films have usefully been compared to other "heritage" films of the Thatcher era, in their nostalgia for an imagined, lush world of Edwardian England that is at odds with the reality of a declining empire (on heritage films, see Higson). Charles Sturridge's *Where Angels Fear to Tread* (1991), much less nostalgic and pretty than the Merchant Ivory films, is the most faithful rendering of any Forster novel. It is also, unfortunately, much less interested in same-sex desire than the Merchant Ivory adaptations, paying almost no attention to Philip Herriton's romantic desire for Gino Carella. David Lean's sweeping, epic adaptation of *A Passage to India* (1984) makes Adela Quested the center of attention, unlike Forster's novel, which is much more concerned with male-male relationships. Lean's insensitivity to the male homoerotic desire inscribed into Forster's text is such that he can transform Forster's ideal of Indian male beauty, the "splendidly formed" (PI 207) punkah wallah at Dr. Aziz's trial, into an aged figure lacking any sexual vitality. Lean's willingness to oversimplify and de-eroticize Forster's novel allows him to replace Forster's complex sense of "the homoerotics of orientalism" (to borrow a phrase from Joseph Boone) with a happy ending in which Aziz and Mr. Fielding are reconciled and become friends on an equal footing with apparent ease, in a symbolic enactment of Indian independence and postcolonial harmony. In contrast, Forster's novel is about the impossibility of such relationships. The "E. M. Forster" constructed through these filmic representations can, therefore, be not only distinct from, but actually at odds with, the (queerer) "E. M. Forster" encountered by readers of his texts.

6. Elizabeth Heine corrects P. N. Furbank's misreading of "draughts" as "drought" (Furbank, *Life* 1:111).

7. Forster himself stressed the priority of class, stating that the phrase "hurt by him" "ought to be written in fainter ink." He continues, "Although it is on my ticket, it is not as vivid as 'perfect union'" (Beauman 302, n.), suggesting that he privileged the ideal over the real.

8. Richard Dellamora, in "Textual Politics/Sexual Politics," provides a very useful survey of the impact of the posthumous publications on Forster criticism.

9. Martin's view of Symonds has been critiqued by John Fletcher, in his "Forster's Self-Erasure: *Maurice* and the Scene of Masculine Love."

10. Another story that focuses on male-male desire, "Albergo Empedocle," which was published in 1903 and largely forgotten until its posthumous republication, is the subject of an important study by Richard Dellamora in his *Apocalyptic Overtures.*

11. See S. P. Rosenbaum, "*The Longest Journey:* E. M. Forster's Refutation of Idealism," for an earlier, more traditional, but fascinating account of Forster as an anti-idealist in the tradition of G. E. Moore and Bertrand Russell.

2

"Queer Superstitions": Forster, Carpenter, and the Illusion of (Sexual) Identity

Gregory W. Bredbeck

We rested outside it while the villagers sang and tried to cover our clothes with red powder: and the women issued from a rent in the mud wall and sat twenty yards off. When we passed them they abused us ritually like the women at the bridge in Ancient Greece. And I expect that *queer superstitions* are mixed up with the merriment and sex generally, & that's why we can't follow either. *Letter from E. M. Forster to Goldsworthy Lowes Dickinson, c. 10 April 1921 (my emphasis).*

1. A LETTER FROM INDIA

On March 4, 1921, E. M. Forster commenced his second passage to India. The times were wrought with political tension. The oppressive Rowlatt Acts of 1919, the massacre at Amritsar in April 1919, and the emergence of Gandhi as a leader of the Congress movement in September 1920 had coalesced into a strident policy of Indian noncooperation with British expansionist policies. The political turmoil closely paralleled personal turmoil in Forster's own life. While in the service of the Maharaja, Forster became the center of a messy controversy when he was found to be involved sexually with a male court servant. Only the Maharaja's support and defense of Forster saved his position—the Maharaja, in effect, enacted a policy of noncooperation with British homophobia. But, more important, the Indian ruler's defense of homosexual behavior seems to have established in Forster's mind a link between Indian culture, sexual permission, and social progress, for Forster subsequently publicized the Maharaja as a genius and a saint.

Forster's correspondence from the time reveals a sexual revelry that contrasts harshly with the somewhat dour and entirely neurotic image of the torn homosexual that so much criticism has perpetuated.[1] The letter from which I take my epigraph is an extreme and informative example. Addressing "Dear Goldie" from Dewas, Forster tells how "it is most interesting and friendly, but very disjointed. Or rather, I fear that I have lost my old power of joining it up." He recounts how a British "husband & wife," being entertained at the Maharaja's palace, become entangled in sexual intrigue:

> There was a farce which I saw again at the Palace next night, so got some idea of. Husband & wife. She: "Can I go and see my people?" He: "Dangerous for you—and for me—and morality generally." She persists, and as soon as she goes the husband says, "I want a eunuch—*at once*"—A tall scraggy man with a moustache then came on, in a pink sari, and paid attention to such members of the audience as His Highness indicated. (This is a recognised turn: the boy-dancers did it too). The "eunuch" squatted beside his victim and sang "do not hurt me"—or "I am not too old yet to remember what we did as boys"—and tried to kiss him amid laughter from the court. Resuming the drama he danced indecently before the husband, made terms with him, bought him sweets, and coming to a conclusion when the news is brought to the ill-advised wife. She returns from her parents. "How can you ruin your health by such a proceeding?" is her arguement [sic]: and I think that's where this particular indecency ended. (SL 2:3–4)

This anecdote is quintessential in the ways it depicts Forster's impression of British subjects in India. The generic man and wife find in the foreign culture a threat, something "dangerous for you—and for me—and morality generally." The prospect of exotic, alien eroticism is viewed as an enemy to the (national) body: it will "ruin your health." This is, quite simply, a classic example of xenophobia and erotophobia.

In contrast to the fears of the British couple, Forster himself finds within the scene of Indian eroticism a troubling but intriguing broach of his own mental and moral faculties. His "old powers of joining it up" fail in the face of cultural difference; he was, as he says, "struck by the remoteness of [the eunuch's] sexual gestures: in most cases I didn't know what was up." For the "Husband & wife" the otherness of Indian eroticism is a foreign intruder against which British culture must mount border patrols; for Forster it is a phenomenon that marks the limited range of British knowledge, for it continually opens a space that extends beyond the conceptual abilities of British thought. In both cases the encounter with India sets a limit for British culture, but there is a crucial and subtle political difference. For the "Husband & wife" the limit is that which becomes all the more important and all the more crucial to defend in the face of otherness; for Forster, otherness provides the impetus for seeing these limits as being, indeed, *limiting*. And Forster's pleasure in the scene comes neither from a wife nor from a eunuch but from a rather queer delight in speculating on the fact that there is always something more that cannot be known.

Forster's letter succinctly demonstrates a style of thought that will be my topic in this essay. Typically speaking, it would be most probable to find views toward alien eroticism falling into a bifurcated pattern. The xenophobia and erotophobia of the "Husband & wife" should form the counterimage of a fetishistic, eroticized desire. The one image of the fear and rejection of difference should parallel another image of a valorization and intensification of difference. Both the denigration of the alien and the eroticization of the alien constitute modes of containment through stereotyping; each constructs a manageable view of difference, through either selective rejection or selective acceptance.[2] There are data within Forster's life to suggest that he was in no way averse to the fetishization of India. One of his longest and most important emotional attachments was to Syed Ross Masood—to whom he dedicated *A Passage to India*—a strapping, handsome member of the Indian elite whom he tutored at Cambridge. As Forster's biographer P. N. Furbank has noted, Masood became one of Forster's first and most trusted confidants about his homosexuality. Like Forster's experience with the Maharaja's support, the relationship, which became overtly romanticized on Forster's part, provided for Forster an image of idealized permission outside of the straitjacket of middle-class English repression (Furbank, *Life* 1: 101–03).

And yet this fetishization of India does not capture the entire dynamic of Forster's letter. For even as the letter constructs an exotic, eroticized other, it does so not with the intention of solidifying the hegemonic power of English thought but, rather, with an eye toward the way the eroticized other limits English hegemony. There is, in other words, a split consciousness to Forster's letter, one that works within the tropes of English colonialism but at the same time works against them. The sources of this split consciousness—sources that extend to a prior encounter with Indian thought Forster negotiated through his friendship with Edward Carpenter—suggest that the "queer superstition" Forster ascribes to India is, in fact, an enabling component of his own art and therefore a vantage indispensable to any critical encounter with Forster.

2. STYLES OF BEING: THE INFLUENCE OF CARPENTER

In a famous passage from the 1960 terminal note to *Maurice*, Forster acknowledges his strong early debt to the radical socialist sexologist Edward Carpenter.[3] As the note says, "In its original form, which it still almost retains, *Maurice* dates from 1913. It was the direct result of a visit to Edward Carpenter at Milthorpe" (M 249). Forster's posthumously published homosexual fiction everywhere shows a debt to his encounter with Carpenter. In one of the most important examinations of the posthumous Forster, "Edward Carpenter and the Double Structure of *Maurice*," Robert K. Martin germinated a theory which still stands as one of the most influential in Forster studies. The love affair in that novel between Alec Scudder (a gamekeeper) and Maurice represents in Martin's theory an embrace of Carpenter's socialist views of homosexuality, and also functions to dislodge the asceticism and classism associated with Maurice's inaugural affair with Clive Durham.

Martin's thesis captures an important facet of the novel. Carpenter's theorization of democratic homosexuality—a theorization deeply informed by Walt Whitman's theory of calamitic democracy—does, indeed, provide the motivational image for the Scudder-Maurice affair. In 1906 Swan Sonnenschein issued an enlarged edition of Carpenter's book *Love's Coming of Age* that included an essay previously only circulated privately, "The Intermediate Sex." Two years later Carpenter extracted this essay, combined it with two magazine articles, "The Homogenic Attachment," and "Affection in Education," written in 1897 and 1899, respectively, and released it as the book *The Intermediate Sex*. The tract is Carpenter's fullest explication of what might best be called nonheterosexual evolutionary democracy. Drawing on a Darwinian model of sexual selection, the tract posits "Urnings"—a term for homosexuals Carpenter derived from the works of Karl Heinrich Ulrichs—as signs of social evolution:

It may be that, as at some past period of evolution the worker-bee was without doubt differentiated from the two ordinary bee-sexes, so at the present time certain new types of human kind may be emerging, which will have an important part to play in the societies of the future—even though for the moment their appearance is attended by a good deal of confusion and misapprehension. (*Sex* 186)

Carpenter posits this evolutionary newcomer as revolutionary, providing the catalyst for new forms of sociosexual organization:

Anyhow, with their extraordinary gift for, and experience in, affairs of the heart—from the double point of view, both of the man and the woman—it is not difficult to see that these people have a special work to do as reconcilers and interpreters of the two sexes to each other   It is probable that the superior Urnings will become, in affairs of the heart, to a large extent the teachers of future society; and if so that their influence will tend to the realization and expression of an attachment less exclusively sensual than the average of today, and to the diffusion of this in all directions. (*Sex* 188)

Carpenter's construction of the Urning as a disrupter of gender relations parallels his intense preoccupation with escaping traditional class relations. His life begins with entitlement and elitism, but its course proceeds toward an active rejection of society and, instead, the adoption of a life of rural seclusion and class difference with George Merrill, a laborer who was his lover (see *Sex* 79).

As Martin suggests, and as this biography demonstrates, the desire to "drop out" of the upper class can also be seen as the central structure of *Maurice,* which, as Martin phrases it, moves from a "false vision of an idealized homosexuality" ("Edward" 38)—chaste, ascetic, and aesthetic—to a poetic "dominated by Edward Carpenter and his translation of the ideas of Walt Whitman" (36). Maurice himself explains to the psychiatrist Lasker Jones his own fantasy of a time when "England wasn't all built over and policed" and when "Men of my sort could take to the greenwood" (M 211–12). The terminal note to the novel reinforces this idea, for in it Forster tells of an original, canceled ending to the novel, in which Kitty, Maurice's sister, "encounter[s] two woodcutters some years later" (M 254). The images of laborers and greenwoods converge to project an idea of classlessness, a romanticized, naturalized image of the outcast that recalls Carpenter's own life with Merrill at the idyllic rural retreat of Milthorpe. Indeed, Forster's own recollections of Carpenter, written originally as an address for the BBC, centralize Carpenter's class revolt as the dominant synecdoche for the bulk of the thinker's work; as Forster phrases it,

With [Carpenter] it was really a case of social maladjustment. He was not happy in the class into which he had been born. He wanted to live and work with the manual labourers. . . . He lived with working-class people, adopted many of their ways, worked hard physically, market-gardened, made and wore sandals, made (but did not wear) a Saxon tunic. He may not have got into another class, but he certainly discarded his own and gained happiness by doing so. . . . (TCD 205–06)

There is no doubt as to the importance of the type of thematic comparisons that can be drawn between Carpenter's work and Forster's— and hence the enduring importance of Martin's work. But I would like to stress a different comparison, one concerned not with themes but with structural, semiotic convergencies. The image of the homosexual presented in both Maurice's fantasies of a Robinhoodesque homosexual life and Carpenter's Darwinian image of the Uranian variety complete a process of bifurcated cultural stereotyping—the same process I discussed in relation to the eroticization of India in Forster's letter to Dickinson. In contrast to dominant strains of British homophobia, which construed homosexuals as stigmatized deviants, both Carpenter and Maurice fetishize the homosexual, positing him not as the debased other, but as the valorized other. Carpenter and Maurice in these instances, in other words, deploy a method of stereotyping that attaches different values to hegemonic denigrations of homosexuality, but that, in so doing, preserve the essential rhetorical form of the discourse of the stereotypical.

It is worth seeing the formal complicity between denigration and valorization, for it is, in point of fact, something Carpenter himself saw and something that, therefore, can stand as a source for the traces of "queer superstition" that color Forster's encounters with Indian eroticism. For Carpenter's theory embeds his deterministic construction of the evolutionary, class-defying Urning within a broader frame of queer thought— a frame derived, again, from a passage to India.

Near the beginning of *Love's Coming of Age,* and preceding his enlightened but more orthodoxly structured explication of woman as serf and marriage as contemporary feudalism, Carpenter offers an extraordinarily idiosyncratic and uncannily (post)modern explanation of sex. He says,

Sex-pleasures afford a kind of type of all pleasure. The dissatisfaction which at times follows on them is the same as follows on all pleasure which is *sought,* and which does not some unsought. The dissatisfaction is not in the nature of pleasure itself but in the nature of *seeking*. In going off in pursuit of things exter-nal, the "I" (since it really has everything and needs nothing) deceives itself, goes out from its true home, tears itself asunder, and admits a gap or rent in its own being. This, it must be supposed, is what is meant by *sin*—the separation or sundering of one's being—and all the pain that goes therewith. It all consists in *seeking* those external things and pleasures; not (a thousand times be it said) in the external things or pleasures themselves. . . . For us to go out of ourselves to run after *them*, to allow ourselves to be divided and rent in twain by *their* attraction, that is an inversion of the order of heaven. (*Sex* 102)

Writing in 1907, Sigmund Freud provided a pithy summary of the pre-vailing viewpoint which this counters: "It is commonly believed that the sexual instinct is lacking in children, and only begins to arise in them when the sexual organs mature" (*Sexual* 19). As Freud suggests—and as many still take as common sense—tradition holds that first comes a body, then come the genitals, then comes sexual desire, all in a congru-ent teleology of developmental steps that are naturally grounded in the matter of the preceding ones. Sexuality in this sense marks the coming-of-age that brings to fruition the "complete" and "finalized" human be-ing. The picaresque development of the traditional sexual subject is, of course, precisely the model Freud famously disrupted by heretically pos-iting that "the new-born infant brings sexuality with it into the world" (*Sexual* 19). Carpenter, too, disrupts this model, but not by writing sex-ual desire as an original component of the subject. Carpenter, rather, labels sexual desire as the disruption of the subject, the unnatural need to yoke the self to something else which then assumes all authority.

When the surface of this formulation is scratched, Marxist theory appears, for the relationship between "I" and "external things" appears as nothing more or less than the relationship between laborer and com-modity, with the commodity marking both the identity and the estrange-ment of the worker who creates it. This theoretical parallel is made al-most explicit by Carpenter himself when he says, "[man's] own passion arises before him as a kind of rude giant which he or the race to which he belongs may, Frankenstein-like, have created ages back, but which he now has to dominate or be dominated by" (*Sex* 97). Sex here becomes capital itself, the excess, self-perpetuating value that exceeds, outlives, and dominates the material conditions that originally created it. Like capital, sex exists not as the means to an end, but as the end itself. Certainly, as this parallel suggests, Carpenter's theorization is deeply in-debted to Marx. By the time of his major writings, Carpenter had thoroughly digested H. M. Hyndman's *England for All,* which popularized Marx's theory of surplus-value, and in his memoirs he states, "However open to criticism the Marxian theory of surplus-value must be (and *every* theory must ultimately succumb to criticism) it certainly fulfilled a want for the time by giving a definite text for the social argument" (*Sex* 50).

But Carpenter's intention is not so much to construct a Marxist theory of sexuality as it is to use Marxist theory to create a new vantage on sexuality. He ends his elaboration of alienated desire with this telling summary: "To this desertion of one's true self sex tempts most strongly, and stands as the type of Maya and the world illusion" (*Sex* 102). *Maya,* the Hindu term for the illusion that is reality and that keeps humans trapped in unenlightenment, becomes Carpenter's ultimate target. His link between sex and economics serves to elaborate both as modes of false existence, much as his use of natural philosophy uses the science of nature to denaturalize both science and nature. Carpenter's use of the term *maya* bespeaks the influence of the British colonization of India. His elder brother had worked in India during the early periods of colonization; an Indian friend at college taught him how to weave sandals, which he produced and distributed to friends worldwide; Harold Cox, another college friend, moved to India in the mid-1880s and kept Carpenter informed of the growing Indian nationalist movement, which Carpenter viewed as proof of the imminent collapse of British imperialism. By 1890 he had completed a full study of the Bhagavad-Gita, one of the central texts of Sanskrit literature, which had first been translated into English in 1785 by Charles Wilkins, and he traveled to India and Ceylon, primarily to study Hinduism and mysticism. While in India he viewed an erotic festival in a Hindu temple and discovered a clandestine English nudist colony in Bombay called "The Fellowship of the Naked Trust"; both experiences he recounts in his book *From Adam's Peak to Elephanata.* Sheila Rowbotham, who has expertly collated these experiences for modern readers, wryly notes that "it was an unconventional passage to India for an English member of the upper classes," and offers this explanation of the influences it had on Carpenter's thought:

In an Indian Gnani he found another Whitman and in Hindu thought he found a way of developing the feelings expressed in *Towards Democracy.* He could see a means of attaining the consciousness without thought, and beyond words, which he felt existed alongside the self-consciousness which was expressed in western rationalism. By touching this consciousness humanity could transcend the "crack" between mind and nature. The realisation of the individual self was not as in Christianity through denial but through merging with the universe. God was within you. (106–7)

What Carpenter found in Hinduism, to elaborate on Rowbotham's point, was an epistemology of *permission*—not in the narrow, moralistic sense, but in a broad religious and philosophical sense. The Upanisads (or Upanishads), which were crucial texts for Carpenter, make this point clear. Opening with an explanation of the syllable Om, the first Khanda of the first prapāthaka of the first Upanisad states, "That syllable is a syllable of permission, for whenever we permit anything, we say Om, yes. Now permission is gratification. He who knowing this meditates on the syllable (Om), the udgîtha, becomes indeed a gratifier of desires" (I, 2). Permission here means entrance into enlightenment and release from the categorical prohibitions that sustain the illusion of maya (reality). Hence to gratify desire is not to find a *thing* that is *lacking,* but is to escape the conditions that make things appear as discrete, discernible and separate.[4] This idea shows forth in the first stanzas of the same Khanda. Giving the "full account . . . of Om," it states, "The *rasa* of all beings is the earth, the *rasa* of the earth is water, the *rasa* of water the plants, the *rasa* of plants man, the *rasa* of man speech, the *rasa* of speech the Rig-veda, the *rasa* of the Rig-Veda the Sâma-veda, the *rasa* of the Sâma-veda the udgîtha (which is Om)" (I, 1–2).

F. Max Müller, who published this translation in 1879 as part of his massive and important series *The Sacred Texts of the East,*[5] translates the word *rasa* as essence. But retaining the original is necessary, for, as Müller explains in a translator's footnote: "Essence, rasa, is explained in different ways, as origin, support, end, cause and effect. Rasa means originally the sap of trees. That sap may be conceived either as the essence extracted from the tree, or as what gives vigour and life to a tree. In the former case it might be transferred to the conception of effect, in the latter to that of cause. In our sentence it has sometimes the one, sometimes the other meaning" (I, 1). The *real* point is that *rasa* means *neither* the one *nor* the other, but both at once. For the hierarchy of the world set up in the definition is not a hierarchy at all, but rather is a type of nonvectored supplementarity that refuses prohibitional order. The categories of thought that allow the very concepts of origin, support, end, and cause and effect to appear as different, discrete concepts are obliterated by the *Upanisads,* for to perpetuate them is also to perpetuate maya and shun enlightenment. This will never serve as an adequate explanation of Hindu philosophy; but what it *will* serve as is an explication of the type of thought patterns Carpenter extracted from his encounters with Indian religion. Carpenter's perception of the division between the "I" and the external world as the source of discontent echoes precisely the sort of perfect permission that characterizes Hindu enlightenment.

Versions of this thought motivate almost all of Carpenter's most important conceptualizations. In *Love's Coming of Age,* for example, Carpenter formulates a famous redefinition of reproduction, one which Forster himself cites in his terminal note to *Maurice* (M 249). The terms of this redefinition demonstrate their link with his study of Hinduism:

Sex is the allegory of Love in the physical world. It is from this fact that it derives its immense power. The aim of Love is non-differentiation—absolute union of being; but absolute union can only be found at the centre of existence. Therefore whoever has truly found another has found not only that other, and with that other himself, but has found a third—who dwells at the centre and holds the plastic material of the universe in the palm of his hand, and it a creator of sensible forms. (*Sex* 106)

Seizing upon the Hindu principle of unification, Carpenter defines the object of generation not as a child, but as the metaphoric approximation of nondifferentiation that, ideally, can be achieved between two lovers. With the biological object of generation removed, all unions, presumably regardless of the genders involved, can be thought of as generative and procreative. Carpenter's encounter with Hinduism provided him a strategy for conceptualizing reproduction outside of the imperative of nature and biology that had empowered so many programs of oppressive, hegemonic sexual regulation. Carpenter derives from Hinduism not a denigrated other, nor a valorized other, but rather a type of epistemological pleasure that foreshadows Forster's letter to Dickinson, a type of pleasure that revels in seeing the limits of British culture not as borders of the proper but as signs of the *limited* and *limiting* status of the British world picture. The contested border between Indian and British culture that colonialism established is replayed here. But while such a replay typically—say for a normative "Husband & wife"—achieves the solidification of national hegemony, for Carpenter the replay serves to expose the impotencies of British thought and its inability to territorialize and domesticate cultural difference. Carpenter derives his knowledge of Hinduism from the British colonial project but deploys it to decolonize the regimes of knowledge imposed on sociosexual organization by colonial British culture. And in this sense, Carpenter's engagement of Hinduism appears as a distinct precursor of Forster's own split consciousness regarding cultural and sexual differences.

3. "ASIAN EGGS": THE LYRIC "I" AND DEMOCRATIC DIFFERENCES

Carpenter's understanding of the "I" provides an important clue about some idiosyncrasies of his "identity" politics. For in point of fact, within an extreme Hindu framework, identity itself is a manifestation of maya. Carried to its full conclusion, Hindu principles as Carpenter perceived them suggest that to even "be" an "I" is already to be a symptom of the problem, not a part of the solution. "Being" itself—the supposedly necessary precondition of an identity politics—becomes something that prohibits the attainment of enlightened liberation. There is, therefore, something inherently oxymoronic in formulating an identity politics based on Hindu philosophy. Carpenter's thought is strongly inflected by and generated from this seeming contradiction. One particularly succinct method of seeing the differences it inserts in Carpenter's theorization is to compare his poetic cycle, *Towards Democracy,* with one by his poetical and political mentor, Walt Whitman.

Whitman, as Carpenter himself frequently acknowledged, was as strong an influence on Carpenter as was Hinduism. In his memoirs Carpenter recalls how one of the Fellows of Trinity Hall entered his room at university in 1869 with "a blue-covered book in his hands"—William Rossetti's edition of Whitman's poems. As Carpenter remembers it, "I remember lying down then and there on the floor and for half an hour poring, pausing, wondering. I could not make the book out, but I knew at the end of that time I intended to go on reading it. In a short time I bought a copy for myself, then I got *Democratic Vistas,* and later on . . . *Leaves of Grass* complete" (*Sex* 88). Furthermore, Forster, in his appreciation of Carpenter, recounts the author's delight at the common derision of his poem cycle as being "Whitman and water" (TCD 206). Yet the similarities that appear between Whitman's poetry are not as important, I believe, as a crucial and vivid difference. Whitman's work inspired Carpenter, to be sure.[6] But Whitman's *lack* of a Hindu basis for his thought also serves to highlight through contradistinction the precise representational dilemma which Hinduism foisted onto Carpenter's theories.

In *Democratic Vistas* Whitman supplies a prose explication of his theories of calamitic democracy which demonstrates their influence on Carpenter. Examining the evolutionary potential that a true American literature will release "those hundred years ahead," Whitman suggests that

Intense and loving comradeship, the personal and passionate attachment of man to man—which, hard to define, underlies the lessons and ideals of the profound saviors of every land and age, and which seems to promise, when thoroughly develop'd, cultivated, and recognized in manners and literature, the most substantial hope and safety of the future of these States, will then be fully express'd. (492)

Whitman here clearly foreshadows Carpenter's more specified and scientific version of the evolutionary, revolutionary Uranian. Whitman's calamitic democracy constructs a mode of bonding that presages Carpenter's Uranian mode of *being*.

Yet, ironically, the style in Whitman which congeals into the thing itself in Carpenter exists in counterpoint to an antithetical conceptualization, for Whitman begins his theorization with a crystallized and determinant idea of being that, ultimately, Carpenter's Hinduism could not fully entertain. As Whitman says early in *Democratic Vistas,*

For after the rest is said—after the many time-honor'd and really true things for subordination, experience, rights of property, etc., have been listen'd to and acquiesced in . . . it remains to bring forward and modify everything else with the idea of that Something a man is (last precious consolation of the drudging poor), standing apart from all else, divine in his own right, and a woman in hers, sole and untouchable by any canons of authority, or any rule derived from precedent, state-safety, the acts of legislatures, or even from what is called religion, modesty or art. (464)

After everything—which really means *before* everything—there is the individual, the "male or female, characterized in the main, not from extrinsic acquirements or position, but in the pride of himself or herself alone" (464), the self-possessed subject existing anterior and causally to everything. Indeed, for Whitman, democracy itself is not a mode of governmental or social organization; it is, rather, a recognition of the inviolate absoluteness of this foundational subject and a nurturing of the conditions which allow him or her to remain autonomous and powerful.

The combination of a determinant subject and an evolving style of male bonding bespeaks the influence of Whitman's own historical moment. Like pre-Freudian ideas of personhood, which posited an asexual, originary creature preceding the emergence of sexual structures, Whitman posits an originary creature that precedes all structures. Hence eroticism—even homoeroticism—can emerge as a *secondary* construct, one that exists between persons but does not necessarily touch a core issue of subjectivity. Eroticism is a style of existence, not a mode of being.

For Whitman, the "I" is a pure, unmarked, and foundational concept that governs all types of representation—political, social, personal, etc.[7]

This foundational place of the unmarked "I" within Whitman's thought is best seen within the poetic closure of "Song of Myself." Recent criticism has tended to stress the *lack* of closure in Whitman. Both Martin and Betsy Erkkila have, to use here Martin's words, noted that "the dispersion of seminal energy is . . . for Whitman a recurring figure for the destruction of all hierarchies, a way through the renewal of the body (of the text as well as the person) to the renewal of the earth" ("Disseminal Whitman" 75)[8] the broader point being, this time using Erkkila's phrasing, that Whitman's poetry typically perpetuates "the image of an open-ended process," one which, through its lack of closure, "incites the reader to the final act of creation" (62–63). Such statements are, I think, by and large correct regarding images of sexuality in the poems. That is, Whitman does not subscribe to a traditionally Oedipalized model of narrative and sexual closure. However, it does not seem as apparent to me that Whitman therefore abandons *all* closure. Whitman's texts radically push a polymorphous range of possibilities on the reader, but at the same time they express a distinctive faith in the ability of the "I" of *Democratic Vistas* to transcend and guide all such destabilizing possibilities.

"Song of Myself" would seem initially to bear a striking similarity to the "permission" of Hindu thought Carpenter found. Its poetic voice is one that refuses the prohibitions and segregations of orthodoxy, putting "Creeds and schools in abeyance" (1.10) and "Welcom[ing] . . . every organ and attribute of me, and of any man hearty and clean" (3.20). It refuses the types of segregations and valuations that typify normative Western ontology, stating instead that "Clear and sweet is my soul, and clear and sweet is all that is not my soul" (3.15): adjectives of value, generally used to draw distinctions, here refuse to make distinctions. And it strongly rejects the simple bourgeois containment of both poetry and eroticism in the domestic sphere of private production.[9] In poem 2, for example, the poetic voice refuses to "let" "houses and rooms . . . full of perfume" "intoxicate me" (2.3,1,3), while in poem 11 the "Twenty-eight young men [who] bathe by the shore," "all so friendly" (11.1–2) are set in enticing opposition to "[the woman who] owns the fine house by the rise of the bank" (11.4). In effect, the poetic imagery sets in parallel motion two separate worlds, one of cultural containment and one of unbounded potentiality.

And yet the cycle is not simply about the dissolution of the bounded bourgeois sphere; it also about how such dissolution results in the emergence of a determinable and determining "I." In poem 15, when the speaker offers what might best be thought of as the poetic charge of the entire cycle, the idea becomes apparent:

> And these tend inward to me, and I tend outward to them,
> And such as it is to be of these more or less I am,
> And of these one and all I weave the song of myself. (15.64–66)

Following as it does an epic catalog of American images ranging from wolverines to coon-seekers, this charge obviously sets up a complicated social space for the "I" that is both preceded by and followed by the "I" itself. From the encounter with experience a tale of the "I"—a "song of myself"—will emerge, but the process of emergence is always already controlled by that very "I"—a poetic presence "tending outward" and controlling the act of weaving. There is a story of the "I" that will emerge from the cycle, but only because there is already an "I" in place to cause it. It is not too extreme to see "Song of Myself" as one long explication of the intransigence, the permanence, and the pervasiveness of this causal "I." From "the city's quadrangular houses" (33.8), to "Where the bat flies" (33.25), to "Where bee-hives range on a gray bench" (33.55), the "I tread day and night such roads" (33.88) suffuses every aspect of the poem, both the bounded and the unbounded realms of existence, with a dominant and sustained organizing principle.

I stress this permanency of the "I" in "Song of Myself" because it puts in question a reading of the cycle as open-ended. Poem 49 initiates a four-poem sequence that traditionally has been read as the conclusion to the sequence. It ends with the poetic voice's description of death as ascension:

> I ascend from the moon, I ascend from the night,
> I perceive that the ghastly glimmer is noonday sunbeams reflected,
> And debouch to the steady and central from the offspring great or small.
> (49.18–20)

This image blends with those in subsequent poems to suggest a shedding of temporality and materiality; in poem 51 "The past and present wilt" (51.1), while in poem 52 the speaker describes how he "depart[s] as air, . . . shake[s] [his] white locks at the runaway sun, / . . . effuse[s] [his] flesh in eddies, and drift[s] it in lacy jags" (52.7–8). The voice "bequeath[s]" itself "to the dirt to grow from the grass" (52.9) and, as Erkkila notes, thereby suggests a "merging with the processes of universal creation" (62). The "myself" of which the sequence has been a song in these examples dissolves.

Yet the dissolution of "myself" which Erkkila so convincingly documents is juxtaposed, again, with a solidification of the "I." Poem 50 begins with a succinct restatement of the "I" from *Democratic Vistas:* "There is that in me—I do not know what it is—but I know it is in me" (50.1) and amplifies this image a few lines later: "I do not know it—it is without name—it is a word unsaid, / It is not in any dictionary, utterance, symbol" (50.4–5). This image of that "I" which persists after all else is said resonates backward to the closing lines of poem 49, and we become retrospectively aware that the ascension of the poet is, in point of fact, governed by a permanent "I": "*I* ascend from the moon, *I* ascend from the night." Death, a process which supposedly objectifies everyone, here is a process to which the "I" still relates as an active and controlling subject. The wilting of past and present in poem 50 similarly becomes an occasion to assert the permanence of the "I's" agency, for it is caused by the "I" itself: "*I* have fill'd them, emptied them, / And proceed to fill my next fold of the future" (51.1–2, my emphasis). In perfect accord with the principles Whitman sets forth in *Democratic Vistas,* the "I" remains intransigent, permanent, and foundational, governing the poetics of the cycle, remaining impervious to the dissolving processes of unification and merger that affect space, time, and even the "myself" that forms the basis of this song. Only the "I" as object—the "myself"—dissolves; the "I" as subject remains autonomous and omnipotent.

The final two stanzas of "Song of Myself" perfectly encapsulate the image of the "I" which I have been explicating and therefore can be used as a summation. In their entirety:

> You will hardly know who I am or what I mean,
> But I shall be good health to you nevertheless,
> And filter and fibre your blood.
>
> Failing to fetch me at first keep encouraged,
> Missing me one place search another,
> I stop somewhere waiting for you. (52.11–16)

The lines create an "activist poetic" (Erkkila 63), foisting onto the newly invoked "you," the reader, a demand for interpretation and action. The reader is challenged to negotiate a cognitive process, one that will achieve access to a new, undefined space—a space that is simply "somewhere." This challenge also, therefore, implies two separate realms, one of that which is already known, and one of that which is to be known through a sort of enlightenment. But these two orders are linked, again, by the intransigent "I" of the cycle; for the route demanded of the reader is *not* new nor absolutely unknown—it is somewhere where the "I" has arrived and is waiting. The "I [who] celebrate[s] myself" (1.1) and causes the poem jumps forward to territorialize and control the projected space of resolution. The task of interpretation placed on the reader, then, is not to know something unknown, but to (re)know something that is always already known, the foundational "I" of American democracy in general and "Song of Myself" in particular.

One reason the foundational "I" of Whitman's cycle has sometimes been overlooked by criticism—even criticism as subtle as Erkkila's—is, I believe, that it is a concept so naturalized within American culture and politics that it is difficult to see it as a representational concept. Yet it is important to see Whitman's "I" as, in point of fact, his greatest and most potently controlling poetic *construct* precisely because this "I" is what Carpenter's Hinduism will *not* allow—at least in the fully naturalized sense with which it appears in "Song of Myself." Carpenter's "Towards Democracy" vividly demonstrates this difference. The cycle, which continued to grow over Carpenter's life, was first published in 1883, fourteen years after Carpenter's crucial encounter with Rossetti's edition of Whitman. Despite its current invisibility, the cycle was extraordinarily popular and went through a number of expanded reprintings. The original cycles of seventy poems was reprinted in 1885 and 1892 with the addition of two other sections, one containing forty-eight additional, individual poems and titled "Children of Freedom," and another, "After Civilization," which collected eighty-three more poems. In 1902 a separate volume of seventy-six poems was published as "Who Shall Command the Heart," and this was included as the final section of the complete edition, *Towards Democracy,* in 1905.

Although the volume changed radically over time, the germinal cycle, "Towards Democracy," was established in its predominant form in the 1883 edition, and it serves as a vivid demonstration of both the debts and differences between Whitman's and Carpenter's thought. Like "Song of Myself," "Towards Democracy" begins with a poetic voice firmly embedded in a highly visible "I." Proclaiming "Freedom at last" (1.1), the voice sets forth a goal for the cycle that recalls Whitman's "activist poetics" (Erkkila, "Politics" 63): "These things I, writing, translate for you— I wipe a mirror and place it in your hands" (1.6). As in the ending of "Song of Myself," where the reader is drawn into the cycle and given responsibility for an active role of interpretation, "Towards Democracy" begins with the ascription of an active role to the reader, who must look at and interpret the "mirror" "place[d] . . . in [his or her] hands."

Also like "Song of Myself," "Towards Democracy" is governed by an idea of ascension; but it is in this idea where differences most strongly appear. Poems 48 through 60 embody the poet's ascension, which begins with the speaker's proclamation that "I arise and pass" (48.1). The phrase is repeated as the opening line of each of the next four poems (49.1, 50.1, 51.1, 52.1), each of which catalogs the material and temporal experiences the speaker encounters as he "passes." In poem 48 the speaker's form dissolves as he merges with the material world: "I am the light air on the hills . . . / I pass and pass and pass" (48.10–12), while in poem 49 the speaker "arise[s] and pass[es]" (49.1) "The old dowager" who "sits" (49.5) "in her tall-windowed sitting room, with its antique pier-glasses and profuse handsome ornaments—alone—" (49.4)—a dowager who strongly recalls the younger woman who "owns the fine house by the rise of the bank" (11.4) in "Song of Myself."

This is a stereotypically Whitmanic ascension of the "I," an explication of the "I"'s ability to extend beyond the exigencies of all contingent experience and to, thereby, emerge in its pure, unmarked, and intransigent form. Poems 53 and 54 make this Whitmanic mode even more explicit, for, like "Song of Myself," they suggest a division between two worlds in the cycle. The "I" which has arisen and passed suddenly changes topics and explicates "Where *you* are" (53.1, my emphasis): "Where the firelight flickers about your room. . . . / Where you sit alone" (53.2–3); "Where you open your eyes upon the world" (53.6); "Where you bend ankle-deep in mud all day in the rice plantations for a few half-pence" (53.10); and "Where the old Hindu feeling the approach of death leaves his family and retires to a hut in the jungle, there to spend his last days in prayer and solitude" (54.10). Where "you" *are* is, in other words, where the "I" *was* but is no longer; for, as poem 55 states, the "I" has "passed away and entered the gate of heaven. [The] I [is] absolved from all torment. All is well to [it]" (55.1). Like Whitman's "I," which flails forward into and territorializes an unknown space of resolution—and there waits for "you"—so too does Carpenter's "I": "On the wind I ride, / And dream the dream of the soul's slow disentanglement" (49.20–21).

But poem 50, which begins with the completion of ascension, at least in Christian terms, also destabilizes this spiritual attainment. For, curiously, this completed ascension does not end the process of ascension:

I arise and pass once more: I travel forth into all lands: nothing detains me any longer. By the ever beautiful coast-line of human life, in all climates and countries, wandering on, a stranger, unwearied, I meet the old faces: I came never away from home. . . .

The arched doors of the eyebrows of innumerable multitudes open around me: new heavens I see, and the earth made new because of them.

I will stop here then. I will not leave the earth after all. I am content and need go no farther. (50.21, 24–25)

Attainment for Carpenter is not attainment of a new "somewhere" where the "I" waits. Rather, the "I" must exist in *this* somewhere, the somewhere of "cottages," "climates," and the "beautiful coast-line of human life." The "I" can exist in this world, in a heightened state of enlightenment; but, ultimately, the "I" does not transcend. It ends up back again where "you" are, in the material world, the world of experience, experiencing differently, but also still building that different experience out of the *same* things as the "you." What dissolves here is not material existence— the world of maya—but rather the *desire* of the "I" to transcend. Unlike the unenlightened "I" of *Love's Coming of Age,* this more enlightened "I" achieves a difference through *indifference,* through the fulfillment of a desire to stop desiring. This is not a personal idiosyncrasy on Carpenter's part, but is, rather, a full embrace of the most central principle of Hindu practice, and of most Eastern religions, the doctrine variously referred to as inaction, indifference, or nongraspingness; it is a doctrine Carpenter perfectly and explicitly states in the cycle:

The path of Indifference—action, inaction, good, evil, pleasure, pain, the sky, the sea, cities and wilds—all equally used (never shunned), adopted, put aside, as materials only—you continuing, love continuing—the use and freedom of materials dawning at last upon you. (6.6)

The point is not to find a new, different place, but to be in this place newly and differently: "Where this makes itself known in a people or even in the soul of a single man or woman, there Democracy begins to exist" (6.12).

Unlike Whitman's "I," then, which comes to stand in the unknown space of a new order, Carpenter's "I" achieves whatever it is it achieves by admitting that this new order *is and remains* unknown, even to the "I." The ascension of the cycle ends within the gate of heaven (50.1), but no description is supplied of what the "I" sees, or even that the "I" has seen anything. For from the moment the "I" enters the gate, it also casts its glance and voice backward to the world of material experience: "A tiny infant am I once more, leaning out from my mother's arms" (55.2); "I am a wild cat crouching at night in the angle of a bough" (55.3); and, most tellingly: "I am Arjuna reasoning on the battle-field with Krishna" (55.30)—Arjuna being the *not yet enlightened* interlocutor of the *Bhagavad-Gita,* the one who, as the cycle notes, is "learning the lessons of divine knowledge" (55.3) but who has not yet learned them thoroughly.

Another particularly striking similarity between "Song of Myself" and "Towards Democracy" is that the final poems of Carpenter's cycle, like those of Whitman's, can aptly summarize the poet's entire conception of this different "I." In a structure of circularity that again strongly recalls Whitman, poem 69 returns almost verbatim to the opening lines of the poem; in its entirety:

I—who write—translate for you these thoughts: I wipe a mirror and place it in your hands[,] look long, O friend, look long, satiate yourself—
I bring you to your own, to take, or leave for a while, as pleases you best. I have perfect faith in you.
And can wait: the whole of Time is before me.

At the end of the poem the "I" is doing the exact same thing as at the beginning, which questions both movement and progress. The "I" and the "you" exist on the same plane and engage in a mutual action. And the "I" who waits does so not beyond temporality, as does Whitman's, but with "the whole of Time" before it, enduring, to be sure, but neither intransigent, permanent, nor transcendent. Moreover, poem 70, the last of cycle, places the entire text in a similar position:

The little red stars appear once more shining among the hazel catkins; the pewit tumbles and cries as at the first day, the year begins again;
The wind blows east, the wind blows west, the old circle of days and nights completes itself. (70.1–2)

The material world of nature, geography, and temporality emerges unscathed from the cycle, with the resolution being an altered consciousness *within this world:* "But henceforth the least thing shall speak to you words of deliverance; the commonest shall please you best." (70.3). Moreover, Carpenter's own text is denigrated as an inferior manifestation of this unenlightened world, for "henceforth" ". . . the fall of a leaf through the air and the greeting of one that passes on the road shall be more to you than the wisdom of all the books ever written—*and of this book*" (70.4, my emphasis). In direct opposition to Whitman's conclusion, the "I" which has "perfect faith in you" (49.2) has no faith in itself or the text it has produced. Indeed, if "Song of Myself" should be read as a statement of the potency of the "I," then it is also appropriate to suggest that "Towards Democracy" should be read as a statement of the impotency of the "I" and of the inability of the "I" to serve as a conduit to a state of pure enlightenment.

In *Democratic Vistas,* Whitman supplies a curious footnote—one of his few direct references to Eastern religions—that is important to consider here. Defending the role of literature in culture, Whitman glosses his assertion of a Greco-European literary continuum with this marginal comment:

See, for hereditaments, specimens, Walter Scott's Border Minstrelsy, Percy's collection, Ellis's early English Metrical Romances, the European continental poems of Walter of Aquitainia, and the Nibelungen, of pagan stock, but monkish-feudal redaction: the history of the Troubadours, by Fauriel; even the far-back cumbrous old Hindu epics, as indicating the Asian eggs out of which European chivalry was hatch'd. (458)

The poet who goes to such extremes to include everything in his poems here activates tropes of exclusion: Vedic literature becomes the infantilized other which precedes European modernity. This is a view neither original nor exclusive to Whitman; F. Max Müller, for example, places "the Sacred Books of the East" at "the dawn of religious consciousness of man" and states that they come from "an age when there was nothing corresponding to what we call literature" (*Upanisads* xi, xiii). This is the discernible language of British nineteenth-century colonialism, the infantilizing and othering of the East in the face of Western expansion. And Whitman's implicit embrace of it should be seen simply as one of those places where the thinker is inextricably knotted to the matter of his historic moment.

But what is striking is the extent to which Carpenter, writing a year before Müller published the second volume of his translation of the *Upanisads,* escapes this mindset. Poem 7 of "Towards Democracy" serves as a good example:

Inevitable in time for man and all creation is the realisation: the husks one behind another keep shelling and peeling off.

Rama crosses to Ceylon by the giant stepping-stones; and the Ganges floats with the flowers and sacred lamps of pilgrims; Diotima teaches Socrates divine love; Benedict plunges his midnight lust in nettles and briars; and Bruno stands prevaricating yet obstinate before his judges. . . .

The great stream of history runs on. (7.1–2, 4)

Preceding cultures do not stand as developmental increments, as steps across which time passes and then leaves behind. Rather, like a true stream, which carries all its water along its course, they exist as possibilities which flow forward and are always present, intermixed yet discrete, and always available. Rama, Diotima, Benedict, and Bruno stand together, delineating a range of possibilities in the present, not a chronological progression of eggs hatching into chickens which will lay more eggs. Carpenter's "great stream" will not allow the reassuring progression of evolution that empowers Whitman's chronology; it is, rather, a stream of indifference which does accept that time has always already differentiated between what was and is gone, and what is and is not available.

Carpenter's evolutionary Uranian, then, exists within a field of thought that repudiates the very notions of time and progress that form the conditions of evolution. Carpenter's Uranian represents the best possibility within this world—but this is not necessarily the *best* of all possible worlds, and it is certainly not the *only* possible world. This split viewpoint also goes far toward suggesting a reason for the differences between the "I" of Carpenter's poetry and that of Whitman's. Empowered by the belief that the past has led incrementally to the present, Whitman can then extend this to a belief that his "I" can lead incrementally to the future. Carpenter's "I," however, can only profess a belief that there will be a future. The most his "I" can do is mark a moment of representation in the present, a moment that is politically empowered by its impotencies, by the conscious flaunting of its limitations and its inabilities. Through suggesting a time to come and denying an ability to know it, Carpenter's "I" also denies the teleology of time and the totalizing assumptions of representation that typify Western poetics of religion and Whitman's poetics of the "I." Carpenter's "I" stands as a thing within his poem, but his poem stands as but one thing within the great stream, a thing subordinate to that stream and unable to control or even to know its myriad currents and self-sustaining flows. Carpenter's "I" represents the best possibility within his text—but his text is not necessarily the best of all possible texts, and certainly not the only text.

4. *MAURICE'S* "QUEER SUPERSTITIONS"

I stress this diacritical difference between Whitman and Carpenter in order to demonstrate that, in point of fact, Carpenter's theorization embodies two relatively discrete revolutions in thought. His construction of the evolutionary Uranian might best be termed a thematic revolution. Sexology had already acknowledged the possibility of a deviant, homoerotically oriented person, and in the figure of the Uranian Carpenter revolts against that concept, establishing strategies for adhering new values to that particular point of content. Indeed, it is this program of social revaluation that has motivated some critics to see the late nineteenth-century construction of the homosexual subject as the historical precursor of gay liberation. But I would like to examine here what I perceive to be a more important and also more overlooked style of thought, one that probably seems more like *queer* liberation to many people. For even as Carpenter advocates the liberation of homosexual subjects from codes of oppression, he also advocates a liberation of *all* subjects from the very system of western subjectivity and meaning. This latter course of action creates a conflicted semiotic stance in his writings, one that demands that meanings be made, but that also, at the same time, suggests that meaning itself is, in fact, a symptom of the problem. On one level, Carpenter *identifies* new meanings in culture; on another, he *disidentifies* with both "meaning" and "culture." I want to focus attention on the *two* projects at work in Carpenter because, I believe, the *dominant* route of influence between Carpenter and Forster happened along this second line of *disidentification,* and that this phenomenon has been clouded in much criticism by an a priori belief in determinant thematics and topical influence. I suggest that when we read the lineage of Carpenter to Forster, we should not be seeking commentary on *what* to think about that *thing,* the homosexual, but should be retrieving, rather, an important rumination on *how* to think about the very idea of a *thing* itself. These ideas are not, of course, mutually exclusive—but I focus on the latter here because it has not often been noted.

Examples of Carpenter's mode of social and epistemological disidentification surface frequently in Forster's posthumously published fiction. In the short story "Arthur Snatchfold," for example, Sir Richard Conway stands in the gentry estate gardens of Trevor Donaldson and spots the ruddy milkman who will become his *al fresco* sex partner. The moment is facilitated by the milkman's boisterous greeting, which he utters "as if they were equals" (LTC 98). The encounter tersely embodies all of the strains of Uranian democracy that Carpenter envisioned, for it suggests a desire motivated by an ideal of equality between classes and based on male homoeroticism. Yet at the same time Conway does not desire just the simple address of class inequalities and the refinement of social structure. He later looks at the milkman and sees that he "was coarse, very much of the people and of the thick-fingered earth; a hundred years ago this type was trodden into the mud, now it burst and flowered and didn't care a damn" (LTC 102). This is not a desire for social progress and reform, but a desire for a nostalgic time *before,* a time which embodies the fantasy of an escape, not a refinement.

Similarly, in the seldom commented-on story "The Obelisk," Hilda, the young wife about to commit adultery, also fetishizes class difference in this split way. The narrative abandons its omniscient viewpoint to deliver this description of her pursuer, Stanhope, a navy sailor, entirely from the woman's perspective:

He told her—it was fascinating. He was of a good family—she had guessed as much!—but wanted to see the world. He had left a soft job in an office when he was eighteen. He told her the name of the office. She had happened to have heard of it in her typist days, and was instantly possessed by a feeling of security. Of course she was safe with him—ridiculous. He reeled off the names of ports, known and unknown. He was not very young when you were close to him, but Hilda did not like very young men, they were not distinguished, and her dream was distinction. These well-marked features, this hair, raven-black against the snowy line of the cap, yet flecked at the temples with gray, suited her best, oh, and those eyes, cruel eyes, kind eyes, kind, cruel, oh! they burnt into your shoulders, if you turned and faced them it was worse. And she so dumpy! She tried to steady herself by her modesty, which was considerable, and well-grounded. (LTC 121)

The dynamic would again seem to suggest a type of class fetishization, except that, in point of fact, Stanhope does *not* represent the lower class. He represents, rather, escape from the bourgeoisie, having been fostered not in the East End, but in the comfortable environs of a professional office. Indeed, the narrative makes this point explicit, stressing how the *similarity,* rather than the *difference* between the two, creates a "feeling of security." Moreover, Stanhope's escape from this class is not—as, say, was Carpenter's—into the lower classes. Rather, in Hilda's imagination, Stanhope becomes enmeshed in a romanticized web of adventurous images. He becomes a sort of Errol Flynn or Douglas Fairbanks figure, alluringly dark and associated with *unknown* ports. The desire here flows not between the classes of the English system, but between the English system and something else altogether.

These brief examples help to set the stage for the most obvious text in this argument, the one which Forster himself most closely associated with Carpenter, *Maurice*. For if "Arthur Snatchfold" and "The Obelisk" demonstrate some distinctly queer notions about the dynamics of class eroticism, *Maurice* centers these same notions onto the topic of sexuality itself. It is worth here rehearsing again and in greater detail Martin's argument about *Maurice,* because it so pithily explicates a reading that is irrefutably embedded within the novel.

It has regularly been supposed that the novel is concerned primarily with an opposition between homosexuality and heterosexuality. . . . In fact, the novel opposes two kinds of homosexuality—one that is identified with Cambridge and Clive, and one that is identifies with Alec and the open air—and uses the opinions on homosexual love expressed by Clive to indicate a stage in Maurice's development, but one that does not represent the author's concept of the final stage of development: this Maurice can achieve only through the encounter with Alec. . . . The first [kind of homosexuality] is dominated by Plato and, indirectly, by John Addington Symonds and the apologists for "Greek Love"; the second is dominated by Edward Carpenter and his translation of the ideas of Whitman. ("Edward" 35–36)

Martin concludes his discussion with the assertion that "Edward Carpenter thus brought an end to Forster's search for a homosexual tradition. For Carpenter seemed to create his own tradition, to offer a world where the homosexual could build a new social order" (44).

While Martin's reading of the Symonds/Carpenter split within Forster's mind—his "dual perspective"—is convincing, I would like to push momentarily his contention that Carpenter *concludes* Forster's—and the novel's—search. Returning to the afterword to the novel, a curious destabilization appears. For while it states that a Carpenter-like resolution, with Alec, Maurice, and nature in perfect commune, is something with which Forster toyed, it also says this is something he specifically rejected:

The chapter after their reunion, where Maurice ticks off Clive, is the only possible end to the book. I did not always think so, nor did others, and I was encouraged to write an epilogue. It took the form of Kitty encountering two woodcutters some years later and gave universal dissatisfaction. Epilogues are for Tolstoy. (M 254)

Instead of leaping forward to a new social order, the novel rejects such resolution, ending, instead, with Clive and at the estate of Penge. Like the strange halt of ascension in "Towards Democracy," which draws the cycle back into the world of maya, *Maurice* draws the narrative and the reader back into the very world Martin suggests it leaves behind. The "dual perspective" between Symonds's platonic homosexuality and Carpenter's socialist Uranism is not, in actuality, the governing binary of Forster's thought in the novel; the governing binary is between this system *in its entirety* and something else altogether.

The movement from Clive/Platonism to Alec/Uranism is not the only course of development for Maurice.[10] Another emerges about half-way through the novel, and its terms are initiated in the scene in which Clive realizes that he has "against [his] will . . . become normal":

Clive sat in the theatre of Dionysus. . . . Here dwelt his gods—Pallas Athene in the first place: he might if he chose imagine her shrine untouched, and her statue catching the last of the glow. She understood all men, though motherless and a virgin. (M 116)

The moment becomes retrospectively fraught with meanings when, in passing, Anne, Clive's wife, asks Maurice, "Are you a disciple of Nietzsche?" (M 169). This light comment resonates for the reader, who, unlike either Anne or Maurice, has observed Clive's agon in Greece. For, of course, the theater of Dionysus is the birthplace of Nietzsche's *The Birth of Tragedy,* in which the philosopher delineates the difference between Apollinian culture, the culture of plastic art and containable form, and Dionysian revelry, the impulse of rupture and rapture that culture must contain, the unboundedness that continually threatens the *principium individuationis* (Nietzsche 36). In this temple, Clive looks toward Athene, a representative of the arts, like Apollo, but female. Moreover, he sees the Goddess as an image of sterility, a woman who, like his love for Maurice, must "end where it begins" (M 97)—as if in this moment of looking away from the Dionysian and toward culture, Clive also sees his homosexuality reintegrated into heterosexuality.

The opposition between Apollinian and Dionysian which this reliance on Nietzsche inserts in the text would tend to suggest some coordinated binarisms. On the one hand there is the upper class, heterosexuality, the Apollinian, and Clive; on the other hand—and this would support Martin's reading—there is the lower class, homosexuality, the Dionysian, and, presumably Alec and Maurice. However, this is not exactly how the text works, for the Dionysian does not become associated with things *in* the text, but rather comes to suggest the possibility of an unknowable and unrepresented space *outside* of the text. After the invocation of Nietzsche, Maurice does, indeed, move progressively toward the

Dionysian. On an evening walk in the gardens at Penge, Alec bumps into Maurice and, "for a moment," holds him "by both elbows" (M 187). When he returns to the house, Mrs. Durham, Clive's mother, compliments Alec on his "exquisite . . . coiffure," which has been glittered by evening primrose pollen, and says, "Oh, don't brush it off. I like it on your black hair . . . [it is] quite *bacchanalian*" (M 188, my emphasis). Bacchus, the Roman equivalent of Dionysus, associates Maurice with the Dionysian, and this association appears again at the end of the novel. Clive, standing on the porch at Penge, stares into the dark garden where he thinks Maurice stands, who has just informed him of his plan to leave with Alec. He lectures Maurice on his responsibility, and then invites him to dinner, "Next Wednesday, say at 7:45. Dinner-jacket's enough." The narrative continues:

> They were his last words, because Maurice had disappeared thereabouts, leaving no trace of his presence except a little pile of petals of the evening primrose, which mournes like an expiring fire. To the end of his life Clive was not sure of the exact moment of departure . . . He did not realize that this was the end, without twilight or compromise, that he should never cross Maurice's track again, nor speak to those who had seen him. (M 246).

This is, as Forster says, the "only possible end to the book" (M 254), and its effects are telling. Readers are left within the boundaries of Penge, within the pages of the narrative, and in the presence of Clive. The only trace of Maurice is also a reminder of Dionysus—the same evening primrose which earlier clung to Maurice's hair—and Maurice himself is simply somewhere *different,* somewhere discernible neither by Clive, nor the reader, nor the narrative itself. For to determine meaning is to work within the boundaries of the *principium individuationis;* and here it should be remembered that just prior to this moment, when Clive thrusts his hand forward to *determine* the location of his friend in the dark, he touches only "a bush of laurels" (M 246), the same bush into which the nymph Daphne transformed in order to escape being raped by Apollo.[11]

   Maurice's use of a Nietzschean motif, then, echoes the poetics of Carpenter's "Towards Democracy." It propagates at the text's end a choice, not between knowable options *within* British culture, but between that culture and something else altogether; it is a choice between meaning and difference, not between different meanings. Forster uses Nietzsche to approximate the same split signifying practice present in Carpenter's thought and in his own letter from India to Dickinson. It is not surprising that Nietzsche would lend himself to such an appropriation, for in *The*

Birth of Tragedy appears this passage, which, when considered in relation to *Maurice,* assumes all sorts of suggestive overtones: "In the Dionysian dithyramb man is incited to the greatest exaltation of all his symbolic faculties; something never before experienced struggles for utterance— the annihilation of the veil of *maya,* oneness as the soul of the race and of nature itself" (40). Nor is it a coincidence that the same line from *Oedipus at Colonus* which so intrigues Nietzsche is the same line with which Clive grapples—and with which he fails to come to terms—just before he accepts his conversion to "normalcy": "Not to be born is best" (M 116; Nietzsche 42). The answer is neither life nor death, but *not being,* an impossible position that refuses to enter and can never enter the very system that articulates it. Death for Oedipus, as the line says, would be a *second* best choice, the best choice being never to have been inscribed into the system which constructs the very conditions of choice (cf. Nietzsche 42)—in effect, never to have been at all. Within Nietzsche, therefore, I find a way to articulate fully the queer superstitions that haunt both Carpenter and Forster: there are ways of being which are better, but these are all the *second* best choice; the *best* choice "is utterly beyond [one's] reach: not to be born, not to *be,* to be *nothing*" (*Oedipus at Colonus* 1224ff; qtd. in Nietzsche 42).

5. QUEER FORSTER: ON THE POLITICS OF NOT BEING

Forster has long haunted criticism as a figure torn between conflicted modes of existence.[12] June Perry Levine, for example, in an uncommonly finessed examination of Forster's posthumously published fiction, claims that the stories published after Forster's death prove the dominance within his writing of one specific motif; as she sees it, "The posthumous homosexual fiction of E. M. Forster indicates a marked impulse in all his work: the tame in pursuit of the savage, oscillating within a field of attraction and repulsion. Although the strangeness is repugnant, the tame pursues the savage because conjunction will be completion" (72). Levine's essay is laudable in that unlike so much work about the posthumous Forster canon it refuses to lapse into easy moralizing or overt homophobia. Moreover, the generality of Levine's binary terms calls to mind any number of more specific binaries that circulate through Forster's canon: the upper class in pursuit of the lower class, the heterosexual in pursuit of the homosexual, the British in pursuit of the Indian, the man in pursuit of the woman.

Levine's general categories of savage and tame echo a passage in *The Birth of Tragedy*—a passage Forster would surely have known. Moreover, this passage crystallizes the queer dynamics that such thematization sometimes represses in Forster's writings:

Where we encounter the "naïve" in art, we should recognize the highest effect of Apollinian culture—which always must first overthrow an empire of Titans and slay monsters, and which must have triumphed over an abysmal and terrifying view of the world and the keenest susceptibility to suffering through recourse to the most forceful and pleasurable illusions. (43)

It is not too much of a stretch to replace the terms naïve and Apollinian with tame and savage, and doing so summarizes crisply my central point: wherever we encounter the savage in Forster we are encountering the highest effect of the tame—and, what is more important, I am suggesting that Forster is *entirely aware of this.* His encounters with Hindu thought, like Carpenter's earlier ones, instilled within him an ability to view *all* choices as manifestations of English culture, as the continually reproduced and reproducing systems of power and knowledge that perpetuate hegemony.

Forster's representational politics, therefore, revolve *partially* around a poetics of identification—a strategy of selecting and promoting options for change and for being—but *primarily* around a poetic of *disidentifica-tion*—a strategy of embedding identifications within an epistemological framework that questions the entire apparatus of "identification," "identity," and "politics." Forster's posthumous fiction exists within a series of split and contradictory goals: to articulate while repudiating, to affirm while disavowing, to speak for while silencing, and, ultimately, to be while not being. It is only, I would claim, a *critical* humanism—both within the academy and within the world of gay and lesbian politics—that has resolved these contraries into a humanist Forster, a champion of the individual and of freedom for all, a somewhat jaded libertarian with a nonetheless overwhelming belief in the ability of culture to overcome. Exposing these contraries, I think, serves a greater political agenda for the present, for it suggests that tensions that have attended identity politics at the end of this century (tensions typified by proliferating identities, imperfect identifications with these identities, and multiple repudiations and disavowals from all fronts) actually are not new, but can be read as participating in a larger history of *disidentification politics*—a history stretching backward from Forster, to Carpenter, and even to the very Greek tragedy that spurs the thinking of Nietzsche and the structure of *Maurice.*

I do not suspect that a specifically situated essay such as this can convincingly make this larger case; I hope, rather, that it might, like Carpenter's poetry, spur a reader to quest for this history that is as yet unknowable—not to move to a place where the "I" already is, but to contemplate the possibility of things that "I" cannot comprehend. Both Carpenter and Forster worked within a framework that always believed there was something beyond the status quo, something that spans before it, after it, and in its own moment, something unrepresentable from any point in the system and therefore of paramount importance. If this essay has motivated anyone to believe in something similar, then I offer only two more words, the epigraph from *Howards End:* "only connect."

Notes

1. For examples of this depressingly frequent mode of commentary, see Jeffrey Meyers and Cynthia Ozick.

2. This is the basic thesis set forward in Homi K. Bhabha's germinal articles; see "Other Question" and "Mimicry" in *Location.*

3. The most important work on this topic is Robert K. Martin, "Double Structure"; but see also John Fletcher and June Perry Levine. For Forster's own description of his debt to Carpenter, see his essay "Edward Carpenter" (TCD 218).

4. I examine this prohibitional mode of knowledge and its functions in Western ontology and in gay and queer activism in depth in "New Queer Narrative."

5. A passage from Carpenter's writings indicates his familiarity with this specific edition and therefore justifies my reliance on it: "In one of the Upanishads of the Vedic sacred books (the Brihadaranyaka Upanishad) there is a fine passage in which instruction is given to the man who desires a noble son as to the prayers he shall offer to the gods on the occasion of congress with his wife. In primitive and simple and serene language it directs him how, at such times, he should pray to the various forms of deity who preside over the operations of Nature: to Vishnu to prepare the womb of the future mother, to Prajápati to watch over the influx of the semen, and to the other gods to nourish the foetus, etc. Nothing could be . . . more composed, serene, simple, and religious in feeling, and well might it be if such instructions were preserved and followed, even today; yet such is the pass we have come to that actually Max Müller in his translations of the Sacred Books of the East appears to have been unable to persuade himself to render these and a few other quite similar passages into English, but gives them in the original Sanskrit! One might have thought that as Professor in the University of Oxford, presumably *sans peur et sans reproche,* and professedly engaged in making a translation of these books for students, it was his duty and it might have been his delight to make intelligible just such passages as these, which give the pure and pious sentiment of the early world in so perfect a form; unless indeed he thought the sentiment impure and impious—in which case

we have indeed a measure of degradation of the public opinion which must have swayed his mind" (*Sex* 104). The Upanisad to which Carpenter alludes is in *The Upanisads,* II.73–227.

6. It is necessary to note that Carpenter harbored some misgivings about Whitman, dwelling primarily on the erotic polymorphism of the poet's work and his disavowal of homosexuality. On this point see Folsom 210.

7. What I am calling the "foundational 'I' " in Whitman finds a critical antecedent in Kenneth Burke's analysis of the cycle, which reads the mystical poems in it as being "the verbal equivalent of a universalized first person pronoun" (74–108 passim). A more recent rumination on this same topic, inflected heavily by French poststructuralism, can be found in Killingsworth.

I am aware here of an unsettling phenomenon, which is that the "I" I here explicate takes me back to the aesthetic "I" of New Criticism, the ungendered, unmarked, universalized subject who justifies "pure" as opposed to "political" readings. This is, of course, the "I" which important gay criticism such as Robert Martin's, Moon's, and Yingling's has so amply displayed as a [ph]allacy. I stress, therefore, that I perceive this "I" to be an intended, constructed effect *within* Whitman's poetry—not a naturalized assumption of my own reading practices. Moreover, I still grapple with the question of how much the necessity of carrying forth an agenda of liberation (and, therefore, an image of a liberated subject) might not at times erase differences and discrepancies within texts themselves. My own argument is entirely knotted in this same crux of issues, and I do not pretend to have answered it any more than any of these other scholars—I want only to contribute to the important debate they have begun, a debate we cannot begin to conclude at this historical moment.

8. Erkkila's work in this essay is a condensation of some aspects of her important book-length study (Erkkila, *Whitman the Political Poet*); Martin's essay represents an interesting theoretical inflection of his germinal arguments about Whitman as a gay poet (Martin, *Homosexual*). I encourage all readers to consult both of these fine books for broader explications of the framework in which I am working.

9. Michael Moon and Eve Kosofsky Sedgwick ("Confusion") trace a similar rejection of domesticity in Whitman's relationship with his mother.

10. This and the next paragraph are modified from my article "The New Queer Narrative: Intervention and Critique"—as such, they owe something to the guidance of editors Jean Howard and Alan Sinfield.

11. I thank Enoch Anderson for bringing this connection to my attention.

12. This paragraph and some of the broader ideas in this section are revised from Bredbeck, "Missionary."

3

"Thinking about Homosex"
in Forster and James

Eric Haralson

One may as well begin with E. M. Forster's lecture on Henry James
in *Aspects of the Novel* (1927):

Many readers . . . cannot grant his premise . . . that most of human life has
to disappear before he can do us a novel. . . . [His characters] are incapable
of fun, of rapid motion, of carnality, and of nine-tenths of heroism. Their
clothes will not take off, the diseases that ravage them are anonymous, like
the sources of their income, . . . no social explanation of the world we know
is possible for them, for there are no stupid people, . . . no barriers of language, no poor. Even their sensations are limited. . . . Maimed creatures alone
can breathe in Henry James's pages—maimed yet specialized. . . . They are
gutted of the common stuff that fills characters in other books, and ourselves.
And this castrating is not in the interests of the Kingdom of Heaven, there
is no philosophy in the novels, religion . . . , no benefit for the superhuman
at all. It is for the sake of a particular aesthetic effect which is certainly gained,
but at this heavy price. (AN 109–11)

Many readers—to turn Forster's phrasing back on him—have been
struck by the severity of this censure, and not a few have wondered
at what Lionel Trilling deemed its lapse of critical "energy" and "intelligence" (Trilling, *Forster* 43).[1] This is not to say that Forster was being

terribly original here; indeed, he himself quotes from H. G. Wells's attack on James in *Boon* (1915), unconsciously cribbing from Wells's own formulas: there are "no poor people" in James, and none with "lusts or whims," but only the "eviscerated"—"all that much of humanity he clears out before he begins his story" (Wells 113). On a simple view, that is, it might be said that Forster was merely joining the company of contemporary Master-beraters, which included, for instance, George Moore, who felt that James "confesses himself on every page . . . a prude" (211); the essayist Frank Moore Colby, who described the adulterous affairs in James's late novels as "the discreditable amours of skeletons" (338); and André Gide, who likewise missed "the weight of the flesh" on James's figures, the sign of "robust touches" in their characterization (258–59).[2] Yet Forster's *was* a special response to James, I will argue, marking less a failure of acumen (it was not, in any case, wholly negative) than an attempt to surmount the artistic and cultural predicament that Forster *shared* with James: the broadly "modern" narrative challenge, first, of "getting the body into writing" or "mak[ing] the material body into a signifying body," in Peter Brooks's terms (1); and the far more vexing problem of getting the *male* material body to signify within a scenario of homosexual desire—the problem of publishing same-sex passion in an era of newly intensified repression.

A watershed here, of course, was Oscar Wilde's plight at law in 1895, which culminated a decade fraught with the social negotiation and political regulation of homosexuality and which left a deep impress on the fictional enterprise of both James and Forster. James attended closely to Wilde's complex relationships with Robert Ross and Lord Alfred Douglas, to John Addington Symonds's writings on behalf of Greek love, and to the machinations of parliamentarian-journalist Henri Labouchère and Solicitor-General Frank Lockwood on behalf of its suppression (see Dellamora, *Masculine*). Capping what James saw as a replay of an earlier "ugly age of English legal or judicial history," the "sickening horribility" and "ghoulish" spectacle of the Wilde trials only reinforced his tendency to treat (homo)sexuality by implication and indirection—a coyness with depths that queer readings are only beginning to sound (James, qtd. in Thwaite 358; see James, *Letters* 9–10).[3] For the young Forster and other "men under that star" (M 89), the orchestrated demolition of Wilde hit even harder. As Richard Dellamora observes, Wilde's fate "devastated hope and destroyed affiliation" for homosexual men generally, and "permanently affected" Forster both as a private person and as an evolving writer (*Apocalyptic* 83).

Their common situation in homophobic England, then, helps us to see a submerged ground of Forster's objections to his predecessor's fiction: his disappointment that James had been willing to go so far, but no farther—to explore "certain selected recesses of experience" into which others did not venture, but not to explicate his findings with complete candor (AN 111). As if imitating Lambert Strether of *The Ambassadors* (1903), which bore the brunt of Forster's criticism, James could apparently suppose "innumerable and wonderful things" about alternative sexualities but "dressed the possibility in vagueness, as a little girl might have dressed her doll" (James, *Ambassadors* 313). This would seem to be the corollary of Forster's insight, concerning *The Turn of the Screw* (1890), that James's very compositional practice depended on a semiconscious titillation of both himself and his audience—that he was "declining to think about homosex, and the knowledge that he is . . . throws him into the necessary fluster" (CB 17–18).[4] Somewhat like Wilde, that is, who found the same novella deliciously "lurid [and] poisonous" but predicted its author would "never arrive at a passion," Forster perceived a hidden motive as well as a resistance to that motive at the heart of James's production (Oscar Wilde, qtd. in Sicker 8).[5] If Victorian sensationalism in the vein of *The Turn of the Screw* functioned "to 'say' certain things for which our culture . . . has yet to develop another language," as D. A. Miller contends, then Forster heard James saying things about "homosex" in an ulterior voice—and not nearly audibly enough (Miller 148).

More precisely: James's novels, of which Forster read many, served as a steady source of provocation—of *constructive* irritation—because he grasped how their typical texture of "cocooning and muffling" registered a simultaneous acknowledgment and concealment of the (male) body's diverse impulses (SL 2:299).[6] At the same time, one may speculate, Forster's scolding of James drew added force from his worry that, as a fiction writer, he had perhaps foundered on the same rock. Had *he* managed to repudiate what Amy Lowell called the "slimy inhibitions" (Lowell 460) of the Victorian inheritance? Were his own characters ample-bodied, or were they (to adapt Stevens) "castratos of moonmash" (Stevens 281)—no better than James's "exquisite deformities" (AN 110)? Had he also declined to "think" out loud about homosex, or too often veiled his thinking behind heterosexual screens? In a revealing entry in his commonplace book for 1927—the ripe period of *Aspects of the Novel*—Forster wondered whether "my ability to write fuck may preserve me from too close contact with H[enry] J[ames]" (CB 29), but it will prove instructive to glance back at two *formative* events that find him broaching the same general question: Forster's meeting with James in Rye in 1908, and his effort to transcend James's matter and manner in *A Room with a View* (1908), a novel bent on fun, rapid motion, and carnality in which masculine bodies and desires notably romp.

| | | |

But the body is deeper than the soul and its secrets inscrutable. *Maurice*

It is not too much to say that Forster's early encounter with Henry James set both the tone and the terms for all of his subsequent criticism of James's fiction. According to P. N. Furbank, when Forster entered Lamb House in January 1908, it was for his "first meeting with a first-rate literary celebrity," and his own account of the "funny sensation[s]" involved bears this out (Furbank, *Life* 1:163–64). After James's initial (and forgivable) misimpression that Forster was the Cambridge philosopher G. E. Moore,[7] the visit came off charmingly, with Forster studying his host's features ("Head rather fat, but fine") and James exuding "civility and warmth" as he clasped the young man's shoulder (SL 1:92)—"that gesture so familiar to those who knew him," as Evan Charteris recalled, in which biographers have seen a blend of avuncular tenderness and muted eroticism (276; Edel 496–98; see also Kaplan). Perhaps fittingly, the jokes turned to gender-bending, as James hailed the late Queen Victoria, whose letters he was reading, as "more of a man than I expected," adding, when another guest faulted her excessive underlining, "Well, she was an underlined man."[8] The topic of the body's artistic uses arose, too, as James discussed the "vulnerable" self-display of a popular stage actress (not unlike his own Miriam Rooth of *The Tragic Muse* [1890]), whom he described as "divesting herself of armour and baring her breast" (Furbank, *Life* 1:163–64). However playfully or obliquely, then, questions of how gender gets inscribed or "underlined" and how physical passions get deployed in art percolated through Lamb House that afternoon.

Forster's summation of the day—"I felt all that the ordinary healthy man feels in the presence of a lord"—conveys his admiration for James as a writer and "a really first class person," while at the same time tweaking him for his drawing-room courtliness (qtd. in Furbank, *Life* 1:164). This last caveat is key, for Forster's pilgrimage confirmed him in an authorial direction opposite to James's. The signal moment of their meeting, in fact, occurred only *afterward,* when Forster noticed a young workman lounging and smoking in the shadows outside of James's residence. The sudden obtrusion of this embodiment of manly ease inspired a poem of vocation (quoted in full in Furbank, *Life* 1:165) that records Forster's relieved transition from the constraint of Lamb House ("the room / Where culture unto culture knelt") to the freedom of the street; from the "presence of a lord" and Master to that of another "ordinary healthy man"; most crucially, from a venue of "high talk" and "subtle experience" to one of simple body language, mundane pleasures, a savored cigarette: "The spark, the darkness, on the walk." With a touch of melodrama, the poem announced that the "reality" Forster sought— and would seek to represent in fiction—would not be James's, but something riskier, more abject, closer to the bone: "Something just darker than the gloom /   / the unknown and the truth."

Forster's reaction to James in person, as I have suggested, patterned his comments on James in print, whether for private or for public consumption. In a letter of January 1918, for example, in terms he would formalize in the Cambridge lectures that became *Aspects of the Novel,* he complained that James required the reader to "throw off the interests of one's larger life, and flatten oneself . . . to crawl down his slots." "Bring muscle or blood to bear"—try to read James with or through the body— "and you stick at once" (SL 1:283). The vocabulary of self-abasement and infantilization here ("flatten oneself "; "crawl") indicates Forster's uneasy sense, while reading James, of reenacting the Lamb House episode of "kneeling" to Victorian high culture. Yet as hinted by the equally arresting imagery of trying to insert himself in the "slots" of James's fictional corpus (only to connect, as it were), this was no ordinary anxiety of influence. Forster's discontent, that is, originated not in his feeling inferior to "the last hectic Edwardian giants" (Robert Lowell's phrase for the likes of James and Hardy [Robert Lowell 4]), nor in his chafing under the Master's mastery (as with Wells), but in his yearning for a greater and a grittier *physicality* both in James's represented world and in the pleasure of the text: "His art is so sure and dominating that it pacifies us while we read. But it doesn't satisfy us" (CB 14).

As will become evident in considering the queer emanations of *A Room with a View,* Forster's composite "us"—like his placid appeal to "many readers" and their "common stuff " in *Aspects of the Novel*—harbors complicated issues of reading practice as it relates to different sexualities and the narratives that are likely to "satisfy" them. But for now I wish to focus, in a more neutral way, on his most basic disenchantment with James: the absent body. Although Forster granted that inhabitants of "the nations of fiction . . . need not have glands," his prejudice was clearly that they should, along with substantial physiologies—as with Moll Flanders's "hard plump limbs that get into bed and pick pockets"

(AN 36, 40). Whether regretting that the English novel neglected "the sensuousness of swallowing" (AN 37) or applauding "an enlightened greediness" toward food in the pages of Virginia Woolf, he set a premium on vividly evoked appetites. Thus we should not be surprised by the insistently corporeal terms in which he criticized James ("maimed," "gutted," etc.), nor, perhaps, by the fact that the "carnality" he missed in James's characters is conceived as fluent and continuous, with sexual satisfaction (the most serious casualty of such "castrating") often figured as gustatory relish—or, in this case, the lack thereof: "There is . . . no savour whatever in any dish of Henry James's" (TCD 246). This felt linkage or slippage between physical pleasures is further illustrated by a puckish entry in Forster's commonplace book for 1926, which envisions James in his garden, "snipping beetroots and spring onions for his salad": "I know he would keep among the vegetables, if only because their reproductive organs are not prominent" (CB 7). Like this squeamish horticulturalist of fancy, the author of The Ambassadors had "pared" from his characters "all that's exciting to body and spirit" and dumped the disjecta membra in "the dustbin or the W.C.," adding to the store of books in which the body seemed to be nothing more than "a sheet of glass through which the soul gazes" (SL 2:73; TCD 241).[9]

To give James his due (or his donnée, as he would say), The Ambassadors takes as its center of dramatic and psychological interest exactly that puritanical wariness of the body that Forster imputes to the author, touring its bemused hero—that "belated man of the world" Lambert Strether of provincial Massachusetts (James, Literary: French 1311)— through a Paris in which the "terrible life" of sex might be lurking behind every smile (James, Ambassadors 121). As a well-traveled, well-read, premature man of the world himself, James had early recognized how "prudish" his compatriots could be when contrasted with products of continental culture, especially the French in their "unshrinking contemplation of our physical surfaces," their "high animal spirits" (James, Literary: French 367, 43). And one staple of his fiction, of course, was the international theme—the entanglement of this almost willful American innocence in the meshes of a Europe charged with sexual power politics. Although The Ambassadors is rather a benign instance, it shows James tallying the cultural liabilities—as well as the less obvious assets—of a New England imagination that labors to sanitize carnal relations (technically, adultery) under the guise of a "virtuous attachment" (Ambassadors 133). In this respect, a character like Strether in a place like Paris might be said to discover—under the pressure of his author's gentle irony— the very facts of experience that Forster saw James as eliding in the pursuit of formal tidiness: more often than not, the body will out, and no creatures on earth are "so wanton as human beings" (AN 110).

But where James's novel really rubbed Forster the wrong way was in apparently *valorizing* this turn from the sexual body (with whatever concession to the costs involved) in favor of more delicate raptures of a "super-sensual," but resolutely nonsexual, kind (James, *Notebooks* 393). On Strether's example, that is, "living all you can" (in the words of his famous outburst) amounts to *displacing* sexuality onto the delectations of the aesthete—visual and memorial mainly, though with an allowance for epicureanism that Forster seems to have overlooked (witness Strether's romance with "thick-crusted" bread, *omelettes aux tomates,* "light cold clever French things," an overprized bottle of Bordeaux (*Ambassadors* 132, 176, 71–72, 133). At best a "compensatory erotic," in Jonathan Freedman's phrase (193), such a mode of being bordered too much on the finicky aestheticism of "fastidious saints" like Cecil Vyse of *A Room with a View,* on the one hand, while on the other its renunciations were simply too tepid for Forster's liking (RV 86). As he editorialized in *Howards End,* the "belief that bodily passion is bad . . . is desirable only when held passionately" (HE 183), whereas Strether's continence held no "superhuman" drama, no discernible payoff for "the interests of the Kingdom of Heaven."

There is more to be said for Strether—for his relational choices, his mild "moral glamour," even his naive Paterian strain (*Ambassadors* 64)—than Forster was willing to admit. In its own circumspect way, that is, *The Ambassadors* offered a subtle challenge to the new discursive and regulatory environment of late-Victorian England—an environment in which, as Christopher Craft observes, social purity campaigners, legal reformers, and the medicoscientific community conspired to ensure that "sex would not just signify, it would signify everywhere," with dire consequences for homosexual emergence (*Another* 27–28). Indeed, the Forster who argued for "the importance of sensation in an age which practises brutality and recommends ideals" should perhaps have sympathized with James's plea on behalf of adventures of consciousness and impressionism, as against more bodily delights (TCD 247). "My poetic and my appeal to experience rest upon . . . *my* measure of fulness—fulness of life and of the projection of it," as James wrote to H. G. Wells in 1915, protesting his rough usage in *Boon:* "For myself I live, live intensely and am fed by life, and my value, whatever it be, is in my own kind of expression of that. . . . It is art that *makes* life, makes interest, makes importance, . . . and I know of no substitute for the force and beauty of its process" (*Letters* 767–70). But Forster can only have

viewed such claims for art as imbalanced and undialogic, with a privileging of exquisite intensities that led precisely away from "one's larger
life"—the life in and of the body—and into "the Palace of Art, . . . that
bottomless chasm of dullness," that "dreadful hole into which the un-
wary esthete . . . tumble[s]" (TCD 240).

As my reference to Pater suggests, and as Joseph Bristow has well
demonstrated, Forster's contestation with Victorian cultural residues
went far beyond his reservations about specifically Jamesian aestheticism
(Bristow, *Effeminate* 55–99). But it is nonetheless striking how James
would recur as a culprit throughout his career, and how consistently
in the context of (homo)sexual representations of the body. Even the
"Terminal Note" to *Maurice* (1960) maintains that, while tracing masculine desire requires "careful handling," still "the art called for . . . is not
of a high order, not as high as Henry James thinks" (M 239). To the
end, it seems, Forster strove to queer the exalted notion of mastery he
associated with James, as if to certify his very *early* conviction that, inas-
much as the Jamesian novel abstracted the body and rarefied the emotions, "that isn't my road" (SL 1:92). Yet difficult questions confronted
the young Forster as he charted his literary itinerary at the start of the
century. Just *how* would he dramatize the counterposition that, as he
urges in *A Room with a View*, "passion . . . should forget civility and
consideration and all the other curses of a refined nature," particularly
when he possessed such a nature (RV 108)? Would *his* accounts of "life"
embrace the full experience of the body and the range of sexualities—
the ways of all flesh?

| | |

So they proceeded outwardly like other men. . . . Behind Society slumbered the
Law. *Maurice*

A Room with a View, published in the same year as Forster's meeting of
James, gives a convenient gauge of his progress along his different novelistic "road," as well as an inventory of the obstacles lying in it. In this
monitory tale in which young lovers transcend "the rubbish that cum-
bers the world," obstructing both emotional and physical expression,
old Mr. Emerson's much-quoted pronouncement that "love is of the
body" seems a staunch rebuttal of the austerity that Forster disliked in
James (RV 134, 202). Further, the novel (unlike James's) boasts characters whose clothes explicitly "take off," as with the three men who disport
themselves in the Sacred Lake, a scene memorably circulated in popular

culture through the Merchant Ivory film adaptation. Already in 1908, that is, Forster found himself searching—in the terms of Bristow's analysis—for "a public and plausible form" of representing homoeroticism in unobjectionable relation to both heterosexist taste and feminine authority; and already his text betrayed a crisis of representation, remaining "regulated—if not, by necessity, mystified—by profoundly heteronormative assumptions" (58–59). As a narrative hot spot, the bathing scene conveys Forster's sense of the male body, in especial, as a "restless captive of culture" that "animates and disrupts the social order" and that the social order struggles always to recontain (Brooks 6). Yet just as the clothes that "take off" eventually go back on—"To us shall all flesh turn in the end," they taunt from the lakeshore, countermanding the Thoreauvian dictum on the Emersons' wardrobe (RV 131)—Forster is ultimately compelled to cloak his critique of the "normal" in the garb of the normal, thus risking the same "cocooning and muffling" he deplored in James.

Before addressing the Sacred Lake episode in detail, however, it will be useful to review Forster's characterization of his three bathers— Freddy Honeychurch, George Emerson, and the clergyman Mr. Beebe— and of the negative countertype Cecil Vyse, who will show up with his intended, Lucy Honeychurch, and her mother to put "a confining and depressing end to the affair," as Samuel Hynes says (qtd. in Fussell 306). Young Freddy, whose letters to his sister Lucy are "full of athletics and biology" and who is seen "studying a small manual of anatomy," can easily be pegged as the earnest, hail-fellow-well-met creature of such homosocial institutions as the British public school and (prospectively) the medical establishment (RV 56, 82). Forster has fun with Freddy's efforts to sever the maternal apron strings ("Oh, do keep quiet, mother . . . and let a man do some work") and permits Cecil to sneer at him as the sort of muscular-Christian "healthy person . . . who has made England what she is," but Freddy also scores points for his glad animal movements: "Apooshoo, apooshoo, apooshoo. . . . Water's simply ripping" (RV 84, 91, 130).

In George Emerson, who will dislodge Vyse as Lucy's true mate, Forster tests out a prototype of the new-age male—a character, as Bristow writes, who incorporates "an idiosyncratic blend of cultural interests . . . where the appreciation of art and 'love . . . of the body' are not separate" (73). Yet, although George is dedicated to securing the heterosexual love-plot, and will emerge from his dip "bare-chested" and "radiant" to smite Lucy's vision (RV 133), Forster simultaneously invites another frame and another kind of gaze—not only by annexing the post-

Whitmanian tradition of bathing-boys scenes but also, and less obviously, by stocking George's library with his own early readings of a homoerotic hue, notably Samuel Butler's *The Way of All Flesh* and A. E. Housman's *A Shropshire Lad,* which, as Forster said, "mingled with my own late adolescence and turned inward upon me" (qtd. in Furbank, *Life* 1:153).

Completing the trio, the "stout but attractive" Mr. Beebe (RV 4) is a slightly more hopeful incarnation of the Victorian bachelor figure whose line of descent, as Eve Kosofsky Sedgwick has shown, includes John Marcher of "The Beast in the Jungle" (1903) and other "poor sensitive gentlemen" (James, *Literary: French* 1250) whose psychic constitution opens onto homosexual panic, if not homosexual possibility (Sedgwick, *Epistemology* 182–212). In a tactful but no longer difficult allusion, Forster notes that Beebe has "rather profound reasons" for responding coolly to women and for seeing them as objects of strictly anthropological curiosity, even though as a "feminized" man of the cloth he lives mainly among them (RV 32). Forster's indirection in describing Beebe, moreover, is inscribed in the cleric's own manner of commentary—or what Freddy calls his "funny way, when you never quite know what he means." Not coincidentally, what puzzles Freddy's amiable but restricted mind is Beebe's contention that Vyse can only *impersonate* a (hetero)romantic suitor, being in actuality "an ideal bachelor . . . like me—better detached" (RV 85). And even though Forster satirizes Charlotte Bartlett's lament to Lucy, bemoaning the death of chivalry ("Oh, for a real man! . . . Oh, for your brother!"), Charlotte's sense of Beebe as "hopeless" in this regard also tags him as exemplifying another style of masculinity (RV 75).

An extra emphasis on "masculinity" is warranted here, for Forster takes pains to discriminate between Mr. Beebe and Cecil Vyse as, respectively, the hearty and mostly *sympathetic* "ideal bachelor"—one who, as Charlotte primly objects, "laughs just like an ordinary man" (RV 9)—and the repugnant variety, one of the "despicable and regressive species of mocking intellectuals" (Bristow, *Effeminate* 72), who combined, for Forster, a precious Paterian-Jamesian aestheticism with a Wildean lassitude and antiathleticism ("I have no profession," says Cecil, "It is another example of my decadence" [RV 91]). It is Beebe, after all, who analogizes Vyse to a Gothic statue, implying "celibacy," where a Greek statue implies "fruition" (RV 87)—who perceives, in a word, that Vyse is insufficiently masculine for *either* heterosexual or "masculine love" (as it will be named in *Maurice*) and thus perniciously opposed to the currents that replenish and "fructify every hour of life" (RV 71). In this way, too, Beebe distinguishes himself from the novel's other clergyman, the Reverend Cuthbert Eager, who fatuously praises Giotto's frescoes for being "untroubled by the snares of anatomy" and for avoiding the corporeal "taint of the Renaissance" (RV 22). Beebe's consent to strip and swim, then, aligns him provisionally with the adversaries of "drawing-room twaddle" and genteel Baedeker discourse (echoes of Lamb House, to Forster's ear), which chastely applauds Giotto's "tactile values" and holds that "a pity in art . . . signified the nude"—as in Charlotte's disdain for *another* water borne being, Botticelli's Venus (RV 127, 19, 40). Like Mr. Emerson, who pontificates about the paradise to be regained when "we no longer despise our bodies," like Lucy Honeychurch, who "by touch . . . come[s] to her desire" and "entertain[s] an image that [has] physical beauty," but decidedly *unlike* Cecil Vyse with his "depths of prudishness," Beebe votes for—and with—the body at the Sacred Lake (RV 126, 30, 143, 107).

What *makes* the lake sacred in Forster's fable is no great mystery, although here again the level of popular, heteronormative signification and reception shades into more covert "messages" and a queerer take on the scene. As a medium of more or less *generic* lubrication, tumescence, nakedness—and notice that Lucy, too, had bathed there until "found out" and reclaimed for gentility by Charlotte (RV 107)—the lake emblematizes Mr. Emerson's projected paradise on earth: "set in its little alp of green . . . [it was] large enough to contain the human body, and pure enough to reflect the sky" (RV 129). Further, to the extent that the episode advances George's conquest of Lucy, the lake reprises the riverine bed of violets in which they first kissed in Italy—that ejaculative "primal source whence beauty gushed out" to "irrigate" the grass with "spots of azure foam" (RV 68). At this level, both the hyperidealized scenery—the "beautiful emerald path, tempting the feet towards the central pool"—and the sacramentalized passion it induces ("a call to the blood . . . a momentary chalice for youth") subserve an Eden whose beckonings and indulgences wear a look familiarly heterosexual, or at the very least "neutral" (RV 129, 133). To put this another way, Forster's obligatory insistence on scenic "purity" and, by extension, on the innocent frolicsomeness of his male bathers does little to retard the normative thrust of the narrative or to disturb the normative valence of the "floods of love . . . burst[ing] forth in tumult" that it seeks to celebrate (RV 71).

Yet as we remarked in sorting through George Emerson's library, in which Housman huddles next to Nietzsche, the heralded bathing scene manages to gesture toward a different call to the blood and a different kind of sexual immersion as well. As hinted by the unidentified "aromatic plant" flourishing near the pond's "flooded margin"—almost certainly a tribute to Whitman's calamus, or sweet-flag—Forster provides a comic, if inevitably veiled, variant of the "greenwood" fantasy of masculine love that concludes *Maurice*. In a setting "beyond the intrusion of man" and nestled in the bosom of nature—in an aqueous vessel, no less, that conjures up both seminal and amniotic associations—Freddy, George, and Mr. Beebe find a social space where not only anticorporeality but also heterosexist presumption and regulation are put in suspense—where for a moment, in the parlance of *Maurice*, the Law slumbers. Whether "rotat[ing] in the pool breast high"—in Forster's campy depiction—like "the nymphs in Götterdämmerung," or "play[ing] at being Indians," or kicking their bundled clothes like schoolboys at soccer, or "twinkl[ing] into the trees," the three men try on alternative genders, ethnicities, and social roles in a temperate carnival of deviance (RV 129–131). In fact, they even try on each other's costumes in a homoerotically coded sequence of exchanges: Freddy, who significantly cannot see the repressed Cecil Vyse "wearing another fellow's cap" (RV 87), here makes off with Beebe's waistcoat, while George dons Beebe's "wide-awake hat" and ends up wearing Freddy's "bags." These often phallically connotative swappings and sharings, in turn, culminate in a figurative instance of male-male conception when Freddy announces, giddily: "I've swallowed a pollywog. It wriggleth in my tummy" (RV 131–133).

But as we know—and as Forster, for all his lighthearted treatment, underscores—the Law only slumbers, soon to arouse and reinstate itself, as the amalgamated powers of the maternal, the domestic, the female-amative, and the bourgeois-respectable intervene to terminate this idyl of masculine adhesiveness. Freddy's weak protest against the restoration of conventional rule ("Look here, mother, a fellow must wash, . . . and if another fellow—") is quelled when Mrs. Honeychurch declares that, being naked, he is "in no position to argue" and gains his compliance by means of a time-honored token of motherly concern: "All these colds come of not drying thoroughly." Meanwhile George, in all his "bare-chested" radiance, gets carefully reinvested in the heterosexual paradigm, calling Lucy to her romantic fate "with the shout of the morning star," and Mr. Beebe finds himself painfully recalled to reality and propriety, imagining—in his paranoia—that "every pine-tree [is] a Rural Dean" (RV 131–134).

Perhaps most telling, from the standpoint of Forster's adjudication of masculinities, is his casting of Cecil as unwittingly arrayed with the feminine forces of normalization—a notion embedded in Beebe's sentinel cry of alarm, "Hi! Hi! *Ladies!*," which seems to collapse Vyse with

his female companions (RV 131). By now well-established as a condescending poseur who "believe[s] that women revere men for their manli-
ness," Vyse here shows even more sharply as a walking parody of the
English patriarch, "who always felt he must lead women, though he
knew not whither, and protect them, though he knew not against what"
(RV 108, 132). To this ersatz version of an already corrupt gender style
the Merchant Ivory film furnishes an added accent, as Cecil—gloriously
overplayed, as hardly seemed possible, by Daniel Day-Lewis—bush-
whacks through the bracken, "ladies" in tow, in quest of new territory to
colonize on behalf of the constrained body, male privilege, and imperial
aggrandizement. We may confidently speculate that Forster, whose later
novels criticize just such a "desire for possessions [and] creditable ap-
pendages," would have appreciated this touch (PI 241).

A Room with a View might be read, then, as a concerted attempt to
reject what Forster saw as the mistaken scheme of values informing
James's oeuvre, as well as a critique of the sociopolitical context that
surrounded and conditioned those writings. In a calculated riposte to
authors like James, who believed fiction should delineate the "elemen-
tary passions . . . in a spirit of intellectual superiority" (James, Criticism:
Essays 857) and who anticipated modernist misgivings about sentimen-
talism's "connection to a sexual body" (Clark 7), Forster set out to give
his third novel a "stifling human quality"—to make it "sogged with humanity" (in the aptly fluid terms of Aspects of the Novel) and not to deny
the "sentimentality . . . lurk[ing] in the background" of much readerly
pleasure (AN 15). As I began this essay by suggesting—and as would
become apparent in the experiment of Maurice—one powerful (if still
hidden) motive of Forster's campaign to make a great good place for the
body and naked feeling in fiction was the hope of clearing a narrative
field for homosexual subjectivity—for the "generous recognition of an
emotion and . . . the reintegration of something primitive into the common stock" (M 240). Not only did the "common stuff" that Forster
missed in James's characters need to be reanimated in the conversation
of culture, but that same move should open a way toward acceptance
of less common—or rather, less commonly acknowledged—sexualities
as well.

In the final analysis, though, we must ask whether A Room with a
View accomplishes or even effectively predicts such a "rout of . . . civilization" in this more ambitious sense (RV 134) or whether instead—as
queer theory posits, and as Forster would perceive with growing acu-
ity—certain costs attach to the traditional "marital teleology of the comic
text" with its policing of nonnormative masculinities (Craft 36). If one

means to contest the cultural position that Forster found inadequately contested in James by asserting that love is "of the body," why stipulate (as Mr. Emerson does) that love is "not the body"? Might stopping this one step shy of fully "carnal embracement" (PI 135)—a last-ditch reticence encountered in all of Forster's fiction, including *Maurice*—involve renewed concessions to a spiritualized "love" that is always in peril of being (re)engulfed in heteronormativity? Doesn't *A Room with a View* forfeit something *politically* vital by deferring to the usual script with its "idiotic use of marriage as a finale," as Forster wrote in *Aspects of the Novel*, repeating an opinion he held even at the time of the novel's composition (AN 26)? Or if one *does* nod, in the same work, toward other possible desires and consummations, how much gets changed, in the realm of the real, when the nod is only to those in the know?

The rhetorical posture of such a line of inquiry is perhaps unavoidably invidious, and as we have seen, Forster's private ruminations were not without self-doubt and self-recrimination on this score. Yet to charge "queer Forster" with not being queer *enough*—or with failing decisively to subvert heterosexist narrative conventions—would seem to miss the point. For how, in fairness, *was* one to "reveal the hidden life at its source" when "mutual secrecy" had always been the enabling premise of society (AN 31), and especially when the state and its agencies of sexual regulation made one pay with one's body for certain disclosures? To leave Forster's perennial quarrel with Henry James simply in the region of psychobiography—the influence of somebody upon somebody, to adapt Woolf—would be to neglect the *collective* testimonial of their works to the efficacy and resilience of homophobia in what is called, evidently without conscious irony, the life of man.

Notes

1. For this and other helpful bibliographic leads, I am indebted to Arthur Sherbo's "Jamesiana." As Alan W. Bellringer says of the passages on James in *Aspects*: "Forster's chatty tone covers a multitude of sins. . . . *The Ambassadors* emerges as an uninteresting exercise in aesthetic formalism" (157).

2. Colby's remarks on James are nicely extrapolated in Litvak.

3. The James-Wilde relation and its artistic registrations have been much discussed; for especially valuable treatments, see William A. Cohen and Jonathan Freedman.

4. In this entry, Forster mainly intends to criticize James's evocation of *evil* in favor of Dostoevsky's or Melville's, even as he characteristically prefers a humbler, more quotidian moral drama than theirs ("I don't believe evil exists"). Curi-

ously, there is some suggestion that (homo)sexuality itself, *as* a bodily aspect, threatens the degree of abstraction needed to evoke cosmic battle between darkness and light: the "goodness" symbolized by Billy Budd seems to be depreciatingly "alloyed by [the] suppressed homosex" of his relation to John Claggart (CB 17–18).

5. See Sicker, chap. 1, generally for the reception history on Jamesian "passion."

6. Even Forster's praise for James had a bodily flavor, as when he finds a particular scene in *The Princess Casamassima* "terrifying in its nakedness" (SL II: 299). For a list of the James's works read by Forster, see Sherbo, especially 217 n. 3.

7. As a comical measure of the problems of generational succession in literature, Forster's identity remained a source of confusion to James's circle; Edith Wharton, meeting him years later, addressed him as "Michael" rather than Morgan; see Wharton's *Letters* 596.

8. According to Adrienne Munich, James, like many others, took Victoria"s "muted sexuality for granted so that he [could] depend on her maternal protection . . . as a folk madonna, . . . open[ing] her ethnic shawl to her peoples" (78).

9. Forster's extraordinary metaphors when discussing James in particular and authorship in general deserve closer attention. Extending the "W.C." motif, Forster saw James's (and others') practice of revising and republishing as "fiddling, masturbational"—a narcissistic and largely fruitless manipulation (CB 74). Perhaps for this reason, he hesitated to number James among the great novelists, whom he imagined (in a fantasy from *Aspects of the Novel*) as "seated together in . . . a circular . . . sort of British museum reading-room," a cadre for whom "the feel of the pen between their fingers"—"the fact that their pens are in their hands" and "their sorrows and joys . . . pouring out through the ink"—was the defining obsession (AN 5, 13). These figurations of writing as either a "bad" autoerotism occurring, say, in a water closet or a "good" micturation occurring in a famous reading room locate Forster in a line of authors from Shelley to Hopkins to Joyce, who "valorize[d] the flow of bodily fluid" (in Richard Dellamora's phrase [*Masculine Desire* 54]) as a homoerotically tinged discourse for artistic fluency, perhaps signaling (once again) Forster's deeper frustration with James for failing to articulate masculine love. On "Joyce's identification of micturition with creativity" and its application to the "symbolic union" of Leopold Bloom and Stephen Dedalus, see A. Walton Litz 401.

4

The Mouse That Roared:
Creating a Queer Forster

Christopher Reed

WE'RE HERE! WE'RE QUEER! WE'RE . . . Forster? Forster, whom Virginia Woolf called "timid as a mouse," explaining "he spends his time rowing old ladies upon the river, and is not able to get on with his novel" (Woolf, *Letters* 2:63)? The man she described as "limp and damp and milder than the breath of a cow" (Woolf, *Letters* 3:266)? The one she several times compared to a blue butterfly, explaining "I mean by that to describe his transparency and lightness. . . . I find him whimsical and vagulous to an extent that frightens me with my own clumsiness & definiteness" (Woolf, *Diary* 1:291; cf. 295; 3:177; *Moments of Being,* 198)? That Forster? And his books? Novels that have become the basis of luscious "Masterpiece Theatre"–style films, which thrill middlebrow audiences with their picturesque ideal of Edwardian England? His stories were like "careful cocoons," Woolf said, "why not say straight out—yes, but what?" (Woolf, *Diary* 2: 304). Forster, of course, was not straight, but neither was he out. He locked away his novel and short stories that dealt overtly with same-sex eroticism, all of which were published only posthumously. It is hard to imagine anyone further from the in-your-face politics of contemporary queer identity than E. M. Forster.

And yet. Yet a high school teacher was fired for teaching *Maurice* to her seniors.[1] Children—even about-to-be-adult children—apparently need to be protected from this mouse, this puff of cow's breath, this blue butterfly. A figure has emerged, with the name E. M. Forster, who is, to the dominant culture, terrifyingly queer. And who made him? Not scholars who write under the banner of queerness. We have not made Forster a role model for high schoolers. As noted in the introduction to this volume, pioneering gay activists rejected Forster as a "traitor"—the "Closet Queen of the Century," who "betrayed other gay people by posing as a heterosexual and thus identifying with our oppressors" (Hodges and Hutter 20–21)—while pioneering gay scholars, such as Robert K. Martin, were careful to situate his writings in their particular historical context. And, as many of the essays in this collection demonstrate, a self-styled "queer" generation has been quick to interrogate Forster's sexual radicalism, citing, even in the stories he found too daring to publish during his lifetime, the lurking presumptions of the white middle class. In an irony that Foucault would have appreciated—or predicted— Queer Forster is a product of those who abhor queerness. Just as legal discourses produce lawlessness and medical discourses produce pathology, so the constant—even hysterical—rehearsal of homophobia has produced the queerness of the "queer Forster."

This construction of the queer Forster began with the critical reception to *Maurice* in 1971. Responding to the revelation of Forster's sexual attraction to men, reviewers scrambled to demote him from the role of spokesman for universal humanistic values to which he had been assigned by the rhetorics of mainstream literary criticism. "Now suddenly with the appearance of *Maurice,* it is clear that Forster's famous humanism is a kind of personal withdrawal rather than a universal testimony," asserted Cynthia Ozick in *Commentary,* asking and answering her own question: "Does it devalue the large humanistic statement to know that its sources are narrowly personal? Yes" (85). Likewise, George Steiner in the *New Yorker* regretted that this new insight into Forster meant that he must be demoted to the rank of a "minor master," "less representative of modern English literature than some critics have argued" (482).

For these reviewers, however, homosexuality was more a limitation than a threat. Homosexuality—or rather its explicit articulation—excludes the speaker from the sphere of the "universal" and "humanistic," but that charmed circle spins on intact. This is an attitude of breathtaking arrogance, epitomized, perhaps, by Jeffrey Meyers's appalling 1977 book, *Homosexuality and Literature,* which opens with the regret that "when the laws of obscenity were changed and homosexuality became legal [in England] . . . the theme surfaced defiantly and sexual acts were grossly described. The emancipation of the homosexual has led, paradoxically, to the decline of his art" (3). By this time, however, other critics were less sanguine. "Gay Liberation" seemed to threaten more than the mechanics of aesthetic obfuscation—and with that, the livelihood of critics who set out to wrest the "truth" of the author's homosexuality from coded texts. In the late 1970s, the complacent condescension of modernist liberal humanism gave way in writings on literature and the arts to rhetorics previously associated with headline-hungry politicians and sensationalists from the behavioral pseudosciences. By the 1980s, the image of the homosexual as a dangerous threat came to undergird critical discourses that seemingly had nothing else in common—indeed, that were in other ways antagonistic. This was the argument of an essay I published in 1991, looking specifically at how Bloomsbury was invoked to signify a pernicious and overwhelming threat in critical discourses of the 1980s ranging from Marxist to neo-Victorian, and even feminist. The editors of the present volume have asked me to provide a version of that article—much abridged and slightly revised—as an account of the context that created a "Queer Forster."

| | |

As early as 1968, Quentin Bell noted that Bloomsbury had been "criticised from a bewilderingly large number of points of view" (*Bloomsbury* 10).[2] The 1980s saw little change in this situation. Bloomsbury's name was deployed to signify everything from the English landed gentry to the hippie counterculture, and from free-wheeling sexual liberation to the most oppressive phallocentric conspiracy. The contradictory nature of the attacks on Bloomsbury suggests a general failure to come to grips with the group in any kind of historical specificity, a failure attributable in part to the breadth of the group's activities, which ranged from aesthetics to economics, and from the most public of political campaigns to the most private of sexual revolutions. Robert Skidelsky has observed that Bloomsbury was the last intellectual movement to sustain itself in England outside of the university system (248), and its disregard for the boundaries of academic disciplines contributes to the imprecision with which modern commentators, trained within those limits, use the group's name.

From the apparent chaos of current critical approaches to Bloomsbury, however, emerges a common anxiety. Consistently behind—or metaphorized within—pejorative descriptions of Bloomsbury is the group's transgression of patriarchy's ultimate prohibition: the feminized man. So primary is this taboo (consider the number of men who wear skirts, as opposed to women who wear pants), it can be used to signify virtually any deviance from any critical norm and to symbolize the most overwhelming of threats. Bloomsbury's deviance from the conventional standards of masculinity allows (or provokes?) critics of all ideological stripes to position the group as a symbol of the dangerous "other" against which their versions of virtue (significantly, from the Latin *vir*, for "man") are defined. In popular and academic culture alike, masculine effeminacy and male homosexuality are conflated, with each serving as the image and proof of the other. On the streets, to deviate from the standards of masculine heterosexuality is to invite the kinds of attacks known popularly as "queer-bashing," a practice that justifies itself as a defense against a threat to morality or public order. In current criticism, Bloomsbury suffers an analogous kind of bashing at the hands of academics in the name of a variety of critical orders and moralities.

The Marxist version of this phenomenon may be represented by Charles Harrison's survey text, *English Art and Modernism,* first published by Indiana University Press in 1981, but rereleased in 1994 under the Yale imprimatur. Here Harrison presents the history of modernism as a competition between "two significant and contrasting interests," the first identified with "the social function of art," while the second associated with "the contrasting point of view that art should be valued in terms of a set of culturally autonomous interests" (13–14). The triumph of the protoformalist painter J. A. M. Whistler over the protosocialist critic John Ruskin—here Harrison refers not to their actual legal confrontation, which ended by bankrupting Whistler, but to the way "history has tended to represent [Whistler] as a martyr in the cause of modernism" (14)—is described as presaging Bloomsbury's subsequent domination of both the social realist Camden Town painters and the quasi-Futurist Vorticists. Not willing simply to chronicle the rivalries among contingents of the London avant-garde, however, Harrison grafts this history onto a Marxist account of class conflict, with Bloomsbury's successes symbolizing the bourgeoisie's domination of the working class.

The absurdity of this project—focusing exclusively on the avant-garde arts subsidized by the bourgeoisie, Harrison ignores the popular visual culture that might be read as an expression of working-class values—necessitates a form of argumentation based on buzzword and innuendo rather than historical analysis. Attempting to exaggerate Bloomsbury's social status, for example, he informs the reader that "the intellectual aristocracy of Bloomsbury" (32) "had the southern English gentleman's habit of shrinking from the consequences of industrialization" (90), phrases carefully crafted to avoid outright falsehood, while nevertheless conveying the erroneous impression that the group was comprised of aristocrats: English gentlemen, not only southern but "shrinking." The flip side of Harrison's presentation of Bloomsbury as upper crust is his portrayal of the Camden Town painters as true sons of Ruskin and Morris, thwarted champions of the worker. To sharpen the comparison rhetorically, Harrison introduces Bloomsbury's Roger Fry as an "amateur" and Camden Town's Walter Sickert as a "professional deeply engaged with the technology of painting" (33) and the author of "workmanlike modern paintings" (26). That Sickert came from the same bourgeois background as Bloomsbury's members—that, in fact, Fry was close friends with his family—is obscured in a rhetoric (the workmanlike professional vs. the shrinking amateur) that evokes not only class but gender.

If Harrison does not actually call Fry prissy, the idea is there in his compulsive repetition of a more polite synonym. Fry, Harrison says, "nurtured a fastidious distaste" for John Singer Sargent's painting (52); his "sensibility" was "too fastidious not to be highly selective in the face of experience" (56); he was even "fastidiously indifferent to German culture" (95). Little wonder that, in Harrison's account, the high road of masculine accomplishment rapidly bypasses Bloomsbury, with its domestic emphasis on "the renewal of decoration," to plunge on to the art of "ideas" represented by the "new and energetic faction" (74) of Wyndham Lewis's competing Vorticist group. Again the class-based distinction between Bloomsbury and its avant-garde rivals is exaggerated and infused with sexual innuendo. The Vorticists are presented as "mostly the children of working men [not women?!], shopkeepers, foreigners or the nouveau riche" (89), although Harrison leaves vague the relationship among these categories of disenfranchisement, and one can only speculate about how the working-class Vorticists interacted with Lewis, a cosmopolitan Canadian, who was born on his father's yacht and educated at Rugby. Moreover, among the Vorticists, Cuthbert Hamilton was, like Fry, the son of a judge, and Edward Wadsworth, heir to a textile fortune, was much more moneyed than anyone in Bloomsbury. While the Vorticists are allied in Harrison's rhetoric with the masculine working class, his acknowledgement of Bloomsbury's political activism is sexualized by the language of courtship: "the intimates of the Bloomsbury circle . . . flirted with radicalism" (88).

The sexual subtext of Harrison's rhetoric breaks through in his thumbnail comparison of Bloomsbury with the Vorticists. Despite the fact that of Bloomsbury's four art critics and painters—Roger Fry, Clive and Vanessa Bell, and Duncan Grant—only Grant manifested any erotic attraction to his own gender, Harrison opens with the generalization: "Where Bloomsbury took pride in its considerable homosexual membership, the Futurists and [Vorticists] struck attitudes of aggressive heterosexuality." This remark is followed by a comparison of two groups' responses to the war: "Bloomsbury was on the whole pacifist, and when conscription was introduced many of its denizens took to the country; among the rebels, on the other hand, there were some eager and early volunteers and several uncomplaining conscripts" (90). One might expect that Harrison's leftist politics might lead him to admire—or at least consider—Bloomsbury's opposition to a war that Clive Bell, in a manifesto seized and burned by the government, condemned as a betrayal of the public interest in favor of "what a small ruling caste considered gentlemanly" (*Peace* 5). Instead, Harrison concludes about Bloomsbury's pacifism: "of the three principal constituent factions within the prewar avant-garde [Camden Town, Bloomsbury, and the Vorticists] the adherents of Post-Impressionism were thus best placed after the war. . . . the friendships and connections within the Bloomsbury set had predictably remained largely intact" (145). With the "predictably" hinting that domination of the English avant-garde motivated Bloomsbury's withdrawal from the mayhem of the front lines, Harrison spares himself consideration of the connections between Bloomsbury's antinationalist pacifism and its rejection of "aggressive heterosexuality."

Doubtless there is an important story to be told about the effects of class on the development of British modernism. Harrison's reductive and inaccurate assignment of the roles of bourgeoisie and proletariat to competing factions of avant-garde painters produces not this history, however, but a simplistic fable in which hardy working lads are betrayed by effeminate aristocrats. Forster, individually, figures hardly at all in this study of painting, of course, although his name is several times mentioned in relation to Bloomsbury. What is most pertinent to this volume, however, is the way the specter of Bloomsbury's "considerable homosexual membership" is put forward to explain the betrayal of the Marxist promise of proletarian triumph over the bourgeoisie.

This drama of subversion and betrayal, staged by the British left, finds its counterpart in the story of Bloomsbury spun simultaneously across the Atlantic for the benefit of the American right. The links between antipatriarchal and antimilitary attitudes, which Harrison ignores, are central to the attack on Bloomsbury in Gertrude Himmelfarb's 1986 *Marriage and Morals Among the Victorians*. Otherwise, Himmelfarb's treatment of Bloomsbury is strikingly similar. Like Harrison, she imputes to the middle-class Bloomsberries a social status they did not have, describing Forster as writing "in good aristocratic fashion" (24) and referring to Bloomsbury's "aristocratic disdain" toward public affairs (39). Also like Harrison, Himmelfarb uses homosexuality to explain Bloomsbury's nonconformist attitudes on a variety of issues. Establishing Lytton Strachey as the "essence" of Bloomsbury for no other reason than his homosexuality, she belittles the output of the group's painters and writers as enervated by "the extraordinary amount of psychic energy that went into their complicated personal lives" (42). Even Keynes's economics are linked to "his homosexuality—what Schumpeter delicately referred to as his 'childless vision'" (37).

Himmelfarb also follows Harrison in her treatment of Bloomsbury's objections to World War I, noting archly that "the First World War . . . left Bloomsbury itself with no casualties" (38). Bloomsbury's pacifism, she explains, was motivated by a "contempt for the masses" she finds "dramatically illustrated" by Strachey's testimony before a tribunal empowered to imprison or exempt from service draft resisters. In a scene recently reenacted in the film *Carrington,* Strachey, responding to the jingoistic question of what he would do if he saw a German soldier about to rape his sister, "solemnly looked at each of his sisters in turn and replied, in his high-pitched voice, 'I should try and interpose my own body'" (39).[3] Although this anecdote demonstrates both Strachey's sexual preferences and his wit, how "the masses" were represented by the military establishment Strachey here confronted is left unexplained, despite the fact that although this was exactly the question Clive Bell's pacifist manifesto was burned for asking. Himmelfarb is no follower of Marx—indeed her identification of Forster as a "fellow-traveler" or "sympathizer" of Bloomsbury (29) self-consciously echoes the red-baiting rhetoric of the McCarthy era, and her complaints about Forster include the charge that he "was not as immune from the 'virus' of communism" as others have claimed (41). The rhetorical appeal to "the masses" here derives not from Marx but from a letter in which Duncan Grant tried to justify his pacifism to his father, a major in the army: "I began to see that one's enemies were not vague masses of foreign people, but the mass of people in one's own country and the mass of people in the enemy country, and that one's friends were people of true ideas that one might and did meet in every country one visited." Anyone seriously interested in the impact of homosexuality on Bloomsbury's position outside mainstream culture would read Grant's remark—which is quite clearly not about "the masses" understood as the proletariat—in the context not only of such obvious historical events as Oscar Wilde's recent imprisonment, but also of Grant's other writings. In a letter to Keynes from a visit to his family in 1908, Grant said:

You are the only person I feel I can speak to. . . . It's not only that one's a sodomite that one has to hide but one's whole philosophy of life. . . . Here I am surrounded by . . . good, honest sort[s] of people but it's so damnable to think that they can only think me a harmless sort of lunatic or a dangerous criminal whom they wouldn't associate with at any price.[4]

But of course Himmelfarb is not attempting to think seriously about the impact of homosexuality on Bloomsbury. Rather she is using Bloomsbury to invoke clichés of a dangerous and powerful homosexual elite. Bloomsbury, she says, founded "an 'adversary culture' strong enough to challenge the bourgeois culture" (32). Glossing Forster's writings on politics, she explains that he considered himself to be part of an "aristocracy that was not beholden to [democracy], an aristocracy . . . who would betray, if need be, their country but not their friends (still less their lovers)"—a footnote here belittles Forster's alienation from a democracy he saw as potentially fascistic, remarking dismissively that "the major example" of such tendencies he could cite "was the censorship of a homosexual novel" (41). Homosexuality, for Himmelfarb, is an all-purpose agent of vilification, leaving those associated with it open to charges of being too queer, not queer enough, or both simultaneously. Forster, for instance, is bitterly blamed for his reticence, evidenced by the fact that "even so perceptive and psychoanalytic-minded a critic as Lionel Trilling was able to write a full-length study of Forster in 1943 without realizing he was a homosexual" (42)—although it is unclear how Trilling would have used this information, given his doubts over the advisability of publishing the original Kinsey report on the grounds it would promote the behaviors it described.[5] Then, herself armed with the recently disclosed facts, Himmelfarb splutters with sibilants and outraged alliteration as she sums up Bloomsbury: "We are only now beginning to recognize how 'queer' that world was—not only homosexual but androgynous, near-incestuous, and polymorphously promiscuous" (45).

Such inconsistency is ultimately unsurprising, however, for Himmelfarb's concern is not to forge a coherent historical understanding of Bloomsbury but to create an account that will act as a parable for our times. Where Harrison used Bloomsbury to exemplify the betrayal of the workers by the upper crust, Himmelfarb deploys the group as a symbol of the threat to bourgeois norms that are frankly neo-Victorian.

Her study is introduced with the observation that "from the perspective of our own time," an unidentified "we" have come to "better appreciate Victorian morality." In an assertion all the more foreboding for the enigma of its complete lack of reference, she says, "Today more than ever, we have reason to be wary of the kind of 'civilization' celebrated by Bloomsbury" (xviii–xiv). Both Harrison and Himmelfarb lend urgency to their historical narratives by casting them as stories about a tiny minority that poses an overwhelming threat. For both, Bloomsbury's deviance from conventional masculinity, epitomized in the figure of the male homosexual, invests the group with subversive strength beyond its numbers—never mind that the social forces the group is made to represent are diametrically opposed.

It is not really news—although it is worth reminding ourselves— that both the political right and left are susceptible to the homophobia inherent in the rhetorics of patriarchy. One might expect that feminist scholarship, recognizing the misogyny underlying prescriptions against masculine effeminacy, might be reluctant to deploy this particular device. But (sadly) this has not always been the case. It is true that pioneering feminists of the 1960s and early 1970s—Carolyn Heilbrun and Germaine Greer, for instance—were fascinated by the coalitions created through Bloomsbury's linkage of feminism with an acceptance of same-sex eroticism. During the late 1970s and early 1980s, however, there emerged in feminist characterizations of Bloomsbury a trend paralleling the one I have traced in left- and right-wing scholarship, in which male homosexuality figures as the index of overwhelming menace.[6]

The tendency can be traced back to Phyllis Rose's 1978 biography of Virginia Woolf, *Woman of Letters.* Rose describes her account as "written in sympathy" with its subject, in an attempt at "an imaginative understanding of a figure who, as the years pass, seems less remote and less aloof" (xix). This attractive-sounding theory results in practice in Rose attributing to Woolf her own highly conventional values, often reading strongly against the grain of Woolf's own letters, memoirs, and fiction. In her last novel, *Between the Acts,* for instance, Woolf offered the following view of women's response to gay men: "They knew at once they had nothing to fear, nothing to hope. At first they resented. . . . Then they liked it. For then they could say—as she did—whatever came into their heads. And hand him, as she handed him, a flower" (135–36). In Woolf's memoirs, the worst effect she recalls from with her youthful association with homosexual men is a feeling of boredom because "there was no physical attraction between us." There are "many advantages" for women in "the society of buggers," Woolf says, "it is simple, it is honest, it makes one feel . . . at one's ease." Nevertheless, with gay men "one cannot, as nurses say, show off," which "is one of the great delights, one of the chief necessities of life" (Moments 194, 196). This passage Rose glosses as Woolf's "traumatic encounter with the young men of Bloomsbury" (47), in which the young Virginia was "hurt" by "her treatment by the Bloomsbury homosexuals" (65).

To present the homosexuality of Bloomsbury men—what she calls "Bloomsbuggery"—as a threat to the group's women, Rose leans heavily on clichés, asserting that Lytton Strachey, in particular, was a perpetual "adolescent" with "atrophied emotions" (92) (it's just a stage) and announcing that for "many of the Bloomsbury homosexuals . . . there was no biological obligation in their youthful preference for men" (it's just a choice). Rose's conclusion that homosexuality in Bloomsbury "was decidedly misogynist" (77) is based on a reading of Forster's Maurice, which, she says "conveys the platonic, Greek spirit of attachments between university men at the turn of the century and their antifemale bias" (77); she neglects to acknowledge that the book is a critique of these attitudes.

In Rose's scenario, the "homosexual conspiracy" of Bloomsbury "represented a real obstacle to [Woolf's] consolidating her self-esteem" (78).[7] Ultimately this is accomplished only by Woolf's "willed commitment to normality" in the decision to seek out straight male associates and ultimately to marry (67). Rose characterizes Woolf's marriage as "a plunge into reality" that allowed her "acceptance of herself as a woman" and "the excitement of . . . discovering that the ordinary adventures of life [were] open to her" (67–68). Where Woolf's autobiographical essays celebrate the influence of her gay friends in helping her escape "the old sentimental views of marriage in which we were brought up" (Moments 196), Rose's version of Virginia's story is a narrative of feminist triumph over the evils represented by male homosexuality.[8] And these evils expand rapidly beyond the arena of sexual politics: Rose informs her reads that "even [Woolf's] prose style is more democratic than [Strachey's]"— this because hers "demands a reader's participation to fill in the gaps" while his "structure[s] response in so totalitarian a fashion that, as we would against any tyranny, we rebel."

As told by Rose, the history of Bloomsbury becomes a fable rousing a readership of democratic feminist "we's" to rebel against the "tyranny" of totalitarian faggots. The only thing more incredible than this scenario is its acceptance into the feminist mainstream. Not only is Rose's Woman *of Letters,* reprinted as an inexpensive paperback by a feminist press, a staple in Women's Studies courses, but its rhetorical conflation of patriarchy with homosexuality with totalitarianism has inspired other feminists in their treatment of Bloomsbury. Jane Marcus, author of numerous articles and editor of two anthologies on Woolf, for instance re-presents Rose's image of Virginia as a woman who "in imagination and in action . . . met misogyny full-face" when she confronted the "homosexual hegemony over British culture," specified later as "E. M. Forster and his ilk" ("Liberty" 60, 61, 64). Identifying the Nazis as a "homosexual brotherhood," Marcus goes on to assert, "The Cambridge Apostles' notions of fraternity surely appeared to Woolf analogous to certain fascist notions of fraternity" ("Liberty" 67).

Marcus's "surely" not withstanding, there is no evidence in Woolf's writing for this thesis, which, in its totalizing conception of fraternity as homosexuality, and homosexuality as fascism, ignores the complexity of relationships between men in general, overlooks the very real historical differences between the homosexual men who were Woolf's contemporaries and their predecessors, belittles the antifascist work carried out in Bloomsbury, and insults the memory of the men killed because of their homosexuality in Nazi concentration camps.[9] Marcus's willingness to put words in Woolf's mouth, moreover, is matched by her anxiety to suppress and erase the evidence of what Woolf actually thought and did. Dismissing Woolf's clear self-identification with Bloomsbury—evidenced in her memoirs, her voluminous correspondence with its members, and her eulogistic biography of Roger Fry—Marcus opens one of her anthologies of feminist scholarship on Woolf with the pronouncement "we do not consider 'Bloomsbury' as an important influence on Virginia Woolf. . . . her work and life ought to be wrenched out of their provincial English Bloomsbury setting" (*New* xvii–xviii).[10] Not content to relive Woolf's life for her, Marcus also objects to Woolf's stated opinions on feminism. "Premature and optimistic, one thinks," is her verdict on Woolf's suggestion in *Three Guineas* that the term "feminism" be consigned to a ceremonial burning ("No More" 154). What Woolf actually said in this powerful passage bears quoting. Allying herself with the suffragist Josephine Butler's claim to be working "for the rights of all— all men and women," Woolf imagined, "The word 'feminist' is destroyed; the air is cleared; and in that clearer air what do we see? Men and women working together for the same cause" (185), for she explains to her male correspondent in 1938, "You are feeling in your own persons what your mothers felt when they were shut out, when they were shut up, because they were women. Now you are being shut out, you are being shut up, because you are Jews, because you are democrats, because of race, because of religion" (186–87).

| | |

Woolf's powerful articulation of the links among categories of oppression exposes the poverty of a feminism that empowers itself through the scapegoating of other afflicted classes. Writing recently in the *Women's Review of Books*, Marcus characterized her approach to Woolf in the 1980s as "a necessary (and temporary) critical strategy, a convenient lie," adding, "And anyway it was fun" ("Tale" 12).[11] Exhilarating it may have been for (certain) women to discover they could wield the master's tools to such satisfying effect, but I would hope that the theorization of "queer" subjectivities that cross the boundaries of sexuality and gender might mark an end to this sort of entertainment.

Nevertheless, there is a certain irony in the effect the scapegoating of homosexuality has had on queer theory. Just as the term "queer" seeks to reappropriate a term of abuse, so queer theory, in trading old "gay and lesbian" rhetorics of marginality and minoritization for claims to centrality and ubiquity (as discussed in the introduction to this volume), attempts to seize control of the enormous powers imputed to homosexuality in homophobic discourse. This conceptual reversal helps to explain the apparent conundrum that queerness, with its roots in "stigmatization" or "shame," should manifest itself as a form of confrontational visibility (here I am thinking of everything from the politics of "Queer Nation," to the look of queer neighborhoods, to the tone of this essay).[12] It seems to me important, however, to insist that this act of jujitsu was neither easy nor automatic. As individuals and as a community, we have (and continue to) run tremendous risks and suffer tremendous losses in our efforts to assert some agency to deploy for ourselves the subversive powers attributed to us, rather than having them deployed against us by those pursuing, apparently, virtually any other agenda.

It is in order to acknowledge the accomplishment of queerness that I have to reply in the negative to the question, "Was Forster queer?" The term is not just historically anachronistic, but at odds with everything we know about his self-presentation through the course of his life. The more interesting question, however, is, "*Is* Forster queer?" Maybe. If so, it is because through the publication of his posthumous writings he— along with the other Bloomsbury men whose homoerotic proclivities were publicly avowed at the same period[13]—allowed his image to be turned into the terrifying specter with which heterosexuality haunts itself. The most interesting question of all, however, is what will become of this queer Forster, what will we do with him? It is this potential— and its limitations—that my colleagues in this volume explore.

Notes

This chapter was published in an earlier version under the title "Bloomsbury Bashing: Homophobia and the Politics of Criticism in the Eighties," *Genders* 11: 58–80, and is reprinted by permission of the University of Texas Press.

1. Eric Alterman's "Neutering America" leads with an account of Penny Culliton's dismissal in September 1995 by the Mascenic [New Hampshire] Regional School Board. The school board later went to court to contest an independent arbiter's recommendation that Culliton be reinstated ("National Briefs").

2. On the persistence of old feuds in English art criticism, see also Simon Watney.

3. Notwithstanding the quotation marks, Himmelfarb here actually paraphrases Joseph A. Schumpeter's obituary notice of Keynes, reprinted in his *Ten Great Economists* (275). Likewise, the quotation she attributes to Strachey was corrected in all editions after 1971 of Michael Holroyd's *Lytton Strachey* to be "I should try and come between them."

4. Both of Grant's letters are quoted by Robert Skidelsky (196, 326), but only the first is referred to by Himmelfarb.

5. Trilling's review of the Kinsey Report, first published in *The Partisan Review* and reprinted in Trilling, *Liberal* (223–42), objected particularly to the report's "idea that homosexuality is to be accepted as a form of sexuality like another, that it is as 'natural' as heterosexuality."

6. As the original version of this essay was in production, Mary Ann Caws's *The Women of Bloomsbury* appeared, countering the trend I identify in biographically oriented feminist approaches to Bloomsbury. Although Caws does not take on previous feminist critics by name, she challenges in general terms their assumptions, arguing strongly for a more nuanced understanding of the choices made by Bloomsbury's women (see Reed, "Review").

7. The phrase "homosexual conspiracy" is footnoted to Noël Annan, which does not make it right.

8. The self-confident heterosexism of Rose's intuitive brand of scholarship continued to animate her writings on Bloomsbury into the 1990s, when, writing in the *New York Times Book Review,* she suggested that Vanessa Bell, Virginia Woolf, and Duncan Grant must have been jealous of Keynes's wife, Lydia Lopokova, because "amid the Bloomsbury minuet of shifting liaisons, sexless marriages and *ménages à trois* and *quatre,* the once-homosexual economist and the hardly virginal ballerina offer a radiant if improbable example of heterosexual devotion and stability" (Rose, "Love" 12).

9. On the difference between the homosexual and the homosocial in male-male relationships, see the introduction to Eve Kosofsky Sedgwick's *Between Men*. For a detailed analysis of Bloomsbury's construction of male homosexual identity in relation to its Victorian predecessors, see my "Making History." On the Nazi persecution of homosexual men, see Heinz Heger and Richard Plant.

10. Marcus claims here to want to place Woolf in a "European" context of "Jews, homosexuals, and radicals." All these identities could be found in Blooms-bury, of course, but Marcus associates them with Woolf's "real contemporaries": Kafka, Brecht, Benjamin, and Proust—the homosexuality of the latter is for some unspecified reason not like the fascist version found in Bloomsbury. This determination to "wrench" Woolf from her own community and into what looks suspiciously like a conventional masculine canon both exploits and condescends to the woman whose legacy as "a guerrilla fighter" against patriarchy Marcus claims to retrieve (see Marcus, *New*).

11. Marcus's comment here responds to a footnote in another essay of mine.

12. On the roots of queerness in stigmatization and shame, see Sedgwick, "Queer Performativity" (*Tendencies* 137). On the visibility of queerness in the urban fabric, see my "Imminent Domain."

13. The "outing" of the other men in Bloomsbury was initiated by Holroyd's biography of Strachey.

5

Camp Sites: Forster and the
Biographies of Queer Bloomsbury

George Piggford

My reading of Queer Bloomsbury—and E. M. Forster's place in it—does not argue for a privileged and central position for the writers of Bloomsbury in a refigured, revisionist construction of modernism. Rather, I seek to accomplish two goals. First, this essay asserts the importance of the connections among the major Bloomsbury writers—Forster, Virginia Woolf, and Lytton Strachey. This project, related closely to a recent reexamination of Bloomsbury inaugurated by the work of Judith Scherer Herz, Perry Meisel, S. P. Rosenbaum, and Christopher Reed, argues for the significance of the influence of these writers upon one another and examines their common traits and topoi. Second, I wish to establish the importance of a significant modernist subgenre explored by the writers of Bloomsbury, a category which I term "camp biography," particularly Forster's employment of this mode. Generally, my examination of this subgenre serves to show that the writings of the Bloomsbury group emphasize the modernist forces of parody and irony that have been recently taken up as central terms in the theorization of postmodernism by numerous critics, most notably Linda Hutcheon. The close proximity of Forster, Strachey, and Woolf to the English literary establishment and particularly to the Victorian biographic tradition allowed these writers to examine closely its faults and fissures and to attack its pretension and sententiousness.[1] Although Forster's writing has not typically been read as campy, his biographical writings share the Bloomsbury camp sensibility that has often been labeled "Stracheyism."

1. BLOOMSBURY AND CONSTRUCTIONS
OF MASCULINIST MODERNISM

Before any attempt to determine the salient features of Forster's relationship with Bloomsbury and with the biographies written by Bloomsberries such as Strachey and Woolf, one must first endeavor to answer a basic question: "What is the Bloomsbury Group?" I use the present rather than the past tense in phrasing this query because "Bloomsbury" remains among us as a significant category in the fields of literary criticism, art criticism, history, and even economics and political science.

Although many of its "members"—including Clive Bell, Leonard Woolf, and E. M. Forster (if Forster indeed was a "member")—attempted to provide textual portraits of the group,[2] Quentin Bell's characterization of the group in his *Bloomsbury* is probably the most influential. Bell asserts that his topic is "almost impalpable, almost indefinable" (103); for him Bloomsbury has "the dimensions of a whirlpool" and "the character of a beast that is half chameleon and half hydra" (21). According to Bell, any conception of Bloomsbury must center on friendship and reasonable talk: "it [Bloomsbury] talked on the whole reasonably, it talked as friends may talk together, with all the license and all the affection of friendship. It believed . . . in pacific and rational discussion" (*Bloomsbury* 103–04). For Bell, Bloomsbury is best understood as a group of friends united by a world view that one might roughly characterize as "humanist."[3] Its emphasis on rationality encouraged its members to produce texts and art that combat what the Bloomsberries perceived as the irrational aspects of the modern world—war, racism, censorship, and intolerance generally.

Bell further argues that Forster cannot be placed anywhere near the center of this cluster of friends[4] for two reasons: his reverence and his optimism (Q. Bell, *Bloomsbury* 106), neither of which is part of the Bloomsbury ethos. Bell points out, however, that "ethically" Forster "seems to me altogether on the same side as Bloomsbury: conscious, deeply conscious of the dark irrational side of life but absolutely convinced of the necessity of holding fast to reason, charity, and good sense" (106). Bell's illuminating portrait of the group correctly positions Forster at the margins of Bloomsbury as Bell characterizes it. But by choosing to "leave Bloomsbury linen . . . unaired" (9), as he puts it, Bell largely ignores a central aspect of Bloomsbury with which Forster closely identified: its queerness.

By downplaying the importance for Bloomsbury of sexuality in all its polymorphously perverse forms—a major topic of rational talk amongst these friends—Bell misses arguably the most important defining characteristic of the group. It is most likely for this reason that Bell appears to be mystified by writers such as Sir John Rothenstein who view Bloomsbury as "a criminal association" (Q. Bell, *Bloomsbury* 11). In defending Bloomsbury against what he perceives as Rothenstein's unfair and unwarranted attack on Bloomsbury, Bell apparently forgets that many of the men associated with Bloomsbury engaged in criminalized sexual acts, and almost without exception its other members were guilty of crimes against Christian morality such as adultery and—most notably in the case of Virginia Woolf—sapphism.[5] Woolf herself associated the spirit of Bloomsbury with sexuality, particularly candid sexual talk, in her memoir "Old Bloomsbury." When in 1904 Lytton Strachey articulated the word "semen" in conversation with the Stephen sisters (as they then were), "A flood of the sacred fluid seemed to overwhelm us. Sex permeated our conversation. The word bugger was never far from our lips" (Woolf, "Old Bloomsbury" 54). This moment might be read as the birth of Bloomsbury as an enclave in which sexual possibilities might be discussed and explored.

The connection between Bloomsbury and queer sexual practices has been noted by a number of critics, some of whom, most famously Carolyn Heilbrun, celebrate the group's sexual practices and discourses as liberatory and subversive (Heilbrun x). Usually, however, critics point out Bloomsbury's sexual experimentation in an attempt to condemn its members as effeminate, enervated, decadent buggers. Ezra Pound was one of the first critics to compare unfavorably the feminine (but not necessarily female) Bloomsbury—especially its textual output—to the masculine writing of the group often termed "the men of 1914": James Joyce, T. S. Eliot, Wyndham Lewis, and Pound himself. My reading of Poundian "masculinist" modernism is indebted to Sandra Gilbert and Susan Gubar's *No Man's Land,* particularly "Tradition and the Female Talent." Here I expand Gilbert and Gubar's terms somewhat so that the "feminine" can represent not only women, but also homosexual men. According to sexologists such as Havelock Ellis and John Addington Symonds, homosexual men, or "inverts," were understood to be "women trapped in men's bodies," feminine men. This construction influenced and informed both the formation of homosexual identity in the modernist period and the virulent attacks launched against homosexuals at this time by Pound and others.

In a series of essays Pound lavishes high praise on the work of his fellow (real) men: Joyce's *Ulysses* provides "an impassioned meditation on life" (*Literary* 416), Eliot's "depiction of contemporary life" in *Prufrock and Other Observations* is "complete" (*Literary* 419), and Wyndham Lewis's *Tarr* "is the most vigorous and volcanic novel of our time" (*Literary* 424). Pound embeds a harsh critique of Bloomsbury in his reading of the U.S.-born Lewis's energetic novel. He commends Lewis for attacking the "Cambridge set" (i.e., Bloomsbury), characterized by Lewis as "the *dregs* of Anglo-Saxon civilization," and its individual members (epitomized by the character Hobson) as crosses between "a Quaker, a Pederast, and a Chelsea artist" (qtd. in Pound, *Literary* 427). Pound sees Lewis's *Tarr* as a justified attack on a "frowsy background of 'Bourgeois Bohemia,' more or less Bloomsbury" (428); this assault on those whom Pound elsewhere termed the "Bloomsbuggers" (qtd. in Scott 94) represents for Pound Lewis's "cleaning up a great lot of rubbish" (429).

What we might now term Pound's masculinist, "phallocentric" view of Bloomsbury as the feminine ("frowsy") and inverted (pederastic) dregs of English civilization became a typical criticism of the group in the 1960s and 1970s, expressed notably in Hugh Kenner's *Pound Era* (1971). Kenner suggests that the "shades" moving about the ruins of London—the "Unreal City" of Eliot's "Waste Land"—are the ineffectual shades of the members of the Bloomsbury Group (in this case, Virginia Woolf and Clive Bell) (382), whose "treacly minds" (553) contrast with the massive intellects of Lewis, Pound, Joyce, and Eliot, architects of an energetic vortex of change in English art in the *Blast* period (245).[6]

Terry Eagleton presents a similar argument in his 1970 *Exiles and Émigrés*. In it, Eagleton asserts that the English literary establishment needed to import its modernists from the colonies (James, Eliot, and Pound from the United States; Conrad from the continent via the Belgian Congo; Yeats and Joyce from Ireland) and the provinces (the working-class Lawrence from the collieries of Nottinghamshire). This importation was necessary because the close proximity of bourgeois English writers to their literary tradition blunted the revolutionary potential of the modernist urge among them. Eagleton contends that "the unchallenged sway of non-English poets and novelists in contemporary English literature points to certain central flaws and impoverishments in conventional English culture itself. That culture was unable, of its own impetus, to produce great literary art" (10). Although Eagleton's reading of modernism represents an insightful examination of the importance of colonial writing for a transnational understanding of the modernist movement, the gender politics of his analysis warrant careful scrutiny.

In Eagleton's reading, as in other masculinist constructions of modernism, the perceived "literary elite" of England (read: "Bloomsbury") is viewed not only as feminine and feminized, but also as second rate. By reading the modernism of Joyce, Eliot, and Pound as the necessary influx of aggressive, virile, revolutionary colonial energy that was needed to revitalize the literature of the passive, decadent "mother" country, Eagleton, in effect, reinscribes a binaristic notion of modernism articulated first by Ezra Pound. Reading within an andro- and heterocentric critical tradition, Eagleton implicitly connects the feminine with the suppressed "other" of a binary which always already privileges the male, heterosexual subject as the potential revolutionary "self."[7]

Post-Lacanian feminist theorists such as Jane Gallop and deconstructionist queer critics such as Judith Butler and Lee Edelman have demonstrated various ways that such simplistic binaries are founded upon pernicious tautological structures of argumentation, structures that erase the complex interaction between phallus and absence of phallus, power and lack of power, signifier and signified, self and other. Gallop's reading of Lacan's seminar of 1972–73 argues that Lacan unwittingly demonstrates that "the phallic order and phallic enjoyment are . . . a kind of failure: a failure to reach the Other, a short circuiting of desire by which it turns back upon itself. The phallic order fails because, although unable to account for the feminine, it would, none the less, operate as a closure, attempting to create a closed universe that is thoroughly phallocentric" (34). Lacan's phallocentric analysis of gender, in other words, attempts to erase the feminine at the moment that "the feminine" is articulated as the Other of the phallic order.

Butler and Edelman apply to the binarized category of sexuality a critique similar to Gallop's analysis of gender. For Butler, a sustained query into the conventional binary demarcating the biological sexes leads to a questioning of the logic of heteronormative sexuality:

If we call into question the fixity of the structuralist law that divides and bounds the "sexes" by virtue of the dyadic differentiation within the heterosexual matrix, it will be from the exterior regions of that boundary . . . , and it will constitute the disruptive return of the excluded from within the very logic of the heterosexual symbolic. (12)

Edelman's reading of the binary of sexuality, like Butler's, calls into question the stability and authority of the "structuralist logic" that underpins analyses such as Eagleton's.[8] In contrast to readings that rely on the phallocentric logic of structuralism (and to feminist readings that ground the notion of difference itself in the notion of gender difference), Edelman calls for a kind of critical writing which inscribes "homosexual difference." For Edelman, "the homosexual difference produces the imperative to recognize and expose it precisely to the extent that it threatens to remain unmarked and undetected, and thereby to disturb the stability of the paradigms through which sexual difference can be interpreted and gender difference can be enforced" (*Homographesis* 195). A mode of textual analysis that lays bare this difference—which is not to be confused with binaristic "otherness"—undermines, at least potentially, the structuralist logic identified by Butler and exemplified in Eagleton's reading of modernism.

By privileging one modernism over another, by centering modernism in the textual projects of, in effect, "the men of 1914," Pound, Kenner, and Eagleton reinscribe the privilege of the "masculine male" and his literary output within a heteronormative construct of literary production.[9] For Eagleton in *Exiles and Émigrés,* the masculine modernists "dominated" (*Exiles* 9) the literature of England in the early twentieth century because they were able to "grasp . . . society as a totality" and thereby "transcend" it (*Exiles* 10). The total cultural authority or phallic power of these authors allowed them to achieve "a point of balance at which inwardness could combine with an essential externality to produce major art" (*Exiles* 10). Eagleton contrasts the major art produced by the modernists who had immigrated to England to the minor art produced by native writers such as Woolf and Forster, who, in their "enclosed and elitist" circle of friends were "marooned from the world of working relationships and wider social institutions" (*Exiles* 13). In Eagleton's reading, the female and feminized upper middle class writers exemplified by the members of Bloomsbury were not able to perceive the "totality" of modern society and are therefore marginal modernists. Indeed, any "us versus them" approach necessarily effects a (re)materialization of the phallus and of the phallic logic which numerous queer and post-Lacanian feminist theorists have attempted so strenuously to escape.

As Christopher Reed has so persuasively argued, the sexual, erotic, and social connections among the members of the Bloomsbury Group, particularly Woolf's complicated connections to the queer male writers associated with Bloomsbury, have been de-emphasized or even disregarded from the perspective of certain masculinist and feminist critical methodologies. Reed has rightly, I believe, associated a particular, fairly recent feminist reading of Woolf with an attempt to "undermine Bloomsbury's fundamental critique of sexual oppression" ("Bashing" 69). That is, a specific tradition of revisionist readings of Woolf, epitomized by Jane Marcus's *Virginia Woolf and the Languages of Patriarchy,* rejects the feminine label given to the male writers of Bloomsbury (by, most famously, a resentful Wyndham Lewis) and instead aligns them with patriarchal authority.[10] This move effectively divorces Woolf from her immediate context, the coterie of close friends who attended informal gatherings for years at which "buggery" was a main topic of conversation. By accepting uncritically the male/female and masculine/feminine binaries on which constructions of Bloomsbury such as Marcus's are based, this feminist revisionism reinscribes the very patriarchal authority that underpins binaristic logic.[11]

In contrast, Reed's reading of the Bloomsbury group allows its irregularities, inconsistencies, and contradictions to emerge. His understanding of the group as a subculture which "constructed sexual identity in much the same way it created aesthetic identity: in the realm of the social and in relation to the past" ("Making" 190) allows for both an analysis of the anxiety of influence of the Victorian period on the artistic and literary output of the Bloomsbury Group and an examination of the very complex interaction between the group's writings and various theories of sexuality predominant in the early twentieth century. Reed's assessment, which focuses on the influence of the aesthetic tradition (Pater, Wilde) and of sexological theories (Symonds, Carpenter) on the group, moves toward a construction of what I would like to term "Queer Bloomsbury."

2. STRACHEYISM AND BLOOMSBURY BIOGRAPHY

Strachey, Woolf, and Forster all utilize irony and camp parody in an attempt to inscribe queer sexualities into their various biographical texts. Strachey has been a privileged figure in readings of the Bloomsbury camp mode; that mode has typically been associated with "Stracheyism." For example, D. H. Lawrence mentions in a letter to Forster that he prefers the "sadness" in *Pharos and Pharillon* to its "Stracheyism" (qtd. in Furbank, *Life* 2:163). Edwin Muir's review of *A Passage to India* asserts that Forster "is inclined toward the ironical school of which Mr. Lytton Strachey is the instructor" (Muir 278). Wilfred Stone labels a number of Forster's short biographical sketches "Strachey-like" (Stone, *Cave* 284).

Further, Woolf's recent biographer James King has associated Woolf's *Orlando* with Stracheyism: "By introducing fanciful elements into her mock-biography, Virginia, like Lytton Strachey, was attempting to revolutionize the art of biography" (King 411). For Lawrence, then, Stracheyism represents the comedic belittling of historical figures; for Muir it indicates irony generally; for Stone Stracheyism seems to represent both the style and the brevity of Forster's sketches; for King it suggests "mocking" (parodic) elements and a "fanciful tone." How might one construct a workable definition of "Stracheyism" from these disparate sources?

Judith Scherer Herz, in *The Short Narratives of E. M. Forster,* explores the significations of Stracheyism in a helpful and insightful way. She associates Stracheyism primarily with irony. Forster's irony is tempered by pathos, a quality she finds nowhere in Strachey. For Herz, the basic tenet of Stracheyism, at least as practiced by Strachey himself, is "irony covers all" (80). Although Herz is correct in pointing to the significance of irony as an important category for any definition of Stracheyism, its most distinguishing feature is its use of parody. Irony is always contextualized by parody in the Stracheyesque mode. For Linda Hutcheon, irony often works in parody, is framed by parody, it is "a miniature (semiotic) version of parody's (textual) doubling" (Hutcheon 4). Herz accurately points to the fact that Strachey's use of irony differs from Forster's, but it is in the parodic mode employed by Strachey, Woolf, and Forster that one might find a shared set of stylistic elements traditionally associated with Stracheyism. These elements—the goal of which is to produce an over-the-top imitation of the Victorian biographic voice—are discussed in detail below. It is the extremeness of the parodic imitations found in Bloomsbury's biographies that produces a "camp effect" in the texts, an effect that is closely related to the possibilities for queer desire suggested by the texts' campiness.

The Bloomsbury Group's camp is intentional, deliberate (contrasted by Susan Sontag to "naive" camp [282]); they knowingly parody established conventions in order to belittle and critique them. Their use of camp strategies further positions them as members of a group Andrew Ross has called elite camp "cognoscenti"; he claims that camp "belongs to those who have the accredited confidence to be able to devote their idiosyncratic attention to the practice of cultural slumming in places where others would feel less comfortable" (63). Only a writer who is a "marginal" (64) member of the so-called "literary elite" is able to utilize the particularly queer parodic mode that is camp; his or her privileged knowledge of the dominant culture enables the subversive camp gestures included in his or her texts. The Bloomsbury writers might be identified, therefore, as what Moe Meyer has termed practitioners of the "strategies and tactics of queer parody" (9).

According to camp theorists such as Ross and Meyer, the use of camp in writing produces an effect which critically comments on the gender system of a particular historical/cultural moment in unpredictable —but readable—ways, thereby threatening social understandings of gender. Ross contends that camp plays "a crucial role in the redefinition of masculinity and femininity" (148); and David Bergman thinks that "camp constantly plays with notions of inside and outside, masculine and semi nine, it does not locate truth in these polarities" ("Strategic" 95). The Bloomsbury writers' use of camp in their biographical texts does not eliminate the category of gender; rather, it dissociates the roles that women and men are coerced into playing in a particular society from the category of biological sex. In this way, camp inscribes the queer as a sensibility, and the "camp sites" locatable in the texts of Strachey, Woolf, and Forster provide evidence for the cohesiveness of the subgenre Bloomsbury camp biography.

Lytton Strachey, certainly the best known biographer associated with the group, utilizes camp to undermine and to parody his own Mandarin style. Barry Spurr has argued that "introducing the vocabulary and cadence of Mandarin, Strachey proceeds subtly and wittily to pervert and violate its conventions, manipulating the solemnity of the Ciceronian, Gibbonian dialect to produce a voice placed, as it were, midway between the male and female ranges and sounding, at once, like both and like neither" (32). Although I generally agree with Spurr's argument, I would rather describe the interplay of male and female voices in Strachey as queer parody, a strategy of sexual subversiveness. Strachey's prose parodies the overblown style of Victorian biography; in their impersonation of Victorian panegyric Strachey's biographies exaggerate its mannerisms, flourishes, and conventions. The campiness of Strachey's Mandarin style is emphasized by the brevity of his historical sketches, particularly those included in *Eminent Victorians* and the even shorter pieces originally found in periodicals such as *The Nation and the Athenaeum* and *The New Statesman;* the short length of these sketches undermines the importance of the personages featured in them.

Strachey's campy subversion of pompous Victorian biographic conventions is revealed in his adaptation of three of its stylistic devices: the aphorism, the use of a series for amplification (used for the "bathos of deflation" in Strachey), and the use of allusion.[12] Strachey's most famous camp aphorism, which reads much like a Wildean epigram,[13] may be found in the preface to *Eminent Victorians:* "The history of the Victorian Age will never be written: we know too much about it. For ignorance is the first requisite of the historian" (9). Strachey's statement, its comedic effect multiplied by its very baldness and directness, makes clear to any reader of this first published biographical text that he plans both to insult historians and their methods and to rewrite the history of the Victorian period. Aphorisms such as this represent camped up and parodic versions of the pithy moralizing common in the British biographical tradition. Elsewhere Strachey writes aphoristically that "It has often been observed that our virtues and our vices, no less than our clothes, our furniture, and our fine arts, are subject to the laws of fashion" (*Biographical* 34), suggesting that the moral "laws" of any period are illusory and subject to critique or even ridicule by writers in successive periods.

Further, rather than using a series for amplification or to pile up heroic epithets for his subjects, Strachey uses them in the "bathos of deflation" (Spurr 37). The medieval period, for example, is for Strachey a time of "prayer, asceticism, and dirt" (*Biographical* 34). He characterizes Joseph Addison as "that charming, polished, empty personality" (*Literary* 246). And Voltaire is "an artist, an egotist, a delirious enthusiast, dancing, screaming, and gesticulating to the last moment of extreme old age" (*Biographical* 51–52). This triadic structure is very common in Strachey's biographical writings. Finally, Strachey frequently alludes to texts such as the Bible and Shakespeare's plays, but very often uses them for comic effect. Strachey asserts in a parodic inversion of 2 Peter 3:8 that in the "sight (or perhaps one should say their blindness) [of human beings] a thousand years are too liable to be not as a day but as just nothing. The past is almost entirely a blank" (*Biographical* 17). And referring to Cardinal Manning, Strachey presents a camp Hamlet: "The time was out of joint, and he was only too delighted to have been born to set it right" (*Eminent* 22). These stylistic devices recur throughout Strachey's biographical writing.

In Strachey's pastiche of Mandarin styles, references to queer sexuality are often inserted as subversive gestures, subtle attacks on presumptive heterosexuality. Situated within the highly parodic and multivocal style utilized by Strachey, isolated sentences suggest, at the very least, queer possibilities. What are we to make of the statement that Dr. Arnold "was particularly fond of boys" (*Eminent* 197–98)? Or that Albert, the Prince Consort, who "had a marked distaste for the opposite sex" (*Queen* 136), "never flirted—no not with the prettiest ladies in the court" (*Queen* 179)? These and other examples clarify Strachey's textual project: to write queerly, in ways that allow the irregularities of desire a forum for textual expression.

Although Strachey's texts are certainly the most striking examples of the subgenre of Bloomsbury camp biography, Virginia Woolf, too, is the author of a number of texts which could easily fit into this category, particularly *Orlando* and *Flush*. With her father's stentorian voice literally ringing in her ears, Woolf, like Strachey, attempted to revolutionize biography. Particularly in *Orlando*, Woolf's camp utilizes the figure of the androgyne to queer notions of writing biography and of inscribing sexual identity. She, like Strachey, impersonates a Victorian biographical voice only to parody it: "Happy the mother who bears, happier still the biographer who records the life of such a one! Never need she vex herself, nor he invoke the help of novelist or poet. From deed to deed, from glory to glory, from office to office he must go, his scribe following after" (*Orlando* 14–15). *Orlando* utilizes this overblown style to camp up the voice of the sententious and florid Victorian biographer.[14]

But it is the report by the biographer's voice in *Orlando* of Orlando's abrupt transformation from male to female that clarifies Woolf's parodic reading of discourses of sexual identity. In an attempt to prepare the reader for the radical change, the biographer's voice articulates hesitations and uncertainties about narrating such an unprecedented metamorphosis:

The biographer is now faced with a difficulty which it is better perhaps to confess than to gloss over. Up to this point in telling the story of Orlando's life, documents, both private and historical, have made it possible to fulfil the first duty of a biographer, which is to plod, without looking to right or left, in the indelible footprints of truth; unenticed by flowers; regardless of shade; on and on methodically till we fall plump into the grave and write *finis* on the tombstone above our heads. But now we come to an episode which lies right across our path, so that there is no ignoring it. Yet it is dark, mysterious, and undocumented; so that there is no explaining it. Volumes might be written in interpretation of it; whole religious systems founded upon the signification of it. Our simple duty is to state the facts as far as they are known, and so let the reader make of them what he may. (Woolf 65)

This Stracheyesque passage utilizes a series for an ultimately deflating effect; the fact that there is "no explaining" the coming metamorphosis provides bathetic comedy through its redundancy. Need the biographer note that there is "no explaining it" immediately after she has indicated that it is "dark, mysterious, and undocumented"? Further, the text employs an aphorism that, similar to Strachey's pronouncement about the "first requisite of the historian" in his Preface to Eminent Victorians, proclaims the duty of the biographer with mock gravity: "to plod . . . in the footprints of truth." The afterthoughts added to this aphoristic statement—"unenticed by flowers; regardless of shade; on and on . . ."—emphasize its parodic nature. The final reference to "the tombstone above our heads" might indeed be as close as any writer in English has ever approached to the camp sublime.

The parodic aspects of the above passage are clear, but its significance must be closely associated with its role as the first announcement of Orlando's coming transfiguration, the text's defining moment of queer sexuality: "He stretched himself. He rose. He stood upright in complete nakedness before us, and while the trumpets pealed Truth! Truth! Truth! we have no choice left but to confess—he was a woman" (137). This seemingly simple alteration from one biological sex to another masks a sustained, if playful, critique of contemporary discourses of sexual identity. As I have argued elsewhere, Woolf's presentation of Orlando's sex change undermines notions of sexual identity, particularly Freud's notion of narcissistic cathexis.[15] Both Woolf's and Strachey's biographical writings, called by Michael Holroyd "deviant fantasy" (Holroyd 606), might also be labeled "camp biography" because both utilize an overblown, parodic style and both inscribe queer characters whose irregular desires implicitly critique simplistic, binaristic notions of sexual identity.

Strachey and Woolf inscribe queer desire into their biographical texts through the stylistics of camp parody, and one might argue that Strachey's Elizabeth and Essex represents a thinly veiled inscription of his relationship with Roger Senhouse and that Woolf's Orlando is a thinly disguised celebration of her erotic love for Vita Sackville-West. Likewise, one might look to Forster's fiction to find subtextual references to his queer relationships—A Passage to India, for example, has been read as a rewriting of his relationship with Syed Ross Masood, the friend for whom Forster expressed erotic desire and to whom A Passage to India is dedicated. Although both Woolf's and Strachey's biographical texts trouble the distinction between reality and fiction (Woolf by writing a fiction as if it were a biography; Strachey, in Elizabeth and Essex, writing a biography as if it were a fiction), their camp biographies claim to maintain some relation to historical fact: Orlando is subtitled "A Biography";

Elizabeth and Essex, "A Tragic History." Forster makes no such claims for his fictional works, and, in any case, he does not typically exhibit a camp sensibility in his fictional writings.

It might also be possible to argue that moments in Strachey's and Woolf's lives provide superb examples of camp performance. Strachey's well known appearance before the Hampstead Tribunal to plead his case as a conscientious objector against World War I provides an iconic camp moment in any history of Bloomsbury. One might term Strachey a "camp pacifist," judging by the comments which he expressed at the hearing, prefaced by his histrionic inflation of a seat cushion to protect his tender posterior (he had piles) from the hard wood of his chair. When asked what he would do if he saw a German soldier attempting to rape his sister, he answered simply, "I should try and come between them" (qtd. in Holroyd 349). This queer, parodic expression of nonviolent resistance underscores the strategy of subversive camp with which Strachey hoped to outwit the tribunal.

Woolf, too, engaged in camp performance, most notably through her willing participation in her brother Adrian's *"Dreadnought* Hoax" (see King 161). The Hoax involved Adrian and Virginia and a small number of their friends, disguised as the Emperor of Abyssinia and his retinue, insisting on and being granted a close examination of the Royal Navy's *Dreadnought,* "then the most secret battleship afloat" (King 160). Virginia's participation in this hoax—for which she "wore a turban, an embroidered caftan and a gold chain" in addition to her face being "blackened with greasepaint" and adorned with a moustache (King 161)—suggests camp pacifism, camp orientalism, and camp androgyny.

No such performance may be found in the biographies of Forster's life; both his pacifism and his anticolonialism were serious and earnest. In his letters, however, he does at times demonstrate a camp sensibility. Writing about his impressions of Ravello to his friend Edward Dent, Forster notes that "the noise of people expectorating in the street is wafted up and my mother wails. She cannot get used to the sunny South" (Beauman 109). The campiness of this passage is both ironic and parodic; that is, the ironic tone of a cliché such as "the sunny South" is framed by an overall attempt to imitate a Victorian epistolary style. One need only replace the highly formal "expectorating" with a term such as "celebrating" and a typical nineteenth or early twentieth century tourist letter emerges. This passage suggests the meeting between North and South which is often expressed with irony and is a constant source of comedy in Forster's novels. Such scenes described in Forster's fiction and nonfiction suggest a camp sensibility not foreign to those which underlie the queer parodic performances of Strachey's tribunal appearance or Woolf's participation in the *Dreadnought* Hoax.

3. FORSTER'S CAMP S/CITES

In order to argue for Forster's place in the campy coterie which I have termed Queer Bloomsbury, and more specifically as an author whose texts belong in the subgenre Bloomsbury camp biography, one must begin with an examination of Forster's lesser-known, early nonfictional writing, particularly the short sketches that he published as an undergraduate at Cambridge. In Forster's writing, the Stracheyesque mode is roughly equatable with the Apostolic mode;[16] Forster first employed a camp-parodic mode of writing as a Cambridge undergraduate to amuse his fellow students and apostolic brothers. In early biographical sketches that appeared in Cambridge undergraduate periodicals such as the *Cambridge Review* and *Basileona,* Forster utilizes parody and demonstrates a marked camp sensibility. This parodic mode persists in Forster's post-Cambridge biographical writings, although as his career develops, the parodic Forster comes more and more into conflict with what one might term the "earnest" Forster. A softening of the parodic spirit of Forster's Cambridge writings may very well have produced the "ironic Forster" familiar to many readers of his novels.

In his very earliest published writing—"On Grinds," "On Bicycling," "The Cambridge Theophrastus: The Stall-Holder," "The Cambridge Theophrastus: The Early Father"[17]—Forster employs parody and satire with no little relish. In them, according to S. P. Rosenbaum, "Forster begins to connect through parody the present with the classics and history he had been studying" (*Victorian* 274). The butt of the satire of these sketches is R. C. Jebb's bowdlerized 1870 translation of *The Characters of Theophrastus.*[18] *The Characters* humorously presents thirty types of men: "The Flatterer," "The Unpleasant Man," "The Offensive Man," "The Stupid Man," etc. The sketch for each type typically begins with a definition of the man's representative quality and then uses various examples to illustrate the relationship between the quality and the man. For example, Jebb's translation of "The Flatterer" begins:

Flattery may be considered as a mode of companionship degrading but profitable to him who flatters.

The Flatterer is a person who will say as he walks with another, "Do you observe how people are looking at you? This happens to no man in Athens but you. A compliment was paid to you yesterday in the Porch. More than thirty persons were sitting there; the question was started, Who is our foremost man? Everyone mentioned your name." With these and the like words, he will remove a morsel of wool from his patron's coat. . . . (Jebb 81)

This pattern is consistent throughout *The Characters,* as is Jebb's stilted and literal style, both of which provide Forster with a blueprint for his earliest satirical writing.

"On Grinds" and "On Bicycling" broadly mimic Jebb's use of definition and example. "On Bicycling," for example, begins with a definition of bicycling before turning its attention to the dominant characteristics of the typical cyclist. The two sketches titled "The Cambridge Theophrastus," in contrast, parody Jebb's translation closely. The opening of Forster's "The Stall-Holder":

A stall may be defined as a place in which dumb animals are penned, and a stall-holder is one who pens them.

She is one who, being at other times generous, straightforward and magnanimous, is able, at the call of Charity, to put all these things away from her and devote herself solely to the acquisition of wealth. She addresses herself chiefly to those who are young and in possession of money that is not their own but entrusted to them by their absent parents, using such expressions as, "Now you must buy something from *me,*" and "Let me pin this flower to your coat," and "If you will take both these egg cosies I will reduce them to four and sixpence." (AE 57)

Forster begins his sketch not with the definition of an abstract quality such as flattery, but with a humorously unnecessary description of a familiar site in Cambridge and elsewhere, a stall. Like Jebb, though, he moves from this definition to the description of a type, including phrases spoken by a typical stall-holder. Forster parodies Jebb's style and transfers the personages described in *The Characters* from the ancient world to contemporary Cambridge.

To be sure, comedy is not scarce in Jebb's *The Characters of Theophrastus,* but much of Forster's humor derives from the use of a style—Jebb's—that seems oblivious to the comedy inherent in Theophrastus' original text. Since the Theophrastian text is already funny, the humor that is original to Forster's "Cambridge Theophrastus" lies in his parody of Jebb's pretentiously literal Victorian style. Importantly for Forster, Jebb's translation is bowdlerized, as Jebb explains in his introduction to *The Characters:* "There are . . . in the Characters about a dozen passages or phrases which I was unwilling to translate, and which I have omitted in the English and the Greek" (ix–x). Jebb lists—in Greek—the chapters from which he has excised passages; if one compares these chapters with those in a more recent translation, one realizes quickly that most of Jebb's omissions refer either to bodily fluids or to sexual acts.[19] By parodying Jebb's text, Forster camps up a text that is exemplary of Victorian prudishness; he thereby wages a subtle war against the attitudes which inform Jebb's translation.

The parodic Forster is also evident in a number of Forster's undergraduate writings that are not biographical. In his "A Tragic Interior" in two parts, for example, Forster presents a camp version of Aeschylus' *Oresteia* that features a cuckolded Agamemnon and an overbearing Clytemnestra. The action of Forster's version of the play takes place entirely "backstage." By focusing on the unlikely goings-on that one is supposed to believe are occurring offstage in a Greek play, he reveals the absurdity of numerous Victorian critics who took these tragedies much too seriously from Forster's point of view. Forster emphasizes his critique of Victorian attitudes through a reference to Dr. A. W. Verrall at the end of the first part of "A Tragic Interior":

AGAMEMNON: Really now, this play might have been written by Euripides.
CLYTEMNESTRA: Or by Dr. V*rr*ll. (AE 67)

As George H. Thomson explains, "Verrall (1851–1912) [was] the indefatigable editor of school texts of the Latin and Greek classics" (AE 41). In these satiric plays, Forster parodies classical Greek tragedy; this mode is also evident in an early short story of Forster's, "The Road from Colonus," which might be read as a parody of Sophocles' *Oedipus at Colonus*. While rewriting the texts of ancient Greece, Forster simultaneously undermines the earnestness and reverence with which Victorian critics approached them.

The undergraduate Forster further parodies the Victorian solemnity of R. C. Jebb, A. W. Verrall, and their ilk in his "Strivings after Historical Style," which presents humorous versions of four styles typical of "a certain series of Oxford textbooks" (AE 77): dramatic, personal, critical, and cosmic. The passages that he provides as examples of these styles are filled with bombastic and pompous sentences, clichés, and mixed metaphors (see Rosenbaum, *Victorian* 276). Judging from his earliest biographical and nonbiographical writing, one might safely assert that Forster the undergraduate employed an explicitly parodic mode in his writing almost exclusively, in both his biographical writings and in other short pieces. His use of this style diminishes as Forster develops his characteristic comic-ironic tone in the novels, with their delightful deflations of pomposity and self-importance.

Sketches written by Forster for the *Independent Review* shortly after his graduation from Cambridge also conspicuously employ a camp parodic mode. Short pieces such as "Cnidus," "Cardan," and "Macolnia Shops," all written within a few years after the turn of the century, have been labeled "Stracheyesque" by critics such as Wilfred Stone and Judith Scherer Herz. Possibly the best example of Forster's utilization of this mode is "Macolnia Shops." This sketch examines the character of Dindia Macolnia, "a wealthy lady" and resident of ancient Rome, who purchased a toilet case for her daughter which eventually made its way to the Kirchner Museum, where Forster examined it in 1903. Forster utilizes a catalog of heroic and prominent ancients in this sketch in ways similar to Strachey's and Woolf's use of such indicators of importance, that is, to undercut and parody them through the bathos of deflation: "Marius was in Rome at the time, or, if not Marius, Sulla, or, if Sulla was dead, Cicero was speaking, or, if Cicero was silent Macolnia might have looked with well-bred curiosity on the face of Augustus Imperator. But Dindia Macolnia was there to shop" (AH 171). Shopping, here the accumulation of decorative objects, functions in this sketch to undercut the more heroic associations that a reader might make with imperial Rome.

Also, as in other examples of this camp biographical style, Forster inscribes queer sexuality into his sketch. Macolnia's gift to her daughter was even for her an antique, a "Greek work [that] tells the story of the punishment of Amycus by Pollux. . . . Pollux, the boxer, has vanquished him and bound him naked to a tree, and round them are a group of admiring onlookers" (AH 171). Forster explains that the decorations on the toilet case represent a paean to friendship, which for him could signify the homosocial, homoerotic, and the homosexual.[20] As in Strachey and Woolf, Forster's use of camp allows this queer gesture to signify multivalently, within an overall context of parody. Like an unknowing, uninitiated reader, Macolnia does not understand the import of Forster's queer reading of the toilet case: " 'Praise of Friendship!' cries the angry shade of Dindia Macolnia, rising on its elbow out of the quaint Etruscan Hell. 'I bought it because it was pretty, and stood nicely on the chest of drawers' " (AH 173). The scene on the toilet case, with its same-sex sadomasochistic overtones, provides a subversive contrast to the portrait of a conspicuous consumer of the "middle class" (a self-conscious anachronism) who attempts to own and to domesticate it.

Another sketch that Forster wrote for *The Independent Review*—but was never published in that journal or anywhere—utilizes a camp parodic mode that bears close resemblance to Strachey's and Woolf's biographies. "Luigi Cornaro" focuses on an Italian Renaissance writer who wrote numerous guides to good living that suggest a proper diet is the secret to a happy, long life. Forster's text includes at least one camp aphorism: "An old man, however advanced, may be a poor companion, and a hygienic old man can be a dreadful bore." Also included in the text is a series used in the bathos of deflation, which occurs in a passage written by Cornaro and translated by Forster: " 'Three bad habits,' [Cornaro] says, 'have come into this Italy of ours during my lifetime. The first is Formality, the second Lutherism, and the third over eating.' " In a device that will become typical in Forster's later biographies, Forster separates himself from this bathetic passage through the use of quotation marks. He is not the author of such campy passages, although his use of them nonetheless authorizes them.

Forster generally admires Cornaro for his vitality and assuredness, and possibly also because Cornaro is for Forster in some sense queer. This possibility is suggested by a comment that Cornaro makes to the Bishop of Aquileia in a letter. Assuring the Bishop that he has a beautiful voice, Cornaro wishes that the Bishop could hear him sing, accompanying himself "meanwhile on the lyre like David." If the Bishop could see and hear this performance, Cornaro assures him that he "would be perfectly charmed." As in "Macolnia Shops" and Strachey's and Woolf's biographies, camp is used to suggest the possibility of irregular desire, characterized by Forster in this sketch as "charm[ing]" a Bishop. Forster does become annoyed with Cornaro and his "uncanny . . . energy," however, at one point in the sketch. He asserts that "inhumanity does peep out at times" in Cornaro's personality. After quoting a passage in which Cornaro blames the poor for their own poverty and concomitant hunger, Forster notes, "At such moments one grows irritated with the old boy, and longs to feed him forcibly. One longs to hear the other side—what his wife thought of his singing for example." This humorous passage causes the reader to wonder what Cornaro's wife thought about his desire to charm the Bishop of Aquileia through his singing. Did she realize, Forster seems to be suggesting, that she could never be a Jonathan to her husband's David? This delightful sketch provides a superb example of the parodic, Stracheyesque Forster.

Unlike Strachey's and Woolf's biographies, Forster's early biographical writings do not typically examine Victorian figures in great detail or the Victorian era directly. Generally, "Macolnia Shops," "Luigi Cornaro," and other sketches—most of which are collected in *Abinger Harvest* and *Pharos and Pharillon*— provide Stracheyesque portrayals of historical figures from ancient history, with titles such as "Cardan," "Gemisthus Pletho," "Philo's Little Trip," and "St. Athanasius." Although he parodies Victorian biographical styles in these pieces, he does not provide a direct critique of the Victorian era. A review from 1910 does, however, suggest that numerous anti-Victorian attitudes inform Forster's writing. "Mr. Walsh's Secret History of the Victorian Movement" is the title that Forster gave to his review of A Manual of Domestic Economy, by J. H. Walsh. Forster reads Walsh's manual, which went through several editions in the nineteenth century, as "not a manual of Domestic Economy but a manual of Victorianism" (AE 110). In this review Forster associates Victorianism with "meanness and naïveté" (AE 112), a world view that "condemns every friendship that one has had or is likely to have" (AE 113). Further, he sees the characteristics of Victorianism, which contrast starkly with his own liberal humanism and its faith in human relations, as a threat to his own post-Victorian culture. Forster fears that "Victorianism may not be an era at all. It may be a spirit, biding its time" (AE 116).

Forster uses his later book-length biographies to parody and undermine this dangerous spirit of Victorianism. In contrast to his earlier short sketches, these works do attempt to rewrite established versions of certain moments and settings in nineteenth-century British history, particularly the world of late-Victorian Cambridge in Goldsworthy Lowes Dickinson and the development and decline of the Clapham Sect in Marianne Thornton. In these texts, Forster does not consistently utilize an overblown style that undermines severely the conventions of biography. Indeed, the voice found in Forster's later biographical writings—as in "Luigi Cornaro"—allows, typically, primary sources to "speak for themselves"; the "camp sites" in these texts are often simultaneously camp citations, or "camp cites."

But texts such as Goldsworthy Lowes Dickinson and Marianne Thornton do employ many of the strategies of parody exemplified by Strachey's biographies, although the examples are neither as numerous nor as pronounced as those one might find in Strachey or Woolf. In Goldsworthy Lowes Dickinson (1934), Forster attempts to parody a Victorian, overly serious diarist style in recounting an episode that occurred when Forster and Dickinson were traveling together to India. During the trip, Forster notes, "We kept diaries. 'The extent of the heat may be judged from the fact that, on descending to my cabin, a tube of Kolynos was found in a semi-liquid condition' is a sentence which Dickinson gave me to put into mine. He said it was the ideal diarist style" (GLD 113). In this passage, the pomposity of the phrase "semi-liquid condition" is deflated by the use of the Kolynos tube to register the increasing heat as the English travellers approach India. This camped version of a traditionally serious and exact style of diary writing represents Forster's attempt, in his own words, to "transcribe . . . nonsense" (GLD 113). Although this passage does not feature the over-the-top and exaggerated style of, for example, the biographical voice in Woolf's *Orlando,* it does suggest a similar emphasis on metabiographical parody in that it attempts to undermine the sonorous seriousness of Victorian biography. Its focus on Dickinson's liquefying toothpaste underlines this playfulness. Generally, however, the tone of Forster's Dickinson biography, like Woolf's tone in *Roger Fry,* is tender and sympathetic.

The parodic Forster also emerges in his 1956 *Marianne Thornton: A Domestic Biography,* which takes as its subject the Clapham Sect generally and the aunt whose financial legacy enabled Forster's career. Glen Cavaliero has noted that at points in *Marianne Thornton* Forster's "tone . . . seems about to turn into the patronizing mockery of Lytton Strachey's *Eminent Victorians*" (30); for Cavaliero, Forster usually avoids Stracheyism, being "anxious to mediate between one age and another" (30). Cavaliero unfortunately reduces parody to mockery and seems unaware of the tenderness with which Strachey could write about the Victorian period. Forster's biography of his great-aunt is more Stracheyesque than it first appears, particularly in the final section of the book, which centers on Forster's birth. For example, utilizing a series for an ultimately deflating effect, Forster describes a letter written by his aunt to his mother: "It was not exactly a patronizing letter, it was not snobbish . . . but it left the victim no outlet and was written without the slightest consciousness that it was appalling" (MT 284); this technique is similar to the Stracheyesque bathetic series. In another passage that utilizes Strachey's typically tripartite structure, Forster, discussing the relationship between his mother and his hostile Aunt Emily, asserts that "Once [Aunt Emily] gave me a Bible, whereupon my mother sobbed with rage. I learnt afterwards that when Emily disliked people she gave them a Hymn Book, and when she detested them a Prayer Book. So a Bible was the limit of limits" (MT 299).

Finally, Forster, like Strachey and Woolf, inscribes at least the possibility of queer desire into *Marianne Thornton.* For example, Forster's text includes a reference, in a letter written by his Aunt Marianne, to a close friend of Forster's father, Edward Streatfeild, who accompanied Forster's parents on their Paris honeymoon. Aunt Marianne feels that is unfortunate that Forster's mother must travel with " 'no lady companion, except Streatfeild, who is very nearly one I own, but not quite' " (MT 285). She later describes Forster's father as "old-maidish" (MT 286). As in earlier biographies, Forster separates himself from this camp style through the use of quotation marks. Although other camp s/cites might be found in Forster's book-length biographical writings, generally his later biographies utilize fewer strategies of queer parody in order to undermine a premodernist tradition of biographical writing. At the same time, Forster developed for his novels a style that employs mimicry of both the narrative voice of serious Victorian novels and the English, suburban voices that surrounded him at home and in his travels. His novelistic style was prepared for and anticipated by the early parodic writings.

Strachey, Forster, and Woolf all express allegiance to a humanist philosophy that allows them both to admire and to parody the biographical writings of their literary forebears and to camp various traditions of British literature. Their biographies utilize camp parody, to a greater or lesser extent. The sense of play in texts such as *Eminent Victorians, Orlando,* and *Marianne Thornton* suggests parodic metafiction, which is frequently asserted as characteristic of postmodern writing. To argue, from a masculinist perspective, that the texts of Bloomsbury writers lack vitality and energy misses a crucial point. Although the writers of the Bloomsbury Group enjoyed privileges concomitant with their class positions, they were engaged in a systematic—if playful and parodic—dismantling of the moral and aesthetic underpinnings of the class system which provided such privilege. My hope is that readings such as this one, which find in Bloomsbury a sustained critique of sexual oppression that crossed and undermined the boundaries between sex and gender, will begin the work of making readable the modernism of queer Bloomsbury and the queerness of modernism itself.

Notes

1. Forster, Strachey, and Woolf were not the only Bloomsberries to evince a camp sensibility in their biographical writings. See, for example, the portrayals of the Council of Four at the Versailles Conference in chapter 3 of J. M. Keynes and the biographical sketches collected in Clive Bell's *Old Friends.*

2. See the section entitled "Bloomsbury on Bloomsbury" in Rosenbaum's *Bloomsbury Group* for an ample sampling of these memoirs.

3. Although "humanism" has become a disparaging term for many recent theorists, it signified in the late nineteenth and early twentieth centuries above all a critique of a Christian, theocratic world view. Bloomsbury's humanism was greatly influenced by the philosopher G. E. Moore, particularly his *Principia Ethica.*

4. Judging from a diagram of the Bloomsbury Group provided by Quentin Bell, its central members were Duncan Grant, Clive Bell, Virginia Woolf, Saxon Sydney Turner, Vanessa Bell, Roger Fry, and Leonard Woolf. Orbiting at various distances from this central cluster are numerous others, including Lytton Strachey and Maynard Keynes. Two figures, Francis Birrell and E. M. Forster, are positioned at the outermost limits of the diagram (see Q. Bell, *Bloomsbury* 15). Although Forster was frequently absent from many Bloomsbury gatherings in the first two decades of the century (as Keynes, among others, has pointed out), he was by the mid-1920s a frequent visitor to the homes of prominent members of the group such as Woolf and Strachey. Roger Poole has demonstrated that Forster's connection with Woolf was particularly strong: Forster was Woolf's most valued critic. Their relationship was also extremely complicated, as Joseph Bristow shows in his contribution to this volume.

5. On Woolf's sapphism, see James King and especially Suzanne Raitt.

6. Bonnie Kime Scott correctly points out that the major drawback of Kenner's view is related to its masculinist bias against Bloomsbury: a "Pound narrative of modernism" such as Kenner's does not "touch in a very productive way upon Bloomsbury" because "Pound's virile ethos clashed with Bloomsbury" (94).

7. Eagleton presented a quite similar reading of modernism at the 1994 MLA Convention in an essay entitled "Modernism in Ireland."

8. Edelman claims, for example, that queer critics should not "reengage in our critical practice this heterosexually inflected inside/outside, either/or model of sexual discriminations"; rather, queer critical analysis "might do well to consider Barbara Johnson's description of a criticism informed by deconstructionist insights in order 'to elaborate a discourse that says *neither* 'either/or,' *nor* 'both/and,' nor even 'neither/nor,' while at the same time not totally abandoning these logics either' " (*Homographesis* 203).

9. Admittedly, it is somewhat difficult to assert that T. S. Eliot and Henry James are representatives of the masculine modernist tradition in any uncomplicated way. In *Exiles and Émigrés,* Eagleton includes them in the list of "the seven most significant writers of twentieth-century English literature" (9), all of whom are, significantly, male: "Lawrence . . . Conrad, James, Eliot, Pound, Yeats, Joyce" (9). These writers are characterized by their power to totalize, to grasp "the elements of a culture in their living and changing interrelations" (10). In his later *Function of Criticism,* however, Eagleton lists Eliot, James, and Forster as "crippled, marginalized, self-ironizing humanists" (*Function* 100), suggesting that these authors might not in fact be the exemplars of phallic authority of Eagleton's earlier characterization.

10. Marcus argues, for example, that "for women like Virginia Woolf, the homosexual men of Cambridge and Bloomsbury appeared to be, not the suffering victims of heterosexual social prejudice, but the 'intellectual aristocracy' itself, an elite with virtual hegemony over British culture" (*Virginia* 177). See Reed, in this volume, and "Bashing," 71–72, for a useful critique of Marcus's reading of the role of male homosexuals in Bloomsbury.

11. Bette London, in "Guerrilla," incisively points out Marcus's complicity in phallic logic: "Marcus constructs her revolutionary paradigm as a simple reversal *within* the terms of the dominant discourse, leaving intact its underlying structures of thought, politics, and meaning" (15).

12. I have borrowed these categories from Spurr's excellent analysis of Strachey's style.

13. Oscar Wilde's camp sensibility and characteristically aphoristic style played a major role in the development of Stracheyism. For an exploration of the important connections between Wildean aestheticism and Bloomsbury, see Reed, "Making" 203–17.

14. In *Flush*, her biography of Elizabeth Barrett Browning's cocker spaniel, Woolf parodies a Victorian biographical style as she simultaneously attacks Victorian prudery and sexual double standards. After noting that "Before he was well out of his puppyhood, Flush was a father," the voice of Flush's biographer continues: "Such conduct in a man even, in the year 1842, would have called for some excuse from a biographer; in a woman no excuse could have availed; her name must have been blotted in ignominy from the page. But the moral code of dogs, whether better or worse, is certainly different from ours, and there was nothing in Flush's conduct in this respect that requires a veil now, or unfitted him for the society of the purest and the chastest in the land then" (13). Woolf seems to be suggesting in this passage that the moral code of the Victorians, like the moral code of dogs, "is certainly different" from her own and that of the Bloomsbury circle.

15. See Piggford for a detailed analysis of the relationship between camp and the figure of the androgyne in Woolf's text.

16. The "Apostolic mode" might be characterized as the mode employed in meetings of the Cambridge Apostles, or Conversazione Society, a secret organization whose members, including Strachey and Forster, presented blunt, candid, and frequently campy papers to each other at monthly meetings. In an talk entitled "A Roman Society" (presented to a meeting of the Apostles on 9 December 1910) Forster utilizes a camp parodic style to describe the Renaissance academy of Pomponius Laetus. This talk might be read as exemplary of the Apostolic style. Unfortunately, it has not yet been published. See Joseph Bristow in this volume for an analysis of Forster's lifelong attachment to the Apostles.

17. These sketches were all originally published in 1900 and are reprinted along with Forster's other undergraduate writing in *Albergo Empedocle and Other Writings*. In the original publications, the author of these pieces is typically listed as "Peer Gynt." The fact that these pieces are "spoken" through the voice of a persona—the rakish hero of Ibsen's play—suggests an attempt on Forster's part to distance himself from these campy texts.

18. Theophrastus (ca. 370 to ca. 285 BCE), a student of Aristotle, wrote *The Characters* ca. 319 BCE.

19. An echo of this attitude might be found in *Maurice*'s Dean Cornwallis,

who instructs the undergraduates in his translation class to "Omit: a reference to the unspeakable vice of the Greeks" (M 51) in Plato's *Symposium*.

20. In *The Longest Journey*, for example, the novel's protagonist, Rickie Elliot, wishes that a "friendship office" existed where he could officially record his erotically charged friendship with Stewart Ansell, a relationship which he compares to that of David and Jonathan. And in *Maurice*, Maurice's dream of a "Friend" suggests in the first half of the text John Addington Symonds's erotic and idealizing, but necessarily sexual, notion of "Greek love" and in the second half a Whitmanian-Carpentarian vision of "comradeship," which Robert K. Martin reads as a code for full physical homosexuality. See Martin, "Edward," particularly 35–38.

6

Fratrum Societati: *Forster's Apostolic Dedications*

Joseph Bristow

When you—or L[eonard Woolf]—replies I want news of e.g. Lytton, James [Strachey], Duncan [Grant], [Harry] Norton, [Saxon] Sydney Turner, [J. M.] Keynes, Sheppard; even Dent. My address is Red X, St. Mark's Building, Rue de l'ancienne Bourse, Alex[andria]. *E. M. Forster to Virginia Woolf, 15 April 1916.*[1]

I

"I knew that there were buggers in Plato's Greece," writes Virginia Woolf in the paper titled "Old Bloomsbury" she delivered to the Memoir Club in the early 1920s. "I suspected," she adds, "that there were buggers in Dr Butler's Trinity [College, Cambridge]" (S. P. Rosenbaum, *Bloomsbury Group* 52). But when pausing to reflect on her earliest encounters with members of the Cambridge Apostles at 46 Gordon Square (the family home that became the focus of the Bloomsbury movement), her memory betrayed an altogether unexpected fact about the visitors to this residence. Regardless of the numerous male homosexuals from both classical and modern times, "it never occurred" to her "that there were buggers even now in the Stephens' sitting room in Gordon Square." The special company she joined from 1904 onward comprised a group of young men, the "majority" of whom "were not attracted by young women." "I did not realize," remarked Woolf, "that love, far from being a thing they never mentioned, was in fact a thing they seldom ceased to discuss." For "love"— of a particular kind—certainly dominated their discourse. No sooner had Woolf recognized this than she was free to participate in what felt like a genuinely liberating forum for intellectual debate. The moment Lytton Strachey entered the room, pointed to a stain on her sister Vanessa Stephen's white dress, and inquired if it was "semen," "all barriers of reticence and reserve went down." So open were the ensuing conversations about sex that the "word bugger was never far from" their "lips" (Rosenbaum, *Bloomsbury Group* 54). Nor would Woolf hesitate to use it in the private world of her carefully maintained diary.

Yet, as Woolf makes plain, the lively talk at Gordon Square—an elegant Georgian development where many of the nicknamed "Bloomsberries" would settle[2]—was not the sort in which women could feel entirely uninhibited. Although one may infer that the "buggers' " lack of sexual interest in women put Woolf at her ease, it was certainly the case that "something" was "always suppressed," precisely because of the absence of such eroticism. If there was relief, on the one hand, there was repression, on the other. Enjoying the freedom to speak of "love" with these men, Woolf recognized she could not "show off." Implicitly, any displays of flirtatious femininity would not achieve the desired effect. While she and Vanessa listened with "rapt attention" to the "ups and downs" of these "buggers' " "chequered histories," she found herself frivolously responding to their love affairs, most probably because her own sexual preference—as her later works would tell—revealed a much greater respect for and interest in women, most notably, the female audience she would address at Newnham and Girton, the two Cambridge women's colleges, when delivering the lectures later published as *A Room of One's Own* (1929).[3] For Cambridge to Woolf remained an overwhelmingly male stronghold. Unlike her father, uncle, and brother Thoby, who both attended the university, Woolf was educated at home, only to marry an Apostle whom she accompanied on his occasional visits back to college to debate a burning issue of the day. If her novel *Jacob's Room* (1923) provides a fair indication of her view of Cambridge, then she found it remarkable that a college as notable as King's should even allow women to attend its chapel services.[4]

Woolf's recollections focus two conflicting concerns that I pursue throughout this chapter. The first is the powerful manner in which her memoir accentuates the avant-garde homosexuality of the men elected at the turn of the century to the Cambridge Apostles, an elite—one might say legendary—debating society first established in the 1820s, and whose earliest members included the devoted friends Arthur Henry Hallam and Alfred Tennyson. The Apostles established an important Victorian trend toward artistic and intellectual brotherhoods.[5] By the *fin de siècle*, the Apostles created its own distinctive and unashamed homoerotic ethos. (This was hardly a propitious time to cement such close emotional bonds, for the taboo against sexual intimacy between men intensified greatly after the trials that led to Wilde's imprisonment in 1895.) E. M. Forster—whose relations with Woolf, as well as Bloomsbury more generally, were on some occasions vexed[6]—became an Apostle in 1901, the year he went down from King's. His subsequent loyalty to this group never diminished. Three of his books—*The Longest Journey* (1907), *The Celestial Omnibus* (1911), and *Goldsworthy Lowes Dickinson* (1934)—bear dedications to the Apostles,[7] men who loyally called each other "brother." There is no doubt that his fraternal Cambridge peers provided an intellectual environment in which Forster was soon able to define his identity as a homosexual writer, one keen to imagine loving relationships that resisted the cultural imperatives to become a conventional married man.

Woolf's memoir, however, has further implications for the apostolic homoeroticism that meant so much to Forster. The second—very different—point to emerge from "Old Bloomsbury" and its memories of the Cambridge "buggers" runs somewhat against the first. For Woolf's essay shows how closely she herself was identified with the set from which she to some degree felt alienated. Forster repeatedly saw Woolf as the central protagonist of Bloomsbury, at times distancing himself from its activities because of the exclusive class values he believed it enshrined. Such values were personified most vividly for him in Woolf—a woman he publicly noted, shortly after her death in 1941, as a "snob" (even if, as he went on to admit, her "snobbery" had more "courage in it than arrogance" [TCD 250]). His frequently irked reactions to Woolf (especially toward her "extreme feminism" [248]) suggest that she came to bear the burden of his blame for the exclusivity of a university where many of his most formative intellectual relations were made, and from which he himself had benefited. As anyone could tell from the biography she published in 1940 of the Bloomsbury artist Roger Fry—himself elected an Apostle in 1887—Woolf was exceptionally intimate with this fraternal group.

Woolf's intimacy with the affairs of the Cambridge "brothers" is evident from the letter Forster wrote her in 1916, shortly after he had taken up his post as Head Searcher for the Red Cross in Alexandria. It is Woolf who is supposed to know all the news about their mutual friends (all of them men, many of them "buggers"), thus suggesting that she—in the midst of the wartime crisis—has better access to these apostolic friends than an Apostle like Forster himself. Such details hint that if the Apostles made Bloomsbury an heir to their Cambridge, it was by placing a woman at its center: a woman who was hardly uncritical of the "buggers" who found her joining in their sodomitical wit. So there is an intriguing tension between Woolf's and Forster's respective positions within the university fraternity that largely comprised Bloomsbury, especially since to each other they would represent—for all the friendship between them—some of the worst faults of Cambridge and Gordon Square, respectively.

Forster was never quite at home in either of these places. Having been elected to the apostolic brotherhood in 1901, he graduated soon after and attended meetings only intermittently. The same was true for his appearances at what had become Clive Bell and Vanessa Bell's marital home. His visits to Bloomsbury only began in 1910, some six years after the Friday Club started holding its regular salons. In an essay written in the late 1960s, David Garnett notes that "Morgan Forster was on the periphery rather than at the heart of this circle" (31–32). Hardly a scintillating presence, he "seemed to turn up when something interesting was occurring." If Garnett's memory revealingly fails to give shape to Forster's role in these events, then he turns to another authority to confirm the rather weak impression Forster made: "The elusiveness that Maynard Keynes notes is very characteristic, and was made more noticeable by the fact that for many years, just as the party was warming up, he had to catch a train back to Weybridge" (32). For some baffling reason, so it seemed, Forster's domestic life with his mother in suburban Surrey took precedence over the intellectual vibrancy of Gordon Square.

The question of Forster's apparent marginality to both the Apostles and Bloomsbury becomes much more intriguing when one realizes that he himself was viewed as emblematic of both groups. Not only was *The Longest Journey* (1907), as S. P. Rosenbaum explains, the "first piece of fiction to be written about Bloomsbury's Cambridge origins, the first to use [G. E.] Moore's philosophy, the first to represent certain values of the Group" (*Edwardian* 226), his early stories were also prominent in the pages of the apostolic *Independent Review*. Established by university friends, the twelve volumes of this impressive periodical ran from 1903 to 1907, providing one of the most progressive perspectives on Edwardian culture. Among notable contributors, for example, was the sex radical, Edward Carpenter. (It may well have been in the pages of this journal that Forster first encountered Carpenter's work, a body of writing that leaves its mark on *The Longest Journey, A Room with a View* [1908], *Howards End* [1910], and *Maurice* [written 1913–14].[8]) Yet at the very point that Forster became the Apostles' and Bloomsbury's most celebrated writer of fiction, he was seeking to set himself at a studied distance from their concerns.

Forster's ambivalence toward both Cambridge and Bloomsbury frequently appears in his writing. Succeeding entries to his *Commonplace Book* for 1929 show where his discomfort lay. Stating that Bloomsbury is "the only genuine *movement* in English civilization," he proceeds to note that it suffers from "contempt for the outsider," even if that "rests on inattention rather than arrogance" (CB 48). "Once convinced" that the newcomer to its ranks "is not a figure of fun, it welcomes and studies him, but the rest of humanity remains in the background of screaming farce as before" (CB 48). A similar insularity afflicts his alma mater: "*Cambridge* . . . attracts my heart but depresses me more because as soon as the train slackens at that eel-like platform it's settled who I can know, who not." "The two [ancient] universities [Oxford and Cambridge]," he adds, "disintegrate and degrade their towns" (CB 49–50). Town and gown—"extortionate manual workers," on the one hand, and "dons and undergraduates," on the other—remain in his eyes appallingly at odds. Perhaps that is why he tried to efface his reasonably well-to-do origins in public. In the words of Frances Partridge, Forster took pains to dress "like 'the man in the street', in impossibly dull grey suits, a woolly waistcoat perhaps and a cloth cap" (83). The cloth cap—hardly in keeping with either Bloomsbury's aestheticism or Cambridge's collegial garb—was the kind of attire that belonged to the ordinary man (unlike himself) who hailed from the lower middle, if not working, classes.

But for all his efforts to maintain a certain distance from Bloomsbury and Cambridge, his work kept being drawn back to both locations, in ways almost beyond his control. In the paper titled "My Books and I" delivered to the Memoir Club (to whose members Woolf had presented "Old Bloomsbury"), Forster claims he could not understand the reaction among his university friends to "The Story of a Panic," which was the first short narrative he wrote after coming down from King's and which was published in the *Independent* in 1904. This eerie fantasy implied that Forster had absorbed much more of the apostolic ethos than he was willing to admit. He recalls how the Cambridge aesthete, Charles Sayle, was somewhat scandalized by the tale:

"Oh dear," he says, to Maynard Keynes, preparatory to discussing "The Story of a Panic"; "Oh dear, oh dear, is this Young King's?" Then he showed Maynard what the Story was about. B[uggered] by a waiter at the Hotel, Eustace [the fourteen-year-old protagonist] commits bestiality with a goat on that valley where I had sat. In the subsequent chapters, he tells the waiter how nice it has been and they try to b[ugger] each other again. (LJ 302)[9]

The story, of course, contains no explicit scenes of buggery or bestiality. But Sayle was not letting his fantasy run too far in pursuit of this subtext. Forster's haunting narrative—which is as richly homoerotic as any of his fictions—features an English teenager who, enlivened by the spirit of Pan in an Italian setting, escapes into oblivion. Eustace's riotous behavior, especially his physically intimate friendship with an Italian boy, disturbs his respectable English companions. Too sprightly for his own good, the boy embodies an erotic spirit that, true to the name of the classical god, puts English culture in a panic.

In "My Books and I," Forster's reflections on his unwitting use of sexual symbols is perhaps a little disingenuous: "I knew, as their creator, that Eustace and the footmarks and the waiter, had none of the conjunctions he visualized." And he continues: "I had no thought of sex for them." But he is willing to concede one point: "I had been excited as I wrote and the passages where Sayle thought something was up had excited me most" (LJ 302). The same went for the climactic moment in *Where Angels Fear to Tread* (1905) when Philip, tortured by Gino, winces with a broken arm. "This too stirred me," observes Forster. In fact, these stirrings had already been awakened for some time. Even in the drafts of his earliest fragment of fiction, editorially titled "Nottingham Lace" and dating from 1899, one can see the impassioned interest in the intimate friendship between young men whose contrastive aestheticism and athleticism the story seeks to synthesize. This is a pattern—one I have traced in some detail elsewhere (see Bristow, *Effeminate* 55–99)—that would be reappear in many of his later writings.

Yet the desire for connection between men—in the erotic terms that titillated Sayle—would take a quite specific form in the fictions he dedicated to the apostolic world of Cambridge. Each of the stories in question lays an extraordinary emphasis on what it means to have and to be a "brother." But rather than confirm Woolf's belief that such brotherhood thrived among the Apostles, with their unending and shameless love affairs, Forster's early writings attempt to transform and relocate this fraternal world to places far from either the ancient university or Woolf's literary metropolis. Neither Cambridge nor London can offer the many "brothers" of Forster's narratives a context that supports their loving bonds and loyalties. This point is of some note, I think, when one bears in mind that Forster belonged to perhaps the only intellectual grouping that could—and, indeed, did—set in motion the homosexual currents that pass barely beneath the surface of his published novels, and which erupt, with startling violence, in the suppressed works—such as "The Life to Come" and "The Other Boat"—that came to light posthumously in 1972.[10] Time and again, Forster's fictional yearnings for brotherhood would lead to places as diverse as Greece, Italy, Sicily, Hertfordshire, Wiltshire, heaven, and sometimes hell, not the Cambridge to which he dedicated many of his stories on this theme. This pattern of narrative escape from and dedicatory return to his apostolic brethren discloses a revealing area of unease. Having arguably greater opportunities than those of any contemporary novelist to develop his writing of male same-sex desire, Forster turned his gaze to landscapes that were ostensibly beyond both the Apostles' and Bloomsbury's reach. In these writings, the Cambridge that shaped and defined his erotic interests—in ways more than he himself would acknowledge—was constantly represented as constraining, so much so that it encourages his young male protagonists to flee abroad.

Yet Cambridge was the place where in late middle age Forster would find a comfortable home, with a set of rooms in which he enjoyed considerable celebrity and privilege. In 1947, he returned there for good, as an honorary fellow of King's. By that time, however, the apostolic world was on the verge of becoming more than a little disreputable. Four years later, the scandal aroused by the defection of two diplomats—one of them, Guy Burgess, an Apostle—to the Soviet Union put a troubling gloss on the consequences of homosexual fraternalism at Cambridge. These defections to communism, as Alan Sinfield notes, caused the national culture to recoil from the despicable treachery felt to be embodied by these intellectual queers (60–85). So during his declining years, should any critic—such as John Bayley—dare in public to point out "the homosexual themes that underlie all his novels" (Bayley, "Cambridge" 7), then that person would certainly elicit Forster's wrath: "Are you aware," wrote Forster after reading Bayley's thoughtful review in the *Manchester Guardian,* "that homosexuality is still a criminal offence, and any public implication of it therefore highly objectionable" ("Letter")?[11] Although there is a political point to Forster's outburst (he was writing in the early 1960s before the Sexual Offences Act partly decriminalized male homosexual relations), his indignation may have as much to do with being identified as one of countless aging Apostles who symbolized certain values that for more than a decade had been prone to harsh criticism.

In any case, if the Apostles were to be criticized, it was from within their own ranks, and Forster would be the first to undertake this task. From the start of his career, he explored the limits to apostolic brotherhood, if in narratives that were emphatically dedicated to fraternal bonding. It may well have been that the Apostles' perspective on life—as "The Other Side of the Hedge" (1904), *The Longest Journey*, "Arctic Summer" (dating from 1911), and *Maurice* all make clear—would only stretch so far. But in each story, the powerful meaning of brotherhood would never dissolve. In what follows, I attempt to show why.

II

If one story, more than any other by Forster that appeared in the *Independent*, gives brotherhood a troubling erotic meaning, then it is surely "The Other Side of the Hedge": a fantastic narrative that presents itself as an allegory of desired departure and forced return. In many ways, this tale shows how brotherhood provides an unsettling figuration for a lasting bond of kinship that cannot be broken, no matter how much one tries to do away with it. "At first," remarks the narrator, "I thought I was going to be like my brother, whom I had had to leave by the roadside a year or two round the corner" (CT 39). Following the path of life with his symbolic "pedometer" in hand, he recalls how his brother had "wasted his breath on singing and his strength on helping others." That is why he left him behind. His own independent journey, however, proves exhausting, and so he takes a rest. While slumbering by the roadside, having reached "twenty-five" miles, he finds himself suddenly pulled through to the other side of the nearby hedge. Consequently, he discovers pastures new, and the phantasmagoria that passes before his eyes fills him with awe.

In this world, "all seemed happy" (CT 43). There are scenes of "singing," "talking," "hay-making," and "gardening." Not surprisingly, the man who escorts him through the fields, remarks that a "Lee-Metford"—a type of rifle—"wouldn't work" in this domain (CT 43). Having espied a man "with a scythe over his shoulder" (CT 48), he approaches what seems to be the grim reaper. But when he seizes the deathly figure's "can of . . . liquid in his hand," the beer he imbibes works its alcoholic magic upon him, and he is lowered down into the arms of the reaper "to sleep off its effects." In his drowsiness, he suddenly recognizes the figure of death as his "brother." So this haunting story—whose elements of fantasy are played out throughout the narratives collected in *The Celestial Omnibus* —dramatizes the uncanny return to a brother that the protagonist initially deserts. Here the desire not to be like a brother turns back to the man he has abandoned. Somehow, the journey follows exactly the trail from which it is supposed to lead away. But this is not a tragic quest. For in the end there is reconciliation, physical intimacy, and—by imaginative extension—erotic connectedness.

In many respects, this pattern provides the template for *The Longest Journey*, whose plot Forster first sketched in 1904,[12] and whose interest in the reclamation of a lost brother would seem to draw on a well known Edwardian visionary narrative, Samuel Butler's *Erewhon Revisited* (1901). But this rather awkwardly handled novel—which met with very mixed reviews—is much more than a reworking of Butler's tale. Here the complex double movement between the desertion of and reconciliation with one's brother makes for an extremely demanding, often contorted, and arguably unmanageable story that repudiates one form of brotherhood based on the Cambridge Apostles while seeking to transvalue it within another model of fraternity allied with the organic heart of England. Although dedicated "*Fratribus*," the novel unforgivingly criticizes the apostolic world represented in its early chapters. But it none the less remains loyal to that group, not just by virtue of its dedication, but also by seeking to relocate those brothers—to preserve them, as it were—in a wider world. This is a world that cherishes the forms of connectedness—ones transgressing conventional erotic lines—already imagined in "The Other Side of the Hedge."

Throughout *The Longest Journey*, Cambridge remains the subject of a repeated philosophic joke. Opening with an undergraduate discussion that touches on Moore's apostolic refutation of idealism,[13] the novel converts the subject matter of the young men's debate into a noteworthy leitmotiv. Adamant to prove that "the cow is there" (LJ 3)—that is, present in his Cambridge rooms—the young Hegelian philosopher Stewart Ansell, hailing from a humble Jewish draper's family, emerges as an intellectual zealot embodying the spirit of the Apostles in their heyday. Ansell is the first of the protagonists to contribute to the novel's ambitious desire to reveal how men need many different brothers to gain a fuller picture of the world. By insisting that the "cow is there" by a subjective act of will, Ansell reveals argumentative power but narrowness of vision. For his decision to claim the "cow" in his midst is assuredly misplaced at Cambridge. Collegial life is remote from the altogether more real landscape that attracts Forster's interest, a landscape featuring farmers, horsemen, and shepherds: exactly the location where it would surely be meaningless to dispute whether or not "the cow is there." So, later, it comes as no surprise to find the narrator slipping inside the consciousness of Rickie Elliot—Forster's weakly antihero—contemplating his dear friend Ansell's shortcomings: "Ansell could discuss love and death admirably, but somehow he would not understand lovers or a dying man" (LJ 57). Yet that is not to say that Rickie himself has an even more privileged position from which to view the world. For, as the story unfolds, he too will need a kind of brotherly support—one that extends beyond Cambridge—to enjoy a more expansive vision.

From the earliest, Rickie is hampered because he "was only used to Cambridge, and to a very small corner at that." Although "he and his friends there believed in free speech," they "would have shrunk from the empirical freedom that results from a little beer" (LJ 111). Even for those who make greatest effort, the Cambridge life of academic endeavor is ultimately disabling. "A person like Ansell," remarks a college friend, Tilliard, "who goes from Cambridge, home—home, Cambridge—it must tell on him in time" (LJ 142). And so it does. Ansell fails to obtain his fellowship on his second and last try in submitting a dissertation. The penalties tell on him considerably. Surrounded by books in the Reading Room of the British Museum, Ansell listens to Rickie's cousin Widdrington bemoan the plight of apostolic types: "What have we done? What shall we ever do? Just drift and criticize, while people who know what they want snatch it away from us and laugh" (LJ 180). It is a hopeless predicament. Indeed, this lamentable situation preyed on the conscience of many young scholars who, since the mid-nineteenth century, discovered they must at last face up to a world of tough professional— not privileged collegial—life. If these young men spurn the university, then where can they go? And what precisely might they set about getting "done"?

The answer, Forster believes, lies in making contact with the soil of a landscape whose very geology figures forth just the kinds of convergence and connection that Cambridge cannot even pretend to achieve. It is at the symbolic focal point of Cadbury Rings in Wiltshire that Rickie for the first time apprehends an idea of community altogether larger than Cambridge. It is at this harmonizing rural location that all disparate parts of the nation are seen to blend together in organic oneness. But there is much more than just organicism in this anthropomorphized environment that captivates Rickie's lyrical, distinctly Romantic, imagination:

The whole system of the country lay spread before Rickie . . . He saw how all
the water converges at Salisbury; how Salisbury lies in a shallow basin, just at
the change of the soil. He saw to the north the Plain, and the stream of the Cad
flowing down from it, with a tributary that broke out suddenly, as the chalk
streams do: one village had clustered round the source and clothed itself with
trees. He saw Old Sarum, and hints of the Avon valley, and the land above
Stonehenge. And behind him he saw the great wood beginning unobtrusively,
as if the down too needed shaving . . . Here is the heart of our island: the Chil-
terns, the North Downs, the South Downs radiate thence. The fibres of England
unite in Wiltshire, and did we condescend to worship her, here we should erect
our national shrine. (LJ 126)

Although it should not need pointing out that England is only one part
of a larger "island," one cannot overlook the nationalistic confidence of
this passage, as it idealistically humanizes every feature of the landscape.
Nor can one fail to notice the strongly masculine connotations to the
name and nature of this locale. The river is called the "Cad," and its
caddish spontaneity figures in the chalk streams that suddenly break the
soil. The same is true of the "great wood," which—like the down itself—
looks as if it needs "shaving." Vitalizing these pastures, then, is an ap-
pealingly rough-edged masculine power that pulls all of England together without any deference to respectability. And it is to the burly
body of this part of Wiltshire that the rest of the novel is drawn.

The person most closely associated with this landscape is Stephen
Wonham, the man Rickie—much to the embarrassment of his wife Agnes—discovers is his illegitimate half-brother. "A villainous young brute
he looked," remarks the narrator, "his clothes were dirty" (LJ 244). Frequently drunk, not disinclined to bad behavior, at home out of doors,
Wonham represents vibrant contact with the earth—if not the veritable
"cow"—that promises to transform the introspective academic values of
Cambridge. Why? Because "class distinctions were trivial things to him,
and life no decorous scheme" (LJ 244). This is equally the case with his
attitude toward love. As they ride together along a Wiltshire road "where
the power of the earth grows stronger" (LJ 270), Wonham declares:
"Rickie, mightn't I find a girl—naturally not refined—and be happy
with her in my own way? I would tell her straight . . . that she should
never have all my thoughts . . . because all one's thoughts can't belong
to any single person" (LJ 271). In other words, Wonham is the antithesis
to the class-bound apostolic ethos. But he is still, as the narrative keenly
insists, Rickie's brother. Like the landscape of Wiltshire itself, Wonham
enables all conflicting currents—of class, physique, ethnicity, and brotherhood—gradually to intersect.

The various brothers, with all their differences, come together most compellingly in the final chapter, years after Rickie—bearing the burden of physical disability—has died while trying to remove the muscular body of the drunken Wonham from a railway track. His brothers-in-law are found arguing about the royalties to his book of stories. "You've done me out of every penny it fetched," protests Wonham. "It's dedicated to me—flat out—and you even crossed out the dedication" (LJ 286). Unable to tolerate Herbert Pembroke's manipulative behavior, Wonham insists that he should take a look outside at the "solid chalk." "Think of us riding at night when you're ordering your hot bottle—that's the world" (286). And, by implication, it is a world in which much more valuable matters than Pembroke (a public-school master) ever imagined might actually get "done." Since the larger "world" of "solid chalk" must win through in *The Longest Journey,* Pembroke eventually capitulates to the fair terms on which Wonham drives his bargain. Reconciled, they have their rightful share of Rickie's volume, whose title, *Pan Pipes,* recalls the scandalous homoeroticism implied in "The Story of a Panic."

Even though *The Longest Journey* is at its most overwrought when trying to combine these differing models of fraternity, there is no doubt that it seeks to recuperate what it can of the Cambridge world about which it voices so much dissatisfaction early on. In fact, one could argue that its whole drive to make its cast of male characters into brothers derives precisely from the apostolic ethos that spent much of its time quibbling on whether or not "the cow is there." Perhaps Cadover House—the home to which the illegitimate Wonham rightly lays claim—is simply a transposed version of those Cambridge colleges where the Apostles thrived and where women were not welcome. This point is worth laboring, since the female characters who intervene in this novel are treated harshly. To be sure, the narrator observes with some compassion that Rickie's mother suffered greatly at the hands of her snobbish husband, and his consequent adultery: "one day, when she bought a carpet for the dining-room that clashed, he laughed gently, said he 'really couldn't,' and departed" (LJ 22). But the women who remain in Rickie's midst do their best to break the fraternal bond. His condescending aunt, Mrs. Failing, does all she can to spoil the brotherly connection between Rickie and Wonham. And Agnes does much the same by dissociating herself from this bastard son of the earth to preserve her marriage to Rickie. So if *The Longest Journey* seeks to reach out toward the real "cow" many miles from Cambridge, it does so on a model that is inescapably tied to the exclusive brotherly ambience of the university it would sharply criticize. No wonder Frieda Lawrence remarked to Forster some eight years after the novel appeared: "Your women I don't understand, *you* seem to dislike them *much*! Rickie was a very domineering young man in spirit! I would have argued with him" (qtd. in Gardner 97). But, as Forster's later works would show, it was not a woman's place to challenge one's beloved fraternity.

III

The fantasies of brotherhood in *The Longest Journey* would haunt Forster's imagination right up the First World War, and on two further occasions they would force a return to Cambridge. Yet it is notable that neither *The Longest Journey* nor the succeeding fictions that feature the university would enjoy the success of his other novels. It is almost as if the more he turned away from his apostolic background the more appealing his fictional world became to the reading public. His two Italian novels—*Where Angels Fear to Tread* and *A Room with a View* (1908)—and his portrait of contemporary England, *Howards End,* were extremely well received. Forster's growing reputation, however, took its toll. The considerable success of *Howards End* was so great that he felt immobilized by the celebrity it brought him. "I don't like popularity," he wrote on 21 November 1910 to his senior apostolic mentor, the classicist Goldsworthy Lowes Dickinson. "It seems so mad," he added (Furbank, *Life* 1:191). It was at this time that he was drawn belatedly into Bloomsbury, reading a paper to the Friday Club that reflected his preoccupation—which was also theirs—with the gendered nature of literary writing: "The Feminine Note in Literature." Yet once back within a circle of largely familiar Cambridge faces, Forster found it difficult indeed to make a start on a further work of fiction. Perhaps because he was once again in apostolic circles he felt compelled to set his narratives in the world of collegial life. Whatever the reason, the first attempt failed.

Begun in 1911, the disparate fragments comprising "Arctic Summer," from which Forster read sections at the Aldeburgh Festival in 1951, hardly add up to a coherent narrative. But one familiar feature emerges on many a page: the enduring interest in brotherhood. In many ways, it appears that "Arctic Summer" was designed to broach the subject of homosexuality, to which fraternal love would be the key. One passage from the "Main Version" is worth examining at some length, since it shows exactly how brotherhood, Cambridge, and homophilia—if not same-sex eroticism—lie in extremely close proximity. This issue emerges most noticeably when we learn how Mr. Vullamy became guardian to his nephews:

When his brother-in-law died, he also took in hand the boys' careers. Lance should have gone into the Army, but his sight was bad, so Clesant went instead; and had just passed out of Sandhurst without discredit. Lance was entertaining on his last year at Cambridge and then would read for the bar. (AS 178)

Once we have noted how a "brother-in-law" is overseeing the futures of two young brothers, the actual relations between Clesant and Lance come to the fore, so resonant is this tie of kinship. Sent to different public schools, the boys "escaped all that makes brotherhood hard and banal" (AS 179). It was for this reason that "they came to each other with a touch of romance." Such "romance" was possible because of "the emotional ease" Lance had acquired at Cambridge. But such "ease" breaks down when the two men set off on their horses for a ride through the country. "Do you go falling in love, Cles?" asks Lance (AS 180). To which his brother replies, "Do you?" But the inquiry is not welcome. "And who's the happy damsel?" Clesant persists. "You've not understood," says Lance. "I don't mean anything decent. It's getting a damned nuisance."

The "damned nuisance" obviously does not disappear. For in a later fragment we discover that Lance has been sent down from Cambridge. Hearing the news, Clesant exclaims: "My brother couldn't act dishonorably" (AS 186). Even if it seems that Lance's crime has been "to take to filth and go with women" (AS 191), it remains unclear whether this is just his brother's naïve surmise. The narrative does not disclose that another sort of "filth" involving homosexuality might be lurking in its depths. All that is left is the spectacle of the brothers quarreling violently, a scene witnessed by Mr. Vullamy and a man named Martin Whitby, who met Clesant while on holiday with his spouse and mother-in-law. Like Lance, Martin is connected with the university. Although now working as a civil servant, he was elected to a Cambridge fellowship. But "he had no inclination to give up London." "Cambridge," remarks the narrator, "may be the nursery of winning causes, but it is seldom their home" (AS 132). No doubt that is why the story develops a sexual scandal at Lance's college. The extent to which Martin may be party to this event remains at best obscure.

Only in Maurice—the novel Forster could not bring himself to publish in his lifetime—would he once and for all meet head-on the challenge posed by these ceaseless returns to Cambridge and its apostolic brethren. Featuring what are among the most resonant sentences in a novel inhabited by ghosts from the past, the penultimate paragraph reveals the Cambridge intellectual, Clive Durham, haunted by an event that he cannot believe ever in fact occurred: the final parting of his erstwhile lover, Maurice Hall, into oblivion. "To the end of his life," we are told, "Clive was not sure of the exact moment of departure" (M 230). All that he denied about his sexual relations with another man while they were both undergraduates at Cambridge preys on his memory: "Out of some eternal Cambridge his friend began beckoning to him, clothed in the sun, and shaking out the scents and sounds of the May Term." This exquisite elegiac moment captures the remarkable ambivalence of the narrative toward the Cambridge that could and did encourage sexual love between young men. For, on the one hand, by letting Clive linger for the rest of his days on this occurrence gives Cambridge an "eternal" quality that cannot be wished away. But, on the other, it assures us that Maurice Hall—against almost insurmountable barriers of class and country—managed to escape. For—as Forster commented in the "Terminal Note" he appended to his manuscript in 1960—Maurice and his working-class lover, Alec Scudder, have made their home in an anonymous "greenwood": "an England where it was still possible to get lost" (M 240). This "greenwood" is, by strong implication, a world altogether larger, freer, and more real than Cambridge could ever be.

By 1913, Forster had been able to reach this position by aid of Carpenter's works, such as *The Intermediate Sex* and "Homogenic Love" (both published in 1908). These radical writings on "Uranian" desire, as Robert K. Martin notes, "brought an end to Forster's search for a homosexual tradition" ("Edward" 44). And it is fair to claim that *Maurice* bears more than a passing resemblance to Carpenter's own life story, a life that led this radical utopian thinker—known for his work with the Independent Labour Party—away from a privileged intellectual life at Cambridge to the north of England where he settled on a smallholding with a working-class male lover. Already in *Howards End,* Carpenter's discourse of "comradeship"—if stemming from socialist sources that Forster's liberalism would repulse—shaped the narrative trajectory that follows the novel's epigraphic imperative: "Only connect. . . ." Not surprisingly, the cross-class fulfillments of *Maurice* pleased Carpenter himself, whom Forster had met—through the offices of Dickinson—in 1912. Having been shown the manuscript, Carpenter wrote to Forster: "I was so afraid that you were going to let Scudder go at the last—but you saved him & saved the story" (SL 1:223). By this time, then, Forster had an affirming model that offered itself as a hope for the "Happier

Year" to which the novel is dedicated. The vitality of "comradeship" allowed him to look to the future, while at the same time enabling the apostolic past to echo on the final page, proving that such brotherly bonds endure, no matter how much one might wish to repress them. So if Clive is left suffering from a conscience bound to a world of institutional privilege, a world that can only continue to decay (his landed estate, Penge, has a leaky roof), he also remains in touch with the homosexual love that he once enjoyed at Cambridge: a place of desire and denial, from which he sought to dissociate himself only to find it return. By comparison, Maurice and Alec do not so much flee from England as disappear into it. Their brotherhood continues the fraternal pastoral that animates much of *The Longest Journey* and notable passages in *Howards End,* perhaps figuring a healthy and thriving male homosexuality in the heart of a nation that sought to banish such desire from its shores.

IV

By its close, then, *Maurice* suggests an ambivalence toward what it chooses to leave behind, no doubt because the brotherhood it identifies in Maurice and Alec's love translates and repeats into an idealized context the apostolic bonds that Forster often found himself the first to defend. For with time, criticism mounted against the Apostles, and Forster was left to guard the reputations of some of its most prominent brethren. Faced with criticism of his own kind, Forster pledged his fraternal loyalty. And his reasons for doing so reveal the power that his Cambridge peers held over the remainder of his life.

It was, without doubt, homosexuality that made the Apostles increasingly vulnerable to criticism as their fame grew and grew. And some of the earliest public scorn for their erotic interests was made by the woman who had been let into their ranks, and who knew their love lives intimately. It is in Woolf's *A Room of One's Own* that a late member of the Apostles comes to typify the sodomitical culture that for her defined the patriarchal oppression of women, especially with regard to the students at Girton and Newnham who had not so many years before been granted the right to take their degrees. The example she holds up for mockery is Oscar Browning—better known as "O. B."—whose presence at Cambridge in his heyday was legendary, not least because of his skills as a talker and his imposing physical presence. He was made an Apostle in 1858. Drawing on details recounted in a biography of "O. B.," published in 1927, Woolf remarks:

Mr. Oscar Browning was wont to declare "that the impression left on his mind, after looking over any set of examination papers, was that, irrespective of the marks he might give, the best woman was intellectually the inferior of the worst man." After saying that Mr. Browning went back to his rooms—and it is this sequel that endears him and makes him a human figure of some bulk and majesty—he went back to his rooms and found a stable-boy lying on the sofa—"a mere skeleton, his cheeks were cavernous and sallow, his teeth were black, and he did not appear to have the full use of his limbs . . . 'That's Arthur' [said Mr. Browning]. 'He's a dear boy really and most high-minded.'" The two pictures always seem to me to complete each other. And happily in this age of biography, the two pictures often do complement each other, so that we are able to interpret the opinions of great men not only by what they say, but by what they do. (Woolf, *Room* 92–93)

Citing exactly the same passage, Jane Marcus is led to ask: "Why does she choose Browning as her scapegoat?" (*Virginia* 183). It would seem that the biography of Oscar Browning by H. E. Wortham crystallized those sexist aspects of apostolic Cambridge that most revolted Woolf, particularly Wortham's disingenuous comment that Browning's remark about the "dear boy" Arthur was a token of the corpulent don's "Franciscan feeling for humanity at large" (Marcus, *Virginia* 182). Marcus speculates that "O. B.'s" closeness to the men of the Stephen family—he taught Woolf's cousin, J. K. Stephen—allowed an outburst of "displaced anger at the Stephen family's misogyny" (*Virginia* 185). In addition, Woolf had by this time—1928—"been living with the illusion that the homosexual and bi-sexual men of Bloomsbury were women's natural allies and fellow outsiders, that they were all fellow-sufferers from Victorian repression and suppression" (*Virginia* 184). Now, argues Marcus, the truth could be told that the "patriarchy protects its own and male bonding seems to transcend all other bonds in society." Perhaps it was the case that these apostolic connections figured patriarchal power in its most virulently misogynistic form.

Certainly, by the late 1920s, Woolf found the men she never ceased to note as "buggers" a little tiresome. Her diary entry for 4 April 1930 sketches out her observations "chiefly upon the atmosphere of buggery," which made her giggle:

Morgan came in from Meleager [the Apostle R. C. Trevelyan's verse tragedy being performed at the Rudolf Steiner Hall in London]. And I went in to see Ronnie [Trevelyan] behind the scenes. He was looking very nice in shorts. Eddy [Hilton Young] came in with his latest . . . Anyhow, he said, Ensor (I forget) looked very pretty in a white suit—the rest oh so hideous. At this point the other buggers pricked up their ears & became somehow silly . . . An atmosphere entirely secluded, intimate, & set on one object . . . A photograph of Stephen Tennant (Siegfried Sassoon goes to the same dressmaker) in a tunic, in an attitude was shown about; also little boys in a private school. Morgan became unfamiliar, discussing the beauties of Hilton Young's stepson. "His skating is magnificent" (then in an undertone deploring some woman's behavior). This all made on me a tinkling, private, giggling, impression. As if I had gone in to a men's urinal. (Woolf, *Diary* 3:299)

Given that Forster was not unknown for making misogynistic asides— Woolf records how in 1928 he, perhaps jokingly, "said he thought Sapphism disgusting, partly because he disliked that women should be independent of men" (*Diary* 3:193)[14]—her light mockery of his behind-the-scenes comments at a London theater is completely understandable. Allowed to laugh at the "buggers'" camp exchanges, she finds herself not so much entertained by this circle of friends but more a potential object of contempt—since her womanhood held no sexual interest for these men. ("Morgan," noticeably, becomes "unfamiliar" once his conversation focuses on the "beauties" of a young man.) It is almost as if she feels Forster and his cronies turned the dressing-room into a men's room whose exclusive gender figures most odiously in the "urinal": the place, after all, where homosexual men—at no uncertain risk—were known to make sexual contacts.

But Forster had good reason not to let Woolf's publicly aired anger with "O. B." go unremarked. In his Rede Lecture, delivered at the Senate House in Cambridge a short while after her death, he elaborated the dissatisfaction with her fictional methods that he had already spelt out in an essay, "The Novels of Virginia Woolf," published in the *New Criterion* in 1926. "She has all the aesthete's characteristics," he told his Cambridge audience in 1941. She "selects and manipulates her impressions; is not a great creator of character; enforces patterns of her books; has no great cause at heart" (TCD 240). This becomes such an unflattering picture that he is led to pose a question, one whose allusions place her work both sexually and politically in antithesis to his own: "So how did she avoid her appropriate pitfall and remain up in the fresh air, where we can hear the sound of the stable-boy's boots, boats bumping, or Big Ben; where we can taste really new bread, and touch real dahlias?" Somehow, the "real" is achieved. Yet it is clear that such reality is not the aim of her writing.

For it would seem that the "stable-boy"—more than probably the Arthur dear to "O. B."—belonged to a homosexual vision that reached out to a world more "real" than he felt Woolf herself could ever bear to imagine. To Forster, hers was a falsifying style that approached the "real" from the narrowest of class perspectives. Asked to give a lecture to honor her name at his alma mater, Forster could not resist deepening his earlier criticisms of what he felt were Woolf's innumerable failings—such as her inability to capture "life; London; this moment in June" (AH 106). Even though he claims "she loved Cambridge," the joke he makes about her relation to the university damns her with sardonic praise: "I cherish a private fancy that she once took her degree here . . . she could surely have hoaxed our innocent praelectors, and, kneeling in this very spot, have presented to the Vice-Chancellor the exquisite but dubious head of Orlando" (TCD 239)—the androgynous protagonist of her fantasy published in 1928. What may at first appear as a compliment to Woolf's virtuosic intellect must surely, in the broader context of his writings, be read as a backhanded remark on her presumed penis-envy toward an apostolic ethos that feared the "dubious" pretensions of such a clever female interloper.

It is highly likely—and, in retrospect, all the more cruelly ironic— that Forster knew how much Woolf respected his opinions of her work. Her diaries are dotted with appreciative comments about the feedback he generously gave on each of her novels as they appeared. In his definitive biography of Woolf, Quentin Bell makes it plain that "Forster was the English contemporary for whom she had most respect" (*Virginia* 2: 132– 33). He "has the artist's mind," she writes in 1919, "he says the simple things that clever people don't say" (Woolf, *Writer's* 21). (Forster was gratified to read such words when they first appeared in 1953 [SL 2: 255].) Six years later, his praise for *Mrs. Dalloway* (1925) seems to have meant more to her than any other response from her associates ("Morgan admires . . . Better than *Jacob* he says" [Woolf, *Writer's* 77]).[15] But when confronted with Forster's allegiance to the Apostles, she was at best dismissive. In 1934, having read Forster's biography of Dickinson, she notes: "The EMF. Goldie thing to me quite futile" (Woolf, *Diary* 4:247). Perhaps her attitude was informed by the brush-off she received several years back from "Goldie": "When people—G[oldsworthy]. L[owes]. D[ickinson]. for instance—put us [Leonard Woolf and herself] off, we are almost shocked, & then feel an amazed relief. Is it possible that there is someone who does not want to see us? Such royalty we have become—in our set, as Ethel [Sands] says" (*Diary* 4:40). Although in 1925 Dickinson had complimented Woolf by telling her she was the "finest living critic" (Woolf, *Writer's* 75), one senses that she did not figure largely enough in his apostolic world. Not even the "royalty" of Bloomsbury could command his attention. His commitment was to fellow Apostles like Forster.

Dickinson's life and works gave the devoted Forster more than one opportunity to defend his brothers to the last. In his seventies, Forster furnished a brief preface for the 1956 reprint of Dickinson's *The Greek View of Life,* a popular study that first appeared when the Apostles were enjoying their renaissance in the 1890s. The book, published in 1896 and running to many subsequent editions, is notable for its unhesitating commentary on "passionate friendships between men" which "occur in all nations and at all times" (*Greek* 168). Dickinson's work, claims Forster, shows how Plato "expounds . . . his belief that the highest love is homosexual" (GLD 214). One is almost led to believe that Dickinson—and Forster after him—would not dispute Plato's claim. The timing of the remark is important. It appeared while the Wolfenden Committee was drafting the groundbreaking report on male homosexuality it would publish the following year (1957).

The Socratic ethos structures much of the impressive body of research that Dickinson completed around the turn of the century and that Forster would reread when writing the biography of this much-loved senior Apostle that Woolf found "futile." (The resulting work, *Goldsworthy Lowes Dickinson,* has received surprisingly little critical attention.[16]) Most of the personal information that Forster needed for his book was supplied by the suppressed "Recollections" Dickinson entrusted to Forster in his will (leaving him "at liberty to publish them or withhold then from publication as he may in his uncontrolled discretion think fit" [Dickinson, *Autobiography* ix]). Throughout this memoir—which records many tales of frustrated homosexual longing—Dickinson nostalgically evokes the apostolic debates he cherished from 1884 onward. "When young men are growing," he enthuses, "when speculation is a passion, when discussion is made profound by love, there happens something incredible to any but those that breathe that magic air" (*Autobiography* 68). "Oh, brethren," exclaims Dickinson, "if ever any of you should read these words, be sure that they are written by one who has never forgotten and never been faithless" (*Autobiography* 69).

It was in this noble spirit that Forster tried his best to make Dickinson's sexual preference as clear as he could to readers, in terms that are neither coy nor explicit: "he was never drawn to women in the passionate sense, all his deepest emotions being towards men" (GLD 47). Given the unapologetic tone of these carefully judged clauses, this was perhaps the closest Forster came in the 1930s to letting the public know that these were his own feelings as well. In other words, Forster sought to emulate Dickinson in his homosexual loyalty to the brothers whose company he adored, and whose enduring influence could at last be recognized in his dedication: "*Fratrum Societati.*" There were no excuses to be made for one's brothers. In this respect, *Goldsworthy Lowes Dickinson* was hardly a "futile" work. It courageously rose against the shame of being represented as a figure of fun—an old "bugger"—who risked sneers and giggles from very close quarters. One cannot underestimate the significance of how this Apostle's biography formed part of Forster's enduring project to bring an end to an era whose hypocrisy was made only too evident in the violent legal sentences laid down against homosexual Englishmen. For it was the case that even if his class peers at times made fun behind the "buggers'" backs, they could—if they chose—also afford their homosexuals friends not a little protection. This point comes through forcefully in the final sentence of the "Terminal Note" of 1960, where he finds good reason to deplore how "Clive on the bench will continue to sentence Alec in the dock," while "Maurice"—a university man—"may get off" (M 241). Only by looking at the privileges and prohibitions that occupy that "may" can we begin to understand the deeper conflicts that dwell within Forster's apostolic dedications.

Notes

This essay was written while I held a Senior External Research Fellowship at the Stanford Humanities Center, 1995–96. The Provost and Scholars of King's College, Cambridge, and John Bayley kindly granted permission to quote from unpublished manuscript sources. My thanks to Robert K. Martin and George Piggford for their helpful editorial advice.

1. The novelist and editor Leonard Woolf (1880–1969) was elected an Apostle in 1902, the year in which he graduated from Cambridge. Soon to be lauded for *Eminent Victorians* (1918), Lytton Strachey (1880–1932) was elected in the same year. His younger brother, James Strachey, renowned for translating and editing the work of Sigmund Freud, was elected four years later. The painter Duncan Grant (1885–1978) was Strachey's cousin. Harry Norton (1887–1936) was elected an Apostle in 1906, and Saxon Sydney-Turner (1880–1962) elected four years earlier. All these men were associated with Bloomsbury, all were bisexual or homosexual, and all were conscientious objectors during the First World War. On Lytton Strachey, see Michael Holroyd; on James Strachey, see Paul Delany and Holroyd; and for a general discussion of the apostolic ethos, see Paul Levy. Dates of election to the Apostles are taken from Levy's "Appendix" (300–311).

2. David Garnett sums who moved into which residences in and around Gordon Square:

If there was a Bloomsbury, it certainly centred round No. 46 Gordon Square, the house in which Clive Bell and Vanessa Stephen went to live after their marriage. . . . Of the others, Virginia and her brother Adrian set up house together in Brunswick Square. Maynard Keynes, Duncan Grant and Gerald Shove took rooms in it . . . Virginia married Leonard Woolf and they had various homes, moving out to Richmond and back to Bloomsbury; Adrian Stephen married and came to live in No. 51 Gordon Square. Maynard Keynes married and took over the lease of No. 46. Clive took a flat at the top of Adrian's house and Vanessa took a lease on No. 37. Roger Fry went to live in Bernard Street, and Morgan Forster had a *pied-a-terre* in my mother-in-law's house, No. 27 Brunswick Square. (30–31)

"According to Clive Bell," writes Rosenbaum, "it was Molly MacCarthy [(1882–1953) the spouse of the literary and dramatic critic Desmond MacCarthy (1877–1952)] who coined the word 'Bloomsberries' around 1910 or 1911 when arranging her friends topographically . . . The term remains useful to distinguish the parts of Bloomsbury from the whole" (*Bloomsbury Group* 157). Bell's remark first appeared in 'What Was Bloomsbury?' (1954) and is reprinted in Rosenbaum, *Bloomsbury Group* 117.

3. Woolf's significant lesbian relationship was with Vita Sackville-West. On their intellectual and sexual intimacy, see Suzanne Raitt.

4. "But this service in King's College Chapel—why allow women to take part it?" (*Jacob's* 32).

5. It is the case that from the outset the Cambridge Apostles—known more formally as the Cambridge Conversazione Society—fostered eroticized bonds between its male members, and the closeness of Hallam and Tennyson is perhaps the most memorable of these early intimate friendships. On the history of the early Apostles, see Peter Allen. For a detailed discussion of the Victorian interest in brotherhoods and all-male communities, see Herbert Sussman.

6. Forster's friendship with Woolf reached a crisis in late 1931, shortly after the publication of her novel, *The Waves*. He informed his old Cambridge friend, W. J. H. Sprott: "The position is that I have got to being bored by Virginia's superciliousness and maliciousness, which she has often . . . wounded me with in the past, and with this boredom comes a more detached view of her work" (SL 2:111). For a perspective on the creative and intellectual relations between Forster's and Woolf's respective writings, see David Dowling 85–94.

7. *The Longest Journey* is dedicated "Fratribus," *The Celestial Omnibus* "To the Memory of the *Independent Review*," and *Goldsworthy Lowes Dickinson* "Fratrum Societati." The editorial board of the *Independent* comprised several Apostles— G. M. Trevelyan (1872–1951, elected 1895), Nathaniel Wedd (1864–1940, elected 1888), and Goldsworthy Lowes Dickinson (1862–1932, elected 1885)—as well as Francis W. Hirst (1873–1953) and the social investigator, C. F. G. Masterman (1873–1928). The most comprehensive account of the Apostles of this era is Levy.

8. Forster's links with Carpenter have been carefully traced in Tony Brown, "Discussion" and "Evolution," and Martin, "Edward."

9. Elizabeth Heine notes that this passage was heavily revised (LJ 303).

10. On the homoerotic violence in Forster's suppressed colonial fantasies, see Joseph Bristow, "Passage," and Christopher Lane, *Ruling* 145–75.

11. The exchange between Forster and Bayley is worth elaborating in some detail, not least because of Forster's remarkable defensiveness about the imputation that "homosexual themes . . . underlie all his novels." In a poor hand, Forster informed Bayley:

I have been thinking over your statements in a recent number of the Guardian that homosexual themes underlie all my novels. Are you aware that homosexuality is still a criminal offence, and any public implication of it therefore highly ~~undesirable~~ objection-able? If ~~your~~ ~~interesting~~ ~~article~~ is ~~ever~~ ~~reprinted~~ ~~I should be obliged~~ will you please see that the statement ~~in question~~ is eliminated.

I ~~should~~ shall be obliged for a reply to this letter.

Forster's letter is unsigned.

Bayley furnished this thoughtful and courteous reply:

I know indeed that in the present state of the law certain kinds of discretion become essential, & of course it would be barbarous not to practise such discretion, but I cannot see that I have failed to do so. What is to become of imaginative literature if we assume at once, & in the most "intelligencing" fashion that a theme or idea or treatment in a book can be traced at once to the author's life?

Bayley adds that he is not in the habit of reprinting reviews (although the one in question was collected in a volume published in the United States in 1966), and he closes by remarking: "for these reasons, I cannot feel that you can fairly ask me to 'see' that the statement you object to will not reappear." Forster began drafting a reply to Bayley, also in a poor hand. The letter opens: "I must not leave your friendly letter unanswered." This incomplete letter was never mailed.

12. Heine reprints the "Plot," dated 17 July 1904 (LJ xlviii–ix).

13. For conflicting perspectives on Moore's influence on *The Longest Journey*, see: P. N. Furbank, "Philosophy"; Brown, "Discussion of the Cow"; Bernard Harrison; and Rosenbaum, *Edwardian* 225–58 and "*Longest*."

14. Woolf and Forster were both rather drunk when he made this (possibly ironic) remark. George Piggford informs me that this is the only instance of anti-Sapphism that he has found in materials recording Forster's conversations with friends. In this context, it is important to note that 1928 was the year that Radclyffe Hall was charged with an "obscene libel" for the publication of her lesbian novel, *The Well of Loneliness*. Writing to Vanessa Bell, Woolf remarks: "I think much of Miss Radclyffe Hall[']s book is very beautiful" (Woolf, *Letters* 3:526), although later that year she declared to Quentin Bell: "we have to uphold the morality of that Well of all that's stagnant and lukewarm and neither one thing

or the other" (Woolf, *Letters* 3:555). Although Forster was willing to use his public influence to defend Hall against censorship, he did so feeling the book was "tedious" (SL 2:86). Together, Forster and Woolf made a public statement about the censorship of Hall's novel ("The New Censorship").

15. For Forster's encouraging comments on *Jacob's Room*, see his letter to Woolf dated 24 October 1922 (SL 2:32).

16. An important exception is Stone, *Cave* 72–98. Stone's is one of the few studies to explore the significance of homosexuality in Forster's apostolic circle at Cambridge at length.

7

"This is the End of Parsival": The Orphic and the Operatic in The Longest Journey

Judith Scherer Herz

One may as well begin with Cosima Wagner's diary, 4 April 1874; after all, it does describe a letter: "A very melancholy [letter] from our friend N[ietzsche], who is tormenting himself. R[ichard] exclaims, 'He should either marry or write an opera'" (1:749). Nietzsche, we know, did neither (nor did Wagner expect him to, for he continued: "though doubtless the latter would never get produced and so would not bring him into contact with life"). But did Forster? Well, he certainly did not marry, nor was he very good at imagining it, especially the physical fact of it (the few children that are born in his fictions, the very few, appear on cue, glow symbolically, and, as often as not, die). But he did make his melancholy operatic, that is, gestural, excessive, extreme. Indeed, Forster's writing can readily be described as Wagnerian in its mythic aspirations, except that in an important sense it is anti-Wagnerian, for despite its often prophetic tonalities, its rites and rituals and woodland deities, its explicit Wagnerian echoes and allusions, it is alert to mystifications and fraudulent redemptions; it is ethical, exact, and humane. In all his writing, but most resonantly in *The Longest Journey*, the operatic and the ethical are implicated in one another. The one mode mystifies desire as the music swells; the other unmasks it, probes it, ultimately deconstructs it through the precision of the prose.

Listening for the music in Forster's writing is nothing new. Forster wrote about it frequently, and critics have discussed it in symbolic, structural, thematic terms at least from the time of Peter Burra's 1934 essay. Burra identified what Forster a decade earlier in *Aspects of the Novel* had asked the reader to listen for, that is the song. Burra argued that the impulse toward abstraction, the move from the symbolic to the fantastic, was for Forster a move toward music. The violent plots, the calculated antirealism as in "Gerald died that afternoon," or of such moments as Ansell declaiming to the assembled boys at their Sunday lunch the story of Rickie's failure to acknowledge his half brother, or Leonard Bast, surrounded by enraged Wilcoxes, felled by bookcase and sword, carry "the sort of declamatory conviction that good opera carries" (Burra 318). For Burra, Forster was a musician, who happened to use words as his medium, but what was important was the something that sounds beyond those words, a something that Burra identifies in succession as "melody," "perception of truth" (both categories derived from *Aspects of the Novel*), anonymous prophecy, the athletic body of Stephen. No wonder Forster thought it a splendid essay, including it in the 1942 Everyman edition of *A Passage to India* (the longest section of the essay was on *Passage*), and again in 1957. Burra "saw exactly what I was trying to do. . . . one grows accustomed to being praised, or being blamed, or being advised, but it is unusual to be understood."

"Declamatory conviction" is an interesting phrase. For Burra it identified a technique that enabled Forster's "intensely passionate imagination [to] work . . . upon closely recorded detail of behavior and conduct" (PI 323). Burra was implicitly rebutting Woolf's argument (published seven years earlier) that Forster ultimately lacked "the power of combination—single vision." But it is a revealing phrase and not so readily tamed insofar as it implies a gap between sound and sense that is immediately covered over, but which nonetheless remains. The excess of the moment empowers assertion; logic follows the trajectory of desire. Often in Forster's writing, when the text gets troublesome, when he cannot entirely follow where his characters seem to be leading, or merely doesn't wish to, the music gets very loud. But even as it obscures, it marks the site of difficulty.

If we take the phrase out of its immediate context (a double one—Burra in 1934 joining a debate and Forster over the next two decades making it frame and in a sense officially represent his fiction) we can read "declamatory conviction" as the marker of the operatic in terms very close to Wayne Koestenbaum's argument that "opera can't achieve the coherences it seeks." For Koestenbaum this is thematized at the moment of opera's birth in the frequently set story of Orpheus and Eurydice, notably in Monteverdi's 1607 opera: "words never clasp music so closely that we forget their difference." The metaphoric resonances for Forster of this Orphic struggle "to cross over into the other world" are multiple. Opera is queer, Koestenbaum argues, "because culture has cast homosexuality . . . as the condition of loss . . . the discourse of homosexuality has defined gay desire as operatic or Orphean" (178–179).

1. THE LONGEST JOURNEY AS ORPHIC FABLE

No more than opera can Forster's fiction achieve the coherence it seeks; that's where "declamatory conviction" comes in, the need to assert, despite the evidence to the contrary, that the quest has been successful. Of course, *The Longest Journey* is explicitly about the failure of such quests, the gap between the words and the music. As it writes large the narrative of Orphic failure, it tells the second half of the fable as well, the spurning of the women of Thrace for the shepherd boys of the Thracian hills, of the silencing of music, of dismemberment and death.

One intertextual marker of this second story is Milton's *Lycidas*. It enters in Mrs. Failing's ironic musings, as she surveys her shepherd nephew, contrasting him to the pensive swain and Cadover to Arcady. In part, Forster is playing here with her self-congratulatory Miltonic allusion set against the naturalized, un-self-conscious Theocritan pastoral that will be associated with Stephen's ride to Salisbury—safe pastoral versus subversive, coded pastoral. There is, too, at the novel's close something of the *Lycidas* ending of the pensive swain twitching his mantle blue as the sun stretches out over the western hills. Stephen watches the day fade on the hillside, as he holds the memory of Rickie and of their mother and the promise of his child in a single revery of continuity and expectation.

Yet more than Arcady, Amaryllis, and the hopeful swain enters with the allusion to Milton's poem. For central to it is Orpheus himself, concentrating all the poem's anxieties in the figure of the poet who is silenced and torn apart by the "rout that made the hideous roar." Rickie's death in this reading is that of a parodic Orpheus. His poetry (stories, of course, but there is little difference) about animate nature charms no one (at least not until his death gives them a whiff of topical interest), the Thracian women are indifferent (he was, wrote Mrs. Failing, "one of the thousands whose dust returns to the dust accomplishing nothing in the interval" (LJ 282), and he, too, is dismembered, but mechanically, randomly, when the train goes over his knee as he wearily saves his brother's life but loses his own.

In earlier versions where the pastoral mode was more extravagantly imagined, Stephen (then still Harold) also participated in the Orpheus myth. As a near maddened figure, he wanders the woods, eating and sleeping "among the bracken, charmed even through dreams by the pattern of fronds against the sky" (LJ 335). He runs "in simple joy," he splashes, sinks, and rises in a forest pool. "Naked and <glorious> \immortal/, he did for one instant attain \to/ it, being himself a god, . . . \unvexed/ by// good or evil" (LJ 336). What remains after the passage was first revised and then erased is neither the event nor the language but the desire that empowered the scene. It is drastically cut down, becoming a retrospective musing over a moment of childhood panic, not a descent into Orphic madness. But it leaves its trace in much the same way that the unwriting of the events in the cave marks *A Passage to India*. There Forster willed his writing mind to remain a blur so he need never know (although he had earlier "known," that is imagined, written) what happened there. In *The Longest Journey* what remains is an Orphic echo: desire, its near attainment, and loss. What is represented is an emotion rather than an episode in a linear narrative. With something of the same arbitrariness whereby characters are sent to their death, Mr. Failing is suddenly brought in, made responsible for focusing the scene. It is his enigmatic recollection, found by his puzzled widow as she arranges his papers, of the young, naked Stephen, calling from the rooftop, that gives the moment its mythic potency far more effectively than the earlier feverish evocations of woodland ecstasy had been able to: "I see the respectable mansion. I see the smug fortress of culture. The doors are shut. The windows are shut. But on the roof the children go dancing for ever" (119).

2. *THE LONGEST JOURNEY* AS WAGNERIAN OPERA

Those who discuss the operatic in Forster's writing tend to talk of it in either structural or thematic terms. Hence Benjamin Britten, who more than anyone was able to recognize Forster's instinctive musicality, comments that "the construction of Forster's novels often resembles that of the 'classical' opera (Mozart-Weber-Verdi) where recitatives (the deliberately un-lyrical passages by which the action is advanced) separate arias or ensembles (big, self-contained set pieces of high comedy or great emotional tension)" (82). His examples include the bathing scene in *A*

Room with a View, the school dinner in The Longest Journey, the trial in A Passage to India, and opera itself, Lucia di Lammermoor, in Where Angels Fear to Tread.

Britten did not mention Wagner, but he is the composer whom critics most frequently invoke. He appears in discussions of Forster's typical use of a tripartite structure, in his use of such motifs as Rheingold's Rainbow bridge in Howards End, as well as in his many references to Wagner characters, especially from the Ring. But more important than local allusions is the larger cultural context. For interest in Wagner at the turn of the century was not just evidence of an avant-garde aesthetic, it was also, for homosexuals, a lightly coded affirmation of sexual preference.[1] Forster would have known, at the very least through his interest in Wilde, of the homosexual cult of Wagner. Dorian Gray "listen[s] in a rapt pleasure to Tannhäuser" (209), leading one critic to remark that "Tannhäuser almost becomes a code word for experimentation with forbidden pleasures" (Sessa 103). These forbidden pleasures may be tragically imagined as in Dorian's case, or comically camped as in Beardsley's Tannhauser whose "dear little coat of pigeon rose silk . . . hung loosely about his hips, and showed off the jut of his behind to perfection" (Furness 40).[2] This certainly does not strike the Forsterian note (although it does evoke Strachey, especially the Strachey of Ermyntrude and Esmerelda), but it does suggest the degree to which a Wagnerian idiom and range of allusion were part of the turn of the century homosexual discourse available to Forster. Stopping at Dresden to see the Ring on his way to Elizabeth's German Garden must have been an interesting stimulant to his Longest Journey musings. He was clearly excited by it: "I doubt whether anything is as stupendous as the end of Rheingold" (SL 1: 68),[3] and possibly, like Beardsley's Chevalier responding to "The Third Tableau of Das Rheingold," he may have "rejoiced in the extravagant monstrous poetry, the heated melodrama, and splendid agitation of it all" (Furness 39). Certainly that sentence is not a bad approximation of The Longest Journey.

Although many Wagnerian allusions and echoes have been noted, the most completely argued structural and thematic likeness has been to Parsifal. John Lucas argued for it as both source and analogue for A Room With a View; Tony Brown worked out the connections to The Longest Journey.[4] Both of these essays make convincing claims for the importance of Parsifal in Forster's imagination while he was writing these novels. I am not interested here in arguing the specifics of their analyses. There's something quite forced, I think, about the linkages and echoes that Lucas proposes. Brown's is by far the more convincing, although again I would disagree about some of his claims. They make it absolutely clear, however, that Forster knew the opera (as Lucas points out, he may have had the piano score; Lucy plays from it in *A Room with a View*), and, as Brown argues, he must have known Trevelyan's play, *The Birth of Parsival*, written while Forster was working on his three first novels (there's no easy answer to the question: which was Forster's first novel?).

What is it that he heard there? Young Forster, old Wagner/young Parsifal, old(er) Forster? Forster was attracted no doubt to the innocent, foolish, athletic, handsome young Parsifal, just as he was, by his own testimony, attracted to Stephen Wonham. Brown emphasizes "the sacredness of male brotherhood" ("Parsifal" 42) as the key element, arguing that *Parsifal* may have "helped release the very personal impulses which are realized most fully in *The Longest Journey*" ("Parsifal" 51). Both observations are, I think, accurate. But they are used too readily in the interests of a therapeutic argument, the novel as symptom. Brown reads the conclusion, for example, as Forster's "rejection of those aspects of himself which we know from his letters and diaries that he hated: his fastidiousness, his indecisiveness, his timidity, his repression, and possibly, his homosexuality. It is both an act of self hatred and another act of emancipation" ("Parsifal" 49). Such a reading assumes far too much about the person (there is no evidence that he hated himself for his sexuality even if Tunbridge Wells did not provide too congenial a habitat for its expression) and far too little about the fiction and the making of fiction. Yet the notion that Rickie is Forster, a creature who had to be violently rejected, literally crushed, is fairly common. Nicola Beauman says as much in her comment: "What kind of feelings of self-hatred did he have that he had to invoke such a sad life, and such a brutal end to it" (180).

Thirty years ago, Wilfred Stone, using a Jungian paradigm, also read the novel through the putatively vexed relationship between Rickie and his creator. "Rickie is the author's ego character as well as his anti-ego" (*Cave* 213), Stone argued, claiming that if the book does not finally succeed, it is in large measure because Forster was doing what he didn't fully understand (a proposition that is doubtless true in some degree for all creative acts, to say nothing of the acts of one's daily life). As with the more recent biographically based arguments, there is too much emphasis here on the writer's buried, unacknowledged, suppressed, repressed "real life." But what is remarkable about Stone's reading is how entirely it enters into the text's twists and turns, and how queer it is.

Putting to one side Stone's ongoing Jungian argument (Rickie illustrates the "infantile hero unable to withstand retrogressive longing for the mother" [*Cave* 212]) and recalling the date of composition and the fact that Forster was still alive when it was written, one is struck by Stone's attentiveness to the disruptions and necessary incoherences of the text and how much he understands these in sexual terms. Further, he is neither censorious nor sentimental. He begins his discussion of *The Longest Journey* with the premise that in Forster's writing "cross purposes seem as active as purposes—and give the hint of impish censors at work" (184). Earlier, in talking of the frequent sudden deaths in his fiction, especially in *The Longest Journey,* he observes that the "characters must be able to come and go like phrases in a musical composition" (109) and then goes on to remark that "there may be some covert malice in using people like musical notes" (110), an observation that has affinities with readings that make betrayal, really the delights of betrayal, the mark of the queer text. This is a point to which I will return, but first, the overture completed, we should look at the opera.

There are multiple points of correspondence. The most obvious are the Rickie/Amfortas, Stephen/Parsifal analogies, although Rickie, like his brother, is also partly imagined in terms of the orphaned holy fool. Insofar as Kundry is a split figure, temptress and instrument of redemption, she is "played" by both Agnes and Ansell (possibly that is why Ansell is Jewish and in ways that reverse Wagner's anti-Semitic equation, for Ansell/Kundry is the redeeming half). Mrs. Failing, in part the dragon of *Rheingold,* also resembles Klingsor, notably in her sterility and as mistress of an enchanted palace. The Rickie/Amfortas link is certainly explicit ("Rickie trusted that to him also benefits might accrue; that his wound might heal as he laboured, and his eyes recapture the Holy Grail" [LJ 153]), and Stephen is, as clearly, intended to be Parsifal (with a dash of Siegfried). The other comparisons are more speculative (Brown equates Herbert with Klingsor, for example), and in any event I don't intend them in more than a suggestive way. More interesting, however, than reading the novel as an opera à clef is the sense one has that Forster had been listening to the music, meditating the story while writing his own, so that its ethos entered his text almost of its own accord. If, as Bryan Magee contends, "Wagner's music expresses, as does no other art, repressed and highly charged contents of the psyche" (Brown, "Parsifal" 62), then we might conclude that as his music entered Forster's imagination, it performed something of the same function, especially if we allow that description to offer a fairly accurate assessment of Forster's novel.

What both the novel and the opera share is captured in a phrase of Arthur Symons, who, describing *Parsifal,* spoke of "the unsatisfied desire of a kind of flesh of the spirit" (300).[5] One can read that phrase as an anticipation of Koestenbaum's claim of the ultimate impossibility of the fusion of words and music, an impossibility that opera is understood to depend on for its Orphic frisson. In Symons's phrase, flesh, spirit, and desire pursue one another in an oddly sexless fashion (can there be sex if you can't tell flesh from spirit?); they circulate in constant deferral, something like the images on Keats's Grecian urn. The plot of *The Longest Journey* enacts this system of deferrals in its narrative circlings, indeed provides an iconography for it in Ansell's circles and in the Cadbury rings.

Thus to the question, what did Forster hear in *Parsifal*, one must first reply Parsifal himself, his innocence, his salvific potential, his androgynous beauty, the words he sings. Indeed, Parsifal's first extended passage bears an interesting resemblance to the canceled scene I looked at earlier, of Stephen/Harold running wildly through the woods:

> Once on the forest edge
> on their fair steeds sitting,
> bright gentlemen came by;
> I would fain have been like them:
> They laughed and thereupon rode off.
> So I followed, though ne'er came up with them;
> Through deserts I have come, mountains and valleys;
> Oft night hath fallen, then day returned:
> My faithful bow alone
> against wild and monstrous men. (94)

Forster not only responded to specific moments, characters, and scenes, but as well to the opera's ethos, in particular to its thematized androgyny. Cosima observes in her diary that the reason for concluding with the chorus is so that "the effect would be neither masculine nor feminine" (C. Wagner 499).[6] And that is certainly the effect of *The Longest Journey*. It is not so much that Stephen is an androgynous figure as that the opera's neither/nor sexuality is carried by the Stephen/Rickie dyad. This reading is similar to the way Syberberg conceives the figure of Parsifal in his film of the opera, dividing the role between a boy and a girl (a split that occurs immediately after Kundry's kiss in the second act), neither of whom possesses the tenor's voice issuing simultaneously from both their mouths. When Rickie sees Agnes and Gerald kiss, the response is also deflected/divided; one might well echo Symons here and describe it as the "unsatisfied desire of a kind of flesh of the spirit." But what is the direction of this (queer) desire? Is it man to man, man to woman, woman to man, flesh to spirit, spirit to spirit, flesh to flesh? Whose voice is issuing from whose mouth? What does the score, here the aria sung by the narrator, have to do with the scene we are observing?

At this point in the novel, Rickie is both Parsifal and Amfortas. The kiss he witnesses occurs soon after the scene in the sacred wood, in Rickie's dell of dryads, fauns, and friendship, where he has told his story, culminating in the death of his mother (the first of the many sudden deaths and as suddenly announced: "while he was out his mother died" [LJ 27]). In the scene of the kiss of Agnes and Gerald, Rickie is both observer and vicarious participant, although immediately after he observes the embrace, he resumes the wounded Amfortas role (interestingly, in the opera, Parsifal's first words after the kiss are "Amfortas. The wound, the wound" [164]). In the opera, Kundry's description of the death of Parsifal's mother occurs shortly before the moment of the kiss. In both opera and novel the kiss provides a musical and narrative climax. Wagner's orchestral setting is not the same as Forster's, who starts with "an obscure instrument," moves to the clarinet, the brass, and then to the violins (40), while Wagner begins with strings, gradually bringing in the other instruments. However, Forster's music in this passage is still Wagner's, as Elizabeth Heine shows in her excellent Introduction, where she argues for its precise resemblance to the "Prelude to *Rheingold*," music already structurally in place through the piano score that accompanied Agnes's first entrance (LJ xiii). Moreover, the narrator's comment at the end of the scene, "It was the merest accident that Rickie had not been disgusted" (LJ 40), glosses Parsifal's disgust and horror at the kiss, his sense of sharing the wound of Amfortas, a moment that recurs in the novel when the kiss scene is replayed. That occurs in the sacred dell: Rickie is Parsifal; Agnes, Kundry; and Parsifal's revulsion at the touch of a woman's lips finds a baffled echo in Rickie's words, "I prayed you might not be a woman" (LJ 73).

The opera provides more than motifs, however; it also lets into the text experience and emotion that have no narrative analogue. Rickie does not, in any literal (that is, narratively realizable) sense, desire Gerald, no more does he desire Agnes (although this will take him a while to understand). Rather he desires their desire, which he responds to from the position of Agnes: Gerald "had drawn the woman on to his knee, was pressing her, with all his strength, against him" (LJ 39). What the music does (both the instrumentation and the singing of the narrative voice) is provide a cover for the queer story; or to put it more precisely, the music is the queer story. There is a basic disjunction here between gender and voice.[7] What we hear and what we see are at odds in something of the way they are in the marvelous tenor and baritone duet in Bizet's *The Pearl Fishers*, "Au fond du temple saint." In it the music we hear speaks male/male love, but the words describe heterosexual desire at war with friendship and brotherhood. Certainly Ansell understands Rickie's story that way: "'War!' cried Ansell,' crashing his fists together. 'It's war, then! . . . I fight this woman not only because she fights me, but because I foresee the most appalling catastrophe'" (LJ 80).

The Bizet effect in Forster's text is mostly carried by the narrator joining his voice with Rickie's in an adaptation of free indirect discourse. The language of the aria responding to the embrace on the lawn of Dunwood House is not really Rickie's, although the passage from Aristophanes' *The Birds* on which this scene is based certainly feeds the "classical enthusias[m]" (LJ 161) that Rickie will attempt to convey to his Sawston pupils. But it is a clear marker of the Cambridge world. Indeed, Forster will use that passage years later in his biography of Goldsworthy Lowes Dickinson to mark his subject's entry into an imaginative realm where "music kept its measure apart from rules or the breaking of rules" (GLD 22). The young Goldie glimpsed this world in his sixth form lesson and found it again at Cambridge (GLD 21–22). The narrator appropriates that language and creates Rickie's response through it, but it remains real only in the music. Paradoxically, the more we hear, the less story there is. We listen to the merging of two male voices singing an aria of the birth of (male) love: "In full unison was Love born. . . . His wings were infinite, his youth eternal. . . . Was Love a column of fire? Was he a torrent of song?" (LJ 40). What we see is a man and a woman embrace.

That language reappears at the final crisis of the novel, when Rickie and Stephen return to Wiltshire. It is in fact materialized. What was metaphor earlier—"the river continued unheeding. . . . Love [was] born, flame of the flame" (LJ 40)—is now enacted. They stop at the river and "played as boys who continued the nonsense of the railway carriage. The paper caught fire from the match, and spread into a rose of flame" (LJ 272). This is indeed a *Pearl Fishers* moment. They talk about marriage, but their music sings of something else. It is never specified or even imaginable on the plane of representation. Words and actions remain separate, but, musically, boyish play becomes romantic union. Stephen watches the flaming rose disappear under the arch of the bridge. He sees "a fairy tunnel, dropping diamonds. . . . [and] declared that it was still afloat . . . burning as it would burn forever" (LJ 273).

There are other operatic moments in *The Longest Journey*; probably the most startling scene of operatic melodrama and loud music occurs when Ansell enters in wrath and denunciation to reveal the truth to

Rickie before the assembled school at its Sunday lunch. But rather than look at opera as high tragedy now, I want to take my last example from a scene where the plotting is ostensibly comic, even though the music gradually strikes ever more dissonant chords. It contains, as well, the novel's most explicit *Parsifal* allusions, the narration of the near death of Mrs. Lewin's dove, a recitative undertaken to mask the confusions of the breakfast gone awry; it is the scene where Rickie surprises Ansell with the announcement of his engagement. Here Wagner's dove appears as Mrs. Lewin's Parsival, the hapless bird that nearly died when his feathers turned bright green from his freshly painted cage (there's a bit of the *Parsifal* swan in him as well). Plucked clean by the confused bantams till he turns entirely bald, he becomes the still point of a swirling scene that is itself operatically plotted, with voice overlying voice, aria alternating with recitative, duet, and trio. There is the jilted lover (Ansell), the bewildered spectator Tilliard), and principals singing their parts by rote (the engaged couple). It is a scene of surprises, reversals, and suppressions. Mrs. Lewin's tale provides a comic counterpoint—"'Hugo look. This is the end of Parsival. Let me have no more surprises.' He burst into tears" (LJ 77)—that confirms the turbulence of the engagement scene it plays against. One operatic moment, the green Parsival, screens another, the young man (here the wounded Amfortas/Parsifal) in the thrall of the flower maidens (Agnes and her chaperone). This scene immediately follows the seduction in the dell, a space that at the start of the novel is an analogue to the forest of the grail knights in Act One of the opera, but is then transformed by the presence of Agnes into the dangerous garden of Act Two. The thralldom continues at the breakfast in Ansell's rooms. It is a typical strategy: something is opened up but as quickly covered over. Here *Parsifal* offers comic relief and, more important, "an atmosphere [where] everything seemed of small and equal value, and the engagement of Rickie and Agnes, like the feathers of Parsival, fluttered lightly to the ground" (LJ 77). One might observe that Ansell's declaration of war occurs immediately after.

3. QUEERING THE QUEER READING: OPERA, ETHICS, AND THE LIBERAL HUMANIST

There is certainly more to the opera than Parsifal's lyric tenor. There is misogyny, anti-Semitism, a sense of sexuality as disease, "a curse," in Nietzsche's words, "pronounced in the same breath on the mind and the senses" (234), a conception of racial purity that, from our late twentieth-century retrospect, chills and frightens. To be sure, the music is gorgeous; Debussy described it as "one of the loveliest monuments of sound ever raised to the serene glory of music" (Beckett 23). Yet it exists in uneasy tension with the narrative (written several years before), which frequently troubles the listener's response to that music.

What if any of this did Forster hear? It is impossible to answer that question with any confidence. He probably "heard" the misogyny without much resistance, and he may well have been aware of discussions of the opera that linked the wound of Amfortas with syphilis, and those that noted the opera's anti-Semitism.[8] He may also have read or known of Wagner's anti-Semitic writings from the period of the composition of *Parsifal*, such as *Religion and Art* (1880) and the much earlier "Judaism in Music" (1850). I think it's possible to argue, as I suggested earlier, that making Ansell Jewish was in part an anti-Wagner move. Of even greater interest, however, are the resistances to the Wagnerian ethos built into the text itself, the way he invokes the Wagnerian heroic, but quizzically, as if unsure of the music he has let sound.[9]

Burra's observation concerning Forster's "intensely passionate imagination work[ing] . . . upon closely recorded detail of behavior and conduct" (PI 323) implies, I would argue, a fidelity to moral discriminations that may well clash with the over determinations of myth. Stephen gets drunk at the end, not because he is some irrepressible force of nature or because, as Rickie mistakenly assumes, he is morally weak and has thus tarnished his heroism forever, but rather in disgust at the eviction of the Thompson family and his realization that he was in part responsible for it (and complicating the ethical analysis is our realization of Rickie's ignorant complicity in this betrayal). Stephen may be constructed out of a mythic desire for the heroic, for the natural, and may be seen as a figure who sups with the gods in Ansell's excited response, but he is accountable for his actions and his words and he becomes an ethical norm for the other characters.

The last chapter holds these varied views of Stephen in imperfect suspension. The romantic imperative, to turn him back into a mythic figure, exists uneasily with the satiric, and that mode collides with the bildungsroman conclusion whereby the protagonist has learned and earned his place in the world. Too much has to be resolved here (but that was always Forster's problem in his last chapters; only *A Passage to India* solves it by swerving away from it, those horses riding single file into the future). There are no doubt "cross purposes" to repeat Stone's phrase. An ethical resistance to closure, to returning the characters to their symbolic functions, clashes with a yearning for the symbolic and redemptive. The Silts, for example, mostly used comically and indifferently over the course of the novel, come into ethical focus. Indeed, they act out the real heroism, for they have turned out the villainous overseer, Wilbraham, and built a bridge over the railway. It might not be a rainbow bridge, it certainly does not lead to Valhalla, but it will save lives. However, their actions exist on a quite different narrative plane from Stephen's sense of salvation through Rickie's death (or, more precisely, Forster's sense of that salvation conferred not too convincingly on his character).

Over the years, as Forster recalled this creature of his imagination and desire in memoir, commonplace book, and diary, Stephen took on a life, a vividness that Rickie never possessed for Forster. His later remark about Rickie, "I could kick him for his lame leg you know" (qtd. in Wilson 55), suggests an ambivalence in his response, allowing critics (too readily) to read self-hatred in his conception, as if Rickie could have had a choice in his maker's despite, as if he had somehow betrayed his maker. Yet it is the lameness (and Forster's double and ultimately un-Wagnerian response to it—his Amfortas is not cured of his sexual wound) that more than anything else queers the text. It disrupts it, not because it codes homosexuality (that's pretty much there uncoded in Ansell, and in Stephen and Gerald as objects of desire), but because it allows entry for the Orphic, for incompletion and loss. Reading the operatic in *The Longest Journey* makes this queerness more audible. The operatic marks the sexually disruptive; the music is the queer story.

That said, however, one should be careful not to let the observation that sexuality functions disruptively in Forster's texts diminish the importance, indeed the toughness, of his liberal humanism. Discovering inconsistency, or observing the erotic in pain (that kick, for example), or noting, with Stone, covert malice in the sudden deaths, need not, must not, undermine the validity of that humane (and admittedly incomplete and class-privileged) idealism. Peter Burra's Forster is no doubt out of fashion today; he is too much his own creation, the "real" voice of a speaking subject, and we have learned to mistrust such humanist notions (save when they refer to ourselves). But the Forsterian subject remains, if not exactly unified, still able to "declaim with conviction," that phrase continuing to carry its contradictions and disruptions, but its optimism, too.

Notes

1. Herbert Lindenberger discusses how the reception history of Wagner differs from that of any other composer; only Wagner, for example, is responsible

for an "-ism." Noting Virginia Woolf's visit to Bayreuth in 1909, he remarks that it "was motivated less by any real enthusiasm for the music than by the influence of a Wagnerian suitor and by her own commitment to a modernist aesthetic, which in England at that time (though no longer in Germany) could count Wagner in the avant-garde" (224). There has been very interesting work recently by Mitchell Morris on the homosexual cult of Wagner. I am indebted to an excellent paper he delivered at the 1996 meeting of the Association of Canadian College and University Teachers of English on "Tristan's Wounds: Homosexual Wagnerians at the fin de siècle."

2. Furness also notes that Beardsley had in his room the photograph taken of Wagner in London in 1877 (63). Both Furness and Sessa provide useful information for the fin de siècle context of Wagnerism.

3. Letter to Arthur Cole, 11 April 1905.

4. See also John Beer, Achievement, William Blissett, and John Louis DiGaetani.

5. Symons also wrote several poems on Wagnerian themes, among them "Parsifal," published in Images of Good and Evil (1889). See Sessa, 103–5.

6. Jean-Jacques Nattiez provides a complex account of Wagnerian androgyny in musical, mythical, cultural, psychoanalytical, and biographical terms. Nattiez analyzes the "triumph [in Parsifal] of an asexual androgyny that transcends all racial differences" (171) and connects this with Wagner's anti-Semitism of purity and resignation.

7. There have been several important studies of operatic travesti in this context, discussing how, for example, operas like Der Rosenkavalier allow women to make love on stage under cover of their fictional roles. See Corrine E. Blackmer and Patricia Juliana Smith, ed. En Travesti; also Philip Brett.

8. See Linda Hutcheon and Michael Hutcheon, Opera, especially chapter 3, "Syphilis, Suffering and the Social Order: Richard Wagner's Parsifal." They trace, as well, the connections among syphilis, female degeneration, and anti-Semitism. See also Nattiez, passim, and Marc A. Weiner.

9. This attraction/repulsion duality persists throughout Forster's life. Quoting from Lord Acton in a 1940 Commonplace Book entry, he worries the relationship between the natural and the civilized. Acton's words—"A speech of Antigone, a single sentence of Socrates . . . come nearer to our lives than the ancestral wisdom of barbarians who fed their swine on the Hercynian acorns" (CB 117–18)—get turned around, tested against politics and personal loyalties, subscribed to but not without acknowledging their cost. I discuss this issue at greater length in my Short Narratives.

8

Breaking the Engagement
with Philosophy: Re-envisioning
Hetero/Homo Relations in Maurice

Debrah Raschke

Forster begins *The Longest Journey* with a debate over whether "the cow is there" or not,[1] over whether objects exist or not, or more generally over a nebulous possibility for certainty that has become one of the deciding marks of modernism. Whether embracing a Nietzschean accolade to untruth or countering this prevailing skepticism, modernist documents regularly engage what and how we can know.[2] Attending Cambridge when such ideas were flourishing, Forster was both exposed to and concerned with epistemological questions. As Furbank comments, Forster had a life-long interest in "whether a case could be made out for Asceticism"—the ideality that generally surfeits Western metaphysics ("Philosophy" 37). Forster's attachment to a particular episteme, however, has been hotly debated. S. P. Rosenbaum in "*The Longest Journey:* E. M. Forster's Refutation of Idealism," for example, sees Forster as heavily influenced by G. E. Moore, while Furbank in "The Philosophy of E. M. Forster" minimizes Moore's influence. Robert Martin in "Double Structure" demonstrates how Forster, through his contacts with Edward Carpenter, progresses from Plato to Whitman. Others, including Gregory Bredbeck in this volume, have speculated on Eastern influences. Whether Forster was directly influenced by any one particular episteme, however, seems less consequential than what all these positions clearly establish: Forster's epistemological curiosity. Thus, to what degree Forster adopted or even rejected a particular episteme, although the source of many enlightening discussions, is less germane to my interests than an emerging metaphysical struggle, one, in particular, that repeatedly links epistemological vision with sexual vision, for it is this rather explicit linking that makes Forster's vision distinctive.[3] In this, I am most concerned with demonstrating how *Maurice* engages Platonism as a site of sexual struggle. And although the Platonism that emerges through Ducie, Clive, and Mr. Grace is Christianized, it is Platonism (as an alternative to Christian judgment) with which the text struggles.

Maurice perhaps more clearly than any other Forster text conjoins issues of sexuality and metaphysics. The specific interweaving of Plato's *Phaedrus* and *Symposium* with Maurice's sexual encounters (both physical and rhetorical) suggests that metaphysics and sexuality are inextricably linked. In *Maurice,* as in other Forster texts, a new conception of sexuality (explicitly homosexual, but implicitly heterosexual as well) depends on a rethinking of Western metaphysics. Forster's style may not rival Joyce's and Woolf's, but his vision, which presages a poststructuralist linking of desire and metaphysical thought, does.

Clearly, as *Maurice* demonstrates, Platonism within some Cambridge circles had its appeal. Clive, always a "scholar" and "awake to the printed word," found in the Greeks, and specifically in the *Phaedrus,* an alternative to the "horrors the Bible had evoked for him": its condemnation of Sodom and his own emergent fear that he was hopelessly damned (M 69–70). As David Halperin notes, Clive is "drawn to the study of the classics" because the "Greeks, especially Plato," allowed him "gradually to accept himself and his desires as he had never been able to do in the course of his religious upbringing." Plato, in effect, provided a reassuring alternative vision that was well known by the time Forster arrived at Cambridge (Halperin 3).

Yet whatever solace Platonism may provide in its counter to a chastising Christian upbringing, its metaphysics present a problem. In this, *Maurice*'s recognition of Platonism as an impediment to physical love and human relationships presages Luce Irigaray's critique of Western metaphysics in *Speculum*. For Irigaray, Platonism (and other Western epistemes) camouflages repeated covert tales. Frequently criticized for essentializing, for metanarratizing, and for oversimplifying important differences between epistemes,[4] Irigaray argues that the insisted differences are a ruse for eliding a composite story, which not only effects a damaging masquerade of universal truth, but also maligns sexual relationships, whether heterosexual or homosexual;[5] her critique of the desire for the self-same pertains not to sexual preference but to a way of thinking that becomes enacted within sexual relationships. For Irigaray, epistemological and sexual vision are inextricably intertwined: neither the one without the other. Irigaray's critique in *Speculum* is not limited to Plato, but her objections to Platonism are akin to Forster's. For Forster, Platonism, in particular, becomes central because of its ostensible promise of a " 'new guide for life' " (qtd. in Halperin 1). Paradoxically, Platonism gives voice to homoerotic expression, but because it situates truth away from the body, it thwarts the physical fulfillment of this alternative expression; it, in effect, becomes a site of struggle for characters who fall under its influence.

For Plato, the body and all materiality become a position of illusion and nontruth. In the *Phaedo,* Socrates notes that the "true philosopher" must "dissever the soul from the communion of the body," that the body provides knowledge of nothing (2:203–206). Anyone in search of truth must evade life and "practice death," for "true philosophers" are "always occupied with the practice of dying" (2:207). In the *Timaeus,* Plato's myth of creation, there is only one real world and that real world of Forms belongs to the eternal, not the material world. In Book VII of the *Republic,* the chained prisoner in the "Allegory of the Cave" must escape the womblike cave to which there is one forced exit if he is ever to see the light or truth. Or in Irigaray's words, the prospective philosopher must "disengage himself from his human double, his female understudy, launching himself into the sky in a philosophical flight, raising his head toward what alone has a real existence. Ideas" (Irigaray, *Speculum* 322).

That the body and materiality (that which is to be escaped) become associated with femininity/passivity further corroborates the difficulty Platonic philosophy poses as a paradigmatic homoeroticism.[6] As Halperin notes, the homoeroticism of ancient Greece differs from the contemporary experience and does not merely "confirm" or "legitimate" desired contemporary assumptions. In ancient Greece, sex (both heterosexual and homosexual) as it is "constituted by public, masculine discourse," is characterized by "active" pleasure, by virility. It is not mutual, not "something one invariably has *with* someone." It is seen as a "deeply polarizing experience" that "effectively divides, classifies, and distributes its participants into distinct and radically opposed categories," based on the "phallic penetration" of one body by another. Hierarchical, it is "thematized as domination": the relation between the "active" and the "passive" sexual partner is commensurate with the relation between "social superior and social inferior" (Halperin 30). What this means is that an adult male citizen of Athens could have legitimate relations only with women, foreigners, slaves, and statutory minors (his inferiors not in age but in social and political status).[7] Thus, dominant sexual behavior is not only an expression of desire but of cultural and legal authority. Maurice and Alec's relationship, which in its initial stages is not free of class, ends with the refusal of those hierarchies and with Maurice's stressing the desire for mutuality, for *sharing* his body.[8] Thus, in terms of literal Greek standards, because both Alec and Maurice at times relinquish positions of dominance, their relationship becomes aligned with the feminine (and subsequently with receptivity, passivity, the body, and nontruth).[9] In the end, it is the body as position of nontruth that *Maurice* attempts to revise.

Whether Forster was aware or not of these cultural restraints on sexuality, however, is rather moot, for its dynamics are played out within a Platonic metaphysics. Just as the " 'sexuality' of the classical Athenians, far from being independent and detached from 'politics,' " was "constituted by the very principles on which Athenian public life was organized" (Halperin 31), it would be bizarre to assume that sexuality could be separated from metaphysics (that which supposedly underlies the social and cultural fabric). Plato's injunction to escape the body is not an isolated, arbitrary command; it is, as Sandra Harding and several other feminist philosophers suggest, its metaphysical foundation or what enables the metaphysical quest to function between men.[10] Paralleling Irigaray's final assessment of Diotima as a potential subversive whose metaphysics is ultimately reduced to a "set-up" (*Ethics* 33), Halperin similarly notes:

Diotima's feminine presence at the originary scene of philosophy, at one of its founding moments, contributes an essential ingredient to the legitimization of the philosophical enterprise; her presence endows the pedagogic processes by which men reproduce themselves culturally—by which they communicate the secrets of their wisdom and social identity, the "mysteries" of male authority, to one another across the generations—with the prestige of female procreativity. (144)

Forster's privileging human relationships, the body, and friendship has been frequently cited as evidence for his humanism. And although this may be so, Forster's preference for the body collides with Platonism, which on one hand proffers a positive expression to homoeroticism, but conversely takes it away by making the body and materiality the site of untruth and, subsequently, the site of nonexistence.[11] Thus, by embedding within the romance narrative two Platonic dialogues (the *Phaedrus* and *Symposium*), *Maurice* demonstrates that the emergence of Maurice and Alec's relationship depends on relinquishing a much cherished Platonism, or, as Robert Martin remarks in "Double Structure," the text itself moves from a "false solution" heavily infused by Platonism to one that moves beyond its restrictions (35).

Platonic love is restrictive, as the *Phaedrus* and the *Symposium* indicate. Both dialogues distinguish between two different kinds of love: the false and vulgar love of the body and the true higher, divine love of the soul. The *Phaedrus* begins with Phaedrus leading Socrates beyond the walls of the city to a hilly slope where three speeches on love and a dialogue on rhetoric will be heard: Lysias' speech (presented by Phaedrus), which argues that the nonlover is superior to the lover; Socrates' first speech, which differentiates the lover from the nonlover and privileges the latter; Socrates' second speech, which recants his former position as an offense against Eros and which then attempts to define what constitutes noble love; and a concluding interchange on the nature of noble rhetoric. Socrates concludes, as he did in his discussion of love, that rhetoric (like love) must be joined to philosophy and the highest love of the soul; or as Benjamin Jowett notes, higher rhetoric is based upon a dialectic, which is a sort of inspiration akin to love (Plato, *Dialogues* 1:404). Set within the context of a feast celebrating the poet Agathon, the *Symposium* similarly provides the occasion for a rhetorical exploration of love: five flawed speeches on love preceding Socrates' speech; Socrates' oration, which through the voice of Diotima purveys love as an intermediary that links and ultimately leads men to the divine; and Alcibiades' drunken interruption, which accuses Socrates of dishonesty, enchantment, and manipulation.

Maurice begins with an implicit allusion to the opening of the *Phaedrus* in which Phaedrus entices Socrates to walk beyond the city walls for a discourse on love. Phaedrus suggests a spot near a "spreading plane-tree" where Socrates, in a pleasing mood, lies down on the grassy slope for the interchange (1:434). In a similar fashion, Mr. Ducie, the "old pedagogue" (M 15), who is "never deterred from doing what is right," sets out to have a " 'good talk' " with Maurice (M 10). Taking him away from the company of Maurice's other school fellows, beyond the academy's walls, Ducie likewise leads Maurice to an isolated spot on the beach and lies down on the sand to draw Maurice into conversation. After briefly querying Maurice about his family, Ducie reveals his true purpose: to impart the "mystery of sex" and greatness of "love" (M 13). Ducie's definition of love, fumbling as it is, then falls into a lofty accolade that recalls Socrates' concluding remarks on the beauty of ascetic love in the *Phaedrus*. Of the lovers who love most ideally, Socrates claims:

At last they pass out of the body; unwinged, but eager to soar, and thus obtain no mean reward of love and madness. For those who have once begun the heavenward pilgrimage may not go down again to darkness and the journey beneath the earth, but they live in light always (1:463).

Similarly, Ducie's talk, couched in Platonic idealism that invokes the heavens, sets up an epistemological dichotomy that haunts the rest of the text. He draws explicit sexual diagrams in the sand, but couches them in ideal and abstract terms: the "ideal man—chaste with asceticism" and "the glory of Woman" (M 14). Somewhat Christianized as it is, Ducie's talk, in conjoining Platonic and Christian asceticism, more poignantly sets Platonism up for a fall, for it aligns Platonism with the condemnations of the body that initially motivate Clive to reject Christianity.

That Ducie, moreover, initiated this conversation with Maurice because he found his formal education at the boys' academy wanting a sexual component recalls Socrates' insistence that complete knowledge must include an understanding of love, which is the subject of both the *Phaedrus* and the *Symposium*. In both dialogues, which for Jowett "together contain the whole philosophy of Plato on the nature of love, the essence of rhetoric and love is conjoined" (Plato, *Dialogues* 1:393). In the *Phaedrus*, the connection is most explicit: what makes a good lover parallels what makes a good rhetorician: both share the love of the soul, the conjoining of which is philosophy: "For *philo-sophy* is at once the highest form of love and the highest form of speech" (Friedländer 242).

The opening dialogue between Maurice and Ducie, however, stages a physicality that will not yield to a higher asceticism, a dynamic that is then borne out in the rest of the text. Maurice rejects Ducie's talk, saying "I think I shall not marry" (M 15), which, in part, conveys his homoerotic desires, but the text goes further, implying that the idealized love Ducie presents is tainted. This taint subsequently threatens to collapse an asceticism whose claim to ideality and superiority lies in its remaining beyond corruption and desire. Implicit in this realization are the means through which to confront the ideality of the law that condemns the the foreign other, the lover with the "wrong desires" (M 165). As Judith Butler notes: " 'the law of sex' is repeatedly fortified and idealized as the law only to the extent that it is reiterated as the law, produced as the law, the anterior and inapproximable ideal, by the very citations it is said to command" (14). It has been in this vein, as well, that much feminist philosophy has contested a metaphysical discourse that condemns the feminine, by virtue of its ideality, to material impurity. No amount of protesting the categorization will suffice, since the protests (according to the law) emanate from "wandering errants," that is, unless of course the ideality of the authority itself can be contested. If the "ideal standard" itself is tainted, the exclusionary labels it foists on the Other are also suspect. And as soon as one "begins to pay attention to the procedures and goals of this authoritarian pedagogy," as soon as one spots physical desire in that which condemns physical desire, one ceases to be sure of the accuracy of authoritative labels, of "what madness or lunacy is" or of what is noble or ignoble in desire (Irigaray, *Speculum* 271). Similarly, the authoritative bearers of the law in *Maurice* (Dr. Barry, Lasker Jones, and Mr. Ducie), in losing their authoritarian grip, lose also the force of their labels.

If, as Lacan maintains, all that which is created through language bears residues of the previous desire-surfeited imaginary, nothing escapes, including philosophy. The exploration of the philosophy of rhetoric in *The Symposium* becomes more like a staging of the "salons of courtly love" (Ragland-Sullivan 730) and the *Phaedrus* more like a scene of seduction (Cummings). The *Phaedrus,* as many have noted, is surfeited with desire. Staged outside the town walls (outside the confinements of the law), it leads quickly to the supposed site where Boreas abducted (raped) Oreithyia. Seduced by the promise of a rhetorical exploration of love, Socrates finds the spot of seduction with its sweet fragrances and pillowy, grassy slope a most pleasant place to lie at length. He talks of Phaedrus' spell, which seemed to bait him as if a "bough or a bunch of fruit" were being waved before him and of reclining comfortably on the grass (1:435). But by the end of the dialogue, this initial physicality has been superseded. Socrates in his allegory of the black and white steeds urges suppression of the animal and physical appetites for the higher pleasures of the soul. As Katherine Cummings notes: "The *Phaedrus* suggests that metaphysics is rather like a good bourgeois: he borrows (sexual violence and/or seduction narratives) to launch his business, but works hard to wipe out all material debts" (45).

Similarly, Ducie wants to bury the aspects of the physical as soon as they are spoken. He declares this will be Maurice's life, for it is the right plot, one which "hangs together" with God "in his heaven" (M 15), an echo of Christianity, but also of the *Timaeus,* Plato's myth of creation, which reveals "the whole eternal plan of God," including the implicit creation of masculine and feminine and the ultimate rightness of this plan instigated by "one creator" (3:718). When Ducie realizes, however, with considerable consternation that he has left his drawings exposed in the sand, it is he who is exposed. The philosopher has forgotten to cover up the sexual components of his idealized theories. Maurice, pondering Ducie's fears, comments: "Liar, coward, he's told me nothing" (M 15). Even at the age of fourteen Maurice intuits that the philosopher is a "liar" and that the Platonic philosophy he espouses is suspect.

Clive is Maurice's second and quite self-conscious Platonic teacher who urges Maurice to read the *Symposium*. Like Ducie, he has a "sincere mind" and a "keen sense of right and wrong" (M 69). And he initially lures Maurice with the physical. He subverts Maurice's beliefs in the Trinity and the Redemption as meaningless tags, because, in the language of the *Phaedrus*, they "dissever" flesh from the spirit (M 49). Like Ducie, however, Clive wishes to cover up any traces of physicality with Platonic idealism. Thus, the outing in the motor car becomes a palimpsest that repeats the earlier incident with Ducie. Clive and Maurice, in venturing beyond the academy's walls, settle on a "grassy embankment" beside a brook that once again recalls the "delicious" stream and "gently sloping" grass of the *Phaedrus* (1:434). The afternoon, like the tale of the charioteer's black and white steeds, is one of restraint. As Maurice later reflects on their outing: "Though restrained by his friend, he would have surfeited passion" (M 82). The motor car, perhaps a metaphor for the chariot that harnesses the two horses, purveys a Platonic afternoon in which the spirit wins out over the flesh.

In urging Maurice to read the *Symposium,* Clive further urges Maurice toward loving Eros in the abstract, toward scaling the ladder of Love. In the *Symposium,* Socrates teaches, through the voice of Diotima, that love begins with beautiful things of the earth, but ends with the "everlasting, without diminution, and without increase or any change": the true lover will "mount upwards for the sake of that other beauty," from beautiful bodies to beautiful notions and practices (1:581). Earthly beauty, in other words, matters only as a stepping stone toward a more etherealized, spiritual beauty. This "succession" will then bring forth "not images of beauty, but realities" of the "immortal" (1:582). For Plato, it is the "'image' of the idea," the "good and beautiful" within individuals that we are to love: the "individual, in the uniqueness and integrity of his or her individuality, will never be the object of our love" (Vlastos 31). The movement is up and out, the launch into the realm of pure ideas (Irigaray, *Speculum* 322).

Clive thus rejects any experiences connected with the sensual. Note the closure of the day Maurice and Clive spend in the woods: " 'I say, will you kiss me?' asked Maurice, when the sparrows woke in the eaves above them, and far out in the woods the ring doves began to coo" (M93). Maurice's request for a kiss is juxtaposed to the birds' mating calls. Clive's refusal signals his rejection not only of Maurice but of the physical world. Clive and Maurice part, in Clive's view, "having established perfection in their lives" (M 93). Clive binds their relationship to the spiritual and subtly makes it clear that their love, "though including the body, should not gratify it" (M 151), a rejection Maurice eventually regrets. Remembering the day he spent with Maurice in the sidecar as the culmination of "the unity preached by Plato" (M 80), Clive makes his own ascent and then tries to take Maurice with him, leading "the beloved up a narrow and beautiful path, high above either abyss" (M 98). Once again, paralleling Ducie's earlier moves, Clive attempts to camouflage through a contrived Platonism the day's negativity. As Martin, in noting the "dirt, noise, and stench" that envelop the ride in the sidecar, suggests, the day signals an ironic warning ("Double Structure" 40). Clive elides the negativity so that only the memory of the ideal remains. What Clive engages here is what Irigaray defines as "autoeroticism"; in love with his own ideas, Clive takes his vision to be emblematic of a unitary oneness that is the mark of universal truth. Here Irigaray's mimicry of the philosopher-acolyte relationship in the *Symposium* as a kind of grand narcissism is particularly pertinent: "Love, indeed, will be insensibly aroused in the loved one because his eyes have been enchanted, without their realizing it, without their suspecting that the 'lover is his mirror in whom he is beholding himself.' Thus he is in love. But what with what? With his image?" (*Speculum* 323).

The *Symposium*, like *Maurice,* is a lesson on love. In the orations that precede Socrates' speech, love is depicted as an inspiration to heroic deeds, as having two natures (one the vulgar love of the body and the other as a catalyst for improving the lover's character), as desire for harmony, as desire for completion or wholeness, and as the love of the "beautiful." Each of these stances on love (with perhaps the exception of Phaedrus') appears in various contexts in *Maurice.* Recalling Pausanias, who sees the lover and beloved as instrumental in healing and self-improvement, both Clive and Maurice initially are inspirations to one another. Clive hopes to improve Maurice, whose character he found "not indeed fine, but charmingly willing" (M 98), and Maurice, once he hears Clive's declaration of "normality" hopes to "heal" his friend. In the initial Cambridge conversations in the mode of Eryximachus, who sees love as enacting the "harmony" of song, Maurice finds love "harmonious" (M 72), and recalling Aristophanes' myth of the divided hermaphrodites,

Maurice describes Clive as his other half. Finally, when Maurice visits Clive at Penge before he is married, Clive, recalling Agathon "who cannot say enough of the 'beauty' of the god of love" (2:566), tells Maurice that it was Maurice's "beauty" that first inspired his love (M 92).

But the lesson of the *Symposium,* the answer to these insufficient stances—to surpass material and bodily form—is not *Maurice's* lesson. What *Maurice* implies is that, in order for the bodily fulfillment of the Alec-Maurice relationship to transpire, Platonism (represented by both Ducie and Clive, who are both cast as having the wrong answers) must be relinquished. When Maurice, in the company of Alec, encounters Ducie in the British museum, Ducie gets Maurice's name wrong. Maurice then comments: "How like Mr. Ducie to get the facts just wrong!" (M 223). The misjudgment, though, extends beyond the misnaming, for Maurice, with Alec at his side, is also remembering Ducie's love lesson.

Likewise, Clive regards Maurice as possessing the "wrong desires" and convinces himself that he has become heterosexual. Yet in the end it is Clive's life that seems to have taken the "wrong" turn. Many critics have puzzled, quite understandably, on Clive's inexplicable turn to heterosexuality. One explanation is that he has seemingly confused the perceived desires of his culture with his own. I agree with this assessment, but would like to suggest that there is more to this enigma than cultural substitution of desire, that it is Clive's Platonism that is both the obstacle thwarting the love between him and Maurice and the catalyst to his pallid marriage. Creating "an inner sanctum out of the wall of language," Platonism produces a barrier between the self and another subject (Charles 67). Clive's marriage, rather than a confirmation of his heterosexuality, seems more an extension of his Platonism. Still ignoring the body, Clive "never saw her naked, nor she him," and they "ignored the reproductive and the digestive functions" (M 164). Anne Woods may be Clive's greenwood, but it is a paled one, which admits no intimacy and seemingly no pleasure. Still in love with the pure spirit, the *puer aeternus,* Clive finds in marriage "beautiful conventions" and temperance (M 165), in other words, containment and control (the lessons of the *Phaedrus*). In the end, when Maurice announces that he loves Alec with his body, Clive is offended and is assured of the rightness of his stance, but in later years Clive stares pensively out of the window of the Blue Room, as Maurice "clothed in sun, and shaking out the scents and sounds of the May term," beckons to him (M 246). Paradise inverted, turned upside down, the spiritual cloister turned prison.

The comic counterpart of this Platonic inversion emerges in Maurice's grandfather, Mr. Grace, who has spent his leisure time developing a new cosmogony whose main tenets are as follows: "God lives inside the sun, whose bright envelope consists of the spirits of the blessed." These "sunspots reveal God to men" and the "incarnation was a sort of sun spot" (137). In other words, sun spots are the shadows from which we recognize the ideal forms: another Platonic playground. The sun, the source of the Good for Plato, provides not only light and illumination toward the path to goodness in the visible world, but it is inextricably connected to the processes of knowledge and understanding. Mr. Grace loses his state of grace and becomes frightfully disturbed, however, when a meteor chips off pieces of Saturn's rings, which later fall into the sun, causing Saturn, traditionally imaged as dark, malefic and karmic, to mix with the good and bright sun. Such an intermingling means there is no clear-cut distinction between dark and light, good and evil (sexual and spiritual, heterosexual and homosexual).[12] The traditionally malevolent Saturn then becomes deeply embedded in the sun, the source of life. God is perhaps not all sun; the incarnation may not guarantee repetition or a mirror vision. Sameness, as some illumined state of grace without any dark spots, is fantasy. Like Aziz's experience in the mosque in *A Passage to India,* epistemological pillars shake when black and white are not so clearly separated.

Amusing as this interlude may be, the "cosmogony" that Maurice dismisses here recalls his rejection of Mr. Ducie and Clive's attempted inculcation. In response to Mr. Ducie's lecture on the ideal man and the glory of woman, the young Maurice replies, "I think I shall not marry" (M 15). Implicit too is a reciprocal rejection of the principles underlying the Socratic-youth relationship: the ascent, the division of light and dark, male and female, the burial of the sensual, and the reification of this path as the ultimate truth. As a child, Maurice feared his room because of the "looking-glass" or mirror, a "mirror" being a conventional metaphor for the metaphysical process: Maurice "did not mind seeing his face in it, nor casting a shadow on the ceiling, but he did mind seeing his shadow on the ceiling reflected in the glass" (M 19). Maurice tries to escape his shadow reflected in the mirror, as if the reflected shadows (like the shadows of Plato's cave in Book VII of *The Republic*) beckon another way of knowing. Likewise, Maurice reluctantly agrees to Clive's asceticism (the denial of the shadow). In the end, however, he tells Clive: "I'm flesh and blood, if you'll condescend to such low things—" (M 243). Informing Clive that he has shared with Alec "all" that he has, which includes his body, Maurice discards the Platonic "cosmogony," which for him means embracing both a different epistemology and a different construction of sexuality.

Conversely, for Clive, the body disrupts. Preferring landscape paintings unhampered by the human form, he desires the serenity of the contained garden. Clive tells Maurice that "landscape is the only safe subject—or perhaps something geometrical, rhythmical, inhuman absolutely," that once the human form is introduced, "you at once arouse either disgust or desire" (M 93). Introduce the sensual and the material, and Clive's whole life philosophy begins to crack (M 73). This clearly becomes not only a faulty way to engage in relationships, but an erroneous way to see the world. Although Maurice is supposedly the "wandering errant," with "the wrong words on his lips and the wrong desires in his heart" (M 165), it is nonetheless his revisionary vision that triumphs. Clive wants to rewrite history, "The Aesthetic Philosophy of the Decalogue," he calls it. Pure speculative philosophy, "out of the senses into the intellect, out of the passions into a harmonious love of truth, out of *doxa* into *episteme*" (Irigaray, *Speculum* 286), Clive's episteme fails him, leaving him in his old age noting the undulating ferns outside the Blue Room and searching for shadows (M 246).

If Maurice is situated within the shadows, he occupies an intermediary space that marks Diotima's earlier remarks on love, one which, in blurring boundaries, resists the severe dissevering of soul and body that is ultimately love's fate in the *Symposium*. Moreover, this intermediary position, by obscuring boundaries, parallels what Homi Bhabha defines as an "in-between space" that thwarts the negative defining of the Other (Dr. Barry, for example, casting Maurice as a perversion). Maurice does remain subject to the threats British law poses, but the text subverts the metaphysical machinery that drives its justifications. In the final scenes between Maurice and Clive, Clive asks Maurice, "Who taught you to talk like this" to which Maurice replies, "You, if anyone" (M 245): rhetoric, love, metaphysics. Butler asks: "What would it mean to 'cite' the law to produce it differently?" (15). Maurice, in effect, does 'cite' the law differently, embracing a different sexuality and a different metaphysics, one that does not "dissever the soul from the communion of the body" (Plato, *Dialogues* 2:203). Altering metaphysics effects conceptions of sexuality; neither the one without the other. It is this kind of "enabling disruption" that could produce for both homosexuals and heterosexuals what Butler terms as a "radical rearticulation of the symbolic horizon" (23). And finally, it is a "radical rearticulation," which in conjoining issues of metaphysics and sexuality, recasts the modernist metaphysical quest, so frequently depicted as absorbed in the throes of philosophical flight and "raising its head toward what [seemingly] alone has a real existence. Ideas" (Irigaray, *Speculum* 322).

Notes

1. See S. P. Rosenbaum's assessment of *The Longest Journey* ("*Longest*") as a reflection of G. E. Moore's philosophy.

2. The centrality of epistemological concerns within modernism has been widely established. Marianne DeKoven uses Jacques Derrida's "formulation of *sous-rature*" to analyze the ambivalence toward change in modernist texts; Michael Levenson in *Modernism* addresses the fate of the autonomous self or autonomous knower, and in *Genealogy* addresses key literary, aesthetic, and philosophical concepts that helped constitute modernism; Tony E. Jackson provides a Lacanian reading of aesthetic representation, examining the difference between purported forms and their disappearance; Bette London, in *Appropriated*, suggests that a collapse in the authority of voice produces a crisis in knowing and in literary form; Perry Meisel examines modernism's "impossible" search for origins; Louis Menand suggests that a "materialist's Platonism" underlies empiricism and imagism.

3. I do not see *Maurice* as an anomaly in this respect, but rather as representative of a recurrent theme in Forster's fiction: For example, in *Passage* the Marabar Caves (whose images allude to the cave of Plato's *Republic* and whose positioning functions as the text's structural center) are both the site of epistemological and sexual questioning.

4. See Naomi Schor's "This Essentialism is Not One: Coming to Grips with Irigaray," Carolyn Burke's "Irigaray Through the Looking Glass," and Margaret Whitford's "Reading Irigaray in the Nineties" in Burke's *Engaging*. This collection, as whole, addresses many of the misconceptions surrounding Irigaray's ideas and establishes her as a central revisionary force in philosophy.

5. In Irigaray's recasting of Western metaphysics, first, the ideal standard (what Plato formulates in the *Timaeus* and in other dialogues) is seen as the "Standard Itself/Himself," the universal that is not universal, or the desire for the self-same: In the Socratic dialogue "nothing can be named as 'beings' except those same things which all the same men see in the same way in a setup that does not allow them to see other things and which they will designate by the same names, on the basis of the conversation between them" (*Speculum* 263). Second, this desire for universality (for the self-same) is seen as plagued by autoeroticism: the philosopher having a love affair with his own mind which he then mistakes for universal truth. Third, Irigaray suggests that this ideal, necessarily fixed, is a desire for fixity and control. If, as Jacques Lacan maintains, naming is an illusory control over the world, naming or fixing categories like "masculine"

and "feminine" are fantasies the subject latches onto in order to create the illusion of control. Thus, it is not that the metaphysical quest is devoid of desire, but that it possesses different (physical) desires.

6. See for example Plato's *Phaedo, Timaeus,* and "Allegory of the Cave." Innumerable studies have addressed how gender cannot be separated from metaphysical constructions, and it would be impossible for me to allude to them all. Thus, what follows are a few key studies, in addition to Irigaray's, that have influenced my own work: Jessica Benjamin queries the seeming inevitability of repression and domination underlying psychoanalysis and Western metaphysics and the infusion of these concepts into our love relationships; Judith Butler identifies femininity as metaphysics' "enabling condition"; Lorraine Code examines the relationship between the knower and gender; see also Burke, Schor, and Whitford; and Hélène Cixous and Catherine Clément, Jane Flax, Sandra Harding and Merrill B. Hintikka, Alice A. Jardine, Ellen Kennedy and Susan Mendus, and Toril Moi.

7. Halperin continues to note that "it would be a monumental task indeed to enumerate all the ancient documents in which the alternative 'boy or woman' occurs with perfect nonchalance in an erotic context, as if the two were functionally interchangeable" (34). In his discussion of why Diotima is a woman, Halperin initially revises this position that links women with boys by including Greek accounts of women enjoying sexual intercourse. However, after working through several different speculations on why Diotima is a woman, Halperin implicitly comes back to his original position. If women enjoy sexual intercourse, it is because they desire what men desire them to desire. Halperin notes that women's sexual pleasure was restricted to the desire for reproduction, what he terms as male desire to reproduce the self, both literally and metaphorically (which corroborates Irigaray's critique). Finally arguing for Diotima's singular importance in the *Symposium* not as "a surrogate for Aspasia, not a prophetess, not an Eleusinian priestess, but [as] a woman" (129), Halperin comes to see Diotima's function as a conduit for male desire that "does not speak for women," but "silences them" (145).

8. See Robert K. Martin's discussion in "Edward" of how Maurice's relationship with Alec recalls Carpenter's vision of a "new social order" in which class would not figure (44).

9. The situation also parallels the constrictions of English law at the turn of the century, which would make homosexuals "outlaws" if discovered (M 127). Clive and Maurice occupy what Karen Klein defines as the "feminine predicament," a situation marked by unpleasant difficulty, perplexity, or danger, in which one's body is "not under one's own control, but subject to the will or force of others" (104). Although women are more likely to find themselves in this predicament, given the privileges patriarchy affords men, men too may find themselves in this situation, if a member of the "wrong" political party, race, religion, or sexual orientation.

10. Many feminist critiques of Western philosophy cite the binary opposition

that links femininity with the body, darkness, formlessness, and nontruth. Referencing Plato's *Timaeus,* Butler takes this position further, arguing that femininity becomes linked with nothingness. As Butler notes, the feminine receptacle in the *Timaeus* receives forms, but is to take no form of its own. The problem is not, according to Butler, that "the feminine is made to stand for matter or for universality; rather the feminine is cast outside the form/matter and universal/particular binarisms" (42). In Butler's casting, as well as Irigaray's, with which Butler's analysis has affinity, the feminine exclusion is even more drastic.

11. See Butler's discussion of the *Timaeus.*

12. Alec's dallying with kitchen maids (M 166) suggests bisexuality.

9

Betrayal and Its Consolations in Maurice, "Arthur Snatchfold," and "What Does It Matter? A Morality"

Christopher Lane

Eros is a great leveler.   *Edward Carpenter,* The Intermediate Sex

Physical love means reaction, being panic in essence.   *E. M. Forster,* Maurice

If we apply Forster's maxim in *Howards End* (1910)—"only connect the prose and the passion" (HE 183–84)—to his *The Life to Come and Other Stories* (1972), the latter text is bound to disappoint us. Although Forster's posthumous collection contains his most explicit accounts of love and sex between men, thus documenting a series of fantasies that Forster refused to publish in his lifetime, the majority of these stories have extremely volatile endings: "The Life to Come" and "The Other Boat" conclude in violent murder; "Arthur Snatchfold," in possible treachery and ethical compromise; "What Does It Matter? A Morality," in political banishment; and "Dr. Woolacott," in likely delirium, even psychosis. Considering these amorous failures, how seriously can we take Forster's 1928 observation in his *Commonplace Book* that "[love] needs must come, but I am against lending it any prestige. I am all for affection and lust . . ." (CB 39)? Later the same year, for instance, Forster offered a perspective on Ibsen that affects our understanding of his own work: "This time sex is the villain" (CB 42).

June Perry Levine usefully observes that in "the serious homosexual stories, one pair suffer[s] no violence, three pairs share death, and only one pair meet[s] separate fates, with the lower-class member the sole victim." For Levine, this list of failures eventually mitigates Forster's "vision of eternal love";[1] allegedly, it modifies Wilfred Stone's observation that "some infuriating inequality" usually stymies Forster's works ("Overleaping" 393).[2] In this essay, I qualify Levine's and others' remarks by arguing that we cannot wholly explain this distress by social opprobrium or cultural homophobia. Nor can we simply conclude, as Stone does, that Forster's characters are manifestations of his self-hatred ("Overleaping" 389).[3] Without ignoring biographical or material registers, I contend that the sexual turmoil prevailing in *The Life to Come* collection warrants serious interpretation on its own terms.

Having carefully shown how Forster transformed John Addington Symonds's account of Greek love and Carpenter's model of homophilia,[4] critics including Levine and Judith Scherer Herz argue that "The Life to Come" (1972 [1922]) and "The Other Boat" (1972 [1915–16]) conclude in redemptive passion. According to Levine, the first story's "romantically triumphant ending . . . moves beyond personal vengeance against the white man and into a vision of redemption through action" (85; see also Herz, *Short* 47). If we place such "romantic . . . triumph" alongside Levine's prior emphasis on the lovers' material and racial inequality, however, we must ask whether one man murdering the other before committing suicide is really "mov[ing] beyond personal vengeance." (Levine writes: "In 'The Other Boat,' it is a white man . . . who jumps to his death. He has just strangled his dusky lover . . ."[85].) Recalling the turmoil of Forster's stories' bizarre conclusions renders unpersuasive such claims of "romantically triumphant ending[s]," yet critics nonetheless face a dilemma in understanding the precise stakes of these narrative resolutions. Although Forster's vision of sexual love scarcely appears redemptive—perhaps especially in stories that magnify the heroism of love and passion—critics who stress only his lovers' material and structural inequality ignore an important point: Forsterian passion partly derives from what is irregular and incompatible about his characters' material conditions (CB 34). While this suggests that material *inequality* can cause desire, the resulting fantasies push Forster's narratives beyond such material explanations as discrepancies of wealth and racial oppression. Forster's stress on material incompatibility clarifies why in *Maurice* (1971 [1913–14]) love and friendship coexist between Maurice Hall and Clive Durham without an overwhelming sexual frisson: Since for Forster "there can be no passion . . . between two tamed creatures" (CB 50), the prerequisite for Forsterian desire is a form of "wildness" that not only destabilizes "tameness" but implicitly shatters it.[5]

To assess how these material and psychic tensions inform Forster's statements on nationalism, colonialism, and comradeship, we must revisit a passage from the manuscript of *Maurice* that Forster excised from the novel's final draft; Levine cites this passage quite early in her article, later to ignore it: "During passion, [Alec Scudder] would have died for his friend, but there had been some time since to reflect that a gentleman lay in his power" (qtd. in Levine 77). Scudder's reflection anticipates *Maurice*'s scene of bungled blackmail, which Forster downplayed at the novel's end to confirm Maurice and Scudder's lasting union. As he acknowledged in the novel's Terminal Note, "A happy ending was imperative. I shouldn't have bothered to write otherwise. I was determined that in fiction anyway two men should fall in love and remain in it for the ever and ever that fiction allows . . ." (M 236).

By reminding us why Scudder "would [*not*] have died for his friend," Forster's Terminal Note usefully challenges existing readings of the novel's benign comradeship and "imperative" sexual happiness. Indeed, Scudder's reflection asks us to consider not only class privilege and cultural homophobia, but also the peculiar eroticism of betrayal that unexpectedly recurs in Forster's writing.[6] Scudder's conflict of interest suggests not that Forster was lying when he made these claims about the novel's "happy ending," but that unconscious elements of his fictional relationships eluded his narrative control. These elements underpin and often ruin—through ambivalence and retribution—the fraternal idealism prevailing in most of Forster's novels, some of which he wrote concomitantly with the *Life to Come* stories. Since Forster repeatedly, if inadvertently, shows that the "fraternal" and "sexual" are nonidentical— perhaps mutually exclusive—categories, we need to assess this sexual difficulty in his *Life to Come and Other Stories*. In this way, we can gauge the conceptual distance between the politics at which Forster aimed and the desire that his stories actually foster. We can also question whether Forster's narratives confirm his professed belief that "two people pulling each other into salvation is the only theme I find worthwhile" (CB 55). *The Life to Come* reveals characters torn in directions that not only preclude salvation but fundamentally question its possibility.

Considering Forster's repeated failure to attain his political ideals and his stories' astonishing turbulence at the level of sexual demand, I want first to examine several political essays that Forster reprinted in *Two Cheers for Democracy* (1951). Written in the late 1930s, these essays engage profound questions about racial prejudice, anti-Semitism, and the possibility of sustaining "tolerance" in times of extreme social hatred. "Racial Exercise" and "Jew-Consciousness," both published in 1939, also display inadvertent turns in Forster's argument that betray unconscious elements of racism precisely when Forster attempts to explain and diminish it in others. These essays highlight the limits of Forster's liberalism by detailing his and our unexamined phobia and malice; they profoundly affect how we read Forster's fiction.[7]

Perhaps the most striking example of Forster's racial intolerance is his brief essay "The Menace to Freedom" (1935), in which he claims that we cannot reduce tyranny and prejudice to external forces or material conditions. The essay concedes that prejudice combines with external and internal forms of violence in a cycle we cannot eradicate by political will or material change:

The menace to freedom is usually conceived in terms of political or social interference—Communism, Fascism, Grundyism, bureaucratic encroachment, censorship, conscription, and so forth. And it is usually personified as a tyrant who has escaped from a bottomless pit, his proper home, and is stalking the earth by some mysterious dispensation, in order to persecute God's elect, the electorate. But this is too lively a view of our present troubles, and too shallow a one. We must peer deeper if we want to understand them, deep into the abyss of our own characters. For politics are based on human nature; even a tyrant is a man, and our freedom is really menaced today because a million years ago Man was born in chains. (TCD 9)

Juxtaposing this passage with Howards End's maxim, "only connect the prose and the passion" (HE 183–84) clarifies why Forster's faith in "connection" rarely succeeds; internal impediments often ruin the hope of complete interpersonal understanding and cross-cultural harmony.

Since psychic conflict surpasses external violence, in "The Menace to Freedom," Forster argues that we cannot reason violence into harmony: "That unfortunate event ['Man's origins'] lies too far back for retrospective legislation; no declarations of independence touch it; no League of Nations can abolish it" (TCD 9). Additionally, Forster's stress on internal conflict and hostility implies that both exist irrespective of external harmony. Like Ernest Jones's claims in his essays on war and sublimation, Forster suggests that the pressure to achieve "peace" may precipitate fresh outbreaks of military conflict, for "peace" compels every subject—irrespective of its conscious desire—to renounce whatever aspects of unconscious conflict a war can represent or abreact.[8] To put this more contentiously, subjects may receive announcements of peace with conscious relief, but these announcements may not necessarily bring lasting happiness or unconscious satisfaction; often the reverse, as Jones, Freud, and even Forster radically imply.[9]

As in "Jew-Consciousness" and "Racial Exercise," Forster's argument in "Menace" makes several unforeseen turns concerning the unconscious. Toward the end of this essay, for instance, when Forster considers that love can assuage an excess of fear and hatred, he modifies the unconscious's previous intractable quality in a hope that it will eventually disappear:

It is difficult not to get mushy as soon as one mentions love, but it is a tendency that must be reckoned with, and it takes as many forms as fear. The desire to devote oneself to another person or persons seems to be as innate as the desire for personal liberty. If the two desires could combine, the menace to freedom from within, the fundamental menace, might disappear, and the political evils now filling all the foreground of our lives would be deprived of the poison which nourishes them. They will not wilt in our time, we can hope for no immediate relief. But it is a good thing, once in a way, to speculate on the remoter future. (TCD 11)

"If the two desires could combine": Forster's political philosophy hinges on this outcome. Like Forster, we might wish to "speculate on the remoter future," but "The Menace to Freedom" insists that "we can hope for no immediate relief." This conclusion recalls the narrator's famous pronouncement in *A Passage to India* (1924) that Aziz and Fielding must defer a full and open friendship: "No, not yet . . . not there" (PI 325). However, the narrator of *Passage* renders *external* the impediments disrupting two otherwise willing friends: "The horses didn't want it . . . ; the earth didn't want it . . . ; the temples, the tank, the jail, the palace, the birds, the carrion, the Guest House . . . : they didn't want it" (PI 325). This projection of hostility differs radically from Forster's understanding in "The Menace to Freedom" that if devotion to another is "innate," so is the "poison which nourishes" the possibility of a different outcome: "We must peer deeper . . . deep into the abyss of our own characters. . . . Even a tyrant is a man." Put differently, "The Menace to Freedom" carefully probes whether characters such as Aziz and Fielding really want to be friends; it asks us to consider their desire for and ambivalence about intimacy. In this respect, "Menace" prevents us and Forster from defining hostility solely as a cultural or political phenomenon; the essay asks us to consider the subtle pleasure a person may experience in his or her hostility to another, a pleasure that complicates—but does not entirely jeopardize—Forster's characters' professions of desire and companionship.

How does this difficulty affect Forster's vision of "connection"? How, moreover, does it alter materialist readings of his work, in which prejudice is historically specific and Forster's "Menace" a clear indictment of mid-1930s European fascism? If Forster could not envisage "personal liberty" combining with "devotion to another person or persons" in 1935, should we interpret his fiction's precarious combination of these factors as a wider indictment of society, or was he also grappling with the possibility that if "even a tyrant is a man," so can a man (or woman) easily become tyrannical?

It is too easy to credit Forster with a radical understanding of political hostility. As Forster remarked of such historical materialism, "this is too lively a view of our present troubles, and too shallow a one" (TCD 9). Beyond improbability, such critical perspectives ignore moments in Forster's writing when outcomes differ extensively from what Forster and his narrators anticipate or intend: interpersonal connection. For instance, if the materialist reading is correct and Forster struggled to represent human tragedy and incompatibility in his fiction, why did he also cling (despite all odds) to a vision of connection and not take the path of such contemporaries as Auden, Isherwood, and Spender? At the same time, if Forster struggled to portray cross-class and cross-cultural harmony in his fiction in liberal ways, as other critics maintain, why does this harmony repeatedly fail? Neither approach seems able to address unconscious pressures and difficulties in Forster's work and life. I think Forster was torn between the hope of achieving "connection" and the realization, undoubtedly magnified by historical circumstances, that in describing "the menace to freedom from within, the fundamental menace," he had alighted on a much greater ontological difficulty about human relations.

Careful readings of Forster's essays and fiction demonstrate Forster's vacillation between explaining and downplaying this ontological problem. My aim is not to dehistoricize Forster's dilemma, but rather to demonstrate what history and the unconscious partially taught him about human relations. That Forster professed a fierce belief in "connection" lies in interesting tension with his realization that altruism and misanthropy are coeval propensities. My essay interprets the conceptual and substantive pressure informing Forster's belief that "connection" must avoid the possibility—and attraction—of human treachery.

Forster's admission in "Menace" that he (and we) often "get mushy" when discussing love is invaluable at least in capturing his short stories' apparent discrepancy between their objectives of reconciliation and interpersonal harmony, and their violent displays of passion and cruelty. Far from transcending or displacing these informing tensions, as Levine, Herz, and Jeffrey Meyers contend, these eruptions of violence seem structurally inevitable; they detail the pressure Forster exerted to erase temporarily these eruptions from psychic and textual vision.

Without a psychoanalytic understanding of unconscious fantasy and the death drive, we gain only a limited understanding of Forster's characters in his posthumously published fiction. The following statement by Meyers is a useful example:

These men overcome racial, social and sexual prejudices, and achieve temporary liberation by sodomizing an obliging and acquiescent farmer, milkman, Indian soldier, sailor, policeman and even an animated statue, before lapsing back into their 'apparatus of decay' or plunging to a violent death. (Meyers 108)

Meyers's claim is not in any simple sense untrue, but it fails to grasp the connection between Forster's characters' "temporary liberation" in sex and their resultant "laps[e] back into their 'apparatus of decay.' "Although the last phrase is Forster's, Meyers ignores Forster's link between sexual liberation and sexual decay; he implies that the relations among sex, liberation, and death are contingent for Forster. For psychoanalysis, however—and at several moments for Forster too—these factors are mutually involved, if not causal.

Forster clarifies this involvement in "The Menace to Freedom" by acknowledging that our obstacles to union, peace, and happiness are chiefly internal. He claims that these obstacles have a "primaeval" (TCD 9) influence on our character. Considering our "evol[ution] among taboos," Forster writes, cultures from ancient Greece to the present are deceptively civilized; they are "abortive morally because of those primaeval chains. The ghosts of chains, the chains of ghosts, but they are strong enough, literally stronger than death, generation after generation hands them on" (TCD 9–10).

"The Life to Come" and "The Other Boat" clarify this implicit equation in Forster's writing between the unconscious and a state of savagery. Based on this argument, which I advance elsewhere,[10] I suggest that Forster's hopes of interracial union and intimacy stumble on elements of distrust and the assumption that every fault line in Western consciousness is "racially" significant. These assumptions add to Kipling's notorious complaints about "the White Man's burden" (1899) (Kipling 321–23): By eluding Forster's attempts at symbolization, this "burden" surfaces in all of his discussions of self-strangeness and weakness. Hence Forster's belief in "Menace" that *if* "the two desires [for personal liberty and devotion for another] could combine, . . . the political evils now filling the foreground of our lives would be deprived of the[ir] . . . poison" (TCD 11). Forster formulates an implicit connection between error and "race" here that turns failure into a self-fulfilling prophecy: If the unconscious—our "error"—is primitive and racial, according to Forster, history traps us in a psychic deadlock and blind repetition of prejudice and pleasure, for race and the unconscious persist.

Considering this repetition, we must return to the Terminal Note of *Maurice*. We have seen Forster insist that "two men [can] fall in love and remain in it for the ever and ever that fiction allows" (M 236). Later in the same paragraph he explains that such a "happy . . . imperative" responds to the British government's delay in decriminalizing male homosexuality by waiting to render as law the 1957 *Wolfenden Report*.[11] This admission fosters speculation about the implications of publishing the novel without legal protection: "If [the novel] ended unhappily, with a lad dangling from a noose or with a suicide pact, all would be well, for there is no pornography or seduction of minors" (M 236).[12]

While true in principle, this statement displays a significant—perhaps even cruel—disregard for his characters' plight. If we suspend disbelief here and treat Forster's characters with the degree of reality with which he apparently invests them, we might note a concern for self-survival that is not only complacently at odds with "a lad dangling from a noose" or with "a suicide pact," but substantively in conflict with Forster's now infamous claim in "What I Believe" that friendship outweighs the value of national loyalty: "I hate the idea of causes, and if I had to choose between betraying my country and betraying my friend, I hope I should have the guts to betray my country" (TCD 68; see Herz, *Short* 109–123, esp. 120).

Since Forster wrote *Maurice* without the legal support of *Wolfenden*, Maurice and Alec Scudder inevitably become "criminals" (this is Forster's word and it confirms his stress on realism). Forster explains: "The lovers get away unpunished and consequently recommend crime. Mr. Borenius is too incompetent to catch them, and the only penalty society exacts is an exile they gladly embrace" (M 236). Forster's posthumously published story "Arthur Snatchfold," which was written years after Forster completed the manuscript of *Maurice,* describes a similar scenario, but although this story's eponymous hero has the same initials as Alec Scudder, he suffers a quite different fate.

Arthur Snatchfold is as bisexual in temperament as Alec Scudder;

both protagonists hail from working-class backgrounds and are symbolically associated with nature (Alec is a gamekeeper, Arthur a milkman). Resembling Maurice as an upper-middle-class stockbroker (although he is bisexual in temperament while Maurice is not), Sir Richard Conway is bored and sexually restless one weekend while staying with Trevor Donaldson and his family. Conway has several daughters (LTC 106, 112) and is said to enjoy "an intrigue with a cultivated woman, which was gradually ripening" (LTC 108). Nonetheless, the narrator informs us, "The female sex was all very well and he was addicted to it, but [he] permitted himself an occasional deviation . . . [for] he believed in pleasure; he had a free mind and an active body" (LTC 101).

Arthur and Conway have sex in a wood on Donaldson's grounds (Maurice and Scudder only eloped to the boathouse together to "roam the greenwood" thereafter [M 236]): "Thus, exactly thus, should the smaller pleasures of life be approached. They understood one another with a precision that was impossible for lovers" (LTC 103). However, Conway hears much later from Donaldson that the police caught Arthur and was able to convict him because of "abundant evidence of a medical character" (LTC 110). Since the police and Donaldson cannot trace Conway, Conway is secretly relieved that he can resume his career and former life: "He was safe, safe, he could go forward with his career as planned. But waves of shame came over him. . . . For a moment he considered giving himself up and standing his trial, however what possible good would that do?" (LTC 112).

Critics have responded in various ways to "Arthur Snatchfold." Meyers endorses the narrator's meditation that the affair was "trivial and crude" (LTC 104; Meyers 110), while George Steiner usefully sees this and other Forster stories as the attempted reparation or sublimation of elements of "self-condemnation . . . , as if [Forster] could never shake off the secrecies, the aura of shame that a prudish, vengeful society had sought to instil in him" (165). Forster's interest in working-class men resembles that of his friend, novelist J. R. Ackerley, who acknowledged that "guilt in sex obliged me to work it off on my social inferiors" (qtd. in Salter 25). These statements all endorse Stephen Adams's objection to *Maurice:* "[Forster's] nostalgia for a simpler way of life . . . invests the physicality of the working man with redemptive power" (Adams 127; see also Malek). Adams captures the magnificent untruth of Forster's claims in "What I Believe," but his reading of "Arthur Snatchfold" ignores various elements of treachery and sexual disloyalty.

Forster represents Conway as pleasure-seeking and eager to have sex with Arthur, to be sure, but he also represents Conway's passing impulse to give himself up to the police. Such an act, Conway realizes, "would ruin himself and his daughters, . . . would *delight* his enemies, and . . . *would not save his saviour*" (LTC 112; my emphases). This last phrase clearly represents Arthur as a redemptive figure whose social position and lack of power are woefully at variance with his imaginary stature. Compare this fantasy to Adams's characterization of Conway as "a smug, well-to-do business man [of] . . . selfish cunning . . . [who] schemes to encounter the milkman in a nearby wood . . . [and who is so] well practised in the art, he is able to bluff his way out of danger" (Adams 122). This condemnation of Conway asks us to consider what Adams would deem an appropriate prelude to cross-class sexual intimacy. Adams writes: "[Conway's] selfish cunning contrasts with the naïve courage that the milkman had shown by stubbornly protecting Conway's identity and by refusing to show any shame in court" (122). Adams is referring to an exchange between Conway and Donaldson during which Conway realizes that Arthur consistently misled the police:

"Tell me," [Conway] said, taking his enemy's [Donaldson's] arm and conducting him to the door, "this old man in the mackintosh [Conway, viewed from behind by the police]—how was it the fellow you caught [Arthur] never put you on his track?"

"He tried to."

"Oh, did he?"

"Yes indeed, and he was all the more anxious to do so, because we made it clear that he would be let off if he helped us to make the major arrest. But all he could say was what we knew already—that it was someone from the hotel."

"Oh, he said that, did he? From the hotel."

"Said it again and again. Scarcely said anything else, indeed almost went into a sort of fit." (LTC 111)

Taking sole responsibility for his and Conway's shared pleasure renders Arthur entirely honorable, but how would we read this scene if Arthur were to cede the correct information to the police? An obvious rejoinder might be that Forster's narrator, by emphasizing Arthur's loyalty, encourages us not to read the story in this way. However, Adams implies that Conway's "selfish cunning" renders him legally responsible for his and Arthur's alleged "crime"; that Conway fails to substitute himself for Arthur makes him, in Adams's eyes, a traitor. Yet Conway *does* contemplate giving himself up for "his saviour" (LTC 112). That he finally decides not to derives from his understanding that such action would have no political impact. Forster's narrator also goes to great lengths to convince us not only of Arthur's willing participation, and thus shared responsibility, but also that pleasure in this legal context renders justice quite impossible: "It was a cruel stupid world" (LTC 109).

How does Arthur's emphatic loyalty square with Forster's briefly de-idealizing account of Maurice and Scudder's relationship in *Maurice*'s blackmail scene? If we recall the excised passage from this novel, in which Alec Scudder realizes that "a gentleman lay in his power," Arthur's insistent derailing of the police investigation would suggest an over-emphasis—"a sort of fit"—that appears to smother and render obsolete Scudder's passing impulse to betray his friend for financial gain in *Maurice*.

Another scene in "Arthur Snatchfold" creates confusion. Although a policeman sees Arthur and Conway having sex and Conway escapes undetected while Arthur's distinctive yellow shirt makes him easy to trace, the policeman, horrified and disbelieving of what he has witnessed, waits before arresting Arthur, who is arrested when he later *returns* to the scene with someone else. The narrator corroborates: "Alas, alas, there could be no doubt about it. [Conway] felt deeply distressed, and rather guilty. The young man must have decided *after* their successful encounter to use the wood as a rendezvous. It was a cruel stupid world, and he was countenancing it more than he should. Wretched, wretched . . . betrayed by the shirt he was so proud of . . ." (LTC 109; my emphasis; final ellipsis in text).

Considering this narrative turn, Conway's behavior may be unheroic, but it is neither treacherous nor "smug." To avow his role in what we imagine is the critical—but what is actually in the story, and for legal purposes, a quite different—sexual scene would offer Conway no guarantee that the police would release Arthur, or, indeed, that Conway would not face similar or greater public humiliation. Adams is surely correct to allude to the wider ramifications of class and self-interest, however, and this rebounds on Forster's statement about *Maurice*'s "happy . . . imperative" and the Terminal Note's concluding remarks:

We [Edward Carpenter and Forster] had not realized that what the public really loathes in homosexuality is not the thing itself but having to think about it. . . . Unfortunately [homosexuality] can only be legalized by Parliament and Members of Parliament are obliged to think or to appear to think. Consequently the Wolfenden recommendation will be indefinitely rejected, police prosecutions will continue and Clive on the bench will continue to sentence Alec in the dock. Maurice may get off. (M 240–41)

The note is dated "September 1960" (the British government partly decriminalized male homosexuality in 1967). Following this prophecy's realization in "Arthur Snatchfold," we could reframe the scenario as "Donaldson on the bench will continue to sentence Arthur in the dock. Conway may get off." Stephen Adams implies that Conway on the bench would try Arthur in the dock. While this suggestion is substantively incorrect, I think there are still grounds for suspecting elements of treachery in Forster's work; let me explain why.

Forster's Terminal Note implies that "Arthur Snatchfold" is the realistic conclusion to Maurice's sexual idealism. All the same, we cannot elide Forster's concern in this novel to show Alec Scudder blackmailing Maurice in the British Museum: "You've had your fun and you've got to pay up" (M 207). Whatever fantasy this conveys about the implied treachery or opportunism of working-class lovers, we can ignore neither the historical frequency of this scenario[13] nor, more pressing for us here, the attempt's internal impact on Forster's accounts of love and friendship. The attempted blackmail belies Forster's subsequent wish to ignore internal obstacles to homosexual love; hence the "happy . . . imperative" conflicts with the general tenor of the Terminal Note.

We cannot resolve this dilemma by invoking competing economic and social interests; these factors explain only one side of the story. The other side is best grasped by Forster's admission that the public's homosexual "loath[ing]" concerns less the act of sex than the thought of it— its perception by others and their ensuing fascination or disgust. Again, it would be tempting to accept Forster's word here and believe that the problem is someone else's: the Other's, the homophobe's, et cetera. But as Steiner and Meyers observe, Forster represents sex as a profound hermeneutic and psychic difficulty.[14] Steiner argues: "[Forster] had found no sensuous enactment adequate to his vision of sex. Gesture recedes in a cloying mist" (166). He continues: "In the light of an intensely spiritualized yet nervous and partly embittered homosexuality, a number of Forster's most famous dicta—it is better to betray one's country than a friend, 'only connect'—take on a more restricted, shriller ambiance" (169).

In ways that corroborate Steiner's reading, Forster avowed to Siegfried Sassoon in 1920: "Nothing is more obdurate to artistic treatment than the carnal" (SL 1:316). This statement partly clarifies the subtle enigmas of "Arthur Snatchfold" and "The Menace to Freedom," yet it also powerfully conflicts with Forster's haunting rhetorical question in "The Beauty of Life" (1911): "Why don't we trust ourselves more and the conventions less . . . ?" (AE 173). The conceptual tension between his declaration to

Sassoon and his earlier rhetorical question informs Forster's story, "What Does It Matter? A Morality," which appears toward the end of the *Life to Come* collection. This story brings to the fore a number of volatile issues concerning sexual and social harmony. As we shall see, Forster's hope of integrating sexual conflict into fraternal happiness proves elusive and impossible, although in the process the story raises a fascinating question about sublimation's relation to utopia.

"What Does It Matter?" is a Forsterian "morality" to the extent that it rejects conventional religious and political assumptions that homosexuality is a crime, pathology, or evil; the story imagines with humor and intelligence a political scenario in which homosexuality—and, indeed, all sexual relations—bear no stigma. Dr. Bonifaz Schpiltz is president of Pottibakia, an imaginary republic that resembles the Balkans or Eastern Europe (the narrator tells us that Pottibakia's "capital city could easily be mistaken for Bucharest or Warsaw, and often was" [LTC 130]). President Schpiltz is married, but he's sexually involved with Mme. Sonia Rodoconduco. Count Waghaghren (Pottibakia "retained her aristocracy" [LTC 130]) is the President's rival, and seeks to depose him, being "perhaps . . . a royalist, perhaps a traitor or patriot, . . . It is hopeless to inquire" (LTC 131). The Count aims to exploit dissension between the President and his wife by precipitating a political scandal over the President's mistress; the plot backfires because Mme. Schpiltz is too urbane or indifferent to mind her husband's sexual affair: "She watched the lovers without animosity and without amusement, occasionally showing concern when they struck one another but not caring to intervene" (LTC 131).

Rueful of his failure, the Count later discovers that the President winked at a handsome gendarme on duty at his quarters, so the Count contrives to arrange a homosexual scandal. The narrator carefully emphasizes, however, that all of this is "based on a misconception. It is true that the President had winked as he drove away, but only because some dust blew in his eye. His thoughts were with the ladies at their *goûter,* not of gendarmes at all" (LTC 132). Thus the planned scandal does not easily materialize, for the President is basically oblivious to all of his male guards, who now wink at him regularly on the Count's orders. The narrator corroborates: "We do not see what we do not seek . . ." (LTC 132).

Mme. Schpiltz detects this unusual mannerism in all the guards and points it out to her husband. But while the "roguish smile" on many of the guards' faces (LTC 133) secretly amuses the President, he is sexually uninterested: "I am a man, aha, no danger in that quarter *for me!*" (LTC 133; original emphasis). When strolling alone in a public park, however, the President "suddenly encountered an incredibly good-looking mounted gendarme, and before he could stop himself had winked back" (LTC 133).

Unable to find privacy in the park, the two men reluctantly forego having sex there. Soon after, the President resumes his affair with Mme. Rodoconduco. On his way to one tryst with her, however, he again meets Mirko Bolnovitch, the gendarme from the park, whom we are told is "a model of Pottibakian manhood" (LTC 135). Captivated by the man's beauty, the President agrees that Mirko should join him in Mme. Rodoconduco's bathing room, knowing that his mistress is not there:

The science of the barrackroom, the passions of the stables, the primitive instincts of the peasantry, the accident of the parallel bars [the bathing room is also a gymnasium, and Mirko a gymnast] and Dr. Schpiltz's quaint physique— all combined into something quite out of the way, and as it did so the door opened and Mme. Rodoconduco came into room, followed by the Bessarabian Minister.

"We have here . . ." she was saying. Neither of them heard her.

"We have here . . . we have . . ." (LTC 137)

The news breaks and a political scandal ensues, but Mme. Rodoconduco "remain[s] in a sort of frenzied equilibrium" (LTC 138). The Count turns out to have been instrumental in getting the President and Mirko together, but when the President asks Mirko of his role in the scandal, the latter remains "half a-dreaming, drowsy with delight. He had carried out the instructions of his superior officer, gratified a nice old gentleman and had a lovely time himself" (LTC 139). By partially rewriting Forster's axiom of national betrayal, Mirko (like Scudder) considers betraying his *lover* for his country before alighting on an altogether different ruse. He asks: "What does it matter?" (LTC 139). This rhetorical question provides Forster's narrator with an apparent solution to such comparable dilemmas in *Maurice* and "Arthur Snatchfold," yet other questions of loyalty and sexual intimacy remain. Stone's remarks about Forster's conception of love are useful to recall: "Forster's favorite medium for connection is *love*. No word in his work gets higher marks—unless it is 'art'—than love. Democracy gets only two cheers, but 'Love the Beloved Republic' gets three" ("Overleaping" 397).

Perhaps conscious of his self-contradiction (Mirko's betrayal clearly undermines the trust informing Forster's vision of love), Forster emphasizes that Mirko's behavior is ingenuous because it is commensurate with his background's sexual honesty: "I am a peasant, and we peasants never think a little fun matters. You [Mme. Rodoconduco] and His Excellency and the head of the police know better, but we peasants have a proverb: 'Poking doesn't count'" (LTC 140). When it turns out that the Count secretly installed a microphone and taped the encounter, Mirko pushes aside that he was acting on orders by insisting: "Still, what does it matter? It was fun. Oh, some things matter, of course, the crops, and the vintage matter very much, and our glorious Army, Navy and Air Force, and fighting for our friends, and baiting the Jews, but isn't that all?" (LTC 141). Following Mirko's rather frivolous question, we are quietly invited to forget that he betrayed his lover and precipitated a national scandal. Such an outcome puts in context Sir Richard Conway's comparable question in "Arthur Snatchfold": "What can it matter to anyone else if you and I don't mind?" (LTC 104). Besides the "fun" of serving "our glorious Army, Navy and Air Force . . . and baiting the Jews," the pleasures of sex in "What Does It Matter?" apparently compensate for the President's lost respect and subsequent humiliation. As the narrator quickly reminds us, however, the President is *not* entirely humiliated, because everyone soon learns to laugh at their folly and prejudice.

This reading partially downplays the story's valuable comedy; there is clearly a dimension in which the affair does not—and should not—matter. With considerable humor, Forster wants us to imagine legal and social indifference to homosexuality, and he seems to draw our attention to other factors such as anti-Semitism and ethnic warfare, in order to parody them. But when does social indifference to homosexuality become a generic indifference to *sexuality?* Later pronouncements about the President's renewed career also ring hollow after Forster's concern to avoid the "humiliation" of publishing *Maurice.* Such concern may tend to outweigh the relative literary victory of Forster's and others' defense of D. H. Lawrence's *Lady Chatterley's Lover* in 1960 and Forster's serving, with T. S. Eliot, as literary representative on the 1958 Select Committee on Obscene Publications (formalized as an Act of Parliament one year later [see Page]). For important political reasons, Forster spent a good deal of time urging us to believe that such issues *do* matter to the public—that sexual honesty carries a price, however heinous or unjustified, *and that this price exceeds political ignorance and superficial bigotry.* Forster implies that the price inheres in every sexual dynamic as an inevitable accompaniment to what is tempting and seductive about physical intimacy.

This price overrides distinctions between realpolitik and Forster's virtual world, making it impossible for us to suspend disbelief and imagine a country with no sexual intolerance. For how do we square Mirko's betrayal with the narrator's quiet insistence that Pottibakia has not yet learned its lesson? (Apparently, Mirko's repeated question "was soon to rend the nation asunder" [LTC 142].) In attempting to avert a scandal and because "it's essential to a stable society" (LTC 143), the President and his lovers issue a public statement:

Fellow Citizens! Since all of you are interested in the private lives of the great, we desire to inform you that we have all three of us had carnal intercourse with the President of the Republic, and are hoping to repeat it.
Charlotte Schpiltz (housewife)
Sonia Rodoconduco (artiste)
Mirko Bolnovitch (gendarme)
(LTC 143)

This is obviously amusing, but what is the precise referent for "it" in the statement "It's essential to a stable society"? Considering the ensuing scandal, which culminates in Pottibakia's (somewhat fantastic) diplomatic isolation from the rest of the world for failing to condemn the President's sexual infraction (LTC 144), we might conclude that by "it" the President is referring to sexual honesty. Yet we alight on a paradox here: Although such "honesty" eventually works in Pottibakia (the President's declaration of his various passions is so remarkable that no one wishes to succeed him), the Pottibakians' initial response is as predictable as the outside world's: "The Chamber of Deputies kept a stiffer upper lip, and there were cries of 'Flogging's too good!' and faint counter-cries of 'Flog me!' No one dared to take office, owing to the President's unmeasured eulogy of the police, and he continued to govern as dictator until the outbreak of the civil war" (LTC 144).

The paradox is that sexual honesty initially does *not* appear as "the only way" or, indeed, as "essential to a stable society" (LTC 143). On the contrary, the narrator admits that Mirko's disclosure "was soon to render the nation asunder" (LTC 142). Were the Count neither envious of the President's power nor sexually voyeuristic, Forster's narrative developments might lead us to consider that *hypocrisy* is in fact "essential to a stable society." This reading would confirm Freud's argument in *Civilization and Its Discontents* (1930) and elsewhere that society is contingent on its subjects' partial renunciation of sexual pleasure. Freud writes: "It is impossible to overlook the extent to which civilization is built up upon a renunciation of instinct, how much it presupposes precisely the non-satisfaction . . . of powerful instincts" (Freud, *Standard* 21:97). Maurice Hall faces this quandary when he ruminates on his "lustful . . . yearning" for Alec Scudder: "He called it lustful, a word easily uttered, and opposed to it his work, his family, his friends, his position in society. In that coalition must surely be included his will. *For if the will can overleap class, civilization as we have made it will go to pieces.* But his body would not be convinced. Chance had mated it too perfectly" (M 191; my emphasis).

When read alongside plot complications in "What Does It Matter?," this passage from *Maurice* highlights Forster's profound difficulty in accepting the strength and radicalism of "will" (sexual and otherwise): "Will" generates sexual pleasure and intellectual excitement; it also destroys civilization and "render[s] . . . nation[s] asunder" by combining communal distress with ontological unpleasure. An entry in Forster's *Commonplace Book* confirms this dilemma: "Until we are tamed we cannot be civilised, and as soon as we are civilised we revolt from civilisation" (CB 50).[15] In this respect, it should not surprise us that a character in Forster's story "The Point of It" realizes, when ruminating on his life's "elusive joy," "It was part of the jest that he should . . . eternally oscillate between disgust and desire" (CT 219–20).

Given this paradox about sexual instability, "What Does It Matter?" produces a conceptual twist of which I do not think Forster is fully aware. Certainly, his narrator gives us a shrewd reading of the effects of sexual intolerance. After the President makes his speech, for instance, various government officials empathize so entirely (or fear such widespread reprisals) that they confess all of their sexual indiscretions in an abreactive—or preemptive—gesture: "The scenes at the conclusion of [the President's] speech were indescribable, particularly in the Senate, where old men got up and poured out their confessions for hours, and could not be stopped" (LTC 144). These scenes portray a joyous unburdening and freedom that render Pottibakia threatening—and attractive—to its neighbors. As the narrator archly remarks, Pottibakia is soon isolated from the rest of the world because its "surrounding powers . . . hold—and perhaps rightly—that the country has become so infectious that if it were annexed it would merely get larger" (LTC 144).

Despite these claims of sexual freedom, we cannot overlook that the President "continued to govern [after his speech] as dictator until the outbreak of the civil war" (LTC 144). This suggests, quite interestingly, that the Pottibakians may have been sexually content while lacking political democracy. The next sentence corroborates: "He [the President] is now dictator again" (LTC 144). This suggests that "the civil war," which the narrator barely mentions, fails as a *social* revolution, although it apparently succeeds in making the Pottibakians happy. In this respect,

Forster's story details a persistent—perhaps even prerequisite—gap between sexual happiness and social harmony that reminds us of his related dilemmas in "The Menace to Freedom."

Although Forster tries to integrate sexuality into social life without prejudice, hypocrisy, or phobia, his story concludes with a bizarre picture of Pottibakians as socially content under a politically benign "dictatorship" and sexually happy because their desire is no longer repressed *or* expressed. Allegedly, their desire is so perspicuous, it is annulled of all social difficulty—which is to say, it is magnificently "sublimated" so that no one in Pottibakia seems to want or have sex anymore. This outcome is obviously contentious, but it is interesting for detailing both a blind spot in Forster's liberalism and a failure in the scope of related sexual utopias that try to excise pleasure—or *jouissance,* which is beyond pleasure—from society in the interests of class harmony and cultural equanimity. These sexual utopias reproduce the dictates of the ego as the agent most hostile to difference and desire (see Bersani, *Freudian* 93; Dean 126; and Biddy Martin).

Following Forster's stubborn ambivalence about sexual desire at moments of its apparent emancipation, the outcome of "What Does It Matter?" is not surprising. Forster's vision of sexual liberation may appear emancipatory, but it is actually closer to what the philosopher Herbert Marcuse called "repressive tolerance" (ix). Indeed, to the disbelief and perhaps horror of many Forster scholars, we could read Mirko's titular question as a complacent remark about Forster's difficult relation to unconscious prejudice and hostility. I base this polemical claim on such extraordinary moments in Forster's autobiographical writing as "Kanaya" (c. 1922), in which he describes how he had violent sex with an Indian boy: "[The] sexual intercourse . . . was . . . mixed with a desire to inflict pain. It didn't hurt him to speak of, but it was bad for me, and new in me, my temperament not being that way. . . . I wasn't trying to punish him—I knew his silly little soul was incurable. I just felt that he was a slave, without rights, and I a despot whom no one could call to account" (HD 324).

In this fragment, Forster expresses genuine surprise at finding power over another sexually arousing. By invoking this incident, I do not wish simply to indict Forster for racial intolerance. Forster admitted, for instance, that the incident did not recur. Such opprobrious readings are anyway of limited value: By distancing Forster's readers from ambivalent involvement, they leave the text "tarnished" and the critic magically exonerated of racism. Rather, "Kanaya" displays a conceptual and substantive gap between Forster's vision of "acceptable" and "unacceptable" politics. Against Forster's implicit claim that Mirko's question, "What does it matter?," gives us a lasting sexual morality, I therefore propose that Forster's "gap" is actually a stronger ethical guide. It reminds us that prejudice can surface in the most unexpected and politically embarrassing moments; that issues concerning psychic enjoyment do not sit easily with mandates for sexual and political tolerance.

To support these claims about Forster and the unconscious, let me cite the story's penultimate paragraph, which captures several conceptual shifts in Forster's argument; it also reminds us of the history of East Germany and the splitting of Berlin:

He [President Schpiltz] is now dictator again, but since all the states, led by Bessarabia, have broken off diplomatic relations it is extremely difficult to get Pottibakian news. Visas are refused, and the international express traverses the territory behind frosted glass. Now and then a postcard of the Bolnovitch Monument falls out of an aeroplane, but unlike most patriotic people the Pottibakians appear to be self-contained. They till the earth and have become artistic, and are said to have developed a fine literature *which deals very little with sex.* This is puzzling, as is the indissolubility of marriage—a measure for which the Church has vainly striven elsewhere. Gratified by her triumph, she is now heart and soul with the nation, and the Archimandrite of Praz has reinterpreted certain passages of scripture, or has pronounced them corrupt. Much here is obscure, links in the argument have been denied to us, nor, since we cannot have access to the novels of Alekko, can we trace *the steps by which natural impulses were converted into national assets.* There seem, however, to have been three stages: first the Pottibakians were ashamed of doing what they liked, then they were aggressive over it, and now they do as they like. There I must leave them. (LTC 144; my emphases)

The story's final paragraph details the fate of the hypocritical Count, who is not banished (as most initially desire) but left to repeat what he has done. In this way, the Pottibakians amuse themselves by recalling their repressive history: "On public holidays his private cabinet (now his cell) is thrown open, and is visited by an endless queue of smiling Pottibakians, who try to imagine the old days when that sort of thing mattered, and emerge laughing" (LTC 145).

In our present times of increasing sexual repression, it is tempting to accept Forster's morality and identify with the Pottibakians, as if we could smile with similar relief on the demise of homophobia and related forms of sexual antipathy. Yet much is questionable about Forster's myth of sexual integration. The Pottibakians have become such adept, compliant citizens that all or most of their "natural impulses [have been] converted into national assets" (LTC 144). In other words—and Forster's narrator puts this in extremely illiberal terms—they have rescinded not only privacy but also sexual pleasure by offering up both as "national assets." The narrator also suggests that Pottibakia's "self-contain[ment]" derives from its uninterest in empires; by corollary, Forster usefully critiques the myth that empires were built on sublimated desire, arguing instead that sexual conflict and distress informed nineteenth-century imperialism. But what of Pottibakian literature? Forster's narrator suggests that creativity requires a measure of sexual discomfort (see also CB 47–48). If Pottibakian literature "deals very little with sex," it is ostensibly because their interpersonal and intrapsychic conflicts have dissolved and they have displaced their passion outward or upward in a magnificent display of esprit de corps.

Given this story's unfortunate aim to foreclose on desire at the precise moment of its apparent social integration, where would we locate pleasure or *jouissance* in this text? The answer, I think, lies in the final paragraph, when the Pottibakians laugh at the Count for his folly. In the suggestion that they line up "smiling" to see him, Forster's narrator tempers the magnitude of this *jouissance* by making it part of a ritual; but why, otherwise, would the Pottibakians concern themselves with this act? And why would it focus on one object that serves as their mirth's *cause?* The point is surely that this annual ritual functions—like related forms of commemoration on public holidays—to remind us of what cannot pass, of what we have not processed, and of what we cannot, or must not, forget.

Thus far, I have written only on betrayal's recurrence in Forster's stories—whether in interpersonal, group, or social forms—and on this phenomenon's inconsistency with Forster's belief in "connection." I want also briefly to consider how betrayal *consoles.* My reading of "What Does It Matter?" gives some indication of what is consoling for Forster (and, allegedly, for the Pottibakians) in such fantasies of controlled sexual pleasure, malice, and mirth. To engage this phenomenon more fully, however, we must resist reading Forster's stories at a level of conscious understanding and narrative enunciation; the satisfaction of betrayal emerges when we address an economy of unconscious pleasure of which Forster was aware but not entirely at ease.

As I earlier described, this economy surfaces in "The Menace to Freedom"; it also returns in a brief fragment that Forster wrote in 1939 on "Jew-Consciousness," which I discuss more fully elsewhere (see my "Psychoanalysis"). In this second fragment, Forster speaks of Londoners "sniggering" at Jewish misfortune when discussing pogroms. Forster

admits that this response is shocking, but he argues that we must acknowledge our "enjoy[ment in others'] misfortunes" (TCD 13). What
makes these essays even more distressing, though, is Forster's understanding of mass hatred and genocide only as instances of personal "silli-
ness"—that is, as setbacks to an otherwise ongoing interpersonal dynamic (TCD 14). According to Forster, we can "stop . . . [prejudice only
by] . . . cool reasonableness" and periodic acts of bravery (TCD 14).
Such phenomena as mass hatred and genocide spiral beyond Forster's
comprehension, leaving him without understanding, and his reader
amazed—given the overwhelming historical evidence to the contrary—
at Forster's naive faith in humanity's concern for individual well-being.

Despite Forster's effort to mitigate these political crises, we can see
their interpersonal constituents recur in such stories as "Arthur Snatchfold," "The Life to Come," and "The Other Boat," allegories about a
wider default in human relations. This explains why Stephen Adams
finds Sir Richard Conway reprehensible in "Arthur Snatchfold," but to
read the story only in this way is to misrecognize a drama about sexual
interest and nonreciprocity that Forster inadvertently—but I think in-
valuably—represents in his writing. Stories such as "The Obelisk" seem
to integrate homosexuality into their protagonists' consciousness, but
these stories nonetheless reveal other fault lines in human contact and
understanding. Despite the humor of "The Obelisk," for instance, in
which two sailors separately seduce a bored husband and wife (Ernest
and Hilda), who later infer each other's passions through instructive
lapses of knowledge, the story is a cynical account of marriage and heterosexual relations. Such readings are obviously useful in themselves,
but related issues about the terms, endurance, or fiction of this marriage
never surface in Forster's text. In his concern to emphasize that Hilda's
sexual pleasure with her sailor equals Ernest's pleasure with his, Forster
elides the type of complicated scenario that David Leavitt, for one, finely
elaborated in *The Lost Language of Cranes* concerning a gay son and his
closeted gay father.

"The Obelisk" downplays provocative suggestions of marital betrayal:
Its stress on the "consolation" of sexual pleasure offsets any difficulty
about infidelity, guilt, or sexual interest in anyone other than one's
spouse. This is not the case in "Arthur Snatchfold," "The Life to Come,"
and "The Other Boat," whose respective accounts of sexuality precipitate
a difficulty about human relationships that Forster cannot resolve by
praising sexual pleasure. These stories bind enjoyment to attempts at
divesting others of pleasure and, in the case of these last two stories, of
life. They represent an economy of pleasure whose source and intensity

is contingent on what one subject can deny another. This dynamic jeopardizes Forster's already awkward project of combining sexual enjoyment with interpersonal harmony. We have seen, for instance, that sexual enjoyment derives for Forster largely from the material *disharmony* of two (or more) lovers. Those aspects of enjoyment's "theft" that we glimpse from the Count in "What Does It Matter?," the concluding remarks of "Arthur Snatchfold," and the blackmail scene in *Maurice* add to this disharmony, rendering such "theft" a precondition for sexual happiness. This takes Forster perilously close to the scenes of racism and anti-Semitism that he denounced in *Two Cheers for Democracy;* it also turns his idea of betraying one's country for a friend into an unlikely, even impossible, proposition. Given these psychic determinants, it is no wonder that Forster's accounts of friendship support an improbable idealism. His stories buckle under the pressure, making his characters more complex and selfish than I think he initially envisaged.

By emphasizing the difficult undercurrents of "Arthur Snatchfold" and "What Does It Matter?," I have tried to clarify why unconscious hostility and aversion inform Forster's narratives of sexual desire. I have no doubt that Forster understood Freudian conceptions of the unconscious. In "What I Believe" and "Anonymity: An Enquiry" (1925), for instance, he addressed the consequences of a split and shattered conception of the mind;[16] in "Inspiration" (1912), he also argued that in the act of writing, "a queer catastrophe happens inside [the writer]. The mind, as it were, turns turtle, sometimes with rapidity, and a hidden part of it comes to the top and controls the pen" (AE 118–19).

Unlike Levine's, Adams's, Meyers's, and Herz's readings of *The Life to Come* collection, I have tried to explore the ramifications of this "queer catastrophe" for homosexual desire. In the final paragraphs of "What Does It Matter?," for instance, Forster redefines community, sublimation, and the relations between art and sexuality, only to conclude that sexual desire has no manifest role to play in his social utopias. Put this way, Forster demonstrates that certain utopias by definition foreclose on sexual desire to advance their vision of social equanimity. This conclusion may be politically unfortunate and conceptually embarrassing, particularly after recalling Forster's desire to represent homosexuality in this story without prejudice, but it culminates in neither a "vision of eternal love" nor a trope of "romantic . . . triumph." If anything, and despite their contrary conception, Forster's stories attribute a nonredemptive dimension to human sexuality and social interaction, in which desire gleefully emerges from the manifest failure of ordinary connection.[17] This disparity between Forster's political and fictional ideals is surely the "queerest" aspect of his work and thought, where "queer" is a dimension of unconscious fantasy rather than a politics or performance of the ego. We would do well to remember this disparity when next we feel inclined to rhapsodize on Forster's art of connection. Indeed, Forster gives us ample warning of this dilemma in his *Commonplace Book:* "In a world where so little is known, how shouldn't we, how should we happen to be friends?" (CB 46).

Notes

I am grateful to Kevin Kopelson, Judith Scherer Herz, and Jason Friedman for invaluable comments on an earlier draft.

1. I must stress this curious about-turn in Levine's otherwise valuable analysis of Forster's short stories. Until the final pages of her article, Levine appears as skeptical of Forster's accounts of sexual equality and "lust" as is Wilfred Stone (see his "Overleaping Class," especially 392–93). Toward the end of her article, however, as I show below, Levine curiously transforms Forster's narrative difficulties with love and "lust" into a redemptive anticipation of interpersonal harmony.

2. Stone is citing the narrator's rueful acknowledgment in Forster's *Maurice*. See also Alan Wilde, "Desire" 114–29.

3. "We know Forster *is* Maurice, at least as a sexual being" (original emphasis). As a consequence of this reading, Stone represents *Maurice* and *The Life to Come* collection as a "program of self-discovery" (Stone, "Overleaping" 389). Considering this assumption, we should recall D. H. Lawrence's interesting observation on Forster: "He tries to dodge himself—the sight is painful. . . . He knows that *self-realisation is not his ultimate desire*" (Lawrence 2:283; my emphasis).

4. Forster's strategy differs from Edward Carpenter's argument that homosexuality in literature and life should be "no exception . . . to the law that sensuality apart from love is degrading and something less than human" (Carpenter, "Homogenic" 340). Given Forster's attempt to resolve Carpenter's decree, questions emerge about the price of this exception and the possibility that Forster's ensuing desire is "something less than human." By engaging these questions, my essay considers this conceptual gap between "love" and "sensuality."

5. For elaboration, see Bersani, *Freudian* 38, and Silverman 200. See also Forster's 1929 entry to the *Commonplace Book,* "Kindness and the Rules of the Game," in which he presents an exchange between "Civis" and "Savage" (CB 50).

6. My focus on the "eroticism of betrayal" owes much to Bersani's superb account of this phenomenon in Jean Genet's writing (see Bersani, *Homos,* especially 151: "*Betrayal is an ethical necessity.*" Considering Forster's avowed ambivalence to representing sexuality in his novels, and that he wrote much of *The Life*

to Come collection while completing *A Passage to India* (1924), these claims invoke Forster's complex publication history. For elaboration, see my "Volatile" 190–192.

7. For an account of Forster's racism, see my "Psychoanalysis." For confirmation of this point about malice, however, consider Forster's admission in his *Commonplace Book*: "Resentment is a plant of tortuous growth. Middleton Murry patronises and attacks my work, and at first I seem uninfected by this contact with him, and see clearly enough that he is lamenting not my troubles but his own. And I think that my feelings remain friendly towards him, and that I pity him. But the pity is not genuine, and, having led me to take unusual interest in Middleton Murry, it evaporates. I now discover that my unusual interest has a hostile tinge, and my heart beats quicker in the hope of him making a mistake, and *I enjoy hearing his enemies speak against him, and am even happier when he loses another of his former friends*. But for appearing petty, I would patronise and attack him" (CB 1–2; my emphasis).

8. See Ernest Jones's "War and Individual Psychology" (1915) and "War and Sublimation" (1915) in Jones. I interpret Jones's argument at greater length in my "Thoughts."

9. In addition to the above references to Forster and Jones, see Sigmund Freud, "Thoughts for the Times on War and Death" (1915) (*Standard* 14:273–302); Freud (with Albert Einstein), "Why War?" (1933 [1932]) (*Standard* 22: 195–212); and *Civilization and Its Discontents* (1930 [1929]) (*Standard* 21:59–145).

10. See my "Volatile" 205, where I advance the argument that both "The Life to Come" and "The Other Boat" represent the ego as a white man and the unconscious as a black man.

11. Although published in 1957, the *Wolfenden Report*'s recommendation that Britain's Parliament partly decriminalize homosexual sex between men was not enacted until 1967. In 1967, Parliament established the age of consent for male homosexual sex at 21 for England and Wales (heterosexual sex and, implicitly, lesbian sex remained unchanged at 16). Despite fierce resistance, Parliament voted on 21 February 1994, to lower the age of consent for male homosexual sex to 18 (the vote was 427–162). For elaboration on *Wolfenden,* see Frank Mort and Jeffrey Weeks.

12. Forster's reference to "a lad dangling from a noose" seems to invoke A. E. Housman's account in *A Shropshire Lad* (1896), "The Immortal Part," XLIV, of a man's suicide because of his homosexuality. Although ironic, Housman's reference to "the household traitor" has valuable bearing on my paper and his account is worth quoting at length:

> Shot? so quick, so clean an ending?
>   Oh that was right, lad, that was brave:
> Yours was not an ill for mending,
>   'Twas best to take it to the grave.

Oh you had the forethought, you could reason,
  And saw your road and where it led,
And early wise and brave in season
  Put the pistol to your head.
Oh soon, and better so than later
  After long disgrace and scorn,
You shot dead the household traitor,
  The soul that should not have been born.
(Housman 66)

13. Regarding this scenario's historical frequency: Henry Labouchère's amendment to Britain's 1885 Criminal Law Act was commonly known as the "Blackmailer's Charter" (Weeks 14, 22). This amendment criminalized all male homosexual acts, whether public or private.

14. Here I refer to Forster's fictional and nonfictional accounts of sex. For an example of the latter, see his "Kanaya" (c. 1922), HD 324, which I discuss below. See also my "Volatile Desire" 207–8.

15. Compare this with Forster's 1927 entry in the same text: "Sketch for a character: a highly civilised man who has deep emotions but has prepared no one to respect them when they come out. Consequently he is reduced to casual lust where he is satisfied and happy until his civilisation has an elevating and redeeming influences [sic] upon his bedfellows. The 'better' he makes people the lonelier he feels. He need not be unattractive physically" (CB 24). See also the entry for 1925: "Isolation is the sum total of wretchedness to man" (CB 1).

16. See Forster, "Anonymity: An Enquiry" (1925): "Each human mind has two personalities, one on the surface, one deeper down. . . . The lower personality is a very queer affair. In many ways it is a perfect fool, but without it there is no literature, because unless a man dips a bucket down into it occasionally he cannot produce first-class work" (TCD 83).

17. Bersani and Ulysse Dutoit finely elaborate this argument in their Introduction to *Arts of Impoverishment*.

10

"Contrary to the Prevailing Current"?
Homoeroticism and the Voice of
Maternal Law in "The Other Boat"

Tamera Dorland

In his posthumously published "The Other Boat" (1972), E. M. Forster seeks to transform proscribed desire into a "confession of the
flesh."[1] Captain Lionel March's "stumbling confession" and "open
avowal" of having " 'fallen for' " his bunkmate Cocoanut (LTC 186–
87) attests to Foucault's rather poetic claim in "A Preface to Transgression" that sexuality exposes "the limit of language, since it traces that
line of foam showing just how far speech may advance upon the
sands of silence" (*Language* 30). Liminally caught between speech and
silence, confession and suppression, the narrative disclosure of Lionel
March's "tribal" transgressions against Victorian puritanism and British imperialism adheres to "the authority of a language that had been
carefully expurgated so that [sex] was no longer directly named" but
was relentlessly "tracked down" (Foucault, *History* 20). In spite of its
post-Victorian context, a rhetoric of indirection and discretion still
inscribes the narrative's scenes of illicit homoerotic intercourse between the quintessential British officer and a "wog" (LTC 175). In
effect, this discrepancy between literary form and pornographic content constitutes an "open avowal" that belies its own openness.

In his critique of Forster's typescript of *Maurice* in *Christopher and
His Kind*, Christopher Isherwood notes in 1932 that his "Master's"

prudish or "antique locutions bothered him, here and there," while he concedes that "the wonder of the novel was that it had been written when it had been written; the wonder was Forster himself, imprisoned within the jungle of prewar prejudice, putting these unthinkable thoughts into words" (126). More than four decades after having completed the original draft of *Maurice* in 1913,[2] Forster appears "imprisoned" by continued prejudice and postwar proscriptions against homosexuality. In "The Other Boat," principally composed during 1957 and 1958, the author still betrays a reluctance to let go of "antique locutions" that expurgate the language but not the contents of the carnal narrative. Fashioned by conventions of euphemism and circumlocution, narrative descriptions of the Captain's acts of sodomy and eventual homicide ironically seem to "date" themselves, despite the author's "franker declaration" of his "faith" (Isherwood 126).[3] In the successive scenes of the lovers' illicit intercourse "below deck," the narrator on the one hand counts on concrete referents that obliquely expose yet mock the squeamish enterprise of finding figurative substitutes for depictions of sexual excitement, as in the following image suggesting intercourse: "Pop went a cork and hit the partition wall. Sounds of feminine protest became audible, and they [Lionel and Cocoanut] both laughed" (LTC 178). On the other hand, the narrator purges the erotic plot of concrete reference and clear personal agency by embedding descriptions of physical orgasm and coitus in mystic abstractions. For instance, the narrative reads, presumably from Cocoanut's perspective: "Meanwhile the other one, the deep one, watched. To him the moment of ecstasy was sometimes the moment of vision, and his cry of delight when they closed had wavered into fear" (LTC 178). Marked thus by shifts in tone and focalization, Forster's narrative vacillates between identifying the various stages of homosexual intercourse and providing a screen for its pornographic content through a stylistics of evasion. Such subterfuge in turn mirrors the secrecy Lionel himself must vigilantly secure about his deviation from the normative ideal—from being "what any *rising* young officer ought to be" in the context of a threatened British imperialism (LTC 171; my emphasis). This subterfuge above all reflects the officer's wary concealment of his transgression from the British sahibs and memsahibs of the story proper.

The final writing of "The Other Boat" closely coincides with the compilation of *The Wolfenden Report of the Departmental Committee on Homosexual Offenses and Prostitution,* which was initiated in 1954 and published in 1957.[4] The fact that Parliament resisted the report's recommendations to decriminalize private acts of homosexuality historically underpins the stylistic subterfuge evident in the story and perhaps informs Forster's continued concealment of "a wrong channel for [his] pen" (LTC xii). In his biographical introduction to *The Life to Come,* Oliver Stallybrass offers an excerpt from Forster's diary, dated 8 April 1922, in which the author confesses that he has "this moment burnt [his] indecent writings" (LTC xii). Whether apocryphal or not, this confession refers to the bulk of his pornographic stories, yet excludes his novel *Maurice,* which nonetheless remained unpublished until 1971, a year after Forster's death. Characterizing these "indecent writings" as obstacles to his development as a recognized novelist, Forster refers to them as a channel for personal excitement rather than literary expression (LTC xii).[5]

Originally composed for a novel, the early pages of "The Other Boat" were drafted about 1913, during approximately the same period as Forster's initial completion of *Maurice* and his first incomplete start with *A Passage to India.* Clearly, these early pages were not among those burned writings, which, as Forster explains, included only "as many as the fire [would] take" (LTC xii). Presumably abandoned until 1948, the initial fragment of "The Other Boat" was published under the titles "Entrance to an Unwritten Novel" in *The Listener* (23 December 1948) and "Cocoanut & Co.: Entrance to an Abandoned Novel" in the *New York Times Book Review* (6 February 1949).[6] Providing the groundwork for the first section of the completed "Other Boat," both publications focus on the childhood encounter of Lionel and Cocoanut on the original or "other boat," but neither features their later homoerotic exchange as adults on the second boat. As the "abandoned" novel evolves into its final form as a story, "The Other Boat" acquires four additional sections that reconstruct the events precipitating Lionel's lapse from rigid British propriety into interracial and homosexual "abandon." While the novel-fragment provides the origins for the reunion of the British captain and the wog as adults, the ensuing four sections that which develop from this brief childhood interaction confirm retroactively the illicit sexuality that lies at and threatens the very surface of a colonial past—a past played out in the voices of "little boys" who don "paper cocked hats" and die "stiffly" as proud soldiers. Moreover, the voice of the abandoned mother, so important in the completed story, can also be heard as she attempts to keep such play within bounds of "what is customary" and proper (LTC 166).

With the "passage" of the Aryan officer and homosexual on board the *S. S. Normannia,*[7] Forster ultimately constructs a narrative that violates and in turn reveals the moral boundaries defined by an absent yet repressive England. Even when concealed from public readership until its posthumous publication in 1972, this five-sectioned story betrays the author's ambivalence toward breaking fully with the Edwardian voice of his published novels. I argue this in spite of James Creech's recent suggestion that Forster "overtly claimed" to try "to speak unprophylactically from, for, or about a homosexual subject position" (54). In *Closet Writing/Gay Reading,* Creech bases his assertion on Forster's contention that he wrote the earlier "indecent" stories of *The Life to Come* "not to express myself but to excite myself" (Creech 55; Forster, *LTC* xii). Using the author's testimony against aesthetic intent, Creech speculates: "to state the obvious, what would Forster's stories themselves have resembled if, in the writing itself, he had felt compelled to perform the prophylactic function which, as it turned out, fell to the homophobic intellectual?" (55). While the homosexual subject matter of "The Other Boat" signifies a resistance toward performing "the prophylactic function," I submit that Forster's stylistics of indirection and abstraction suggest otherwise. I propose, rather, that it is the mother, "Mater," or imperial memsahib who is posited as an agent of the son's conscience and Law; her ostensibly marginal yet critical position in all five sections of the story signals the figurative presence of a cautionary agency that still inhibits attempts to confess or "speak unprophylactically" in the "homosexual subject position." In effect, with the mother's presence as an indirect arbiter of imperialist and British propriety, Captain March's "open avowal" proves instead a "stumbling confession" that never loses sight of the heterosexual or "homophobic intellectual."

From an orthodox perspective on morality, the fatal resolution to the homoerotic plot of "The Other Boat" conforms to contemporaneous proscriptions against homosexuality. By contrast, Forster's *Maurice* unconventionally provides a "happy ending" of bucolic exile for its homosexual lovers. In its well known "Terminal Note" (1960), dated nearly a half-century after the novel's original completion in 1913 and a decade before its posthumous publication in 1971, the author characterizes this "keynote" of "happiness" as a virtual "crime." Despite societal demands for retribution, the lovers manage to evade punishment by way of a more permissive fiction that allows them "still [to] roam the greenwood" existing beyond the boundaries of the law and the printed text (M 250). The final form of "The Other Boat" offers the alternate ending that Forster rejects for *Maurice.* In his retrospective "Note" to that novel, he reflects on the unhappy finale that might have led to earlier publication: "If it ended unhappily, with a lad dangling from a noose or with a suicide pact, all would be well, for there is no pornography or seduction of minors" (M 250). Addressing the demands of the orthodox reader, Forster's story does conclude unhappily, with the murder of the seductive "wog" and the suicide of the transgressive officer. In spite of the discretion of its language, the story nonetheless works against these demands and violates a condition of publishability because of the pornographic content it implies.

In effect, "The Other Boat" bears the long-standing legacy of Victorian vigilance over sexual normalization, namely that of bourgeois heterosexuality. Its focus on Lionel's deviation documents Foucault's claim that homosexuality responded with a "reverse" discourse: "homosexuality began to speak in its own behalf, to demand that its legitimacy or 'naturality' be acknowledged, often in the same vocabulary, using the same categories by which it was medically disqualified" (*History* 101). The narrative confessions of Lionel's sexual transgression thus reflect the indirection, if not ambidirection, of the post-Freudian writer's attempt to write within yet against a heritage of sexual conduct paradoxically characterized by "an injunction to silence" and an "incitement to speak" the truth of sexuality (*History* 4, 18). The posthumous publication of "The Other Boat" (not to mention that of *Maurice* and the remaining stories of buggery in *The Life to Come*) testifies to Forster's own inability to transgress publicly the boundaries of a social conscience or repression signified by an England most notably represented by the maternal figure. Here, Forster's final censorship of any direct evidence of Lionel March's homosexual activities parallels the author's necessary suppression of these homoerotic texts from his record of conventional literary publications.

While Captain March's disclosure of homosexual transgression tests and exposes the limits of British codes of normative sexuality, it also reveals the extent to which the officer's conscience is held in check by the chaste and chastising mother. The maternal image of Mrs. March hence becomes both sign of and impetus for suppression. But it is through her son's guilt-ridden projection that she personifies both individual and British social conscience. Allotted a peripheral part in the actual plot, she nonetheless proves to be a potent phantasm of her transgressive son's tormented psyche, an image signifying both repressed desire and repressive prohibition. As the preoedipal and postoedipal single parent, Mrs. March is still identified only by her marital and maternal names; by virtue of her procreating in the name of the father, she secures a position in the symbolic order that formally locates her on the side of

the sociosymbolic community.[8] Absent from the social and family structure because of his own transgression of "tribal" codes of propriety, Lionel's father exists in name only since the patrilineal surname alone survives, the father's Christian name having been expunged from social
discourse because of his disgraceful abandonment of this community.
On board the *S. S. Normannia,* such community and "tribal" order are
chiefly held in check by an ad hoc group of British passengers who,
reports Lionel in his correspondence with his mother, "make up two
Bridge tables every night besides hanging together at other times, and
get called the Big Eight, which I suppose must be regarded as a compliment" (LTC 171).[9] Referring to the "Big Eight" as a gauge for social
propriety and an agency of exclusion, Lionel relates to Cocoanut how
his own name has been purged of his father's identity: "He has made
our name stink in these parts. As it is I've had to change my name, or
rather drop half of it. He called himself Major Corrie March. We were
all proud of the 'Corrie' and had reason to be. Try saying 'Corrie March'
to the Big Eight here, and watch the effect" (LTC 183–84).

Aboard the "other boat," Mrs. March must assume single-handedly
the central position as parent and sign of the sociosymbolic community.
Confronted with an endangered family order, she alone must preserve
a semblance of social harmony and structure, and uphold the law of
prohibition against so-called "pathological" sexualities. In this narrative
context, the name of the mother (or *nom de la mère,* if you will) comes
to signify conscience, the Law, or the Phallus.[10] This signification, however, is not based on a direct representation of the mother; rather, it
derives from the fatherless son's reconstruction of her as a "phallic
mother." Paraphrasing Lacan, Jane Gallop characterizes this conception
of the mother as "the silent interlocutor, the second person who never
assumes the first person pronoun, . . . the subject presumed to know,
the object of transference" (115). In the last four sections of "The Other
Boat," Mrs. March, as the phallicized mother, never directly assumes the
first-person subject position, in spite of her sociosymbolic position as
the central parent. (Only the childhood scene of the first section offers
an unmediated presentation of Mrs. March among her children; located
at the very beginning of the second section, Lionel's overseas correspondence to the "Mater" instantly signals the disappearance of her physical
presence from the narrative.[11]) Textually, she represents the "silent interlocutor" or "second person" that harrows the adult son's conscience, but
she does so with a voice projected only in terms of an indirect subjectivity focalized through either the son or the narrator. Invoking the figure
of the mother, this narrative of sexual transgression fabricates a dialogic

relation between son and mother that reflects the "Idea of Mother and Son" Forster explained in his 1930 entry in *Commonplace Book:*

She dominates him in youth. Manhood brings him emancipation—perhaps through friendship or a happy marriage. But the mother is waiting. Her vitality depends on character, and asserts itself as the sap drains out of him. She gets her way and reestablishes his childhood, with the difference that his subjection is conscious now and causes him humiliation and pain. Is her tyranny conscious? I think not. Could the same relationship occur between father and daughter? No. (CB 55)

Ultimately, the mother-son relationship proves to be as tyrannical between son and conscience as between self and culture, because the narrative of Lionel March reconstitutes the biological mother as an internalized voice of conscience. Although unconscious of "her tyranny," the "waiting" mother inhabits and inhibits "the great blank country" (LTC 193) of the son's textual "confession of the flesh" (Foucault, *History* 19). As disembodied voice and Paternal/Maternal sign of conscience, the marginalized mother of Freudian psychoanalytics symbolically delineates the limits of the discourse of sexual transgression. In this sense, the "confession of flesh" in Forster's text effectively fixes on the indivisible dyad of transgressive son and symbolic mother—of son and an inescapable Maternal Law reinforcing the limits of Victorian England, that censorial and far-reaching "blank country."

As the silent interlocutor, the figure of the mother in "The Other Boat" signifies an absolute arbiter of culture through whom the transgressive son condemns or harrows himself. In *Freud and the Crisis of Our Culture,* Lionel Trilling locates this dialogue or "standing quarrel" between the modern self and culture/mother within a broader literary context (58). Crediting "the layman Freud" with the notion that the self is implicated in the culture and "that the surrogates of culture are established in the mind itself," Trilling elaborates: "By what he said or suggested of the depth and subtlety of the influence of the family upon the individual, he made plain how the culture suffuses the remotest parts of the individual mind, being taken in almost literally with the mother's milk" (36–37). Trilling figuratively defines the lactating mother as the nurturing agent of cultural suffusion; he further characterizes the Freudian and post-Freudian self as one who ambivalently resists yet submits to culture as an absolute (or surrogate God) by which the self is constituted and judged (*Freud* 58). Forster's Lionel March, through his own narrative and psychical "standing quarrels," exposes the extent to which the "surrogates of culture" become irrevocably implanted in the "remotest parts of the individual mind," quite literally through the trope of the mother.

In a letter to Lionel Trilling, dated 1 August 1955, Forster cites Trilling's *Freud and the Crisis of Our Culture* (SL 2:259–60); and, in a subsequent letter to William Plomer, dated 12 December 1957, he describes his secondhand access to the literary Freud:

I had an interesting day's reading yesterday, with the sudden sensation of being in close contact with what I was reading. It doesn't often come to me. What I read is not important, but it radiated ("believe it or not") from Freud. Trilling[']s cluttered-up meditation on him switched me over to Auden's poem ["In Memory of Sigmund Freud"]. (SL 2:268)

Forster's reading of Trilling's and Auden's tributes to literary interpretations of Freud precedes his 1957–58 revision of "The Other Boat" by no more than a few years. The internal or "standing quarrel" that Lionel March undergoes with his mother, the omnipresent and absolute sign of culture, narratively illustrates Trilling's perspective on Freud and the "crisis" of culture; in this light, it seems plausible to trace Lionel March's name, not to mention literary paternity, to Lionel Trilling himself.

As a biographical parallel with the mother-son dialectic between Lionel and Mrs. March, Forster perceives his own mother as the source of his repression as a writer. In a letter dated 10 August 1915, the thirty-six-year-old author equates the presence of his mother (or his infantilized presence within her household) to a form of writer's block:

I am leading the life of a little girl so long as I am tied to home. It isn't even as if I make mother happy by stopping—she is always wanting me to be 5 years old again, so happiness is obviously impossible for her, and she never realises that the cardinal fact in my life is my writing, and that at present I am not writing. (SL 1:229)

In this instance, the maternal figure not only signifies an obstacle to the identity and development of the adult male (the "little girl" possibly suggesting a counterpart to Freud's "little man" in his discussion of the initial stages of female development), but also as an obstacle to those of the author. Biographically, this role links the topos of "the great blank country" with Lionel's repressed sexuality and with Forster's blank pages while living at home, for the mother's presence is targeted as a direct agent of the son's inhibition and self-censorship.

As testimony to Freud's influence, the narrative of "The Other Boat" posits Mrs. March as the center of Lionel's continual negotiations between a "long long ago" of colonial and sexual innocence and a fallen present marked by his turn away from those ideal codes of decorum that putatively held such innocence in check. Captain March's "stumbling confession" in effect manifests two conflicting desires. His first desire is to continue with his culture; therefore, he maintains a link with his mother through overseas correspondence and secures social ties with the British caste, the Big Eight, through participation in their nightly bridge games. Conversely, his second desire is to go against the sexual and racial codes of his imperialist caste—that is, it is a desire to "see England recede" not only from the horizon but from his psyche (LTC 175). In a figurative sense, the contrary directions of the two boats reflect the officer's contrary responses to being "stabled" with a "dago," a setup that is "too damn awkward for words" (LTC 174). In the story's first section, the original or "other boat" of a nostalgic past travels the Red Sea with its bow directed toward the motherland; in the last four sections, the S. S. Normannia journeys through the same waters, but in the opposite direction, with its stern turned on England. With either direction, the imperial motherland remains a geographical and, above all, cultural or moral referent of which the Aryan officer never loses clear sight. The opposing directions of the two boats toward and away from England, although separated by a ten-year gap, parallel Captain March's own ambivalence toward those British precepts of "tribal" decorum he chooses to turn his back on. Whereas his first home-bound passage grounds his cultural conscience in the maternal injunction to "play properly" at soldiering, the second passage during early adulthood documents the extent to which repressive ties to past lessons are inseverable for the officer/homosexual. Critical to a psychoanalytic consideration of the narrative, the opening section from childhood offers a direct context for the reminiscences Lionel later has of his mother as she censures Cocoanut for his immoral influence on "her doomed offspring" (LTC 169). This first section consequently provides the foundation for Lionel's internal conflicts between an awakened or induced (homo)sexuality and an inescapable conscience represented by the embedded voice of his mother.

Since Mr. March had abandoned the family or ship, so to speak, and gone "native somewhere out East" (LTC 183), the childhood scene suggests a preoedipal or imaginary stage during which the mother-son relationship appears unchallenged by paternal authority. The authority of the abandoned mother over her children is nonetheless challenged by a prevailing patriarchal or masculine order that strictly observes gender divisions in terms of territorial space:

A sailor—an Englishman—leapt out of the hatchway with a piece of chalk and drew a little circle round her where she stood. Cocoanut screamed, "He's caught you. He's come."

"You're on dangerous ground, lady," said the sailor respectfully. "Men's quarters. Of course we leave it to your generosity."

Tired with the voyage and the noise of the children, worried by what she had left in India and might find in England, Mrs. March fell into a sort of trance. She stared at the circle stupidly, unable to move out of it, while Cocoanut danced round her and gibbered. (LTC 170)

As sole responsible parent, Mrs. March must serve as both nurturer and head of the household; yet, based on "what is customary," she is barred from following her sons into "Men's quarters" (LTC 170). In this first and fleeting staging of Mrs. March, the narrative selectively portrays her restricted role as both mother and father in a society that upholds "the old custom" of distinguishing "ladies" from "gentlemen" by rigidly preserving masculine territory (LTC 170). As the only direct presentation of her more human aspects, this scene reveals her fatigue as the abandoned parent, along with her apparently unquestioning surrender to custom. Her relative helplessness against the "independent" though "rapacious" English sailor and the gibbering Cocoanut clearly signals her ineffectual authority over her son's later seduction into "dangerous ground." By contrast with this perspective on the mother, in which her paternal authority is temporarily undermined, the narrative's earlier view exposes a less compassionate and relenting figure. Shifting from distant third-person narrative to free-indirect discourse, the narrator characterizes Mrs. March's familial and moral concerns in terms of a high-browed imperialist racism: "A clergyman's daughter and a soldier's wife, she could not admit that Christianity had ever been oriental. What good thing can come out of the Levant, and is it likely that the apostles ever had a touch of the tar-brush?" (LTC 169). This caricature echoes the discussion by Mahmoud Ali and Aziz of a Mrs. Turton, whose "haughty and venal" supremacism characterizes the "average" Englishwoman in *A Passage to India* (PI 8). Purporting to represent Mrs. March's internal thoughts, which are signaled by a shift to a relatively informal or colloquial tone, the narrator establishes her as a model of moral and racial, if not supremacist, conscience, the basis for Lionel's guilty consciousness of British propriety. But Mrs. March never directly voices a distinct imperialist stance; her imperative to "play properly" and her commitment to doing "what is customary" nevertheless reinforce this severe stereotype of the Englishwoman and diminish her relative leniency toward her children's playing with Cocoanut during the voyage outside the formal boundaries of British territory (LTC 169–70).

As the progenitor of "doomed offspring" and agent of family dishonor and shame, Lionel's father remains a covert topic of conversation in the adult sections of "The Other Boat." In his place, Lionel has posited his mother as the voice of authority ("Mother said so" [LTC 166]) that attempts but fails to shield her vulnerable children from a potentially hostile environment and threatened colonial world. He addresses her as the "Mater" and endows her with an omnipotence projected not through her own minimal actions within the narrative, but through his intensification and recuperation of her controlling image from his own repressive conscience—a conscience founded on the highly emblematic childhood scene of the first section. In line with her initial characterization as a racist, Forster's account of the adult Lionel casts Mrs. March as an Arachne spinning entangling "filaments" as extensive as British imperialism:[12]

Behind the Army was another power, whom he could not consider calmly: his mother, blind-eyed in the midst of the enormous web she had spun—filaments drifting everywhere, strands catching. There was no reasoning with her or about her, she understood nothing and controlled everything. She had suffered too much and was too high-minded to be judged like other people, she was outside carnality and incapable of pardoning it. . . . From the great blank country she inhabited came a voice condemning him and all her children for sin, but condemning him most. There was no parleying with her—she was a voice. God had not granted her ears—nor could she see, mercifully: the sight of him stripping would have killed her. He, her first-born, set apart for the redemption of the family name. (LTC 193)

Lionel March renders his own mother as unresponsive and "catching" as the image of a Mother Hag, perhaps resembling Pound's depiction of England as "an old bitch" in "Hugh Selwyn Mauberley." This potent yet misogynist trope links with an earlier brief allusion to an imagined threat of castration occurring when, left alone, Cocoanut covers his nakedness in fear of the hag: "Jealous of what she sees, the hag comes with her scimitar" (LTC 191–92).[13] The potential castration or emasculation of male characters in turn parallels the masculinization of female characters. Whereas the narrator reveals that Lionel was "nearly unmanned" by a past battle injury (LTC 179) and Cocoanut is proclaimed "unmanly" by an angered Mrs. March (LTC 170),[14] a female member of the Big Eight is notably named "Lady Manning" and Mrs. March must assume the absent father's role within the March family, not to mention the role or "voice" of imperialist conscience and racial/moral propriety.

Because of her son's conflicts with his conscience, Mrs. March is both aligned with "the great blank country she inhabited" and reduced to a disembodied "voice" from the past. She thus symbolizes untainted British propriety, purity, and omnipotence, ideals of the Empire (and perhaps a carry-over of the "*divina virago*," Queen Elizabeth I[15]) that his own sexuality transgresses. Characterizing his mother as having "suffered too much" and as being "too high-minded," Lionel envisions her as a type of *Mater dolorosa* who appears both immune to and therefore unforgiving of "carnality," especially that involving a "wog" or "half-caste." As an obverse image of the father, who, as Lionel euphemistically asserts, "went native" (LTC 183), she is imagined by Lionel as witnessing and passing merciless judgment on his acts of sexual transgression. Because of her moralistic stance, he remains conscious of jeopardizing both personal and genealogical redemption, his own chastity previously atoning for his father's "unspeakable" sin. Lionel's homosexual and interracial copulation with the "half-caste" Cocoanut retroactively informs the expression, "He went native." In mocking his lover's hypocritical resistance to acknowledging the possible details of his father's transgression, Cocoanut suggests Lionel's father's defection may have been as illicit as Lionel's own when he asks whether the man went

"With a girl or with a boy?"

"A boy? Good God! Well, I mean to say, with a girl, naturally—I mean, it was somewhere right away in the depths of Burma."

"Even in Burma there are boys. At least I once heard so. But the Dad went native with a girl. Ver' well. Might not therefore there be offspring?"

"If there were, they'd be half-castes. Pretty depressing prospect. Well, you know what I mean. My family—Dad's, that's to say—can trace itself back nearly two hundred years, and the Mater's goes back to the War of Roses. It's really pretty awful, Cocoa."

The half-caste smiled as the warrior floundered. (LTC 183)

Lying in bed with the "half-caste" Cocoa, "in the depths" of the boat heading East, Lionel side-steps his lover's claim that "even in Burma there are boys," ironically denying the implied homosexuality of his "unfortunate parent" (LTC 184).[16] In response to the suggestion of miscegenation, however, Lionel disparages but does not dismiss the "depressing prospect" of his father adulterating the family's pure lineage. The floundering "warrior" banks on genealogical longevity to preserve British imperialist notions of caste and continual progeny. Obliquely aligned with the "hostile" sun whose "mighty power" signifies doom to the unprotected offspring of the "Ruling Race" (LTC 169), Cocoanut, as the narrator claims, has "no scruples at perverting Lionel's instincts" nor "at endangering his prospects of paternity" (LTC 182). Homosexual intercourse with the "half-caste," rather than "with a girl, naturally," violates normative, biological, or Darwinian codes of sexuality. To the conscientious Lionel, who regards himself as the sole means of redeeming the sullied "family name," it also threatens extinction of acceptable patrilineage, since "his surviving brother was too much a bookworm to be of any use, and the other two [siblings] were girls" (LTC 193).[17] His fostering extinction also implicates the self; regaining his sense of self-composure on deck, Lionel favorably surveys the Big Eight sahibs and acknowledges the conditionality of his own social survival: "How decent and reliable they looked, the folk to whom he belonged! He had been born one of them, he had his work with them, he meant to marry into their caste. If he forfeited their companionship he would become nobody and nothing" (LTC 192). This thought clearly counters an earlier assertion that his "colour-prejudices were tribal rather than personal, and only worked when an observer was present" (LTC 174). Public and private sexual identities ultimately prove inextricable in terms of a family honor and moral stance already jeopardized by the father's fall into the "depths of Burma" (LTC 183).

Both son and narrator cast Mrs. March, in contrast to Mr. March, as the Jehovah-like arbiter of the inextricable codes of normative sexuality, morality, and culture required for ensuring caste affiliation and public honor. Presented through the son's guilt-ridden conscience, her disembodied voice denotes both condemnation of and suffering from the past and present falls of father and son. Simultaneously, the adult Lionel venerates his mother's high-mindedness, while denigrating her self-righteous and condemnatory presence in his conscience. Based on a distortion of childhood reminiscence, his veneration and denigration objectify the maternal figure as both ideal mother and ideal Ego. Aboard the "other boat" of childhood, Mrs. March is featured as a woman who has allowed the colonial restraints of the "Ruling Race" to relax while at sea (LTC 167–69); even so, in Lionel's reminiscence, she becomes desexualized and, as his image of sexual restraint and conscience, is internalized as a "Mater" or disembodied Mother.

Significantly, the first section of "The Other Boat" serves both as a crucial foreshadowing of "this particular night" depicted in the fourth section and as a foundation for the self-generated strife the adult Lionel undergoes with a mother who is absent, but present in his consciousness (LTC 177). Although narrated *in medias res,* with the immediacy of dialogue and free-indirect discourse, this opening scene aboard the "other boat" designates a distant past of "long long ago" (LTC 166) "in those far-off days" (LTC 169).[18] The "other boat" thereby symbolizes a nostalgia for a childhood located in the colonial past, when "little boys" postured as "soldiers" who "still went to their deaths stiffly" (LTC 166); yet it also refers to a biblical or archetypal past when Old Testament male progenitors codified the world. Here, in this first section, the subtext of sexuality and potential fatality underlies the narrative's innocent tone and adumbrates the fatal outcome of the homoerotic relationship between Lionel March and Cocoanut, who in playing soldiers is the "only one who falls down when he's killed" (LTC 166). Retreating from this opening battle play among the March children, Cocoanut directs himself toward what he coins the "m'm m'm m'm" inhabiting the bow of the ship. In response to the Marchs' curious inquiries about this cryptonym, he inscribes chalk marks on the ship's planks—a cipher that he decodes as the "M'm," which he insists "have no name" (LTC 167). Cocoanut's reference to these imaginary "m'm m'm m'm" challenges the inculcated belief of the March children that all God's creations have been securely codified. The young Lionel then holds up Adam and Noah—those male progenitors of a "long long ago" whose biblical accounts illustrate the imperative of naming everything, not to mention organizing the world heterosexually for regeneration:

"They must have a name," said Lionel, recollecting, "because Adam named all the animals when the Bible was beginning."

"They weren't in the Bible, m'm m'm m'm; they were all the time up in the thin part of the sheep, and when you pop out they pop in, so how could Adam have?"

"Noah's ark is what he's got to now."

Baby said "Noah's ark, Noah's ark, Noah's ark," and they all bounced up and down and roared. (LTC 167)

The "half-caste" Cocoanut's conception of the "m'm m'm m'm" violates this archetypal imperative, for "they" evade the authority of language (or the Divine Word) to systematize the world. As the narrator follows the March children into the ship's bow, "where the m'm m'm m'm were said to be" (LTC 168), the intradiegetic but indeterminate narrator shifts from a third-person to a second-person perspective that implicates the reader in the pursuit of these unnameables:

Here opened a glorious country, much the best in the boat. None of the March children had explored *there* before, but Cocoanut, having few domesticities, knew it well. That bell that hung in the very peak—it was the ship's bell and if you rang it the ship would stop. Those big ropes were tied into knots—twelve knots an hour. This paint was wet, but only as far as there. Up that hole was coming a Lascar. But of the m'm m'm he said nothing until asked. Then he explained in offhand tones that if you popped out they popped in, so that you couldn't expect to see them. (LTC 168; my emphasis)

The elusive and cryptonymic "m'm m'm m'm" are disjointedly designated as both "here" and "there," "in" and "out" of the holes of what Cocoanut locates as the "thin part of the sheep," or ship (LTC 167). The half-caste's vocalic mispronunciation of "ship" in itself betrays a biblical notion of bestial sodomy, while implying an area of this "other boat" (and perhaps of carnal knowledge) that is shared by Cocoanut and the Lascar but not by the innocent and vulnerable March children. Consequently, the "new game" of "m'm m'm m'm," once reported to Mrs. March, is promptly checked by her injunction to "Go back and play properly" at soldiering (LTC 169).

Suggesting a game of unspeakable impropriety, Cocoanut's sounds take on multiple meanings. The bilabial utterance of "m'm m'm m'm" sounds like a rapid repetition of "mum" if we replace the apostrophe with the more common English schwa and represent this substitution with the grapheme "u." The term "mum" thereby subjects the contraction "m'm" to various denotations: the suppression of speech or the injunction to be silent; the act of masquerading, or masking oneself; or, thirdly, the informal yet chiefly British reference to "Mama." Given this potential multivalence, the unnameable "m'm m'm m'm" conflates the idiomatic expression, "mum's the word," with notions of concealment and mother; hence, as the March children reveal the "new game" to their mother, they phonetically and syntactically link her name with this cryptonym of suppression and deception: "M'm m'm m'm, mummy" (LTC 169).[19] This effectively, although innocently, adumbrates Captain Lionel March's vigilant efforts to mask any word of his "offence against decency" aboard the *S. S. Normannia* (LTC 174). In addition, Cocoanut's neologism works with the notion of "mummery" ("a pretentious or hypocritical show or ceremony"), which aptly portrays the upstanding officer's conscious attempts to keep up appearances and continue playing at soldiers, so to speak, for Colonel Arbuthnot and the Big Eight sahibs—not to mention for his "mum," with whom he corresponds while at sea.

Lionel's overseas correspondence with his mother functions as primary evidence of his contrition and his need to allude to yet mask his reunion with Cocoanut: "He is on board too, but our paths seldom cross" (LTC 171). Most notably, this epistle to the "Mater," which opens the story's second section and signals the narrative's transition from the "other boat" to the second boat, constitutes the core of Lionel's "stumbling confession." In projecting his mother as his confessor, as a Jehovah-like "voice condemning him and all her children for sin, but condemning him most," Lionel necessarily locates her "outside carnality" and deprives her of senses, sensations, and sensuality (LTC 193). He is mocked by Cocoanut because, by idealizing his mother as "the very soul of purity," Lionel denies the possibility of her sexuality and establishes her as the absolute gauge by which to condemn and restrain his own (LTC 185). Lionel later reveals his self-repulsion as he confesses his attempt to imagine his mother engaging in sexual intercourse: "Earlier in the evening, when Cocoa mentioned her, he had tried to imagine her with his father, enjoying the sensations he was beginning to find so pleasant, but the attempt was sacrilegious and he was shocked at himself" (LTC 193). That Lionel appears shocked at the vicarious sexual sensations the image of parental intercourse incites falls in line with Freud's discussion of *"primal phantasies"* commonly generated by neurotics (*Introductory* 371). Syntactically ambiguous, the phrase "enjoying the sensations" may refer to Lionel and to either the mother or the father, any of whom may be enjoying sexual pleasures. But Lionel's sense of profaning his puritanical mother arises from his locating her inside carnality and vicariously identifying with either her or the father as lover. If his identification is with the father as the mother's lover, then the image clearly suggests oedipal and perhaps incestuous implications. But if his identification is with the mother, then it appears equally sacrilegious, yet more "unnatural," and more clearly posits her as the son's object of transference. Lionel envisions his mother, as the cynosure of his fantasy, in his own sexual position. More significantly, he locates himself in the position of his mother, the feminine object of a male lover, as had Cocoanut in the earlier scene.[20] His shock then appears a response not only to the incestuous implications of this imagined scene of parental intercourse, but also to the feminization of his role as homosexual lover.

In his letter to his mother, Lionel addresses her as "Mater." While typical of nineteenth-century English schoolboy slang, this term of endearment suggests the various dimensions of her role as the mother, the matriarch, and, in an ironic sense, one who breeds. Beginning with a capital "M," Lionel's colloquial reference to his mother also seems to invoke the venerable figure of the Madonna, whose virginity and procreation secures her as the pure composite sign of maternity and femininity to the Son.[21] In line with this icon of the immaculate breeder, if you will, the asexual image of Mrs. March hence surfaces as a son's fabrication, which Cocoanut derisively discloses. As Lionel isolates the figure of his mother from "carnality," he essentially sublates her into a symbol of moral superiority that can only prove damning for his own transgressive actions below deck. For, not only endowed with the purity of a "Mater," she is granted the power of Judgment, by which she condemns "him and all her children for sin" (LTC 193).

Cast as an all-controlling spider, the conception of Mrs. March "in the midst of the enormous web she had spun" may well derive from Freud's essay on "Femininity." Here, Freud figuratively discusses the aggressivity of the female spider in order to deconstruct the binarism of female passivity and male aggressivity, and to suggest an alternate figure of the phallic mother (*Standard Edition* 22:115). In *Thinking About Women*, Mary Ellmann extends this imagery of mother and spider:

As the stereotyped ideal grows intolerable, reaction against it takes the form of emphasis upon those who misapply it. It is, after all, Freud who described, simultaneously, the duty of the mother to sacrifice herself to the children and her demand that they sacrifice their wishes to her. Properly, she weaves her life about the children, and then in the children's dreams she is a spider (or, for Jung, a serpent or sarcophagus or specter). The more ideal the conception of a human function, the more resentment and suspicion it arouses: we are entirely accustomed, in the consideration of maternity, to this jolting between soul and damnation. We are as familiar with the accusation of consumptive attachment as with the praise of selfless care. In this sense, women are at once the child makers and breakers; no idea is more commonly fixed than that of the filocidal influence of the mother. (135)

In his own "consideration of maternity" and his "jolting between soul and damnation," propriety and condemnation, Lionel transmutes his mother into an omnipotent yet "blind-eyed" ideal against which to judge his own guilt for having violated sexual as well as racial norms. Simultaneously, he praises and disparages his mother for a purity that he finds both repressive and critical to his own consciousness of imperialism and a genealogy that "can trace itself back nearly two hundred years" (LTC 183).

In the colonial context, Mrs. March, with her imperial "filaments drifting everywhere," represents not only the Empire but its surrogate, the "memsahib," a male construct designed to preserve the genealogical purity and political supremacy of the "Ruling Race."[22] Prior to the memsahib's introduction into India, the British colony was depicted as a "Moloch" primarily populated by males who engaged in interracial as well as homoerotic promiscuity (Hyam 91). This historical image of an exclusively male territory is symbolically portrayed in the scene aboard the "other boat" when Mrs. March enters the area of the boat designated as "Men's quarters" (LTC 170). There, the English sailor draws a circle around her and proscribes her movement into a portion of the boat in which male intercourse can transpire without "the sounds of feminine protest" (LTC 178). As Mrs. March agrees to pay for her trespass, Cocoanut, later described as "like a monkey" (LTC 173) and ironically as one who is "influential in shipping circles" (LTC 171), mockingly supersedes her position within the circle, to which Mrs. March retorts: "You never will play any game properly and you stop the others. You're a silly idle useless unmanly little boy" (LTC 170). Within this narrative context, the "game" most directly refers to Cocoanut's enigmatic game of "m'm m'm m'm"; but within a colonial context, it suggests the Indian male's political means of subverting the British imperialist hierarchy through homoerotic bonding. In his article "Forster's Friends," Rustom Bharucha insists upon not only the rebellious yet clandestine role homosexuality played in England against "the authoritarian and paternalistic rule of [the] government," but also the role it served in India as the Indian male's stratagem for "defeating the British at their own game" (109–10):

In psychoanalytic terms, Indians had begun to "identify with the aggressor." Elaborating on this phenomenon in his brilliant study *The Intimate Enemy,* Ashis Nandy situates the opposition between *purusatva* (the essence of masculinity) with *klibatva* (the essence of hermaphroditism) as the essential conflict in the colonial psychology of Indians. "Femininity-in-masculinity," he claims, "was perceived as the final negation of a man's political identity, a pathology more dangerous than femininity itself." (110)

Attempting to bring "the feminine instincts of man to the surface" (Bharucha 112), to shake or negate the British officer's solid identity as "entirely the simple soldier man" (LTC 174), Cocoanut nearly enslaves Lionel through tactics of homoerotic bondage. Possessed of "thick fairish hair, blue eyes, glowing cheeks and strong white teeth," "a combination irresistible to the fair sex" (LTC 172), Lionel epitomizes the virile Aryan officer and perhaps mirrors Herman Melville's "Handsome Sailor," the "pristine and unadulterate" object of desire, of *Billy Budd, Sailor* (331), which Forster had recently converted into a libretto with Eric Crozier (*SL* 2:223).[23] The "fair sex" attracted to Lionel ironically proves to be the unfair—that is, dark—"wog" who engages in foreplay "like a monkey" (LTC 173). Initially, Lionel maintains his conventionally masculine role as he "manhandle[s]" and "close[s] on" the physically weaker, effeminate Cocoanut—the act of manhandling referring not only to the lover's manpower but to his object of handling (LTC 173). In the penultimate act of sodomy, however, Lionel reverses his role. As visual evidence of Cocoanut's effeminizing the British soldier, Lionel ascends to the boat's deck, unconsciously attired in "effeminate pyjamas" (LTC 195). Previously described as "being built like a brute" (LTC 180), Lionel, or "Lion of the Night" (LTC 189), proves disarmed by the stratagems of the "monkey" (LTC 181); the half-caste Cocoanut unmasks (or unmans) the latent sexual identity of the "Nordic warrior" (LTC 174) and reveals it to be "half Ganymede, half Goth" (LTC 178)—giving an ironic half-caste distinction to the blue-blooded Aryan. The final evidence of Cocoanut's snakelike seduction and successful exposure of the British officer's "femininity-in-masculinity" comes from Lionel's previous identification with his mother; comparing her pleasures of lovemaking to his own, he progressively breaks with his rigidly defined masculinity and accepts Cocoanut's feminine gifts as would a prostitute. The appearance of the image of Mrs. March, however, serves as continual self-reproof of his deviation from normative manhood and racial supremacy.

Throughout the course of his seduction, Cocoanut foresees Mrs. March as the primary obstacle to his homoerotic bonding with (or bondage of) Lionel. Historically, this viewpoint represents that of the Indian male who, according to Bharucha on *A Passage to India*, viewed the memsahib as his primary rival for the British colonialist: "The real antagonists of Indian men were not their sahibs but the memsahibs who . . . saw themselves, as Nandy puts it, as 'the sexual competitors of Indian men with whom their men had established an unconscious homoeroticized bonding'" (110). In the fourth section of "The Other Boat," Cocoanut recalls the memsahib March as "[t]hat vengeful onswishing of skirts" that disrupted a "trivial collision" between Cocoanut and Lionel, the collision an adumbration in childhood of their adult homoerotic relationship (LTC 182). This metonymic denigration of the maternal figure as swishing skirts echoes Forster's critical assessment of the "barrenness" of the characters in his earlier novel *Howards End* (1910) and his preference for "*Where Angels* Gino, in *L. J.* Stephen, in *R. with V.* Lucy, in *P. to I.* Aziz . . . and Maurice and Alec. . . . and Lionel and Cocoa" (CB 204; Forster's ellipses). Dated the same year he completed "The Other Boat," Forster's entry in *Commonplace Book* reflects his distaste for the "onswishing of skirts" and provides an insight into his finding no pleasure in his "best novel": "I feel pride in the achievement, but cannot love it, and occasionally the swish of the skirts and the non-sexual embraces irritate. Perhaps too I am more hedonistic than I was, and resent not being caused pleasure personally" (CB 203–04).

In Lionel's own internalized diatribe against the power of his mother, Lionel, or "lion" (the British emblem), envisions the scene of his transgression and ultimately castigates himself for violating filial duty. We are told: "the sight of him stripping would have killed her. He, her first-born, set apart for the redemption of the family name" (LTC 193). According to Oliver Stallybrass's footnote to the text, Forster was originally more sexually explicit: he has substituted "stripping" for "topping a dago" (LTC 193n). In censoring out direct evidence of homoerotic as well as interracial copulation, Forster in turn has edited or suppressed his initial impulse to offend flippantly both mother and culture (or potential reader). Lionel's disclosure of his "hedonistic" (CB 204) sexuality at first seems to represent the primary "offence against decency" (LTC 174). Narratively, he shifts his concern, however, to "the redemption of the family name" that has been sullied by the "unspeakable" fact that his "hundred percent Aryan" father had abandoned both family and caste in order to go "native" "in the depths of Burma" (LTC 183–84), an act implying miscegenation or—if Cocoanut is right—homosexuality. Condemning his own libidinal and social lapse, Lionel resolves that he "must keep with his own people" for personal, as well as genealogical and imperial, survival (LTC 195). In spite of his resoluteness to submit to cultural norms of sexual conduct, Lionel's "standing quarrel" between erotic desire and "tribal" affiliation can only be extinguished, personally and textually, by the death of both lovers. As Cocoanut is purportedly strangled to death by Lionel, the "scandal" of homicide and suicide, that "sweet act of vengeance," subsequently undergoes its own form of "strangulation" or suppression of details (LTC 195–96). Following three elliptically narrated paragraphs, stylistically mirroring the Big Eight's censorial efforts, the narrative ends with Mrs. March's final act as repressive mother: "she never mentioned his name again" (LTC 197). With this statement, the text itself becomes "silent" or as "blank" as the "country she inhabited" (LTC 193).

"Confessions of the flesh" in "The Other Boat" are not only silenced or mummed by the censorial and decorous memsahib and Big Eight sahibs—and by the childhood game of "m'm m'm m'm," which the adult Lionel enigmatically recalls as the "oddities on the other boat," but ultimately by Forster's own euphemistic rendering of homoerotics. Forster reduces the final sadomasochistic scene leading to Cocoanut's murder to the point of syntactical and emotional abstraction. He says only, "ecstasy hardened into agony" (LTC 195). Similarly, he translates Lionel's submission to Cocoanut's sexual advances into compressed abstract nouns: "Resistance weakened under the balmier sky, curiosity increased" (LTC 177). Stallybrass remarks that in the story the figurative "a muscle thickened up out of gold" comes closest to corporeal description (LTC 173). But through sexual innuendoes, Forster makes the postcoital "ritual" of smoking a cigarette stand for the entire course of an act of fellatio or sodomy:

> [Smoking] was an established ritual, an assertion deeper than speech that they belonged to each other and in their own way. Lionel assented and lit the thing, pushed it between dusky lips, pulled it out, pulled at it, replaced it, and they smoked it alternately with their faces touching. When it was finished Cocoa refused to extinguish the butt in an ashtray but consigned it through the porthole into the flying waters with incomprehensible words. He thought the words might protect them, though he could not explain how, or what they were. (LTC 178–79)

Indeterminate nouns and pronouns, "the thing" and "it," replace "cigarette"; such referential indirection allows for alternate yet otherwise unspeakable readings of the lovers' "ritual" or "assertion deeper than speech." As Cocoanut pitches the live but finished butt into the "flying waters" with words as "incomprehensible" as "m'm m'm m'm," Lionel, in his postcoital act of suicide and "with the seeds of love on him," later pitches himself into the Red Sea, where his body "quickly attract[s] the sharks" (LTC 196).

As the "native crew" then consigns the murdered Cocoanut "to the deep with all possible speed," his corpse floats "contrary to the prevailing current" (LTC 196). Here, I read "the prevailing current" as a metaphor for imperialist decorum and British law that proscribes homosexual conduct. Lionel earlier alludes to the legal consequences of homosexuality and describes such illicit behavior as "the worst thing for which Tommies got the maximum" (LTC 175), as Oscar Wilde's conviction in 1895 proved. In *Sexual Anarchy,* Elaine Showalter historically documents the *fin-de-siècle* criminalization of this "pathology" by the Labouchère Amendment to the Criminal Law Amendment Act of 1885 (14). Positing Stevenson's *Dr. Jekyll and Mr. Hyde* as a "fable of *fin-de-siècle* homosexual panic, the discovery and resistance of the homosexual self," Showalter further explains that death (suicide and/or homicide) provided such stories the "only form of narrative closure" (107), for "it is self-destructive to violate the sexual codes of one's society" (*Sexual* 113).[24] Perhaps drawing on this "Gay Gothic" finale, Forster also chooses to end with passionate murder and suicide. Forster's narrator attributes Lionel's guilt to the inexorable "power" of the arachnoid, phallic "Mater," whose sociosymbolic link or "filament" to her son is confirmed by a letter that he has written out of a sense of filial duty. The "red English pillar-box" in which he deposits this letter or masked confession serves as a signpost of the law—of his mother's and/or Britain's inseverable bond and imperialist network even at sea (LTC 187). The letter to "Mater" provides textual evidence of the son's self-inflicted need both to confess and translate his sexuality into acceptable discourse; Forster's story, also posthumously disclosed, offers evidence of a similar need. The prevalent mediation of the maternal figure in this closing scene complicates the author's bold claim that his intent was to end narratively on a climactic note of romantic tragedy, "when both crash at the height of their powers" (*Letters to Donald Windham* qtd. in Beauman 369).

In "The Other Boat," Lionel March's repeated invocation of the sociosymbolic mother reflects the son's association of mother with cultural and sexual repression—with imperatives to "keep with his own people" (LTC 195) and, as voiced by Colonel Arbuthnot (whose possible namesake published the satirical *Law Is a Bottomless Pit* [1712]), to "come and sleep . . . like the rest of the gang" (LTC 194). Lionel establishes a solitary "communion with the Mater" (LTC 195) and promises his absent mother " 'Never again' " (LTC 193). Submitting to maternal/cultural "imperatives," the son discovers that the mother's repressive voice is ultimately his own, for, as Trilling's Freud asserts, "the surrogates of culture are established in the mind itself" (*Freud* 36). The son's inexorable voicing of Maternal Law can therefore be silenced only by death or the inaudible act of writing—by the "silent, cautious deposition of the word upon the whiteness of a piece of paper, where it can possess neither sound nor interlocutor" (Foucault, *Order* 300).

Notes

This chapter was first published in *Style* 29 (1995): 474-97, and is reprinted by permission of the editor of that journal.

1. In his discussion of the "repressive hypothesis" in *The History of Sexuality,* Michel Foucault translates the "good Christian" act of confessing "the flesh" into a laconic second-person imperative (19): "Not only will you confess to acts contravening the law, but you will seek to transform your desire, your every desire, into discourse" (21).

2. See June Perry Levine's "The Tame in Pursuit of the Savage: The Posthumous Fiction of E. M. Forster" for an informative analysis of the various manuscripts of *Maurice* (76–79).

3. I borrow this issue of the dated text from Christopher Isherwood's own personal account of his "Master," Forster, in *Christopher and His Kind:* "At their meeting in 1932, the Master had raised the Pupil. This time, the Pupil was being asked by the Master, quite humbly, how *Maurice* appeared to a member of the thirties generation. 'Does it date?' Forster was asking. To which Christopher, I am proud to say, replied, 'Why shouldn't it date?' " (126).

4. Using contemporaneous biographies and memoirs and the findings of *The Wolfenden Report,* Antony Grey, in *Quest for Justice: Towards Homosexual Emancipation,* depicts the period between the 1890s and the 1950s as the "silent years," during which transpired "a great deal of homosexual behaviour, most of it discreet and undetected" (19). Because legal proscription did not deter homosexual activity, *The Wolfenden Report* advocated its decriminalization when performed in private by consenting adults.

5. Norman Page, in *E. M. Forster's Posthumous Fiction,* finds this assertion implausible: "Self-excitation hardly demands so evident an exercise of art, and one has the sense of their being written for an appreciative audience" (54).

6. Representing earlier, stylistically more formal versions of the first section of "The Other Boat," both publications mark the author's first appearance in print since the publication of his novel *A Passage to India* in 1924. In the *New York Times Book Review,* the editor also mentions that the "fragment" was originally broadcast by the BBC "a short time ago." Most interestingly, the editor alludes to a concealed yet nameless novel, presumably *Maurice:* "It is known that there reposes in the British Museum the manuscript of a completed Forster novel, but the impression is general that he will never consent to its publication" (6 February 1949). (See Forster, "Cocoanut.")

7. The *Normannia* is also evident in *Maurice* as the ship on which the gamekeeper, Alec, intends to emigrate to the Argentine (M 232, 234). In light of Captain March's internal and social struggle with normative ideals, the ship's title also appears an implicit pun on "norm" and "man," if not "mania."

8. See Julia Kristeva's "The Virgin of the Word" in *About Chinese Women* for a further discussion of the participation of the mother in the symbolic Christian order (25–33).

9. The formation of the exclusive Big Eight sahibs parallels that of the "Cambridge group" on board the 1912 voyage that provided the "germ" for Forster's story (Furbank, *Life* 223). "The Other Boat" clearly adapts biographical elements of this memorable voyage to the East as well as Forster's intimate and lifelong relationship with Syed Ross Masood, the Oxford undergraduate with whom Forster initially posed as Latin tutor. Ostensibly, the character of Captain March borrows from the "fair-haired Byronic-looking" officer who boldly announced his homosexuality to the author while voyaging in 1912 toward his station in India (Furbank, *Life* 224). While Cocoanut inherits the "volatile" (Furbank, *Life* 143) and "despotic" (Bharucha 107) features of Masood's personality, he contrasts with the educated Indian with upper class advantages and physical magnificence. In this light, Cocoanut signifies a hybridized or composite caricature of the perverse seducer and the racial pariah; while his diabolic features perhaps mirror British societal (or Big Eight) conceptions of both the aberrant homosexual and the liminal "wog," such views would clearly oppose the author's own homoerotic attraction to Masood. In turn, "The Other Boat" proves a hybridization of Forster's narrative of homosexuality in *Maurice* and his focus on issues of Anglo-Indian sexuality and Oriental seductiveness in *A Passage to India.*

10. In *About Chinese Women,* Kristeva describes the rationale behind conceiving of a mother with the Phallus: "In a symbolic productive/reproductive economy centered on the Paternal Word (the Phallus, if you like), one can make a woman believe that she *is* (the Phallus, if you like), even if she doesn't have it (the serpent—the penis): Doesn't she have the child? In this way, social harmony is preserved: the structure functions, produces, and reproduces. Without it, the very foundation of this society is endangered" (22).

11. As Herz observes in *The Short Narratives of E. M. Forster,* Mrs. March only appears as a " 'character' in the conventional sense" in the beginning; yet she evolves into a "pure symbol" and, by apparent contrast, a "purely negative creation" (an inferior inversion of Mrs. Moore) in the end.

12. Etymologically related to "Arachne" and "arachnid," the term "arachnoid" denotes the delicate (cobweb-like) membrane enclosing the spinal cord and brain, and significantly located between the *pia mater* (Latin for "tender mother") and the *dura mater* ("hard mother"). This anatomical polarity of tender and hard mother parallels Lionel's construction of Mrs. March as both the unimpeachable caretaker of her fatherless children and the "power," if not backbone, to the imperial "Army."

13. Forster's complete sentence reads: "Jealous of what she sees, the hag comes with her scimitar, and she. . . . Or she lifts up a man when he feels lighter than air" (LTC 191–92; Forster's ellipses). The image of the hag lifting up a man connotes the image of the mother as bird, an image perhaps related to Leonardo da Vinci's fantasy of his mother as a vulture endowed with a penis. Freud aligns this androgynous or phallic mother image with the Egyptian maternal goddess "Mut," a symbol of parthenogenetic motherhood who was iconographically depicted with breasts as well as an erect penis (*Standard* 11:88–89, 94). Freud

likens da Vinci's fantasy of the "vulture-child"—the paradigm of the fatherless son or bastard child of the "vulture mother"—to the virginal conception of Christ (11:90).

14. Mrs. March's invective against Cocoanut's unmanliness biographically recalls Masood's recorded experience with a similar charge when Oxford undergraduates denigrated his "unmanly" use of scents (Furbank, *Life* 144). This in turn links with Cocoanut's "aromatic smell" (LTC 173).

15. See Winfried Schleiner, "*Divina virago:* Queen Elizabeth as an Amazon." Also, Louis Adrian Montrose's " 'Shaping Fantasies': Figurations of Gender and Power in Elizabethan Culture," argues that Queen Elizabeth I, as the gynarchic paragon of virginity and power, proves to be Britain's own complex configuration of the sublime and perhaps phallic mother figure (or Mater) of the growing Empire. See Montrose 79–80.

16. While I have reservations about Forster's most recent biography, Nicola Beauman's account of the immediate Forster family concurs with the implicit depiction of the Marches as homophobic. In several instances, Beauman characterizes Forster's mother, Lily, as not simply one who was dominating or overprotective, but as one who was vigilant against her son inheriting his father's legacy of putative homosexuality: "It may not have been chance alone that took her and Morgan abroad in the very month of the Oscar Wilde trials: might it have been her long repressed feelings about Eddie [her husband] and Ted that prompted her first holiday in France since Paris, 1878?" (69–70); elsewhere, Beauman writes, "Homosexuality was something she would rather not think about, yet she [Lily] must have seen for herself that her son was, like Eddie (about whom she had had her doubts), lacking in some of the characteristics of the active heterosexual" (94–95).

17. Clearly, Lionel's family structure only resembles Forster's in terms of the absent father; the marked absence of Forster's father is, however, related to his premature death from a family disease, as recorded in the author's autobiographical segment of *Marianne Thornton: A Domestic Biography*. In this curious combination of his great-aunt's biography and his early autobiography, published a year before his writing of "The Other Boat," Forster describes his female relatives' overindulgence of him after his father's death: "They centred round me. I succeeded my father as the favourite nephew. . . . I received the deplorable nickname of The Important One, and when my mother showed signs of despondency she was reminded that she had me to live for" (MT 289). In spite of the presence of three other siblings, Lionel also succeeds his own father and, in a similar sense, carries the moral and genealogical burden of being "The Important One."

18. In his fragment of an "abandoned novel," Forster more directly refers to a time when "war had not yet assumed its colonial aspect" ("Cocoanut" 3); this phrase has been edited from the final version of "The Other Boat."

19. Lionel's "open avowal" of his homoerotic desire for Cocoanut can, in this light, be read as a clever play on the open(-ended) vowel of "m'm m'm m'm" (LTC 187). I credit Kathryn Stockton, at the University of Utah, with this insight.

20. In "The Hand That Rocks the Cradle," Coppélia Kahn discusses the son's feminine identification with the mother; borrowing from Adrienne Rich, she describes this potential transference in terms of " 'matrophobia'—not the fear of one's mother or of motherhood, but of becoming like one's mother as in the original identification of the child with its mother, and thus losing one's gender identity as a male" [(M)other Tongue 79].

21. Kristeva refers to this condensed if not incestuous configuration of the trinitarian Virgin in "Stabat Mater": "Indeed, mother of her son and his daughter as well, Mary is also, and besides, his wife: she therefore actualizes the threefold metamorphosis of a woman in the tightest parenthood structure" (Tales of Love 243).

22. In Empire and Sexuality (118–119), Ronald Hyam documents the historical phenomenon of the "memsahib."

23. The snake imagery incorporated into the narrative of Lionel's seduction by Cocoanut ("The bolt unbolted, the little snake not driven back into its hole" [LTC 190]; "the body curved away seductively into darkness" [LTC 195]) and the purity initially ascribed to the "half Goth" Lionel ("He had stepped on board at Tilbury entirely the simple soldier man, without an inkling of his fate" [LTC 174]) link Forster's short story with Melville's in terms of their homoerotic adaptation of man's Fall: "Billy in many respects was little more than a sort of upright barbarian, much such perhaps as Adam presumably might have been ere the urbane Serpent wriggled himself into his company" (Melville 330–31).

According to Mary Lago and P. N. Furbank's biographical introduction to the final phase (1947–70) of his letters, Forster was invited by Benjamin Britten to collaborate on an opera; with Eric Crozier, he produced the libretto for Billy Budd, which premiered on 1 December 1951 (SL 2:223, 246n2). Boosey & Hawkes published two versions of the libretto: Billy Budd: Opera in Four Acts (1951) and the revised Billy Budd: Opera in Two Acts (1961) (SL 2:240n2). These two dates frame the year(s) Forster worked on "The Other Boat" (1957–58).

24. Both Levine and Herz describe Lionel's suicide as an "inevitable" resolution to his internal division between caste affiliation and homosexuality or homoerotic desire for Cocoanut. But given that the narrative comes to a halt with the censorial mother, I can view the fatal outcome neither as an easy reconciliation of psychic conflict nor as a triumphant escape into boundless eternity for the two lovers. (The latter, I believe, more aptly reflects Vithobai's final triumph in "The Life to Come.") Levine's textual illustrations focus on Lionel's relationship to the Big Eight, suggesting that this "story" views them as symbolic if not allegorical representatives of the world's social institutions. But her brief consideration of "The Other Boat" does not include the mother as an agency of social conscience and censorship as well. On the other hand, Herz does associate the mother with Lionel's "fatal split" between "deck" and "cabin." I agree with this direct association, although our readings of the mother as a symbol differ in the end. Examining Mrs. March's "felt presence throughout the story," Herz aligns

the mother with the sea, into which Lionel eventually dives to his death. I am more inclined to agree with her subsequent consideration of Mrs. March as a "purely negative creation" who "consume[s]," or rather censors, the final story of her son (*Short* 55; see note 11); but, since I ascribe primary agency to the son and narrator in their construction of the maternal image, I would not venture to place the mother in the position of an implied omniscient narrator.

11

To Express the Subject of Friendship: Masculine Desire and Colonialism in A Passage to India

Charu Malik

As Adela Quested enters the courtroom for the trial of the Indian she has charged with attempting to rape her, she is distracted by the "person who had no bearing officially upon the trial," the "almost naked" punkah wallah (PI 207). Her attention immediately captured by the punkah wallah, Adela cannot resist thinking that "he seemed to control the proceedings" (PI 207). In his naked yet splendid, and humble yet beautiful form nourished by the city's garbage, in his "strength," "physical perfection," and "aloofness," the punkah wallah's figure "prove[s] to society how little its categories" (PI 207) matter. With every pull at the rope he swirls air for everyone in the room but remains excluded from any of it himself; nevertheless, he seems to refocus and relocate, for Adela, the central action to his humble, marginal position. From his excluded, aloof, yet beautifully compelling form, the punkah wallah rebukes "the narrowness of [the] sufferings" (PI 207) of this girl from middle-class England and challenges the civilizing presence of her compatriots:

In virtue of what had she collected this roomful of people together? Her particular brand of opinions, and the suburban Jehovah who sanctified them—by what right did they claim so much importance in the world, and assume the title of civilization? (PI 207)

Jolted in her perspective by a glimpse of subservient yet unknown, unconquered human beauty, Adela begins to question her own charge of rape. Later in the legal proceedings, as she envisions the scene at the caves, finding that she could see herself both inside and outside the cave but failing to locate Aziz following her into it, "the airs from the punkah behind her wafted her on. . . ." (PI 217). Soon after this recollection, Adela withdraws her charge.

This figure of the punkah wallah, mechanically blowing cooling air into the courtroom, provides the impetus that makes Adela change her mind. The punkah wallah disrupts the entire legal proceedings, which had been largely initiated so that the English could damn and convict as criminal an Indian, a conviction that would legitimize and prove their moral superiority to rule over the natives of India, the "darker races" (PI 208). But the punkah wallah not only makes the disruption of the trial possible. In his aloof servility and humbleness muted by striking physical beauty, he presents a contradictory figure who simultaneously reinforces colonial authority and disturbs it. In his study of colonial discourse, Homi Bhabha theorizes about such a contradictory figure in terms of "mimicry." He describes mimicry as a trope of partial presence that masks a threatening racial difference only to reveal the gaps in colonial power and knowledge, a "double vision which in disclosing the ambivalence of colonial discourse also disrupts its authority" (Bhabha 86).

But although the punkah wallah precipitates a resistance to colonial authority by disrupting and making ambivalent its representative, the system of justice—concurrently demonstrating that in this case law was being regarded as a matter of control, not justice—he does so in a manner somewhat different from Bhabha's mimic man, who is an imperfect double of the English gentleman, inhabiting the space of "not quite/not white" (Bhabha 92). In his menial, servile position, the punkah wallah does embody colonial authority. But through his physical perfection, his aloofness, his non-Anglicized person, he denies this authority in his refusal to mimic and in his lack of aggression. Strategically positioned across from the Indian assistant magistrate, who is seated on a platform as a sign of colonial authority, the punkah wallah offers an opposition to the "good" colonial subject. The punkah wallah, an untouchable, negates everything that characterizes the magistrate—a Western-educated native, who is a "cultivated, self-conscious, and conscientious" Indian civil servant (PI 207). The punkah wallah initiates disruption of the legal place that legitimizes colonial authority through his contrast to the educated colonials: the magistrate; the urbane barrister from Calcutta; the Nawab Bahadur; Hamidullah; and even Aziz himself, a trained medical doctor—all of whom are the apparently privileged subjects of the colonizing mission. The punkah wallah is "exorbitant" in Derrida's sense—an exteriority that is irreducible, cutting across the binary opposition of civilized and barbaric that allows the birth of the arrangement of colonizer and colonized (Derrida 162). He embodies that complete difference between the white and the dark races that makes possible the rule of the former over the latter but that also remains suppressed, its narrative untold. The courtroom dissolves into chaos after Adela's withdrawal of her charge. However, "the beautiful naked god," the punkah wallah, although the only one with nothing to say during this "scene of . . . fantasy," continues "to pull at the cord of his punkah, to gaze at the empty dais . . ." (PI 219) and creates a moment "of subversion that turn[s] the gaze of the discriminated back upon the eye of power" (Bhabha 112).

Forster's *A Passage to India* enunciates this disruption of colonial authority by making visible "the colonized other who is the essential other component or opposite number" of the "imperial world system," to use Fredric Jameson's version of modern imperialism (50). If colonialism constitutes a loss of meaning because "a significant structural segment of the economic system as a whole is now located elsewhere, beyond the metropolis, outside of the daily life and existential experience of the home country, in colonies over the water whose own life experiences and life world—very different from that of the imperial power—remain unknown and unimaginable," it is the situation of just such a loss of meaning that, paradoxically, *A Passage to India* tries to reveal, to make visible in its narrative (Jameson 51).[1] However, in order to imagine fictionally this colonial space—different from, yet essential to, the formation and identity of empire—without turning his own novel into an imperialist narrative, Forster desists from speaking for the punkah wallah, even at the price of leaving his story untold. In *A Passage to India,* we witness moments that the text refuses to master, disrupting the plenitude of representation and allowing difference to seep up to the surface.

In deliberate omissions, as figured in the incomplete narrative, the unknowable, opaque foreignness of the punkah wallah, *Passage* attempts not to create "the other" as exotic—since it does not try to speak for the punkah wallah—but to leave gaps in representation for "otherness" to show through. *Passage* thus presents an analysis and critique of the discourse of colonial authority in terms of the Indian situation. The text of the novel reinforces this critique in its ambiguities, gaps, secrets, and uncertainties, which disrupt and make ambivalent both colonial authority and an imperialist narrative. But Forster's awareness that positing a monolithic experience may constitute an act of imperialism, whether in the colonies or in the text, may be traced finally to the marginal vantage point dictated by the author's homosexuality, this enforced "otherness" making urgent to him the dangerous possibility of excluding other experiences in privileging one kind of certainty. This frame of reference adds another resonance to the punkah wallah's marginal figure, on whose "splendid form" and "untouchable" beauty the text lingers lovingly, seeing the "almost naked" "Indian of low birth" as a "beautiful [all] naked god" (PI 219) by the end of the chapter. The narrative makes this moment of resistance to colonial dominance, provoked by the dignified and sensual presence of the punkah wallah, also a site for homoerotic desire.[2] In using sexual ambivalence here to show the ambivalence of colonial authority, Forster not only questions the dominant discourse that appropriated his own sexuality but also shows its complicity with colonial power and unitary narratives that are based on imperialist, exclusionary models. And may we not also view as the novel's counter to these models both the queering of desire, as witnessed in the comradeship of Aziz and Fielding, and the feminizing of masculinity made possible in the narrative's undulating, sinuous movement of affection and gentleness between Aziz and Ralph Moore? This moment, often overlooked, provides the framing context for the final horse-riding scene of expansive inconclusiveness and deferment.

The disruption that finally becomes embodied in the figure of the punkah wallah reverberates through the town of Chandrapore, echoing in its people and in particular in the courtroom before and during the trial: "A new spirit seemed abroad, a rearrangement, which no one in the stern little band of whites could explain" (PI 204). This rearrangement of the familiar structure of power is manoeuvered by the "spontaneous forms of [rebellious] activity" that spurt up in Chandrapore, among its most disempowered and disenfranchised groups, disturbing the daily life of the city. As the Collector makes his way to the court, a pebble thrown by a child strikes his car in greeting. But it is the young students of Government College, the Collector's "pawns" for whom "he retained a contemptuous affection" (PI 204), who take special delight in their "sly civility"—another one of Bhabha's terms for insurrection (97)—and taunt the authority of the officer. In their sly resistance, they prevent the Collector's assertion of power by disallowing his entry into the front of the Courthouse and countermand the mark of his official privilege.

In the courtroom, the proceedings of the trial are interrupted from the very start with disruptive comments that sometimes seem to "[fall] from nowhere, from the ceiling perhaps" (PI 208). The Englishman's tendency to regard the situation of the attempted rape and this "formal" trial as an appropriate staging of "Oriental Pathology" (PI 208) invites resistance that results in painful and naked revelation of the pathology of empire itself. Thus, when the Superintendent, in his testimony, declares as a "general truth" that the "darker races are physically attracted by the fairer, but not vice versa," the Indian side of the Courtroom erupts with this rejoinder: "Even when the lady is so uglier than the gentleman?" (PI 208). Although present in the courtroom to punish the perpetrator of an assault on her body, Adela's body nevertheless trembles in resentment as it registers this (re)mark of undesirability. And in this trembling, Adela's body signals itself as a site for the play of colonial authority, emphasizing colonialism's mixed economy not only of power and domination but also of pleasure and desire that prevents its authority from being total or complete.[3]

The charge of alleged assault made by an English woman against an Indian man makes concrete the polarized relationship between the Indians and the English. For the English, the situation reinforces their sense of mission and superiority reflected in their communal sense of outraged virtue: "All over Chandrapore that day the Europeans were putting aside their normal personalities and sinking themselves in their community. Pity, wrath, heroism, filled them" (PI 156). For the Indians, it serves to unite Hindus and Muslims, the privileged and the ordinary, into a "confederacy" (PI 182) for a common cause against a common enemy. Thus the trial, seen by the English as a vindication of the moral impulse underpinning the imperial power's civilizing mission, also becomes an occasion for the English to exhort each other to keep fueled the colonial enterprise, with its now evident heterosexual, masculinist rhetoric and ideology:

And remember it afterwards, you men. You're weak, weak, weak. Why, [the Indians] ought to crawl from here to the caves on their hands and knees whenever an Englishwoman's in sight, they oughtn't to be spoken to, they ought to be spat at, they ought to be ground into the dust, we've been far too kind with our Bridge Parties and the rest. (PI 206)

In these vicious sentiments of Mrs. Turton, the novel enacts a twisted parody of the colonial situation: the civilizing mission of the imperial power—experienced by the subjected people as ravishment and pillaging—when threatened is defended by the outraged British as an assault on *their* virtue. What should have been rightly an appropriate appeal for the Indians to make is appropriated here by the English to promote their own cause. As Salman Rushdie comments: "It is useless, I'm sure, to suggest that if a rape must be used as the metaphor of the Indo-British connection, then surely, in the interests of accuracy, it should be the rape of an Indian woman by one or more Englishmen of whatever class . . ." (70).

The answer, or nonanswer (to use a term which *Passage* nudges us toward), to why the trial and the courtroom become such contested sites for colonial, heterosexist authority lurks within the Marabar caves and is suggested by Adela's panic in one of them. In the novel, which finds both the Indian landscape and its people finally beyond its utterance, the circular Marabar caves and what does (or does not) happen in them offer a hermeneutical frame for the elusiveness and sexual ambivalence troped in the figure of the punkah wallah and for the comradeship between Aziz and Fielding, as for the questions of masculinity and relation between races determining the fate of this comradeship.

The text concedes that it cannot ultimately master these caves, suggesting that by age alone—since in their outlines the sun may recognize "forms that were his before our globe was torn from his bosom" (PI 116)—the caves lie before the discernment that is necessary to bring into play binary oppositions (self/other, inside/outside) upon which hinges Western knowledge. These caves, which have (only) nothing attached to them, are "empty as an Easter egg" (PI 118). In their "terrifying echo. . . . entirely devoid of distinction" (PI 138) and their kissing/expiring flames that testify to the alienation at the heart of identification, these caves become a means by which *Passage* recognizes and confronts the racial and sexual other as "other," while it attempts not to participate in the fundamental imperialist structure of (literary) colonial appropriation. In this novel, then, India, as the "other imperial nation-state," "as the colonized other who is [the imperial system's] essential other component or opposite number," occupies the space of the "prototypical paradigm of the Other" (Jameson 49, 50); but, India becomes visible in the structure of the caves as an autonomous entity that has its secrets and that cannot be known in its entirety.

Adela, fond of stories, enters one of these caves that have resisted any "telling" and rushes out of it in a panic and with a story to tell. The story is about her experience of feeling assaulted in the cave by Aziz. However, when the two part at the entrance to a big group of caves they enter separate ones. Moreover, the narrative bears witness to Aziz's nonparticipation as it follows him, allowing us to be with him the whole time. All the same, it is also evident that something did happen to Adela: she becomes so upset that she leaves the Marabar Caves to return to Chandrapore without informing the rest of her party, and she feels violated enough to lodge a complaint against Aziz, who is then arrested upon his arrival back into town. Adela's panic is unmistakable, but all else at this point in the narrative seems incomprehensible and baffling, invites speculation, and in its indeterminacy the novel allows questions to rush in about the spuriousness of stories and dominating discourses (imperialism and compulsory heterosexuality), their lack of authority, and their questionable origins and motives.

The narrative significance of Adela's panic may be enhanced by seeing it as a complex variation of the figure of Pan as it appears in some of Forster's other, more European, fiction. Through the figure of the "fantastic" Pan, these novels and short stories attempt to force the main character to acknowledge his true sexuality and to disperse socially formed, unified selves, but the characters typically either fail in this or resist this very possibility. Alan Wilde develops this argument, explaining that "Pan is . . . above all an *idea*—the abstraction of desire, an urgency made comfortable to the demands of consciousness" ("Naturalization" 196).[4] But if in these other fictions, including *Maurice* and *The Longest Journey,* "Forster manages through his Pan figure to intimate sexuality . . . and at the same time to desexualize it" (Wilde, "Naturalization" 197), then the change from pastoral, fantastic Pan in these earlier novels to the "panic" of the caves in *A Passage to India* also accomplishes another change: sexuality, in the last novel, is not desexualized, but historicized and politicized. While Forster's short story, "The Story of a Panic," and the novels *The Longest Journey* and *Maurice* provide a "blueprint of desire" (Wilde, "Naturalization" 198), desire ending in abstraction as it flees to fantasy, *Passage* confronts sexuality within history, the history of empire, of relations between races, of desire, even as it accounts for the possibility of lack of ultimate union and success in relationships. Thus, if in Forster's earlier work Pan, together with his disruptive impact of sexual panic, stands for "Forster's need to harmonize in the face of chaos at no little cost to the integrity of the novels" (Wilde, "Naturalization" 199), then in the author's last full-length fictional narrative, Pan as panic—firmly attached to earth—realizes desire in all its poignancy and historical reality, witnessed most effectively in the novel's final words: " 'No, not yet,' . . . 'No, not there' " (PI 312).

Similar to Forster's questioning of the chivalric code, the panic in the caves—preceded as it is by Adela's doubts about her engagement and her passion for Ronny—offers an oblique, but undermining, commentary on the limitations of the heterosexual model. We see it in Adela's "formal" response to her engagement: "I don't feel a bit excited—I'm just glad it's *settled up* at last, but I'm not conscious of any vast changes" (PI 88, emphasis added). The official and exclusionary nature of (hetero)sexuality is the subtext, so the novel suggests, of the panic in the caves and of Adela's inability to interpret it positively, for "its message . . . avoided her well-equipped mind" (PI 128). It is largely this inability to relinquish her hold on "settled," knowable reality that carries over the disruptive effect of the caves into her relationship with Ronny, becoming both the cause and effect of her panic, for Adela realizes that the more she and Ronny discussed the misadventure in the cave, the more "intimacy seemed to caricature itself" (PI 186).

But this sexual panic also addresses narrative concerns. Not only does Adela come out of the cave with a story to tell, which is open to speculation, but it is a narrative that is turned into capital by the English, to be used to consolidate their imperious rule. Furthermore, the value of this anecdotal-colonial capital can be maintained only by controlling its audience and interpreters because, as Catherine MacKinnon puts it, "whose subjectivity becomes the objectivity of 'what happened' is a matter of social meaning, that is, it has been a matter of sexual politics" (654). The novel signals its awareness of this imbrication of story telling, power, and sexuality in the exchange between Fielding and the Superintendent of Police, after the former's request for a direct talk with Adela on grounds of sympathy for both parties—the apparent victim and the Indians—has been denied.

The panic in *A Passage to India,* with the novel's probings into the nature of sexuality and its self-reflexivity about narrative imperialism, is also a panic about empire and *its* molestations. Nicholas Potter explains how the incident with Adela brings into focus the colonial "other":

The outrage has brought the English into being, and this has two aspects. On the one hand there is much fine feeling within the embattled group, and on the other hand there is an intensification of hostility toward the 'other.' This has the effect of bringing the 'other' into being, firstly for the English as their myth of the 'Native' seems given solidity by their sense of themselves as a coherent group, and secondly for the Indians themselves, united against a common op-pressor. (210)

For such an explanation to be complete, however, one must also recog-nize the critique of empire implicit in this episode, conveyed through the grim fact that making the "other" visible in this way usually entails hostility and violence.[5] Moreover, the fraudulence of the civilizing mis-sion of colonialism is underlined by the ambiguity about the apparent act of ravishment (Adela's rape) responsible for the inevitable violence. Perhaps the text can represent the "other" without violence and without aesthetic or political colonization only by recognizing its own limitations in fully knowing the foreign subject. Thus, when Brenda Silver con-demns *Passage* for eliding Adela's experience through an act of periphra-sis that opens up "unbridgeable gaps," the critic fails to grasp the novel's commitment to these very gaps in its narrative: its "cracks in the uni-verse" (95) are *its* way of representing the "other."[6] In the disruptive and descriptive indeterminacy of the caves and what transpires in them, Forster's novel accepts that India, the colonial "other," cannot be seen merely as a trope of the "truth" of Western perception.

Not only the Marabar caves, but the inarticulate immensity of the entire Indian landscape, designate humanity as a minority, rendering moot humanity's need for racial and sexual minorities and subverting the domination of its decisions: "It matters so little to the majority of living beings what the minority, that calls itself human, desires, or de-cides. . . . in the tropics the indifference is more prominent, the inarticu-late world is closer at hand and readier to resume control . . . " (PI 105). In allowing this formlessness of the Indian landscape to resist narrative structuring, Forster's text, moreover, defies simple categories of identity formation. It affirms, instead, a complex and fluid model of relations based on inclusiveness yet difference suggested in the Indian land at once split by an infinite number of fissures yet harboring an inclu-siveness that blurs all distinctions and defies human categories.

In alluding to the possibility of such nonresolution in its text, the novel also conveys a subtle rejection of a conventional social paradigm. Mrs. Wilcox in *Howards End* bypasses her immediate family to hand over her inheritance to Margaret Schlegel (and the latter's sister, Helen). Mrs. Moore too does not pass on her legacy to Ronny and Adela, that is, to a heterosexual continuation. Instead, she recognizes Ralph and Stella as heirs who forward her legacy, particularly through Aziz's (partial) reconciliation with Fielding brought about by the nonimposing interven-tion of Ralph, and through Stella (now married to Fielding). *The Longest*

Journey, Howards End, and *Maurice* all struggle for heirs of same-sex lovers who would inherit the earth, inherit England. And all resort to fantasy to achieve this end: Stephen's child in *The Longest Journey,* as she grows up in the English countryside, bears the weight of history, human destiny and Rickie's tortured love for Stephen. In *Howards End,* because Helen will not marry and Margaret will not have children, these dearest sisters/friends will live on together, with Helen's son as Margaret's and England's heir. The infant will also have a lifelong comrade, Miss Avery's grandson Tom, and in their union these boys will be like Maurice and Alec at the end of *Maurice.*[7] *Passage,* however, confronts political and social reality that determines personal relationships; that is, the novel presents us with the qualified comradeship of Aziz and Fielding.

Aziz himself, in his affinity for and hostility toward the British, presents resistance to colonial authority. As such a figure of resistance, Aziz seems to act as what Bhabha has called the "mimic man" more consistently than does the punkah wallah. Aziz figures predominantly in the narrative action because both his background of traditional ethnicity and his status as a Western-educated man make him very mobile in his interaction with other Indians and the British, resulting in a conflicted and contested site of resistance to colonial authority. And, also like the punkah wallah but once again in a more complicated fashion because of his larger role in the narrative, Aziz demarcates a zone of homoerotic desire. The rhetoric of the British, however, judges Aziz's adaptability as duplicity: "The prisoner is one of those individuals who have led a double life," says McBryde (PI 213). Perhaps as significant, poignantly so, is Aziz's own ambivalence toward his social status and role as someone in whom an indigenous and a foreign culture commingle. Because he is an educated professional, he can defy, for instance, the English ceremonial hospitality and refuse to go to their bridge party. But as a colonized subordinate, the "complexion of his mind turn[s] from human to political" and he suffers from doubts and fears about his slight insurgencies (PI 53). The poignancy of the situation lies in Aziz's own painful awareness and conflict over the "double life" he leads (PI 10–11). It is difficult not to hear in Aziz's anxiety echoes of Forster's own keen and agonizing awareness that he too led a double life. As a homosexual, Forster lived and compromised with the gaps between "private desires and impulses and actions" and the "civilization" of the outside world, compromises which can be read in the subterfuges of his literary creations.[8] *Passage* connects colonial subject and sexual "deviant" as suppressed "others," designated as minorities by dominating discourses of political or sexual imperialism. Thus the resonating evocativeness of Aziz's hesitancy in boldly approaching his superior's house: "He compromised, and stopped the driver [of the tonga] just outside the flood of light that fell across the veranda" (PI 11).

What is deepest, if never fully realized, in Aziz's heart is perhaps best expressed in his affiliation with Fielding. When he urges Fielding for complete confidence ("It is far better you put all your difficulties before me, if we are to be friends for ever" [PI 242]), Aziz reveals his unorthodoxy and defiance of set Western norms about sex and intimacy. Such nonconformity characterizes the initial act of generosity that forms the basis of their friendship when Aziz, pretending to have a spare collar stud, gives one of his own to Fielding at the latter's party. The particular expansiveness of this relationship, its freedom from reductive racial and sexual generalities, also presents a model for a democratic, a more "representative," relationship between races. Not based on any particular similarity of interests or backgrounds, their friendship stems from mutual trust and understanding expressed in Aziz's instinctive sharing of his dead wife's picture with the Englishman ("All men are my brothers, and as soon as one behaves as such he may see my wife" [PI 108]), and in Fielding's staunch support of his Indian friend in the face of his compatriots' accusations. Aziz, unimpressed by rational explanations, would describe their friendship as resulting from "the secret understanding of the heart" (PI 14). *A Passage to India* implies that a shift in the paradigm, which privileges heterosexuality as "normal," to include same-sex relationships could help eliminate the structure of dominance prevalent in the meeting of two races. The friendship between Aziz and Fielding, with its coded pattern of erotic attraction, may be seen to present an instance of deviant, socially disapproved desire as the basis for new, free nations, which, for many modern nations, necessarily means independence from the yoke of colonial rule. But the novel also celebrates the "otherness" of the Indian (or non-Western) context, which fosters understanding between men, without recourse to the subterfuge of splitting the beloved into a sensual dark man or peasant and an intellectual friend, as in *Where Angels Fear to Tread* (Gino and Philip), *The Longest Journey* (Stephen and Ansell), and *Maurice* (Alec and Maurice).

However, just like the poem "which should be acclaimed by multitudes" that so inspires Aziz but which never gets written because "In what language shall it be written? And what shall it announce?" (PI 256), the friendship between Aziz and Fielding is also finally not fully realized. And, once again, the novel views the social and historical difficulty of relations between men in terms of the complexity of interaction between races. The one "Aphrodite with a Janus face" of *The Longest Journey,* which shows the oppositional splitting of Eros into the social and sensual, represents that novel's inability to image a convincing union between the two as it steers itself into fantasy in the teeth of history and resorts to the subterfuge of a symbolic mediation that involves Rickie loving Stephen only because their mother lived again in him. In *Passage,* the lack of union between Aziz and Fielding at the end marks instead the inclusion of history, "the divisions of daily life" (PI 311), in the novel, an acknowledgment that also prevents any character from the unreality that undermines Stephen as an independent character. Moreover, narrative subterfuge now manifests itself as *Passage*'s displacement of the "other"—a suppressed desire or subject—on to its formal aesthetics in order to realize the autonomy of the "other," as suggested in the undefinable caves, their indeterminable echo, the unconquerable punkah wallah, or enigmatic Godbole.

It is Godbole's song, open-ended through its appeal and expectation and not dependent on fulfillment of promise for completion, which suggests that we read as unconstricted the separation between Aziz and Fielding at the end of novel. As they ride toward their parting, Aziz and Fielding also ride into an open vista where there may not be immediate union but which is still unenclosed. And, Godbole's song of appeal, the echo of the caves, and the open ending of the narrative all image Forster's own acceptance of the difficulties of completion, whether sexual or textual. Moreover, the "Come" of Godbole's song echoes the "come" that Maurice hears in his dreams and that he himself utters just before Alec Scudder's entry into his room through the window. Maurice's "come" is answered by the friend he desires, but the appeal of *Passage* is to "the Friend who never comes yet is not entirely disproved" (PI 97). Perhaps this is why in the earlier novel Maurice and Scudder wander off into a fantasy "greenwood," away from community or society, and *Passage* ends with the unrestrained celebrations of the birth of Krishna, who can never be born and is always already born, at the Temple in Mau. In fact, the "greenwood" of *Maurice,* where Scudder and Maurice "must live outside class, without relations or money," finds the chance to become a part of society at Mau, with the Hindu state's unfamiliar and tantalizingly liberal communal character glimpsed in the celebrations of the birth of Krishna.

We witness Godbole's total abandonment to sounding the name of Krishna as he sings and dances in celebration of the god's birth, a god who is also cast in the role of the beloved.[9] The religious festivities supply the narrative with a matrix that not only accommodates amusement but also welcomes a variety of human folly enacted at a communal level.[10] The novel does not pretend to understand completely or know the nature of such activity, reveling only in the diverse proliferation of "the World's Desire" (PI 280) and consequently maintaining the authentic, separate human(e)ness of this otherness. But since "perhaps all birth is an allegory" (PI 280–81), such a combination also appealed to the marginalized Forster because he could find a queer space in this exuberant, anarchic social order and the potential to include his own deviation as a variant of human diverseness and "folly." The suggestion of "affection, or the possibility of it, [that] quivered through everything, from Gokul Ashtmi down to daily human relationships," as Forster notes in *The Hill of Devi*, is also made evident in the tentative, restrained, and considered representation of the interaction between Aziz and Ralph. Ralph, whom Aziz found to be "beautiful" (PI 301) and "not a type that is often exported imperially" (PI 299), reaches out to and finds a response in Aziz, a response that impels Aziz to acceptance and expansiveness. The nature of their relationship is perhaps best imaged through their chance and visionary encounter with the king's canopy as they row on the lake:

[Aziz] had heard of the image—made to imitate life at enormous expense—but he had never chanced to see it before, though he frequently rowed on the lake. There was only one spot from which it could be seen, and Ralph had directed [them] to it. . . . [Aziz] knew with his heart that this was Mrs. Moore's son, and indeed until his heart was involved he knew nothing. (PI 303)

Furthermore, as if signaling the triumph of the homoerotic male form in the comradeship of Aziz and Ralph, a servitor appears in the lake to preside over the immersion of the God. Echoing the unfettered beauty of the punkah wallah, the servitor stands "naked, broad-shouldered, thin-waisted—the Indian body again triumphant— . . ." (PI 304).

When Aziz walks in on Hamidullah and Mahmoud Ali in the opening scene of the novel, "they were discussing as to whether or no it is possible to be friends with an Englishman" (PI 5). The rest of *A Passage to India* addresses the possibility of friendship between races, as between men, and the question of how to represent it. In the process, it overturns the imperialist "Oriental Pathology" upheld by the British, a subversion epitomized in Aziz's designation of both Mrs. Moore and Ralph, at the beginning (PI 17) and end (PI 301) of the novel, respectively, as "orientals." This inversion becomes particularly significant since, as Edward Said maintains, "The Orient . . . is one of [Europe's] deepest and most recurring images of the Other" (1). The novel's disorienting dominant perception in this way relocates oriental to denote now the universal values of kindness, sympathy, and friendship, and it also reinstates femininity-in-masculinity as a basis of masculine identity.

Notes

1. Fredric Jameson uses Forster's *Howards End* as his main literary example to illustrate the modern text's ultimate failure to be modern in either style or its critique of modern culture. Nevertheless, I find his formulations regarding the intricate relationship between modern politics (building of empire) and modern literary imagination to be quite helpful in my reading of *A Passage to India*. Incidentally, this latter novel, which I find very closely demonstrates Forster's modernity according to Jameson's precepts, is dismissed from any consideration in a most unconvincing, because peremptory and seemingly willfully inaccurate, manner: "About *A Passage to India,* what needs to be said here is (a) that Forster's luck lay in the fact that one of the many Indian languages is the one called Indian English, which he was able to learn like a foreign language; and (b) that the novel is restricted to British and Muslim characters . . ." (65).

2. Jenny Sharpe, among other readers, recognizes the figure of the punkah wallah as a site of homosexual desire (150–151). However, I do not agree with her reservation that "Forster's representation of the untouchable is decidedly inadequate and, as a model for subaltern resistance, it ultimately fails" (152). When Forster, she claims, "does not speak in the place of the subaltern who cannot speak for himself, . . . he risks representing the punkah puller as nothing but the object of an Indian nationalist discourse and the construct of a Western (homosexual) desire" (152). But in trying to posit only understanding and enunciation as attributes of freedom, Sharpe privileges "speech," making the punkah wallah subject to a Western concept of determining individual freedom. Furthermore, she fails to realize that the punkah wallah does not speak or have cognition because he does not know English, the language of his conquerors, and in this way escapes the most insidious form of colonization.

3. For a theoretical analysis of this economy of colonialism, see Bhabha 156–161.

4. I largely agree with Wilde's reading of *A Passage to India;* however, I am unwilling to go along with his conclusion that in the "aesthetic coldness of Forster's gaze, Pan receives a mortal blow" (Wilde, "Naturalization" 204). My discussion, in fact, argues quite the opposite.

5. Quite often overlooked in readings of the novel is the alarmingly horrifying act of actual violence, and homophobia, that occurs while everyone's attention is caught up with the trial. Nureddin, "an effeminate youth" (PI 90), after a minor car accident is admitted into the hospital where he finds himself in Major Callendar's hands. The white doctor, who has made no pretense of his

hatred for the Indians, feels especially vicious toward this beautiful young boy. Implying to his fellow Englishmen that Nureddin is a homosexual and deserves physical disfigurement, Callendar mutilates the Indian boy's face (PI 206).

6. Moreover, Silver fails to see that this periphrasis belongs to the British, and not to the author.

7. See Robert K. Martin's article in this volume for a more extensive treatment of this point.

8. These phrases are part of Forster's own sentiments expressed in a letter from Alexandria, quoted in Watt.

9. I think the novel compels us to notice its subtle combination of the religious and the (homo)erotic in the descriptions of the festivities. Forster first became fascinated with this order—which allows a form of realization of impulses whose very existence was an affront to the social order he had inherited— at Dewas, as expressed in the person of its Maharajah, and in the sentiments of the Maharajah of Chhatarpur. While the Maharajah of Dewas "sang Hindi love-songs to [him] in the Indra Sabha cave," Forster records the Maharajah of Chhatarpur's feelings in *The Hill of Devi*: ". . . I can meditate on love, for love is the only power that can keep thought out. I try to meditate on Krishna. I do not know that he is a God, but I love Love. . . . *I worship and adore him as a man*" (HD 158, emphasis added).

10. See J. Birjie-Patil for the significance of Forster's stay at Dewas with regards to his sexual inclination and needs as a writer.

12

Colonial Queer Something

Yonatan Touval

Kindness, kindness, and more kindness—yes, that he might supply, but was that really all that the queer nation needed? *E. M. Forster,* A Passage to India

The Orient becomes a living tableau of queerness. *Edward Said,* Orientalism

The interstices of nationalisms and sexualities occupy a queer space—if we take "queer" to mean the mapping out, and in the process the demystification, of relations and identities that a hegemony of the normative would rather keep unexamined. In the climactic final chapter of *A Passage to India,* Aziz opens up just such a space, in a rhetorical performance that perceptively exposes the insidious collusion between colonial imperialism and Western sexuality. Addressing Fielding, but really addressing the British colonial regime in India at large, Aziz says:

[It is the o]ld story of "We will rob every man and rape every woman from Peshawar to Calcutta," I suppose, which you get some nobody to repeat and then quote every week in the *Pioneer* in order to frighten us into retaining you! We know! (PI 312)

As a target of what ultimately proves to be a false accusation of attempted rape, Aziz is speaking, of course, from personal experience.

For in the aftermath of the incident in the Marabar Caves and up until the termination of the trial, Aziz becomes the raison d'être of British colonial rule—of, more exactly, a tightening of that rule. In a discussion at the Club immediately following the incident, there is a plea among the members to "Call in the troops and clear the bazaars" (PI 178). "The crime was even worse than they had supposed—the unspeakable limit of cynicism, untouched since 1857" (PI 178). In collapsing sexual into nationalist (and military) violence, the reference to the Mutiny of 1857 also phobically abstracts the alleged sexual crime of one individual to the possibility of a nation-wide rampage. "It's the time for action," declares Major Callendar, echoing the sentiments of the Collector who "wanted to flog every native that he saw," but whose resistance to doing so hinges on one peculiar reason: "The dread of having to call in the troops was vivid to him; soldiers . . . love to humiliate the civilian administration" (PI 178, 174).

There is doubtless something begging of (demanding?) humiliation in a colon(ial) muscle that's not flexed tightly enough . . . at any rate, the allegations of rape, fear of insurgent nationalism, racial typologies and epistemologies, all collude in order to prevent the formation of any such (queer) space within the totality of the colonial—Oriental—project at large. Yet the queerness in Aziz's knowledge lies not only in a forceful understanding of how these different discursive regimes tighten ass, but also in the ability to destabilize the very coherence of the accusation—the accusation *of* the accusation—itself. "We will rob every man and rape every woman": what seems like an unproblematically straight pairing of two different kinds of violence (rob/man; rape/woman) immediately breaks down by the sheer insistence upon that unproblematicality, as "rape" and "rob" prove to be tongue twisters of a particularly dangerous kind. As labials differentiated in the English solely by whether they're voiced ("b") or voiceless ("p") plosives, "p" and "b" come close to performing a "punning" that—in Christopher Craft's words—"becomes homoerotic because homophonic" (Craft 38).[1] Or better still, that becomes queer because symphonic: for the binaric differential that breaks the plosives into two in English further breaks them into four in Urdu-Hindi, as each gets split into its aspirated and unaspirated variants. These labials which aren't—are no longer—two thus threaten to mismatch verb with object, rendering not only a woman robbed, but also, and far more problematically, a raped man.[2]

Even for the Westerner unschooled in the tricks of deconstruction, however, Indian sexuality would seem stunningly queer;[3] a single glance at the *Kama Sutra* should put *The Joy of Gay Sex* to shame. Still, to romanticize Oriental sexuality would be to reify the worst kind of Western assumptions and ignorances—ignorances especially striking in light of a long history of (to adopt the idiom of the American) "abusive relations" among imperialism, nationalism, and Indian bodies. Much of the reading that follows will chart such relations as they map the scope of *A Passage to India*, but the extent to which these relations reach beyond the confines of the Marabar Caves is important to emphasize. In her recent essay, "Indian Nationalism, Gandhian 'Satyagraha,' and Representations of Female Sexuality," Ketu H. Katrak delineates Mahatma Gandhi's "uses of women's bodies" in the modeling of his crusade for passive resistance:

Female sexuality was essentialized through Gandhi's appeals to the "female virtues": chastity, purity, self-sacrifice, suffering. . . . These "female" virtues were an "investment" in his nationalist, nonviolent strategy. "To me," Gandhi stated in 1921, "the female sex is not the weaker sex; it is the nobler of the two: for it is even today the embodiment of sacrifice, silent suffering, humility, faith and knowledge" (Katrak 396–98).

While Gandhi may have ultimately "essentialized" traditional stereotypes about womanhood—in a campaign, moreover, that was foremost concerned with national rather than women's liberation—it is important to note that within the parameters of gender politics qualities such as sacrifice and suffering are never so much essential as *relational:* to whatever extent womanhood "is" sacrifice or "is" suffering, womanhood is always sacrifice for another, or suffering in the interest of another, where "another" is presumed to be male. In calling upon men (as well as upon women) to embrace these supposed qualities of womanhood, therefore, Gandhi takes womanhood outside the domain of gender politics and, in so doing, neutralizes the political sphere within which womanhood is no longer "essentialized" so much as transformed into a platonic ideal: henceforth, all Indians are *like* women, all women are *like* Indians, all men are *like* women, and womanhood is *like* India just as India is *like* womanhood. Only during the years when Prime Minister Indira Gandhi had achieved the status of (nothing less than) an ego-ideal would the simile "like" be finally disposed of—in the famous line: "India is Indira and Indira is India."

If the Mahatma's vision of womanhood was therefore associated with passivity, it was a notion of passivity that—whether naively or brilliantly—was integral to an entire philosophy of resistance and, finally, independence; and by the time India felt comfortable assimilating its national identity to the figure of a woman, Indira had already established a reputation for being, at the very least, tough and dictatorial. In light of such touchstones in twentieth-century Indian history, it would be tempting to draw a narrative that would begin, say, with Gandhi's feminization of men and end with the masculinization of Indira. Katherine Mayo's famous *Mother India* (1927), which argued that Indian men's oppression of women had created a social psychology that had somehow made Indian society particularly susceptible to colonial rule, would fit neatly into the beginning of such a narrative, while Indira's sterilization program of the early 1970s would stand as that narrative's most spectacular conclusion.[4] And—why not?—into the middle of this narrative (say, into the months leading to Partition) we might as well interject a long-time Pakistani suspicion: that the British finally let India have Kashmir because the wife of the last viceroy (himself famously queer[5]) had Nehru. The value of such a sketch, of course, would lie chiefly in its formalism: as though the feminization of men would conversely precipitate a masculinization of women; as though, too, the Mahatma's wish to become "God's eunuch" would temporarily be answered by a hustling Nehru and finally be granted (*gratis,* we might add, plus a transistor radio!) by a castrating Indira.[6] But if history doesn't follow formalism, *A Passage to India* depicts a community—and I mean the Anglo-Indian one—that does. And the value of our imaginary narrative would lie precisely in the rhetorical force that, as Aziz would learn first-hand, sustains the very logic of the British Raj. Hence Ronny could theorize an India in which "the younger generation believe in a show of manly independence" (PI 27)—a remark that not only captures the uneasy paradox of a dual expectation that Indians at once put on a "show of manly independence" and still remain (in actuality?) in a position of womanly dependence, but also portends the epistemological quagmire that the specific incident in the Marabar Caves will inevitably posit: how can Aziz, simultaneously as it were, act the man and woman both?

This is ultimately what the trial is about, and the burden on the prosecution will be to resolve the apparent contradiction into a coherent formula that would neatly accommodate popular racism, evidential facts, political interests, and imperial misogyny. Something of the drift of that formula we begin to detect in the official charge against Aziz as outlined by the prosecution: "That he followed her into the caves and made insulting advances. She hit him with her field-glasses; he pulled at them and the strap broke, and that is how she got away. When we searched him just now, they were in his pocket" (PI 158–59). But it is Adela herself, who, though presumably lacking in the political shrewdness that makes for imperial sophistication, unwittingly stages the case for the prosecution's dazzling performance:

I went into the detestable cave . . . and I remember scratching the wall with my finger-nail, to start the usual echo, and then, as I was saying, there was this shadow, or sort of shadow, down the entrance tunnel, bottling me up. It seemed liked an age, but I suppose the whole thing can't have lasted thirty seconds really. I hit at him with the glasses, he pulled me round the cave by the strap, I escaped, that's all. He never actually touched me once. It all seems such nonsense. . . . Naturally I'm upset, but I shall get over it. (PI 184–85)

For all the professed outrage over what allegedly happened in the Marabar Caves, at least part of the charge seems to derive—does it not?—from its own immateriality.[7] Not only, that is to say, was a woman assaulted, but—and here is the real violation—she was not assaulted enough. Yet let us be clear again about the context: popular racism *expects* Aziz to be a rapist; evidential facts show that, even if attempting to act on that racial stereotype, Aziz *failed* to rape; political interests demand that Aziz continue to emblematize a certain kind of threat; and imperial misogyny fuels this fantastical chain from the start with sincere wishes that Adela had been raped—or how else to read the aftermath of a trial in which everyone's greatest irritation seems to lie less in the fact that Aziz is vindicated than that Adela wasn't raped after all? Indeed, even Adela's physical recuperation upsets no other than the Civil Surgeon who—the novel makes explicit—"appeared to resent his patient's recovery" (PI 176). If Adela had only closed her eyes and thought of England, perhaps the British Raj would have found justification to maintain its grip for another hundred years. It is within precisely such an overdetermined colonial sphere, I'm arguing, that the prosecution goes on to reformulate the charge against Aziz, so that Aziz will now stand trial not for attempting to rape Adela *but for failing to rape her.*

Of course, if (as in most discursive regimes) the conditions most demanding of change are those which have already made it conceivable, the prosecution in Aziz's trial can likewise be said not to impose a formula so much as to draw it from the field of colonial discourse. Consider this exchange between Fielding and McBryde over the presence of Adela's field-glasses in Aziz's pocket:

Fielding: "It is impossible that, having attempted to assault her, he would put her glasses into his pocket."

McBryde: "Quite possible, I'm afraid; when an Indian goes bad, he goes not only very bad, but also very queer. (PI 160)

So fully rationalized is the evidence that, more than simply refuting any hopes of undermining it, McBryde gives it a spin that only tightens the claim to truthfulness. Meanwhile if we, like Fielding, "don't follow" (PI 160), let the cosmopolitan British Superintendent of Police remind us of our provincialism: "How could you? When you think of crime you think of English crime. The psychology here is different" (PI 166). The paradigm through which Aziz will now be newly imagined, it turns out, has always already existed.

Or let us go one step back: What is different? How is the "psychology" in India "different" from the "psychology" in England? Where does that difference lie, and how is it constituted? The distinguishing mark, of course, has already been offered by McBryde: the Indian can go "not only very bad" (like the English), "but very queer" (like no one else). *Things queer:* there is the "queer valley" by the Marabar Caves (PI 140), Godbole's "queer little song" (PI 125), and Fielding's "queer vague talk" with him later (PI 166). Aziz finds Fielding to be "a queer chap" (PI 113), there are "queer reports" circulating through Chandrapore in advance of the trial (PI 204), and the victory that emerges from it is registered as "a queer one" (PI 222). Adela Quested herself is referred to as "the queer cautious girl" (PI 19), and (after the trial) as "the queer honest girl" (PI 237). Mrs. Moore, too, becomes increasingly "disagreeable and queer" (PI 208), and her ghostly presence at the courtroom as "Esmiss Esmoor" provokes Adela to shudder, "Isn't it all queer?" (PI 215). Even, finally, at the end of the novel, when Fielding and Aziz seem for a moment to have become "friends again," they take their last ride together in a scenery described as "park-like as England, but"—perhaps foreshadowing their final rift—"it did not cease being queer" (PI 308).

The landscape, the talk, the trial, the echo, the reports, the song, the people: it's as though queerness is the stuff things Indian (or, like Fielding, Adela, and Mrs. Moore, things *gone* Indian) are made of, the very essence of Indianicity. Or if not India's essence, at least its identity. And like all forms of identity, India's will by definition be rather elusive. "But nothing in India is identifiable," the novel cautions, "the mere asking of a question causes it to disappear or to merge in something else" (PI 78). Queerness seems to spring everywhere and therefore also nowhere, although it usually (if not always) springs in order to qualify some relation (*the* relation?) between Englishness and Indianness. Set against a normative standard of what is expected from things English, queerness thus becomes constituted by its *difference* from the English. "The psychology here is different," says McBryde, as though by marking it as "different" he has sufficiently done the work of describing it. But of course the function of McBryde's statement is not to describe so much as to perform, for his statement intends to convey that no small share of his duties as Superintendent of Police is based on a superior epistemology that enables him, but not Fielding, to do what the police do (or are supposed to do) best: to know. And while queerness is never more explicitly defined than in the assertion that it lies somewhere in the difference between things Indian and English (but on the side of the Indian), McBryde's know-it-when-you-see-it brand of epistemology, as vague and arbitrary as it seems, is indicatively shared by the entire Anglo-Indian community. "I really do know the truth about Indians" (PI 21), declares one woman at the club in a statement that implies more than simple cosmopolitanism. In fact, if queerness is that difference in the Indian which the quality of being English enables (entitles?) one to know, that ability may well in fact also secretly constitute a correlative ability: the ability of the Anglo-Indians to imagine (or identify) themselves as a community.

Hence, Adela and Mrs. Moore are ultimately banished from Anglo India for refusing an identity politics that hinges on identifying Indians. Mrs. Moore, who from the start disassociates herself from the Anglo-Indian community, identifies with Indians rather than, transitively, identifies them, and so must be hastily shipped away at the crucial moment when she begins to shake Adela's confidence in, precisely, the *identity* of her assailant. Adela's confidence is lost altogether during the trial, and it bears repeating that it's that loss of confidence in identifying her Indian assailant that formally ends Adela's short tenure in Anglo India. "The prisoner followed you, didn't he?"—"I am not quite sure" (PI 217). Adela refuses to identify Aziz—even as the one who would have failed to rape her. But she does something even more dangerous than simply fail to identify by admitting to mistake an earlier identification: "I'm afraid I have made a mistake" (PI 218). Since in misidentifying the Indian, the Anglo-Indian calls into question her own self-identification, Adela's remark is greeted by calls to "stop these proceedings on medical grounds" (PI 223): Adela simply can't be herself. For the threat to the Anglo-Indian's constitution *as* an Anglo-Indian in the dramatic ending of the trial lies in the possibility that, if Adela was mistaken in the process of identification, the very politics of identity might have to be rethought. "But nothing in India is identifiable, the mere asking of a question causes it to disappear or to merge in something else." If queerness finally isn't identifiable (and hence, by implication, also containable) within things Indian, there's no telling with what and with whom queerness might choose to merge—especially when a hyphen persistently reminds us of the provisional bridge that no more separates than conjoins the "Anglo" and the "Indian."

The terror of the Indian—what incites an Anglo-Indian community to playing the police—lies to a significant degree in the impossibility of telling ahead of time the place and the medium through which queerness might strike, or creep. "They give me the creeps" (PI 22), Mrs. Callendar says about the Indians, coming close to admitting her inability to specify why. That specificity can never be fixed, of course, but for that reason alone it most demands to be theorized. In the Anglo-Indian community of Mrs. Callendar, vulnerability is answered by conviction, even if in the form of fiction; identity, after all, needn't be true, it simply mustn't be shown to be *untrue*. Hence, perhaps, the great stakes in Aziz's trial, for in failing to rape Adela lies an implicit negation of at least two scientific theories dear to McBryde's heart (as well as, more generally, to Orientalism at large): first, McBryde's "theory of climatic zones," which, echoing something of Richard Burton's theory of the Sotadic Zone, states that "All unfortunate natives are criminals at heart, for the simple reason that they live south of latitude 30. They are not to blame, they have not a dog's chance--we should be like them if we settled here" (PI 158); and second, McBryde's "favorite theme" of "Oriental pathology," which claims that "the darker races are attracted by the fairer, but not vice versa—not a matter for bitterness this, not a matter for abuse, but just a fact which any scientific observer will confirm" (PI 208). What is interesting about these theories is the absence of gender (or sex) as a possible point of contamination, even when (sexual) attraction is raised to the fore. Since only race here charts the law of desire, the queerness of the Oriental extends precisely to the possibility that the Oriental might also be homosexual. And if Aziz had failed in his assault on Adela—or even if he had never launched one in the first place—the worse for him. For to refute one charge is invariably to produce another: if Aziz had merely *robbed* Adela of her field-glasses, there's no telling that he wouldn't *rape* the City Magistrate next.

McBryde's theories would prove flexible enough to accommodate the prosecution's reformulation of Aziz's crime as long as they aren't challenged head-on. But they are challenged—challenged when, for instance, someone in the courtroom suggests that it was Adela who was after Aziz rather than the other way around, since "the lady is so uglier than the gentleman" (PI 208); challenged, too, although somewhat less decisively, by Adela herself when she finally withdraws the charge. We might even say that, outside the courtroom, the narrative too seems eager to tear apart McBryde's theories, taking care to cite Aziz's dislike of Adela's looks—"Adela's angular body and the freckles on her face were terrible defects in his eyes, and he wondered how God could have been so unkind to any female form" (PI 61)—and Adela's (albeit tentative) attraction to Aziz:

What a handsome little Oriental he was, and no doubt his wife and children were beautiful too. . . . She did not admire him with any personal warmth, for there was nothing of the vagrant in her blood, but she guessed he might attract women of his own race and rank, and she regretted that neither she nor Ronny had physical charm. It does make a difference in a relationship—beauty, thick hair, a fine skin. (PI 144)

Desire flows from fair to dark—against McBryde's theories, against (we might generalize) a Northern racial aesthetic that, almost fifty years after formally letting go, still shapes (doubtless by that invisible hand that adroitly brushes the faces even of, as Bombay's film industry is known, Bollywood) contemporary Indian ethic: for why else the furor, the scandal, and the threats, over a kiss actress Shabana Azmi had placed on the cheek of Nelson Mandela at a recent function? And why do bachelors advertising their eligibility in the weekly matrimonials section of the *Times of India* so often cite—next to their fortunes, Green Cards, and other worldly possessions—their "fair" and "wheatish" complexions?

In *A Passage to India,* so threatening is darker skin that a predictable defense mechanism habitually averts the Anglo-Indian's thoughts from dark to fair. The novel itself performs such a shift when, during the trial, Aziz disappears from the narrative almost altogether.[8] As for Adela, she is paradoxically ignored by a community that prefers to abstract her particular case to a general panic over "women and children":

They had started speaking of 'women and children'—that phrase that exempts the male from sanity when it has been repeated a few times. Each felt that all he loved best in the world was at stake, demanded revenge, and was filled with a not unpleasing glow, in which the chilly and half-known features of Miss Quested vanished, and were replaced by all that is sweetest and warmest in the private life. (PI 174)

If part of the rhetorical force of this abstraction lies in the muddling of the specific charge of assault, that strategy, however, must ultimately fail. For whatever unspecifiable queerness is said to endanger English family values, such values turn out to be as unspecifiable as that against which they are so religiously shored up: we are left wondering what an Anglo-Indian exempted from sanity might actually *do* . . .

| | |

A QUEER EXCURSUS

If only we knew what the unspecifiable was: on the one hand, the queerness that threatens—on the other— the "sweetest and warmest." Let our hunch guide us through between the enchanting and the dangerous of a double bind that can't quite speak its name. Or let us, rather, attempt something infinitely more liberating: recognize that, for all the paranoia invoked, no double bind need actually exist; that the dangerous and enchanting aren't two walls that threaten to close in on us, shut us for good, but a modern mirage of competing aesthetics. Let us, in other words, for one precious moment, enjoy homosocial bonding without suffering from homosexual panic. Let us, I propose, jump into Aziz's bed.[9]

We won't be alone (what would be the point?) or, more snugly, alone *with* Aziz (let us postpone that to our wilder fantasies). Aziz is sick but entertaining guests ("One, two, three, four bumps, as people sat down upon his bed" [PI 94]), and we, too, if there's any room left—though particularly if there isn't—are invited to join in. And I mean, of course, not as some kind of *fifth* column, but as faithful participants in all that will be going on—in all, it bears repeating, without a tinge of paranoia. If we *must* be late (by playing the Indian, or, what at least in this novel amounts to the same, adhering to queer chic), then fine, just as long as we don't miss a word beyond the first few exchanges (whose topic on the ill health of Hindus isn't part of our lesson here anyway), and plunge into the scene right in time for Aziz's recitation of a poem by Ghalib. "It had," happily enough, "no connection with anything that had gone before, but it came from his heart and spoke to theirs" (PI 96):

They were overwhelmed by its pathos; pathos, they agreed, was the highest quality in art; a poem should touch the hearer with a sense of his own weakness, and should institute some comparison between mankind and flowers. The squalid bedroom grew quiet; the silly intrigues, the gossip, the shallow discontent were stilled, while words accepted as immortal filled the indifferent air. . . . Of the company, only Hamidullah had any comprehension of poetry. The minds of others were inferior and rough. Yet they listened with pleasure, because literature had not been divorced from their civilization. The police inspector, for instance, did not feel that Aziz had degraded himself by reciting, nor break into the cheery guffaw with which an Englishman averts the infection of beauty. . . . The poem had done no "good" to anyone but . . . it voiced our loneliness nevertheless, our isolation, our need for the Friend who never comes yet is not entirely disproved. (PI 96–7)

So intimate a scene, and all in bed—pathos, weakness, flowers, the pleasures of literature, the beauty of recitation: all emblematic of a certain (why not quote the text?) "fundamental gaiety," the kind that Aziz "reached when he was with those whom he trusted" (PI 48). If we still haven't got it, Ghalib's Urdu verse belongs to an ephebophilic tradition, as does the motif of the "Friend who never comes."[10]

| | | |

While Aziz's masculinity may strike an Englishman like McBryde as rather "queer," the quest for the "Friend who never comes" is much more than simply permissible for the presumptively heterosexual Indian male, but is rather expected as part of the institution of Indian maleness. To read this institution from an Anglo-European perspective, however, may still prove revealing, if not exactly of Aziz's sexuality, then of Anglo-Indian homophobia. Thus, for instance, we may note that Aziz's "queer effect" is drawn as much from an apparent absence as from a conspicuous excess of masculine self-consciousness. On the one hand, by cultivating the figure of the Mughal Emperor Babur, Aziz reveals a capacity for the kind of self-fashioning typical of the European veneration of St. Sebastian; on the other hand, Aziz exhibits a kind of natural abandon that emblematizes a different (but no less recognizable) kind of personage—the one whose maleness is reckoned all too *lightly* under guard. This type would be read into an Aziz who cries out, "Fielding! Oh, I have so wanted you!" (PI 146), or later, "Cyril, Cyril, don't leave me" (PI 221). Yet to the extent that the queerness of Aziz is, by definition, Anglo-European, it ultimately attaches itself most profitably to the Anglo-Indians themselves. To ask, therefore, who Aziz's friends are (or better: who among these friends isn't an Indian male? Or simpler yet: if not Indian, can he still be male?) betrays an interesting pattern, not least because Fielding stands out as its odd exception: if Indian, then the friend is necessarily male; if not Indian, which is to say English, then the friend is either Mrs. Moore, to a lesser extent Adela, or Fielding. In other words, the basic temperament required for friendship with Aziz is either that of an Indian male (or, in British terms, "queer") or that of an English woman (although that must be qualified by her being exceptionally nice and particularly unattractive). So that while Mrs. Moore and Adela can become Aziz's friends by being affined to the category of Indian men—"Aziz found the English ladies easy to talk to, he treated them like men" (PI 61)—Fielding is left to choose between two categories whose algebra *ugly English woman = queer Indian man*, even for so liberal a guy, must be hard to take. If only he hadn't been English, Fielding's masculinity might just have been spared.

As an Englishman, however, Fielding can't fool anyone, not least the astute Anglo-Indian women whose stake in identifying Fielding's kind is understandably the highest. "They disliked him. He took no notice of them, and this, which would have passed without comment in feminist England, did him harm in a community where the male is expected to be lively and helpful" (PI 56). A bachelor who isn't merely disinterested in looking for a wife but is clearly hateful of the wives of others, Fielding and his preferences must be deemed suspicious. That, moreover, even after having "discovered that it is possible to keep in with Indians and Englishmen, but that he who would also keep in with Englishwomen must drop the Indians" (PI 56), Fielding should sacrifice the company of Englishwomen for that of the Indians', bespeaks more than a simple break of convention. The novel, in fact, presses the point: "Most Englishmen preferred their own kinswomen," but Fielding "had found it convenient and pleasant to associate with Indians and he must pay the price" (PI 57). Where proper male decorum dictates dropping the company of either Englishwomen or Indian men, still "to keep with" Indian men is—for whatever racial, racist, sexist, British standards of behavior—necessarily reducible to, and can only be explained by, a desire for Indian men, a desire strong enough, at any rate, to be entirely consistent with "dropping" the women. (A note on my own "keeping with" several Pakistani friends: the very plurality of my having more than one friend from Pakistan has given occasion among my white, liberal friends to jokes—jokes certainly unhomophobic but less certainly unracist—that I'm into "Pakistani boys." Now what salacious logic has transformed the category "Pakistani *friends*" into "Pakistani *boyfriends*," or, more simply, into "Pakistani *boys*"—period? And how, I dare not wonder, would Sadia Abbas respond to being thus unsexed? As though to have more than one "such" friend violates, on the one hand, the bigoted sensibility of having even one, and, on the other, the politically correct sensibility of daring to have more than one. Less a predisposition on my part than, to diffuse any gay sentimentality, "a stroke of good luck," I've become, nevertheless, a curry queen.) Similarly, in *A Passage to India*, chumming with the Indians isn't merely socially queer (although it is), but must also be explainable by a queer predisposition.[11]

Not, however, that once he categorically drops the women Fielding is free of homosexual panic. A bachelor, who at least until the end of the novel seems intent on remaining one, Fielding may have rehearsed a retort for the pertinent question—Q: "Why are you not married?" A: Because I have more or less come through without it" (PI 110)—but can't finally contain his panic at the slightest provocation:

"Why don't you marry Miss Quested?"
"Good God! why, the girl's a prig. . . . Of course, I don't know her, but she struck me as one of the more pathetic products of Western education. She depresses me." (PI 110)

"Any suggestion that he should marry always does produce overstatements on the part of the bachelor" (PI 111). What begins as a little ritual of male bonding—by Aziz's "great compliment" to Fielding of showing him the photo of his late wife (PI 109); by Fielding confiding in Aziz "a little about myself" (PI 110)—soon develops into a moment of remarkable divisiveness, where the priorities and desires of an Indian male are revealed to be wholly different from those of an Englishman. At the very least, Aziz can, and often does, express his feelings (as when he talks about his late wife), while Fielding only "wished that he too could be carried away on waves of emotion" (PI 109). But Aziz is also quite lustful for women, whereas on this count too Fielding can't but remain somehow dumb. Thus even as Fielding dismisses Adela for being what he calls a "prig," Aziz (who tellingly doesn't even know the word) sees her fault—her *only* fault?—in having "practically no breasts" (PI 111), thereby throwing the label "prig" onto the embarrassed Fielding himself. "There is always trouble when two people do not think of sex at the same moment" (PI 263).

Unlike Aziz, whose desire for women is continuously invoked in lecherous fantasies of taking a trip to the brothels of Calcutta, Fielding's idea of sex remains circumscribed within the institution of marriage. True, the novel seems careful to intimate that it had not always been so with Fielding, but it relegates any such suggestions to mere innuendos. "His career," we read of Fielding, "though scholastic, was varied, and had included going to the bad and repenting thereafter" (PI 55). And when

McBryde later calls Fielding's attention to a letter Aziz wrote a friend "who apparently keeps a brothel" in Calcutta as proof that Aziz "was fixing up to see women," Fielding momentarily suspends his usual discretion: "I dare say you have the right to throw stones at a young man for doing that, but I haven't. I did the same at his age" (PI 161). Significantly, it is upon the occasion of Fielding's visit to Aziz that the narrative allows for this singular revelation:

He looked back at his own life. What a poor crop of secrets it had produced! There were things in it that he had shown to no one, but they were so uninteresting, it wasn't worth while lifting a purdah on their account. He'd been in love, engaged to be married, lady broke it off, memories of her and thoughts about her had kept him from other women for a time; then indulgence, followed by repentance and equilibrium. (PI 109)

But it is a revelation more homosocial than heterosexual, for it emerges from Fielding's desire to reciprocate Aziz's gesture of showing Fielding the photograph. "What had he done to deserve this outburst of confidence," wonders the half-panicked Fielding; "and what hostage could he give in exchange?" (PI 109).

If marriage continues to trouble Fielding up until, as well as after, his own at the end of the novel, it does so only in relation to, and the extent to which, his bachelorhood affects his relationship with Aziz. "It is on my mind that you think me a prude about women," Fielding writes to Aziz just before heading to England. "I had rather you thought anything else of me. If I live impeccably now, it is only because I am well on in the forties—a period of revision" (PI 268). And although he ultimately marries, Fielding's view of marriage is sinister at least:

Marriage is too absurd in any case. It begins and continues for such very slight reasons. The social business props it up on one side, and the theological business on the other, but neither of them are marriage, are they? I've friends who can't remember why they married, no more can their wives, I suspect that it mostly happens haphazard, though afterwards various noble reasons are invented. About marriage I am cynical. (PI 250–51)

Still, even after his marriage to Stella, Fielding's heterosexuality continues to be challenged, at once by Aziz's blunt question—"Is Stella not faithful to you, Cyril?" (PI 308)--and by the reality of that marriage itself: "He was not quite happy about his marriage. He was passionate physically again—the final flare-up before the clinkers of middle-age—and he knew that his wife did not love him as much as he loved her, and he was ashamed of pestering her" (PI 308). Ironically, if at first Fielding is to some degree separated from Aziz for lacking a desire for women, Fielding is now forever to remain separated from Aziz for finding such desire: "Fielding has thrown his lot with Anglo-India by marrying a countrywoman" (PI 309).[12]

One reason why Fielding's friendship with Aziz fails to improve even after Fielding's marriage is that, once *too* interesting as a bachelor, Fielding is now less than interesting as a married man. "I was thinking of telling you a little about myself some day if I can make it interesting enough," he confides to Aziz before his marriage (PI 110). Yet if whichever way Fielding goes he finds himself unable (as people of his kind often try so hard) to "get it right," it is because Fielding never will. For the sad fate is that precisely when he is most sure of having reached "it," Fielding is destined for that dramatic slip (or is it, incurred by its own internal slippage, *lisp?*) that will keep him outside the mode of normality by the sheer self-consciousness that has overdetermined, not to say curiously *mispronounced*, what is at best a highly delicate code. When it comes to marriage, Fielding completely misreads that code, failing to recognize that the state clearly privileged in *A Passage to India* is neither to get married nor not to get married, but rather *to have been married*. Such, certainly, is the example of both Aziz (who marries once) and Mrs. Moore (who marries twice), whose close friendship with each other serves as one clear indicator of the many benefits the novel wishes to advertise about the status of widowhood.[13] The other benefit, just as important, is that widowhood wields the needed authority for legitimating the rebuke of marriage, a rebuke that makes itself a project in all of Forster's novels with the exception of *A Room with a View*.

| | |

To end, but with this queer paradox: at a certain section of Bombay, a section known as Dongri, just steps from a local mosque, a modest door leads to an ancient establishment. Whether one is tempted to call it a bathhouse, or (as the sign over the door declares in Urdu) an "Irani hammam," its function and tradition remain the same. It has been there for over a hundred and fifty years, catering to a bustling male clientele. They flock there in the hundreds, especially on Fridays before prayers— men who, for ten rupees, procure a treatment of exquisite pleasures. In a large hall, just before the inner sauna, they unbutton their shirts and undress. Some then lounge in discreet alcoves, while others wrap around their waists the lungis provided for them to wear in the baths. As they enter the main bathing area, they are met by professional masseurs who, for time unspecified, rub and scrub their bodies in the thick mist. Signs on the stone walls warn: "Those suffering from V.D. or heart disease are strictly not permitted." Some distance away, not far from the Taj Mahal–Intercontinental Hotel, in the touristy section of Bombay's waterfront, one of the city's increasingly open gay bars is packed. In its air-conditioned room, men, some dressed in fashionable jeans, but all aptly dressed, spend an evening with friends. They drink beer, listen to music, chat, make plans for the following day. Perhaps a lucky few will later have sex.

The queerness of "East meets West": not merely in the sense that both of these institutions exist side by side, but also that the ancient one, the bathhouse (the bathhouse that, once part of medieval Europe and closed by the Church in its efforts to curtail male prostitution, later became part of gay liberation only to be shut down by the State in its attempt, equally zealous, to curtail gay sex) seems so much sleazier than its modern counterpart, the gay bar. For while in the first, naked men rub naked men, in the second, although ("Kama Sutra") rubbers might be on hand, any actual rubbing is postponed for another location. And while the Irani hammam becomes the simulacrum of hybridity itself, offering ancient luxuries (the cleansing ritual) in the face of modern realities ("heart disease," "V.D."), the gay bar exemplifies the paradox of a clientele more frank about what it seeks but also less likely to find it there. Still more, the Irani hammam, whose most regular bathers are precisely those most likely to deny the very thing they are there to enjoy, represents a culture (if not a religion) with relatively few injunctions against homosexuality; the gay bar, meanwhile, the prototype of a specifically Western emergence of a distinct gay culture (where *khush,* for happy or gay, is the new code word), represents the historical reason for its own precarious existence: gay sex is illegal in India only as a holdover from the British colonial statutes.

Notes

An early version of this essay was presented at the First Québec Lesbian and Gay Studies Conference in November 1992 as part of a panel on "Sex, Nation and Metaphor." I'd like to thank the chair of that panel, Judith Scherer Herz, as well as the respondent, Jody Berland, for exceedingly helpful suggestions. I'm also grateful to Robert K. Martin for taking an interest in my own interest in E. M. Forster, and for doing so even before I dreamed my thoughts were interest-

ing enough to "make public." Additional helpful advice came from John Mc-
Clure, Samina Najmi, Sadia Abbas, Sarah McKibben, Amir Najmi, Eleanor Kauf-
man, and L. Ramakrishnan.

1. "Aurally enacting a drive toward the same, the pun's sound cunningly
erases, or momentarily suspends, the semantic differences by which the hetero
is both made to appear and made to appear natural, lucid, self-evident" (Craft,
"Alias" 38).

2. Similar confusion has extended itself in Forster criticism to the sexual
significance of the Marabar Caves with at least two competing interpretations:
Frances L. Restuccia, for one, in an essay otherwise devoted to indeterminacy
in *A Passage to India,* confidently proceeds to determine the gender of the caves:
"The Caves are not only female morphologically but perhaps linguistically as
well" (Restuccia 122); and Sara Suleri, in an alternative reading, suggests that
"the category 'Marabar Cave' roughly translates into the anus of imperialism"
(Suleri 132).

3. I say would "seem" queer, since we should remain wary of the unqueer
(because misogynist) drift in numerous Hindu traditions—including that, of
course, of *sati.* As Ketu H. Katrak points out, "The notion of female suffering in
the Hindu tradition is dangerously glorified through such use of mythological
models" (Katrak 398). Still, some of these mythological models encompass
countless different forms of sexual dualism (as, for instance, the half-male, half-
female Siva), triadic structures (as in the notion of yoni, of female twins conjoining a third point representing earth), and diverse kinds of polymorphism (as in
the Tantric philosophy of the six *chakras,* or nerve centers, whose basal one lies
in the region of the rectum). Perhaps because of its monotheistic origins, Islamic
culture has been unable to compete with the sexual diversity of the Hindu tradition; but it, too, especially in the literature that has emerged from the Mughal
era, provides complex histories of sexual behavior. For a unique collection of
essays on South Asian traditions and sexualities, see Rakesh Ratti; for the more
academic stuff, see also the essays by R. Radhakrishnan and Gayatri Chakravorty
Spivak in Andrew Parker et al.

4. Katrak rightly points out that "Mayo's orientalizing approach focused
solely on the most dramatically visible forms of abuse—heaped upon Indian
women by Indian men. She did not discuss at all the colonizer's role in women's
oppression" (Katrak 403).

5. There is no "proof" that the last British viceroy to India was queer, but
the flamboyance of Lord Mountbatten of Burma has earned him a place in Roland
Barthes's journal in an entry that rustles with its own Barthesian queerness:
"—En rentrant, à la radio, j'ai appris l'attentat de l'IRA contre Lord Mountbatten.
Tout le monde est indigné, mais personne ne parle de la mort de son petit-
fils, gosse de quinze-ans" (—Returning home, on the radio, I learned of the
assassination of Lord Mountbatten by the IRA. Everyone is indignant, but no
one mentions the death of his grandson, a fifteen-year-old) (Barthes 88).

6. Ignored by such a narrative would be the precarious position of women in

India especially in times—as in today—of "Hindutva," or Hindu fundamentalist resurgence. For an excellent overview of contemporary legal debates in India, see Ratna Kapur and Brenda Cossman 35–44.

7. In her subtle reading of the novel, Restuccia argues that it's "Eastern indeterminacy in *A Passage to India,* which keeps alive the theoretical possibility of an attempted rape whose vagueness precludes the act from being prosecutable" (Restuccia, 111). I wish to carry her reading onto a different trajectory and suggest that Eastern indeterminacy more than simply "keeps alive the theoretical possibility of an attempted rape," but in effect *constitutes* it.

8. For this, as for a whole host of invaluable insights into the novel's narrative, style, history, and criticism, see Herz, *Passage.*

9. On "homosexual panic," consult Sedgwick, *Epistemology,* especially the chapter on "The Beast in the Jungle," 181–212; see also her *Between Men.*

10. See Tariq Rahman, "Significance" and "Homosexual."

11. For a consideration of personal relationships within a cross-cultural framework and biographical analogies between Aziz's friendship with Fielding and Forster's with Ross Masood, see Rustom Bharucha.

12. We might speculate that if Fielding had run his school in England rather than India, his bachelorhood would have provoked considerable anxiety from quite another direction. Compare his fate to that of Herbert Pembroke in *The Longest Journey* (1907) whose status as a single man prompts the parents of his charges to "demand that the house-master should have a wife" (LJ 63).

13. The novel creates the possibility that Aziz in fact remarries at the end of the novel, but the elusive suggestion seems to raise more questions than answers, including whether the new attachment is not a bride so much as a mistress:

Life passed pleasantly, the climate was healthy so that the children could be with him all the year round, and he had married again—not exactly a marriage, but he liked to regard it as one—and he read his Persian, wrote his poetry, had his horse, and sometimes got some shikar while the good Hindus looked the other way. (284)

Restuccia rightly notes: "We may wonder if this nonchalance is a matter of Aziz's lack of interest in his mate or if the narrative complies with Aziz's desire to protect his treasured mate from aliens" (Restuccia 121).

13

"It Must Have Been the Umbrella"; Forster's Queer Begetting

Robert K. Martin

Forster's famous comment about *Maurice,* that "a happy ending was imperative" (M 236), can be read as a political statement attacking the social reality that even under state repression one can talk about anything sexual as long as those who participate in forbidden pleasures get punished in the end. It may also send us back to the other novels to examine their endings and degrees of happiness. Only *A Room with a View* seems to end in a conventionally happy manner, while the other novels offer some form of recuperation, a life emerging out of death (the pattern of *The Longest Journey* and *Howards End*).[1] All of them offer a strong sense of structural closure, tying up the loose ends and anticipating the future, although perhaps with reduced expectations. One way to look at these happy endings is to examine their apparently Hegelian triads. Characteristically, in Hegel, two opposed principles (male and female, mind and heart, city and country) come up against each other, resulting in a new third principle that can draw from, even while transforming, its original binary opposites.[2]

For Forster, however, such triads must not be seen as successful sublimation (or *Aufhebung*), or even as transcendentalizing. Forster's ironic tone works to prevent such readings, except perhaps in *Mau-*

rice. But Forster's use of such structures is not simply philosophical. Instead he works toward a reorganized vision of human relations in order to allow continuance without physical conception, to provide continuity without heterosex and without nuclear family parenting. At the same time, Forster's texts reveal a drive toward an idealized male couple that could operate against the boundaries of class and nation. The endings of his texts thus more often than not enact this tension between union and community. So too the utopian vision of ideal love, often inscribed as friendship, must be reconciled with an erotics that is grounded in struggle and domination.

Much Forster criticism has obscured these tensions. Claude Summers describes the ending of *Where Angels Fear to Tread* this way: "as Caroline and Philip return to England, he realizes that he is in love with her. But just as he is on the verge of proposing marriage, she confesses her love for Gino [Philip's Italian brother-in-law]." The two are left "resign[ed] . . . to the fact that 'all the wonderful things had happened.' " Summers calls this ending "tenderly ironic" (*Forster* 30). Summers's description of the novel's conclusion indeed makes the text seem a tender acceptance of loss, and underscores a likely echo of Henry James's "The Beast in the Jungle," with its ironic account of an unlived life. But, as with James, matters are not that simple. The resignation is largely Philip's, just as it is he who leaves his would-be passion unspoken. Philip's attempted acknowledgement of his love for Caroline indicates his wish to efface his own desire for Gino, while Caroline at least is able to say, "If he had asked me, I might have given myself body and soul" (WAFT 147).

Summers's reading of this scene is in fact far too "tender": Philip's presumed inability to avow his love for Caroline is juxtaposed to his more clearly asserted love for Gino, in a comedy of misunderstanding. Philip asks Caroline to "say the word," by which he presumably means to agree to marry him, but to which she replies "that I love him" (WAFT 145), thereby prompting Philip to reflect on his "glad[ness] that she had once held the beloved in her arms" (WAFT 147). As the last quotation makes clear, Philip's apparent love for Caroline is in fact a displacement of his desire for Gino; if Caroline (and Lilia) had held Gino, then Philip can achieve his goals, indirectly, as part of a homosocial triangle of desire, like those described by Eve Kosofsky Sedgwick in *Between Men,* embracing Gino *through* Caroline. Philip's implied reproach (somewhat hypocritical at that) to Caroline's passion for Gino, "what ever have you got in common?" (WAFT 146), is echoed in Lytton Strachey's comment to Forster about *Maurice* that Maurice and Alec shared only curiosity and lust. They were not, for Forster, factors to be taken lightly.

Where Angels Fear to Tread is Forster's first sketch of a pattern that would play a large role in almost all his major works, with the striking exception of *Maurice*—the construction of a triangulated love that can be imagined as ensuring continuity through time without necessarily including sex. In many cases this love is represented in a revised family grouping centered around a child, often the child of a dead parent, who represents a radically new future. It is important to see that this pattern is distinctly *not* the simple recreation of a pattern of heterosexual, monogamous family, but instead an attempt to deal with the problem of continuity without direct physical begetting. As the constellation of "parents" works against the kind of romantic reading exemplified by Summers, so too the role of physical desire and physical pain in the construction of the sexual relation works against a sublimated notion of the ideal couple.

Philip's thought of Caroline and Gino together causes him to "smile bitterly" (at his own exclusion, presumably) and to reflect that "Here was the cruel antique malice of the gods, such as they once sent forth against Pasiphae" (WAFT 146). The allusion to bestiality reflects Philip's misogyny and his sense of rivalry; it leaves no doubt that the desires in this complex triangle are of the flesh. What the novel gestures toward, and later works will rewrite, is the formation of a circle of desire around a child who can symbolically displace the dualisms that dominate the texts. We can see it first in the consequence of the carriage accident: "Round the Italian baby who had died in the mud there centred deep passions and high hopes" (WAFT 133). In this early effort, Forster could not quite name those passions, but the mad quest to steal the baby, resulting only in death, is surely a crucial expression, albeit in comic opera form, of his desire to find an alternate genealogy, to acknowledge ties of support and influence that may exceed the claims of physical begetting, without, of course, accepting the alternate claims of the Herritons, who speak for a "family" obligation even in the absence of affection.

Philip and Caroline, who share a less judgmental, or "Hebraic," view of Italy, are more fitting parents for the child, through love rather than through family, and appropriate mates for his father, Gino, even if this can only be expressed through an appeal to a heterosexual tradition of unfulfilled passion. That Philip feels intensely toward Gino is made clear in that remarkable moment when Gino tortures his broken arm and Philip knocks Gino down, "raise[d] him up, and propped his body against his own. He passed his arm around him. Again he was filled with pity and tenderness. He awaited the revival without fear, sure that both of them were safe at last" (WAFT 136). The language is remarkable in its placement immediately after the scene of pain and in its utopian strains ("safe at last"). Unfortunately, these utopian moments, which became a staple of pro-gay Forster criticism after the publication of *Maurice,* have too often come to silence a more complicated notion of desire and pain. If the Philip who thinks of proposing to Caroline is an early Prufrock, anticipating Eliot's ironic hero in his aestheticism and world-weariness, it is another Philip who is sexually aroused by Gino and his violence.

In a related, posthumously published story, "Ralph and Tony" (1902–1903), Forster addresses a triangular and sadomasochistic love more directly. Although Summers has called the story (or fragment, as he considers it) "crude" and "inept" (*Forster* 292), it locates Forster's search for renewal of the body and integration with the spirit in the context of *fin-de-siècle* theories of heredity and health, topics later expanded in *The Longest Journey.* Forster's repeated presentation of a desire for abjection before a handsome athlete has its origins in such sources as Pater's celebration of the Greek athlete and Housman's laments for the "athlete dying young." Although the exploration of masochism in the origins of desire has been seen in terms of personal neurosis in hostile studies, such as Meyers's (104), it should rather be examined as a sickness of (over-)civilization, a rejection of the purely intellectual that was a part of the cultural shift to neopaganism in the period.

Although it is clearly true that the essential relation in the story is that between the two men, Elizabeth Heine goes too far when she argues that "Margaret functions as an entirely transparent medium for Ralph's love for Tony" (x). Ralph's love for Tony and his love for Margaret, although possibly of different intensities and different corporealities, are meant, at least, to be equally valid. Margaret is not a "transparent medium" so much as a guide and intermediary who can, like her namesake in *Howards End,* work toward connection, providing both companionship with a woman and passionate love with a man.

As in *Howards End,* where the apparently sterile Schlegels assure a continuity that is evidently beyond the capacity of the ostentatiously fertile Wilcoxes, so in "Ralph and Tony" it is the "unhealthy" Ralph who can ensure the survival of the "healthy" Tony, in an acknowledgement by Forster that health is not identical with physical appearance. A story that appears to be about the manly virtues thus concludes, without abandoning an attraction to the robust male, by acknowledging a need for the unhealthy, or indeed their union. The terms of the contrast are taken directly from the discourses of eugenics, and their connections to sexology. Tony is "a beautiful half-wild animal" (AS 70), while Ralph is, in

Tony's words, "affected, decadent, morbid, neurotic" (AS 69). The question is how to locate Tony's animality in the world without abandoning his passionate freedoms. It is Margaret who is able to bridge these worlds, realizing that Ralph, despite his "affectations," "was not insincere" (AS 70). Forster indicates that Ralph is indeed alert enough to understand Tony's accusations against him, that he is "not a man—soft and rotten through and through" and that his head isn't "oversound" (AS 72) and to reply with a sharp political sense, "Sanity is the focus of the majority" (AS 73). What Ralph knows is that his difference is the result of a social judgment: he is condemned to difference by a measure of normality, here masculinity, that he cannot meet in himself but instead must seek in others.

Tony's initial response to Ralph is homophobic, reflecting a fear of contagion: "we catch him like a disease, and become affected and unnatural like himself" (AS 73). Ralph has accepted a self-loathing view of himself as sick, with "a sore place" that causes others to "shudder" at the sight (AS 75), like Rickie's lame leg in *The Longest Journey*. Ralph wants justice, and not mercy or pity, as he explains to Margaret. If he accepts a *fin-de-siècle* sense of homosexuality as disease and maiming, he refuses to plead for tolerance. He knows that his performance of insincerity—of not feeling—is but a masquerade. Margaret's desire to pursue Ralph's friendship in London is interrupted by Tony's return from the mountains, arrayed as the hunter and warrior dripping blood from "a dead chamois slung from a pole" (AS 78). Tony has realized the possible threat to his relationship with his sister (who had seen him as a "radiant demigod" [AS 68]), and he is prepared to assert his manhood, "feeling his muscles and practising his strokes" (AS 79) in a way that conflates gender performance and autoeroticism.

Ralph's rather surprising proposal of a polyandrous *ménage-à-trois* in which he wants to "marry" Margaret but "live with" Tony (AS 80) might be read as a search for a cultural androgyny, or, more pertinently, as a way of reconciling affection and desire, tenderness and brutality, but is also part of Forster's attempt to escape from heterosexual monogamy. He seeks an alternative to a hierarchy of relations, in which marriage must take priority over friendship, or vice versa. In this rather fantastic world, Forster attempts to preserve the values of what he terms "the new love" (AS 80), what we might call queer affections. Such affections run throughout his fiction, where they occupy an important place, questioning the assumption of the ideal couple. They do not preclude a sense of subjection or an act of physical submission.

After Tony's refusal of Ralph's proposal, Ralph "fell prone on the floor at Tony's feet, crying, moaning, imploring to be loved. And Tony, without a word, set his teeth and kicked him with all his force, again and again" (AS 81). This masochistic abjection is almost embarrassing in its frankness, revealing a side of Forster's imagination that gay critics have often sought to efface, but it is also crucial as an expression of the need to escape from conventionality and rationality. As the "Kanaya" text from 1922 indicates, Forster was not excited by weakness, but sought to provoke a violent erotic response, even in the context of imperial power. Ralph's submission is the acknowledgement of his desire without a Greek pretext, and it forces Tony into an engagement with his body, even if it is one of attack. Ralph himself becomes capable of passion, just as Tony, whose heart condition is discovered, must develop a rationality that can replace the merely physical. In the logic of sadomasochism, Ralph's "submission" is also his domination of Tony, who is forced into an act of physical desire and expression, albeit in a disguised form as aggression. The two are now able to unite and to join with Margaret, who, refusing traditional femininity, remains "unladylike to the last" (AS 92), to form a threesome of desire. It is as if George Emerson were to marry Lucy Honeychurch *and* Cecil Vyse at the end of *A Room with a View*.

In this very early sketch, the concern is with the triangle and the desire for masculinity. What is increasingly added to the portrait is the child, in Forster almost never linked simply to its biological parents. As I shall argue, for instance, the parental scene at the end of *The Longest Journey* unites Stephen with Ansell and Stephen's child, while *Howards End* concludes with the two sisters and "their" progeny (actually of course Helen's child by Leonard). Over and over again Forster worries about the problem of continuation, or what I. A. Richards calls the "survival theme" (19), hinting at possible biographical sources of this question in his references to Forster's "special preoccupation" and "peculiar personal preoccupation" (18, 20). For Forster the issue is not simply personal but social: how can one praise the single life and question monogamy without addressing the issue of continuation? In *The Longest Journey* this is in effect the largest question and most pervasive theme.

Its roots may be traced back very far: Plato has Diotima argue for the kind of man who longs "to beget and generate" in the soul. Such a man, keeping in mind the beauty of his friend, brings "forth that which he had conceived long before and in company with him tends that which he brings forth," in a partnership based on a "nearer tie [of] friendship" (*Dialogues* 1.541). Plato has in mind children as metaphors for creative work and production, but the passage testifies to a desire for a life that can continue beyond death, in a Paterian "subjective immortality." It is a desire to be remembered, to leave something memorable behind. The child may also be understood as a project of reconciliation of opposites, a new bisexual being that can pass beyond gender or class, a model for which Trilling finds convincingly in the Euphorion of Goethe's *Faust* (*Forster* 100). It is important to note, though, that the search is not for the reunification of difference in a single character (that is, the traditional model of personal androgyny). The search is rather for a connection that brings alternate modes together without the loss of either and that characteristically in Forster finds expression in the triangular (both erotic and structural) and its complications of the binary.

Much of this material is rehearsed in *The Longest Journey*, Forster's contemplation of friendship and inheritance, where suburban, feminine Sawston must join with homosocial Cambridge in a rural Wiltshire. The relation between Rickie Elliot and Gerald Dawes repeats that between Ralph and Tony, with Agnes as a less sympathetic version of Margaret. The lame Rickie is simultaneously attracted to and repulsed by Gerald, the school bully. Gerald's physical attraction is clear: he has "the figure of a Greek athlete and the face of an English one." That ironic contrast is echoed in the narrator's wistful remark, "Just where he began to be beautiful the clothes started" (LJ 35), indicating the suppression of "the Greek" under cover of respectability and heterosexuality. To see "the Greek" Rickie must (imaginatively) see through the clothes to the naked athlete's body. He can have no access to that body, though, except through the mind. Can this vision of the beautiful athlete, like the vision of the beautiful youth in the *Phaedrus*, lead to the contemplation of the Beautiful? Rickie is in any case incapable of understanding the question: for him Plato is "too difficult" (LJ 46).

Despite (or because of) the power of an anglicized Hellenism, represented in its degenerate form in the Pembrokes' bust of Hermes, Rickie can inherit the figure of the heroic male body as the source of all beauty, but he can engage with that body only through an identification of himself with the female. He sees Gerald and Agnes together and recognizes with confused envy the submission of Agnes, now made over into a generic battle of the sexes: "The man's grip was the stronger. He had drawn the woman on to his knee, was pressing her, with all his strength, against him. Already her hands slipped off him, and she whispered, 'Don't—you hurt —'" (LJ 39).

Rickie's response to the scene and his own voyeurism, echoed by Agnes's "thrill of joy when she thought of the weak boy in the clutches of the strong one" (LJ 50), is to propose marriage—to *both* Gerald and

Agnes. As Gerald indignantly puts it, "Marry us—he, you, and me" (LJ 49). This is, for Gerald, at once "unhealthiness" and a threat to his masculine power. For Rickie it is both a way of ensuring continuation without begetting and a way of loving Gerald. For Rickie has accepted the idea that his lameness is congenital and that "he daren't risk having any children" (LJ 50). Once again a eugenicist view of the healthy body and the need for sound breeding coincides with a sexological view of innate homosexuality. Unlike the Freudian model of family relations or traumatic experience in the origin of "neurosis," the sexological model being invoked here[3] sees sexuality written on the body in a way that anticipates current theories of genetic origins of homosexuality. Rickie's response, although read as illness by Gerald, and by the sexologists, is also a result of the glorification of the young male body and the internalization of his own sense of inadequacy. He must die out, but he must also find some way of continuing. This he accomplishes by what the narrator calls "deflect[ing] his enthusiasms," transfiguring "a man who was dead and a woman who was still alive" (LJ 60).

As with the reversal of roles in "Ralph and Tony," it is the unhealthy Rickie who survives while Gerald dies, "broken up in the football match" (LJ 51). This sudden discovery of mortality at the core of aggressive masculinity casts in doubt Rickie's sense of his own inferiority. What is at stake is Forster's probing of gender roles and the meanings of masculinity. Rickie, much like the autobiographical Forster, feels excluded from patriarchal values and the imposition of the male will at the same time that he desires to move beyond observation to participation, as Wilfred Stone correctly puts it (*Cave* 183). To participate requires that Rickie *become* the athlete that he desires, but since he can never achieve this transformation he is bound to remain the athlete manqué. Rickie wants in some sense to *be* both Agnes and Gerald, as well as to marry them both. As a feminized subject, he seeks to celebrate his own submission as the constitution of subjectivity, as well as to demand his right to participation in a world of heterosexual privilege.

As Stone puts it, what is at stake for Rickie is "the discovery of his true nature" and his decision whether, in light of this nature, to defy or endure convention (*Cave* 192–3)—in other words, to acknowledge his homosexuality and then to decide whether or not to live in function of that sexuality. Such language of "nature" will seem oddly dated to many queer theorists, for whom nature is never that clear. It must be remembered that Forster inherits—partly from his mentor Whitman—and works with a model of a fixed self that is discoverable beneath the surface of convention. At the same time he offers a very complex view of human behaviors and desires. Desire, as we see with Rickie's attraction to Gerald, is a very dubious guide to friendship or even love, although a life without it would be lean indeed. As Forster celebrates passion, as an antidote to a passionless conformity, he remains sufficiently ironic to be aware of the uses to which hero worship may be put, in militarism and patriarchy. This conflict underlies all his political writing. Part of the problem of a liberal view is its inability to register aggression and power except as other, as inherently evil. This blindness can lead to a naïve view of representation and desire. Forster, in his texts, wants his utopian love and also wants a strong, forceful partner. This tension, crucial to Forster's work, should not be seen as simply personal and not cultural— for the desire for a strong, passionate other is part of a move toward the recuperation of the body and the intuitive. To be whipped, as Forster's friend T. E. Lawrence was, was in many ways to use aggression against the self as a form of self-(re)constitution.

The kind of intense physical relationship that is present, although in problematic form, in Rickie's admiration and hatred for Gerald, is present in a much more conventional or sublimated form between Ansell and Rickie, signaling another way of reconciling the desire for the body and the needs of the mind. The two young men "play at" a kind of sadomasochistic encounter that follows immediately on Rickie's reflection on the need for a "friendship office, where the marriage of true minds could be registered" (LJ 64). He seeks a public record and hence implicit approval of male love at the same time that he draws on a Platonic idealism via Shakespeare.

That meditation indicates that Rickie is aware of his situation as the homosexual outsider who "shall only look at the outside of homes" (LJ 63). Forster is after all part of the first generation of "homosexuals," according to much contemporary thought derived from Michel Foucault; what had preceded were homosexual acts without identity. Rickie wishes "we were labelled" (LJ 64) at precisely that historical moment when homosexuals were indeed being labeled, a process that brought at once a greater ability to control sexual activity (since the homosexual was now visible, even if only metaphorically lame) and a counterdiscourse, to borrow Foucault's term, of homosexual self-affirmation. If *The Longest Journey* does not precisely label (the word "homosexual" does not appear in the text), Rickie's plea with its invocation of David and Jonathan and of Shakespeare's sonnets takes part in a barely coded discourse of difference and historical continuity.

The problem for Rickie is a need to survive, to have access to a history, what Forster in a letter called "the yearning for permanence" (qtd. in

Widdowson 57). Instead, though, people like Rickie cannot have a place in Nature, unless they act as "dutiful sons, loving husbands, responsible fathers": men's roles are related to the family, and they must give up their friendships when they marry and produce children. In this, the minority situation of homosexuals is, Rickie suggests, unlike that of the Jews, whose persecution, as in the Dreyfus trial to which he alludes obliquely as the "seed" of Abram and Sarai that "disturbs the politics of Europe" (LJ 64), is a part of a long history; the homosexual, having no way to record his love, is destined to die out in each generation.

Rickie's idealized view of the homosexual couple runs, of course, against the Shelley poem "Epipsychidion" from which the title of the novel is taken. Rickie wants a life companion but is unable to recognize one in Ansell. The two men lie together in a Theocritan meadow, from which Rickie will flee, in apparent confusion and terror, to Agnes. Ansell holds Rickie's ankle, even as Rickie asks, "Lemme go," reflecting, with echoes of Gerald, "It's amusing that you're so feeble. You—simply—can't—get—away. I wish I wanted to bully you" (LJ 65). Ansell gets pleasure from holding Rickie prisoner, but only in a playful way. Rickie's masochism is channeled away from the erotic to the cultural. Ansell cannot hold Rickie back, particularly from going to Agnes and making a disastrous marriage of conventionality, from which even the memory of Gerald has faded. The purely intellectual companionship that Ansell offers, although it has its playful sexual moments, may still be seen as only partial: like Maurice in the later novel, Rickie needs to go beyond this idealized Cambridge friendship. Although Stephen in his rural working class attributes provides this novel's analogue to *Maurice*'s Alec, when he calls out to Rickie in a crucial scene, his call is interrupted by Agnes, "the woman who had conquered" (LJ 138). Forster does not seem able (or willing) to make that leap toward a committed homosexual coupling—indeed his pattern of triangulation must argue against it. It is the othering of the homosexual that makes his erotic experience become a means to a larger freedom, a multiplication of desires and experiences, what we may think of as a queer différance.

In the absence of Gerald, the obvious triangle would be Ansell, Rickie, and Agnes, but that is precluded, and not only by Agnes's intense dislike for Ansell. Rickie asks Ansell, "Can't I love you both?" and in the same letter tells Ansell that their friendship is now "registered" (LJ 83), apparently not recognizing that a registration office imposes a model of exclusivity and permanence that works against loving "both" of them. Rickie is apparently unable to see the effect of the inscription of marriage as normal and compulsory. Marriage and the subordination of friendship are, as Ansell's friend Tilliard says, "ordained by nature" (LJ 80). Rickie faces this kind of objection, even within the circle of Cambridge friends (Tilliard rejoices that Agnes may make Rickie "manly, for, much as I like Rickie, I always think him a little effeminate" [LJ 79]—but then he will later be Agnes's spy). Thus, Rickie is unable to pursue both individual and group friendships and instead falls into a triangle with Agnes and her brother, in which Herbert plays the traditional patriarchal authority, in his case a bully without sex appeal.

In this novel about legitimacy and inheritance, considerable attention is given to the role of the family as a social institution. The two half-brothers, Rickie and Stephen, represent respectively the legitimate paternal line and the illegitimate maternal line. Part of the function of this contrast is to put into question the nature of "legitimacy" and to see how sexual politics become the basis of property rights. Although there are important family ties throughout, none of them may be said to be obviously "natural," except perhaps the lower class, Jewish Ansells, who are beyond the pale for reasons of class and ethnicity. The Pembrokes form a brother-sister union that persists even after Agnes's marriage, while Herbert's attempt to marry for reasons of his career leads only to a refusal by his potential wife "with a violence that alarmed them both" (LJ 150). And the widowed Mrs. Failing acts as a very strange aunt/mother figure for Stephen, who is treated as a menial. Family is valued as a concept, but ignored in fact, except when it accomplishes a social purpose. Forster makes it clear that elective human relations based on affection or passion (as in Mrs. Elliot's love for Robert) have a claim much greater than that of family, although he renders Rickie incapable of understanding this. In that, Rickie is a true product of what Forster always sees as the suburban mind.

The family serves, then, to control the sexual behavior of its members, particularly the women, and to ensure the limitation of the rights of succession, in the interest of the conservation of property. It has no inherent interest: as Stephen puts it, "One must be the son of some one" (LJ 216). Although he maintains that ancestry is "trivial" (LJ 244), Stephen himself is the "child of poetry and of rebellion" (LJ 242), and a means of perpetuating the spiritual legacy of their mother, her moment of resistance to her husband and to the proprieties. Even in his relation to Rickie, he refuses to lay his claim on the basis of biological brotherhood, insisting that he be accepted as a man, "not as a brother" (LJ 257).

The novel thus opposes a codified law based on property and a "natural" law based upon desire. After Rickie's death, Stephen and Ansell find themselves together with Stephen's child and Agnes. Herbert departs in a fury after attempting to steal Rickie's royalties from Stephen, charging that Stephen had "filched" from his house "a faded photograph" (LJ 286) of Stockholm, the testimony, along with Stephen himself, to Mrs. Elliot's moment of romantic rebellion. The photograph belongs by a kind of natural law to Stephen as the product of that moment, and only the narrowest legal interpretation would see it otherwise. It is Mrs. Elliot whose spirit prevails at the end, not as a physical parent but as a guide to passions that defy convention. Against Herbert's percentages and calculations, there remains a world of natural renewal ("Sweet peas offered their fragrance" [LJ 287]) and harmony with nature (Stephen says of his daughter, "It is time that she learnt to sleep out" [LJ 288]). The "family" that surrounds the child, its "unnatural" character now becoming a sign of its naturalness, or escape from the code, is composed of the three whom Rickie has loved in different ways, and together they continue him spiritually, publishing his stories, as Stephen is continued physically. Sleeping outdoors like her father, or so the utopian text fantasizes, the child will grow up without a fear of the natural or an overestimation of culture and inheritance. Forster's insistence on the mythological patterns, his desire to get beyond rationality, forces him ultimately to reject the domination of the domestic and the domination of the collegial. If he and Ansell had fought about the priority of wife and friend, the vision of the conclusion attempts to assert their equality, to prove that one can love both wife and friend. Although the book is dedicated "Fratribus," its nod is not simply to the "brothers" of Cambridge, but to a form of ascending fraternity, including physical brotherhood, in the sense of Schiller's Ode to Joy. The novel ends with Forster's apparent resolution of his dilemma about continuity: as Claude Summers has memorably put it, "fraternity has begotten progeny" (Forster 72).

Howards End works out many of the same patterns, although without the presence of Cambridge (Tibby's Oxford takes its place only very ironically). The question of property is addressed more directly through the house whose name is the title of the book, as well as through the question of fixed incomes and investments. It is Forster's only book in which both of the main characters are women, and in which the female (as well as the feminine) contests male privilege. Ruth Wilcox brings together her role as fertility goddess with her role as spirit of place to challenge the world of absentee ownership, whether of houses or countries. Her legacy of Howards End to Margaret Schlegel operates as a central expression of the contrast we have already seen between codified law and spiritual law. If Ruth gives Howards End to Margaret, it is because she believes it already belongs to Margaret by a kind of spiritual succession. But the hand-written note that she leaves to express this gift is not legally valid, as the Wilcoxes know. The members of the family comically multiply their reasons for finding the document invalid—it was not prepared by a lawyer, it was written in pencil, it was not signed, it was not Ruth's handwriting (HE 95). But none of these reasons addresses the real issue, not recognized in law, that Ruth should be able to give the house to its "rightful" owner Margaret, as someone who will know how to appreciate it, and understand its history. It is in any case a part of a matrilineal heritage—Ruth's property that is lost on her marriage to a Wilcox. The Wilcoxes have imposed a phallic masculine mode on the feminine house, and this narrowness is reflected in their violation of "natural" law. After in effect stealing Howards End from Margaret, Henry Wilcox tries to prevent her from spending the night there, asserting, in an ironic reversal, the rights of property as "something far greater" (HE 323) that will permit him to pass the house from his own "illegitimate" ownership to Charles's.

Weddings serve as the external sign of patriarchal power, and it is thus telling that the guardian of the house should be Miss Avery, who had refused Tom Howard's offer of marriage. If Dolly, whose principal occupation seems to consist of bearing children and whose nickname indicates her childishness and conventional femininity, can classify Miss Avery, and thereby dismiss her, as an "old maid" (HE 200), Margaret recognizes a kinship with the older woman. Miss Avery is Forster's presentation of a spirit of the land, a chthonic deity as well as a guardian of the matrilineal. Whatever Forster's personal misogyny, the novel is feminist in its concern for spiritual inheritance and continuation and against unnatural, or male, ownership. At the same time his insistence on Margaret's lack of interest in children and desire not to have any sets her apart from any earth-goddess view of the feminine. Like Miss Avery's, Margaret's feminism does not require physical begetting.

If weddings hold the family together and symbolically reënact male ownership, they also celebrate the nation and the empire, and Forster makes Margaret wonder about the simultaneous desire of the family to be together and to be safely distant. This paradox she links to colonialism, the desire to celebrate the nation by leaving it: "They had the colonial spirit, and were always making for some spot where the white man might carry his burden unobserved" (HE 201). Forster seems already to be thinking about his next novel, *A Passage to India,* when he has Lady Edser comment about Evie's wedding, which Margaret cuttingly thinks of as a "blend of Sunday church and fox-hunting," that it is "quite like a Durbar" (HE 220). Colonialism enters the novel, not simply as the source of income, but as a mode of possession analogous to compulsory heterosexuality.

The Wilcoxes' name is almost too obvious a symbol, but their identification with both the will and phallic possession is crucial to the novel's exploration of gender. At the same time, Forster keeps trying to avoid an essentialist idea of the "feminine" (to which, as I have already said, Margaret does not adhere) in part by recognizing the ways in which women such as Dolly and Evie may serve the purposes of the patriarchy. The Wilcox men may be phallic, but their sexuality remains physical and never spiritual. This can be seen most clearly in the comic bathing scene, with its ironic echoes of *A Room with a View*. While the wedding party is gathered, Charles and Albert Fussell set off for a bathe, only to encounter obstacles—the key to the bathing shed cannot be found, there is "a difficulty about a springboard" (HE 216)—that prevent them from swimming, or even undressing, until Margaret's voice sends them scurrying for cover. Unlike the scene in *A Room*, there is nothing even remotely erotic about this scene. The missing keys are an obvious phallic symbol whose lack indicates clearly the inability of the men to find access to the water: they are totally the products of culture alienated from the body. They are the possessors of the natural, by their claim to possess the land, and by their orthodox sexuality, whose conventionality they read as natural, but they are completely excluded from nature in the form of the pond, where they cannot function without the aid of servants. Margaret's position as silent voyeur echoes the scene's source in Whitman's famous "Twenty-eight young men" section of *Song of Myself* (section 11) while signaling the distance of this moment from its origins. Throughout the novel, keys represent possession and property; true owners such as Margaret do not need them. Whitman's romantic optimism and celebration of the body operate ironically, and control the novel's tendency to idealize.

Hay fever operates in a similar manner. From the beginning this allergy points toward an alienation from nature. Helen's first letter, in which she announces her engagement to Paul Wilcox, already suggests the impossibility of such a pair by its reference to Charles's hay fever, which apparently also afflicts Tibby, rendering him a comic, deflated version of the sickly aesthete (Wilfred Stone rather acidly calls him a "withered sissy" [*Cave* 252]). As Miss Avery explains, "not one Wilcox . . . can stand up against a field in June" (HE 270), as she shows Charles thwarted in his desire to give orders to the farmhands by a tickling that comes "from his father," a patrilineal succession. The Wilcoxes may "keep England going," as Margaret argues, but only by "breed[ing] like rabbits," in Miss Avery's terse commentary. The disease of alienation recurs at another crucial moment, when Henry Wilcox announces that he will leave Howards End to Margaret. The room the Wilcoxes use is "dark and airless," closed off against the hay, while Margaret, Helen, and the children are down in the field, celebrating the mowing. Forster's great accomplishment here is to make the "unnatural" Schlegel sisters, products of London, with their suggestions of lesbianism and incest, be the true inheritors of nature, while the Wilcoxes are now barred from the land by a congenital failing—hay fever, in a wonderful deflation of Fisher King myths of the sacred wound.

The fertility symbolism of the final scene owes something to anthropological studies of the early years of the century, which Forster also used in the earlier novels, particularly in the English mythology of *The Longest Journey*. Such symbolic stagings of reconciliation and absorption into the patterns of the seasons and natural growth run through early modernist texts, from Pater to Joyce and Eliot. They find crucial expression in Frazer's *The Golden Bough* with its account of the sacrifice of the tree god, a ritual that lies behind much of *Howards End*. Such patterns are found in the wych-elm, for Margaret a comrade, promising "hope on this side of the grave" (HE 203), not in some afterlife, and in the scene of the pollarding of the elms, intercut with Ruth Wilcox's funeral. Death and life intersect, death indeed is necessary to life, and even though surrounded by death the young woodcutter proceeds to his "mating" (HE 87), his easy masculinity a diversion to the mourning below, and a narrative distraction. The problem that Forster faced was how to employ this mythological material, with its celebration of fertility, without betraying his commitment to same-sex relations, to what the novel repeatedly, echoing Whitman, calls "comradeship," by which Forster seems to have meant to celebrate a sexuality that went *through* the sexual toward a transcendence that was still based in the body. Part of his solution to the dilemma of the heterosexuality of mythology was to diminish actual sexuality and conception, by, for instance, having Evie breed dogs as Dolly breeds children, while simultaneously maintaining a symbolic fertility that is not linked to physical reproduction.

The field suggests the fertility of the female body (from which men like the Wilcoxes or Tibby must be shut away) and can yield its hay to the two sisters and the children. It is a spirit of the garden that Ruth Wilcox, on the model of the Biblical Ruth, represents and passes on. In contrast, the men are identified by their inability to bloom, by their limitation to the phallus as weapon. Leonard's inability to tell Margaret that he has heard *Tannhäuser* lest he mispronounce the opera's title is painful social comedy at the expense of Leonard's feared inadequacies. Indeed, the use of the umbrella as a stand-in for Tannhäuser's staff, which eventually blooms, with the Schlegels' house as a very inadequate Venusberg, is a comic diminishment that displays the problem of the mythological in a world of real poverty. Helen's otherwise comic confusion about Leonard's tattered umbrella, which is "all gone along the seams" (HE 39) takes on additional meaning and anticipates Helen's later sexual encounter with Leonard, when one thinks of the umbrella as a sign of a reduced male potency.[4]

Similarly, the Schlegel sisters' sword, inherited from their father, and ultimately the weapon that brings down the bookcase and the weight of Western culture on Leonard, is an ironic rewriting of Siegfried's sword Nothung, forged out of the fragments of his father's sword. If the accumulation of capitalist wealth through colonial enterprise is an apt equivalent to the stolen Rhine gold, Leonard is a vastly inadequate avenger or lover. Siegfried's passion for his sister may, however, help determine the novel's insistence on sororal love. It is sufficient, though, that Henry should see Leonard as a sexual threat for him to respond to "the magic triangle of sex," which is specified as "a woman and two men" (HE 144). Seeing Leonard as a rival, Henry is "thrilled," both by his desire to possess the woman and by a rivalry, as between "two angry cocks," that is tinged with the erotic.

Leonard's general ineptness makes him an unlikely figure of male sexuality, as Katherine Mansfield noted in her journal: "I can never be perfectly certain whether Helen was got with child by Leonard Bast or by his fatal forgotten umbrella. All things considered, I think it must have been the umbrella" (121). Mansfield's *mot* obscures the extent to which *Howards End* "seeks to deconstruct" a phallic mode, in Elizabeth Langland's incisive account (256). If Leonard has often seemed "perfunctory" (*Forster* 136), in Summers's term, it is because Forster wants to establish a new kind of relation outside physicality. The union, or connection, at the heart of *Howards End,* is that between Helen and Margaret, and it is they who, acting on behalf of Ruth, can form a female sacred family assuring continuity.

There are few fathers in Forster's family constellations—the relations are those of aunt or uncle. This "avunculate," as Eve Sedgwick terms it (*Tendencies* 52–72), is not only a reflection of Forster's own situation as a fatherless man—although a godfather—but a political project that seeks to redefine a nonpatriarchal family that can efface or at least complicate the binary between friendship and marriage. Helen's flight from the Wilcoxes is also her flight from the masculine, to many of whose values her sister adheres. A flighty romantic from our first glimpse of her, Helen seeks to be controlled, but not by men, whether by her brother-in-law, her lover, or the doctor sent by the Wilcoxes. The doctor promises science to oppose Margaret's love, and she responds with anger. For Margaret doctors can only "label" and ask of the Schlegels, "Were they normal?" (HE 286).

The "labelling" that Rickie wants comes now as a brand, not a promise: to define a gay identity is to be defined by one's identity. Helen's exile from England takes her to Germany, appropriately enough, as the home of the sexology that wants to see in the independent woman the "invert" even if her sexual "crime" has been with a man. Magnus Hirschfeld's scientific committee[5] and its fight for the rights of the homosexual (sexual intermediate) offered a model of political action but at the same time normalized and physiologized. The identification of sexology with Germany was widespread—in *Maurice* Dr. Barry knows nothing about homosexuality, since anything published on the subject was "in German and therefore suspect" (M 147). Helen's stay in Germany during her pregnancy indeed brings her together with Monica, a journalist with whom she shares a flat. Margaret states pointedly "you are very fond of her then," to which Helen replies more ambiguously "she has been extraordinarily sensible with me" (HE 290). Monica's model, apart from its clear suggestion of lesbianism, is deracinated. Although she lives in Germany, she is Italian by birth, and Margaret sums her up as "the crude feminist of the South," "*Italiano Inglesiato*" (HE 291). *Howards End* wants desperately to locate its mythologies, like its loves, in England, so that the house can find its rightful owner and the fields flourish, so that sexual dissidence can be restored as part of the world of nature from which it has been expelled.

The last scene is of the sisters and the child, joined by young Tom, a kind of John the Baptist to the baby's secular Jesus. Tom, the namesake of the "last" Howard, and representative of the values of the small farm being crushed by expansion and industrialization, had been sent by Miss Avery to offer milk and eggs to Helen and Margaret at Howards End, gifts that suggest the succoring, maternal quality of the house and its traditions. Forster's abiding love was for that kind of inheritance that could not stand up in a court of law and that need not be based on physical begetting. It was for friendship, whether within one sex or between the sexes. It could extend across generations, and give fertility to the childless. It could be located in a house, like the Hertfordshire house that served as a model for Howards End. And it could, as Marianne

Thornton's legacy did, "make my career as a writer possible" and thereby let love "follow me beyond the grave" (MT 325).

Even readers sympathetic to Forster have often worried about the apparent fleshlessness of his fictions and particularly of Leonard's relation to Helen. Less friendly critics such as Samuel Hynes have argued that Forster's own sexuality means that he "cannot handle" heterosexuality convincingly. For Hynes, Forster as a homosexual "was incapable of recording deep currents of feeling" (117). Without denying the somewhat programmatic nature of Forster's depiction of Leonard's conception of a child with Helen, I want to see the relation between Helen and Leonard in the context of a search on Forster's part for a queer kind of begetting that can lead to the construction of a queer "family." How to give permanence and continuation in time for the homosexual or anyone who does not biologically reproduce was one of Forster's most abiding concerns, echoed in life in his friendship with the Buckinghams and his godson and finding an ultimate expression in "Little Imber," written when he was 82.

This last story is a fantasy set in a bleak future marked by the virtual absence of men. The few remaining men are in demand to impregnate the women and produce boys. By mistake, two of these human studs arrive at the same time. They are at first competitive rivals, with the older man Warham, a vain and misogynistic former soldier, knowing "how to please [women] and to defer to them, even to skilfully simulating acts of rape" (AS 227), and the title character resenting the possible implications of his epithet "little" ("I can fertilize and I've got my certificate with me, but I won't be called little" (AS 228). Later, rivalry gives way to desire. In a comic display of bodies that expresses their male rivalry and anxiety, "hatred passed into wrestling" (AS 230), in a scene that marks Forster's surprising affinities with D. H. Lawrence's "Gladiatorial" in *Women in Love*. After this encounter with Imber, Warham is unable, as he puts it, to "consummate any intimate relationship unless Imber said fuck" (AS 232). When Warham returns to the "Birth House" and Imber, he realizes that their wrestling orgasm has given rise to a living organism—that two sperms have begotten! It is not, of course, the fantasy biology that is of interest here, but rather the agonistic relationships between men that had by now preoccupied Forster for 60 years. Warham now recognizes "how erotic that wrestling had been and how obscene its outcome" (AS 232), thus providing an unspoken subtext to relations such as Ralph and Tony's, or Philip's and Gino's. Forster's utopian fiction reveals an underside to his idealism, in his recognition of the erotic power of male rivalry and his desire to produce not a replica of heterosexuality but a "pleasing confusion" in which the "sons [get] raped by the wild boys and bugger their daughters, who [bear] sons" (AS 235), a queer babel of sexual desire. Although cast in a comic and sometimes misogynistic mode, the story is in many ways a continuation not only of the erotic desires of *Maurice* (whose love story apparently requires no progeny) but also of the other novels and their preoccupation with the intersections of death and desire.

Forster's insistence on an organic succession (such as that from Ruth Wilcox to Margaret Schlegel) in the context of early twentieth-century ideas of ritual and fertility meant that he could not situate his homosexuals in the city (where, despite the pastoral myth of *Maurice* they increasingly fled to find a social space), but that he must seek to locate them in the rhythms of nature, as he imagined them. This emphasis on fertility and the natural was part of his heritage from Walt Whitman and his English disciple Edward Carpenter, but it also reflected his need to see his aunt Marianne Thornton as the fundamental mother, enabling his life, even if she lived as a spinster. For Forster, begetting removed conception from the body to the mind and proposed a kind of elective inheritance.

Notes

1. *A Passage to India* follows this pattern, although in a more complicated manner. Aziz and Fielding are unable to perpetuate their friendship, but there is a physical continuation, through the "son and heir" (PI 298) of Fielding and Stella Moore, along with the continuation of the spirit of Mrs. Moore. This physical birth is intercut with scenes of "the Birth" of Krishna (PI 294) presided over and midwived by the "enigmatic" (PI 65) Brahman Godbole. The Hindu ceremony emphasizes a theology of incarnation in which the body/soul split is countered by the emergence of life out of death. As the narrator puts it, "religion is a living force to the Hindus," and in the festival "all men loved each other" (PI 294).

2. As Wilfred Stone has shown, Hegel was important for the idealism of the Cambridge Apostles, of which Forster was a member (Stone, *Cave* 48, 58). Stone calls particular attention to triadic patterns, present in Comte, Hegel, and Marx. Such triads are for him fundamental to the structure of *The Longest Journey* (*Cave* 189-90); Gertrude White has argued for the importance of Hegelian dialectics in *A Passage to India*.

3. See Heine's introduction to the Abinger LJ.

4. On the umbrella, see J. H. Stape.

5. A British branch of the Committee was not founded publicly until 1914; Forster was a member (Weeks 136).

Works Cited

Adams, Stephen. *The Homosexual as Hero in Contemporary Fiction*. London: Vision, 1980.

Allen, Peter. *The Cambridge Apostles: The Early Years*. Cambridge: Cambridge UP, 1978.

Alterman, Eric. "Neutering America." *Nation*. 19 Feb. 1966.

Bair, Deirdre. *Samuel Beckett*. New York: Harcourt, 1978.

Bakshi, Parminder. "The Politics of Desire: E. M. Forster's Encounters with India." In Davies and Wood 23–64.

Barthes, Roland. *Incidents*. Paris: Éditions du Seuil, 1987.

Bayley, John. "The Cambridge Humanist." *The Guardian*. 22 June 1962: 7.

———. "Letter to E. M. Forster." Ms. N.d [29 June 1962?]. Modern Archive Centre, King's College, Cambridge U.

Beauman, Nicola. *Morgan: A Biography*. London: Hodder & Stoughton, 1993.

Beckett, Lucy. *Richard Wagner: Parsifal*. Cambridge: Cambridge UP, 1981.

Beer, Gillian. "Negation in *A Passage to India*." In J. Beer, *Passage* 44–58.

Beer, John. *The Achievement of E. M. Forster*. London: Chatto & Windus, 1962.

———, ed. *A Passage to India: Essays in Interpretation*. London: Macmillan, 1985.

Bell, Clive. *Old Friends*. London: Chatto & Windus, 1956.

———. *Peace At Once*. London: National Labour, 1915.

Bell, Quentin. *Bloomsbury*. New ed. London: Weidenfeld & Nicolson, 1986.

———. *Virginia Woolf: A Biography*. 2 vols. London: Hogarth, 1972.

Bellringer, Alan W. *The Ambassadors*. London: Allen & Unwin, 1984.

Benjamin, Jessica. *The Bonds of Love: Psychoanalysis, Feminism, and the Problem of Domination*. New York: Pantheon, 1988.

Bergman, David, ed. *Camp Grounds: Style and Homosexuality.* Amherst: U of Massachusetts P, 1993.

———. "Strategic Camp: The Art of Gay Rhetoric." Rpt. in Bergman, *Camp Grounds* 92–109.

Bersani, Leo. *The Freudian Body: Psychoanalysis and Art.* New York: Columbia UP, 1986.

———. *Homos.* Cambridge, MA: Harvard UP, 1995.

Bersani, Leo, and Ulysse Dutoit. *Arts of Impoverishment: Beckett, Rothko, Resnais.* Cambridge, MA: Harvard UP, 1993.

Bhabha, Homi K. *The Location of Culture.* New York: Routledge, 1994.

Bharucha, Rustom. "Forster's Friends." *Raritan* 5.4 (1986): 105–22.

Birjie-Patil, J. "Forster and Dewas." *E. M. Forster: A Human Exploration.* In Das and Beer 102–8.

Blackmer, Corrine E., and Patricia Juliana Smith, eds. *En Travesti: Women, Gender Subversion, Opera.* New York: Columbia UP, 1995.

Blisset, William. "Wagnerian Fiction in English." *Criticism* 5 (1963): 239–60.

Boone, Joseph A. "Vacation Cruises; or, The Homoerotics of Orientalism." *PMLA* 110 (1995): 89–107.

Bradbury, Malcolm, ed. *E. M. Forster: A Collection of Critical Essays.* Englewood Cliffs, NJ: Prentice, 1966.

Bredbeck, Gregory W. "Missionary Position: Reading the Bible in 'The Life to Come.'" *Journal of Homosexuality,* forthcoming.

———. "The New Queer Narrative: Intervention and Critique." *Textual Practice* 9 (1995): 477–502.

Brett, Philip, ed. *Queering the Pitch.* New York: Routledge, 1994.

Bristow, Joseph. *Effeminate England: Homoerotic Writing after 1885.* New York: Columbia UP, 1995.

———. "Passage to E. M. Forster: Race, Homosexuality, and the 'Unmanageable Streams' of Empire." In Chris Gittings, ed. *Imperialism and Gender: Representations of Masculinity.* Hebden Bridge, UK: Dangaroo, 1996.

Britten, Benjamin. "Some Notes on Forster and Music." In Stallybrass 81–86.

Brooks, Peter. *Body Work: Objects of Desire in Modern Narrative.* Cambridge, MA: Harvard UP, 1993.

Brown, Tony. "Edward Carpenter and the Discussion of the Cow in *The Longest Journey.*" *Review of English Studies* ns 33 (1982): 58–62.

———. "Edward Carpenter and the Evolution of *A Room with a View.*" *ELT* 30 (1987): 279–300.

———. "E. M. Forster's *Parsifal*: A Reading of *The Longest Journey.*" *Journal of European Studies* 12 (1982): 30–54.

Burke, Carolyn, Naomi Schor, and Margaret Whitford, eds. *Engaging with Irigaray: Feminist Philosophy and Modern European Thought.* New York: Columbia UP, 1994.

Burke, Kenneth. "Policy Made Personal: Whitman's Verse and Prose-Salient Traits." *Leaves of Grass One Hundred Years After: Essays by William Carlos Williams, Richard Chase, Leslie A. Fiedler, Kenneth Burke, David Daiches, and J. Middleton Murry.* Ed. Milton Hindus. Stanford: Stanford UP, 1955. 74–108.

Burra, Peter. "The Novels of E. M. Forster." *The Nineteenth Century and After.* Nov. 1934. Rpt. in PI 315–27.

Butler, Judith. *Bodies That Matter: On the Discursive Limits of "Sex."* New York: Routledge, 1993.

Butler, Samuel. *Erewhon Revisited.* London: Dent, 1932.

———. *The Way of All Flesh.* London: Penguin, 1947.

Cadmus, Paul. Letter ("Cadmus on 'Gay Artists' "). *Art in America*, Feb. 1993: 23.

Carpenter, Edward. *From Adam's Peak to Elephanta: Sketches in Ceylon and India.* London: Allen & Uwin, 1921.

———. "Homogenic Love." 1894. Rpt. in *Sexual Heretics.* Ed. Brian Reade. New York: Coward, McCann, 1971. 324–47.

———. *Selected Writings.* Vol. I: *Sex.* London: GMP, 1984.

———. *Towards Democracy.* London: GMP, 1984.

Cavaliero, Glen. *A Reading of E. M. Forster.* London: Macmillan, 1979.

Caws, Mary Ann. *The Women of Bloomsbury: Virginia, Vanessa, and Carrington.* New York: Routledge, 1990.

Charles, Casey. "A Horse Is a Horse: Love and Sex in Plato's *Phaedrus.*" *Literature and Psychology* 38 (1992): 47–70.

Charteris, Evan. *The Life and Letters of Sir Edmund Gosse.* London: Heinemann, 1931.

Cixous, Hélène, and Catherine Clément. *The Newly Born Woman.* Trans. Betsy Wing. Minneapolis: U of Minnesota P, 1975.

Code, Lorraine. *What Can She Know: Feminist Theory and the Construction of Knowledge.* Ithaca: Cornell UP, 1991.

Cohen, William A. *Sex Scandal: The Private Parts of Victorian Fiction.* Durham: Duke UP, 1996.

Colby, F. M. "The Queerness of Henry James." *Bookman* (United States) 15 (1902): 397–407. Rpt. as "F. M. Colby on James's Bloodless Perversity" in *Henry James: The Critical Heritage.* Ed. Roger Gard. New York: Barnes & Noble, 1968. 335–38.

Craft, Christopher. "Alias Bunbury: Desire and Termination in *The Importance of Being Earnest.*" *Representations* 31 (Summer 1990): 19–46.

———. *Another Kind of Love: Male Homosexual Desire in English Discourse, 1850–1920.* Berkeley: U of California P, 1994.

Creech, James. *Closet Writing/Gay Reading.* Chicago: U of Chicago P, 1993.

Crews, Frederick C. *E. M. Forster: The Perils of Humanism.* Princeton: Princeton UP, 1962.

Cummings, Katherine. "A Spurious Set (Up): 'Fetching Females' and 'Seductive' Theories in *Phaedrus,* 'Plato's Pharmacy,' and *Spurs.*" *Genders* 8 (1990): 38–61.

Das, G. K., and John Beer, eds. *E. M. Forster: A Human Exploration: Centenary Essays.* London: Macmillan, 1979.

Davies, Tony. "Introduction." In Davies and Wood 1–22.

Davies, Tony, and Nigel Wood, eds. *A Passage to India.* Philadelphia: Open UP, 1994.

Dean, Tim. "On the Eve of a Queer Future." *Raritan* 15.1 (1995): 116–34.

DeKoven, Marianne. *Rich and Strange: Gender, History, Modernism.* Princeton: Princeton UP, 1991.

Delany, Paul. *The Neo-Pagans: Rupert Brooke and the Ordeal of Youth.* New York: Free Press, 1987.

de Lauretis, Teresa. "Queer Theory: Lesbian and Gay Sexualities." *differences* 3.2 (1991): iii–xviii.

Dellamora, Richard. *Apocalyptic Overtures: Sexual Politics and the Sense of an Ending.* New Brunswick, NJ: Rutgers UP, 1994.

———. *Masculine Desire: The Sexual Politics of Victorian Aestheticism.* Chapel Hill: U of North Carolina P, 1990.

———. "Textual Politics/Sexual Politics." *MLQ* 54 (1993): 155–64.

Derrida, Jacques. *Of Grammatology.* Trans. Gayatri Spivak. Baltimore: Johns Hopkins UP, 1978.

Dickinson, G. Lowes. *The Autobiography of G. Lowes Dickinson and Other Unpublished Writings.* Ed. Dennis Proctor. London: Duckworth, 1973.

———. *The Greek View of Life.* London: Methuen, 1896.

DiGaetani, John Louis. *Richard Wagner and the Modern British Novel.* Rutherford, NJ: Fairleigh Dickinson UP, 1978.

Dowling, David. *Bloomsbury Aesthetics and the Novels of Forster and Woolf.* London: Macmillan, 1985.

Eagleton, Terry. *Exiles and Émigrés: Studies in Modern Literature.* London: Chatto & Windus, 1970.

———. *The Function of Criticism: From The Spectator to Post-Structuralism.* London: Verso, 1984.

———. "Modernism in Ireland." MLA Convention. San Diego Marriott, San Diego, 29 Dec. 1994.

Edel, Leon. *Henry James: A Life.* New York: Harper, 1985.

Edelman, Lee. "Homographesis." *Yale Journal of Criticism* 3 (1989): 189–207.

———. "Queer Theory: Unstaging Desire." *GLQ* 2 (1995): 343–46.

Ellis, Havelock, and John Addington Symonds. *Sexual Inversion.* London: Wilson and Macmillan, 1897.

Ellmann, Mary. *Thinking About Women.* New York: Harcourt, 1968.

Erkkila, Betsy. " 'Song of Myself' and the Politics of the Body Erotic." *Ap-*

proaches to Teaching Whitman's Leaves of Grass. Ed. Donald D. Kummings. New York: MLA, 1990. 56–63.

———. *Whitman the Political Poet.* New York: Oxford UP, 1989.

Flax, Jane. "Mother-Daughter Relationships: Psychodynamics, Politics and Philosophy." *The Future of Difference.* Eds. Hester Eisenstein and Alice Jardine. New Brunswick, NJ: Rutgers UP, 1985. 20–40.

Fletcher, John. "Forster's Self-Erasure: *Maurice* and the Scene of Masculine Love." *Sexual Sameness: Textual Differences in Lesbian and Gay Writing.* Ed. Joseph Bristow. New York: Routledge, 1992. 64–90.

Folsom, Ed. "Whitman's Calamus Photographs." *Breaking Bounds: Whitman and American Cultural Studies.* Eds. Betsy Erkkila and Jay Grossman. New York: Oxford UP, 1996. 193–219.

Forster, E. M. *Abinger Harvest* [AH]. 1936. New York: Harcourt, 1966.

———. *Albergo Empedocle and Other Writings* [AE]. Ed. George H. Thomson. New York: Liveright, 1971.

———. *Arctic Summer and Other Fiction* [AS]. Ed. Elizabeth Heine. Abinger Ed. 9. London: Edward Arnold, 1980.

———. *Aspects of the Novel* [AN]. London: Edward Arnold, 1927.

———. "Cocoanut & Co.: Entrance to an Abandoned Novel." *New York Times Book Review,* 6 Feb. 1949: 3, 31.

———. *Collected Tales of E. M. Forster* [CT]. 1947. New York: Modern Library, 1968.

———. *Commonplace Book* [CB]. Ed. Philip Gardner. Stanford: Stanford UP, 1985.

———. "Entrance to an Unwritten Novel." *The Listener,* 23 Dec. 1948: 975–76.

———. *Goldsworthy Lowes Dickinson* [GLD]. 1934. Abinger Ed. 13. Ed. Oliver Stallybrass. London: Edward Arnold, 1973.

———. *The Hill of Devi* [HD]. 1953. Abinger Ed. 14. Ed. Elizabeth Heine. London: Edward Arnold, 1983.

———. *Howards End* [HE]. 1910. Abinger Ed. 4. Ed. Oliver Stallybrass. London: Edward Arnold, 1973.

———. "Letter to John Bayley." Ms. N.d. Modern Archive Centre, King's College, Cambridge U.

———. *The Life to Come and Other Stories* [LTC]. Abinger Ed. 8. Ed. Oliver Stallybrass. London: Edward Arnold, 1972.

———. *The Longest Journey* [LJ]. 1907. Abinger Ed. 2. Ed. Elizabeth Heine. London: Edward Arnold, 1984.

———. "Luigi Cornaro." Ts. Vo 8/22, fo 52–63. Modern Archive Centre, King's College, Cambridge U.

———. *Marianne Thornton: A Domestic Biography* [MT]. New York: Harcourt: 1956.

———. *Maurice* [M]. New York: Norton, 1971.

———. *A Passage to India* [PI]. 1924. Abinger Ed. 6. Ed. Oliver Stallybrass. London: Edward Arnold, 1978.

———. "Prefatory Note." *A Passage to India*. By E. M. Forster. London: Everyman, 1957. Rpt. in PI 313.

———. *A Room with a View* [RV]. 1908. Abinger Ed. 3. Ed. Oliver Stallybrass. London: Edward Arnold, 1977.

———. *Selected Letters of E. M. Forster* [SL]. Ed. Mary Lago and P. N. Furbank. 2 vols. Cambridge, MA: Harvard UP, 1983, 1985.

———. "That the Mere Glimpse." Ms. Vo 8/19, fo. 76. Modern Archive Centre, King's College, Cambridge U.

———. *Two Cheers for Democracy* [TCD]. 1951. Abinger Ed. 11. Ed. Oliver Stallybrass. London: Edward Arnold, 1972.

———. *Where Angels Fear to Tread* [WAFT]. 1904. Abinger Ed. 1. Ed. Oliver Stallybrass. London: Edward Arnold, 1975.

Forster, E. M., and Virginia Woolf. "The New Censorship." *Nation and Athenaeum* 43 (1928): 726.

Foucault, Michel. *The History of Sexuality*. Vol. 1: *An Introduction*. Trans. Robert Hurley. New York: Vintage, 1990.

———. *The Order of Things*. New York: Pantheon, 1970.

———. "A Preface to Transgression." *Language, Counter-Memory, Practice*. Ed. Donald F. Bouchard. Trans. Donald F. Bouchard and Sherry Simon. Ithaca: Cornell UP, 1977. 29–52.

Freedman, Jonathan. *Professions of Taste: Henry James, British Aestheticism, and Commodity Culture*. Stanford: Stanford UP, 1990.

Freud, Sigmund. *Introductory Lectures on Psychoanalysis*. Trans./ed. James Strachey. New York: Norton, 1966.

———. *The Sexual Enlightenment of Children*. Ed. Philip Rieff. New York: Macmillan, 1963.

———. *The Standard Edition of the Complete Psychological Works of Sigmund Freud*. 24 vols. Trans./ed. James Strachey and Anna Freud. London: Hogarth, 1953–81.

Friedländer, Paul. *Plato: The Dialogues*, Vol. 3: *Second and Third Periods*. Trans. Hans Meyerhoff. Princeton: Princeton UP, 1969.

Furbank, P. N. *E. M. Forster: A Life*. 2 vols. New York: Harcourt, 1977, 1978.

———. "The Philosophy of E. M. Forster." In Herz and Martin 37–51.

Furness, Raymond. *Wagner and Literature*. New York: St. Martin's, 1982.

Fussell, Paul. *The Great War and Modern Memory*. London: Oxford UP, 1975.

Gallop, Jane. *The Daughter's Seduction*. Ithaca: Cornell UP, 1982.

Gardner, Philip, ed. *E. M. Forster: The Critical Heritage*. London: Routledge, 1973.

Garnett, David. "Forster and Bloomsbury." In Stallybrass 29–35.

Gide, André. "Henry James." *The Question of Henry James: A Collection of Critical Essays*. Ed. F. W. Dupee. London: Allan Wingate, 1947. 251–53.

Gilbert, Sandra M., and Susan Gubar. *No Man's Land: The Place of the Woman*

Writer in the Twentieth Century. Vol. 1: *The War of the Words.* New Haven: Yale UP, 1988.

Grant, Kathleen. "*Maurice* as Fantasy." In Herz and Martin 191–203.

Greer, Germaine. *The Obstacle Race.* New York: Farrar, Straus, Giroux, 1979.

Grey, Antony. *Quest for Justice.* London: Sinclair-Stevenson, 1992.

Halperin, David. *One Hundred Years of Homosexuality.* New York: Routledge, 1990.

Harding, Sandra, and Merrill B. Hintikka, eds. *Discovering Reality: Feminist Perspectives on Epistemology, Metaphysics, Methodology and Philosophy of Science.* Dordrecht: Reidel, 1983.

Harrison, Bernard. *Inconvenient Fictions: Literature and the Limits of Theory.* New Haven: Yale UP, 1991.

Harrison, Charles. *English Art and Modernism, 1900–1939.* Bloomington: Indiana UP, 1981. Rpt. New Haven: Yale UP, 1994.

Heger, Heinz. *The Men with the Pink Triangle.* Trans. David Fernbach. Boston: Alyson, 1980.

Heilbrun, Carolyn. *Toward a Recognition of Androgyny.* New York: Knopf, 1964.

Heine, Elizabeth. "Editor's Introduction." In LJ vii–lxv.

Herz, Judith Scherer. "The Double Nature of Forster's Fiction: *A Room with a View* and *The Longest Journey. ELT* 21 (1978): 254–65.

———. *A Passage to India: Nation and Narration.* New York: Twayne, 1993.

———. *The Short Narratives of E. M. Forster.* New York: St. Martin's, 1988.

Herz, Judith Scherer, and Robert K. Martin, eds. *E. M. Forster: Centenary Revaluations.* London: Macmillan, 1982.

Higson, Andrew. "Re-Presenting the National Past: Nostalgia and Pastiche in the Heritage Film." *Fires Were Started: British Cinema and Thatcherism.* Ed. Lester Friedman. Minneapolis: U of Minnesota P, 1993. 109–29.

Himmelfarb, Gertrude. *Marriage and Morals among the Victorians.* New York: Knopf, 1986.

Hodges, Andrew, and David Hutter. *With Downcast Gays: Aspects of Homosexual Self-Oppression.* London: Pomegranate, 1974.

Holroyd, Michael. *Lytton Strachey: The New Biography.* New York: Knopf, 1994. (Revised ed. of *Lytton Strachey: A Biography,* 1967.)

Housman, A. E. *The Collected Poems of A. E. Housman.* New York: Holt, 1965.

Hutcheon, Linda. *Irony's Edge: The Theory and Politics of Irony.* London: Routledge, 1994.

Hutcheon, Linda, and Michael Hutcheon. *Opera: Desire, Disease, Death.* Lincoln: U of Nebraska P, 1996.

Hyam, Ronald. *Empire and Sexuality.* Manchester: Manchester UP, 1990.

Hynes, Samuel. *Edwardian Occasions: Essays on English Writing in the Early Twentieth Century.* London: Routledge, 1972.

Irigaray, Luce. *An Ethics of Sexual Difference.* Trans. Carolyn Burke and Gillian C. Gill. Ithaca: Cornell UP, 1993.

————. *Speculum of the Other Woman.* Trans. Gillian C. Gill. Ithaca: Cornell UP, 1985.

Isherwood, Christopher. *Christopher and His Kind: 1929–1939.* New York: Farrar, Strauss, Giroux, 1976.

Jackson, Tony E. *The Subject of Modernism: Narrative Alterations in the Fiction of Eliot, Conrad, Woolf, and Joyce.* Ann Arbor: U of Michigan P, 1994.

James, Henry. *The Ambassadors.* Ed. S. P. Rosenbaum. New York: Norton, 1964.

————. *Letters.* Ed. Leon Edel. Vol. 4. Cambridge, MA: Belknap/Harvard UP, 1984.

————. *Literary Criticism: Essays on Literature, American Writers, English Writers.* New York: Library of America, 1984.

————. *Literary Criticism: French Writers, Other European Writers, The Prefaces to the New York Edition.* New York: Library of America, 1984.

————. *The Notebooks of Henry James.* Eds. F. O. Matthiessen and Kenneth B. Murdock. New York: George Braziller, 1955.

Jameson, Fredric. "Modernism and Imperialism." *Nationalism, Colonialism, and Literature.* Ed. Seamus Deane. Minneapolis: U of Minnesota P, 1990. 43–65.

Jardine, Alice A. *Gynesis: Configurations of Woman and Modernity.* Ithaca: Cornell UP, 1985.

Jebb, R. C., ed. and trans. *The Characters of Theophrastus: An English Translation from a Revised Text.* London: Macmillan, 1870.

Jones, Ernest. *Essays in Applied Psycho-Analysis.* Vol. 1. London: Hogarth, 1951.

Kahn, Coppélia. "The Hand That Rocks the Cradle: Recent Gender Theories and Their Implications." *The (M)other Tongue.* Eds. Shirley Nelson Garner et al. Ithaca: Cornell UP, 1985. 72–88.

Kaplan, Fred. *Henry James: The Imagination of Genius.* New York: Morrow, 1992.

Kapur, Ratna, and Brenda Cossman. "Communalising Gender/Engendering Community: Women, Legal Discourse, and Saffron Agenda." *Economic and Political Weekly* 24 Apr. 1993: 35–44.

Katrak, Ketu H. "Indian Nationalism, Gandhian 'Satyagraha,' and Representations of Female Sexuality." In Parker 395–406.

Kennedy, Ellen, and Susan Mendus. *Women in Western Political Philosophy.* New York: St. Martin's, 1987.

Kenner, Hugh. *The Pound Era.* Berkeley: U of California P, 1971.

Keynes, John Maynard. *The Economic Consequences of the Peace.* New York: Harcourt, 1920.

Killingsworth, M. Jimmie. "Whitman's I: Person, Persona, Self, Sign." *Approaches to Teaching Whitman's Leaves of Grass.* Ed. Donald D. Kummings. New York: MLA, 1990. 28–40.

King, James. *Virginia Woolf.* London: Penguin, 1995.

Kirstein, Lincoln. *Paul Cadmus.* San Francisco: Pomegranate Arts, 1992.

Kipling, Rudyard. *Rudyard Kipling's Verse: The Definitive Edition*. Garden City, NJ: Doubleday, 1942.

Klein, Karen. "The Feminine Predicament in Conrad's *Nostromo*," *Brandeis Essays in Literature*. Ed. John Smith. Waltham, MA: Department of English and American Literature, Brandeis U, 1983. 101–16.

Koestenbaum, Wayne. *The Queen's Throat: Opera, Homosexuality, and the Mystery of Desire*. New York: Poseidon, 1993.

Kristeva, Julia. *About Chinese Women*. Trans. Anita Barrows. London: Marion Boyars, 1977.

———. *Tales of Love*. Trans. Leon S. Roudiez. New York: Columbia UP, 1987.

Lacan, Jacques. *Écrits, A Selection*. Trans. Alan Sheridan. New York: Norton, 1977.

Lane, Christopher. "The Psychoanalysis of Race: An Introduction." *Discourse* 19.2 (1997): 3–20.

———. *The Ruling Passion: British Colonial Allegory and the Paradox of Homosexual Desire*. Durham: Duke UP, 1995.

———. " 'Thoughts for the Times on War and Death': Militarism and Its Discontents." *Literature and Psychology* 41.3 (1995): 1–12.

———. "Volatile Desire: Ambivalence and Distress in Forster's Colonial Narratives." *Writing India, 1757–1990: The Literature of British India*. Ed. Bart Moore-Gilbert. Manchester: Manchester UP, 1996. 188–212.

Langland, Elizabeth. "Gesturing toward an Open Space: Gender, Form, and Language in E. M. Forster's *Howards End*. *Out of Bounds: Male Writers and Gender(ed) Criticism*." Eds. Laura Claridge and Elizabeth Langland. Amherst: U of Massachusetts P, 1990. 252–67.

Lawrence, D. H. *The Letters of D. H. Lawrence*. 7 vols. Ed. James T. Boulton. Cambridge: Cambridge UP, 1979–.

Leavis, F. R. "E. M. Forster." *Scrutiny* 7.2 (1938). Rpt. in Bradbury 34–47.

Leavitt, David. *The Lost Language of Cranes*. New York: Knopf, 1986.

Levenson, Michael. *A Genealogy of Modernism: A Study of English Literary Doctrine 1908–1922*. Cambridge: Cambridge UP, 1984.

———. *Modernism and the Fate of Individuality: Character and Novelistic Form from Conrad to Woolf*. Cambridge: Cambridge UP, 1991.

Levine, June Perry. "The Tame in Pursuit of the Savage: The Posthumous Fiction of E. M. Forster." *PMLA* 99 (1984): 72–88.

Levy, Paul. *Moore: G. E. Moore and the Cambridge Apostles*. London: Macmillan, 1979.

Lindenberger, Herbert. *Opera the Extravagant Art*. Ithaca: Cornell UP, 1984.

Litvak, Joseph. *Caught in the Act: Theatricality in the Nineteenth-Century Novel*. Berkeley: U of California P, 1992.

Litz, A. Walton. "Ithaca." *James Joyce's Ulysses: Critical Essays*. Eds. Clive Hart and David Hayman. Berkeley: U of California P, 1977. 385–405.

London, Bette. *The Appropriated Voice: Narrative Authority in Conrad, Forster, and Woolf*. Ann Arbor: U of Michigan P, 1990.

————. "Guerrilla in Petticoats or Sans-Culotte? Virginia Woolf and the Future of Feminist Criticism." *Diacritics* 21.2–3 (1991): 11–29.

Lowell, Amy. *Complete Poetical Works of Amy Lowell.* Boston: Houghton Mifflin, 1955.

Lowell, Robert. *Collected Prose.* Ed. Robert Giroux. New York: Noonday, 1987.

Lucas, John. "Wagner and Forster: *Parsifal* and *A Room with a View.*" *Romantic to Modern Literature: Essays and Ideas of Culture 1750–1900.* Sussex: Harvester, 1982. 206-31.

MacKinnon, Catherine. "Feminism, Theory, Marxism, and the State: Toward Feminist Jurisprudence." *Signs* 8 (1983): 635–58.

Malek, James S. "Forster's 'Arthur Snatchfold': Respectability vs. Apollo." *Notes on Contemporary Literature* 10.4 (1980): 8–9.

Mansfield, Katherine. *Journal of Katherine Mansfield.* Ed. J. Middleton Murry. London: Constable, 1954.

Marcus, Jane, ed. *New Feminist Essays on Virginia Woolf.* London: Macmillan, 1985.

————. "Liberty, Sorority, Misogyny." *Representation. of Women in Fiction: Selected Papers from the English Institute, 1981.* Eds. Carolyn Heilbrun and Margaret R. Higonnet. Baltimore: Johns Hopkins UP, 1983. 60–97.

————. " 'No More Horses': Virginia Woolf on Art and Propaganda," *Women's Studies* 4 (1977): 265–89. Rpt. in *Critical Essays on Virginia Woolf.* Ed. Morris Beja. Boston: G. K. Hall, 1985. 152–71.

————. "A Tale of Two Cultures." *Women's Review of Books* 9.4 (1994): 11–13.

————. *Virginia Woolf and the Languages of Patriarchy.* Bloomington: Indiana UP, 1987.

Marcuse, Herbert. *Eros and Civilization: A Philosophical Inquiry into Freud.* New York: Random House, 1955.

Martin, Biddy. "Sexualities without Genders and Other Queer Utopias." *Diacritics* 24.2–3 (1994): 104–21.

Martin, Robert K. "Edward Carpenter and the Double Structure of *Maurice.*" *Journal of Homosexuality* 8.3/4 (1983): 35–46.

————. "The Disseminal Whitman: A Deconstructive Approach to 'Enfans d'Adam' and 'Calamus.' " *Approaches to Teaching Whitman's Leaves of Grass.* Ed. Donald D. Kummings. New York: MLA, 1990. 74–80.

————. *The Homosexual Tradition in American Poetry.* Austin: U of Texas P, 1979.

Mayo, Katherine. *Mother India.* Delhi: Anmol Publications, 1986.

Meisel, Perry. *The Myth of the Modern: A Study in British Literature and Criticism after 1850.* New Haven: Yale UP, 1987.

Melville, Herman. *Billy Budd, Sailor and Other Stories.* Ed. Harold Beaver. London: Penguin, 1970.

Menand, Louis. *Discovering Modernism: T. S. Eliot and His Context.* New York: Oxford UP, 1987.

Meyer, Moe. "Reclaiming the Discourse of Camp." *The Politics and Poetics of Camp.* Ed. Moe Meyer. London: Routledge, 1994. 1–22.

Meyers, Jeffrey. *Homosexuality and Literature 1890–1930.* Montreal: McGill-Queens UP, 1977.

Miller, D. A. *The Novel and the Police.* Berkeley: U of California P, 1988.

Moi, Toril. "Representation of Patriarchy: Sexuality and Epistemology in Freud's Dora." *In Dora's Case: Freud—Hysteria—Feminism.* Eds. Charles Bernheimer and Claire Kahane. New York: Columbia UP, 1985. 181–99.

Montrose, Louis Adrian. " 'Shaping Fantasies': Figurations of Gender and Power in Elizabethan Culture." *Representations* 1.2 (1983): 61–94.

Moon, Michael. *Disseminating Whitman.* Cambridge: Harvard UP, 1993.

Moon, Michael, and Eve Kosofsky Sedgwick. "Confusion of Tongues." *Breaking Bounds: Whitman and American Cultural Studies.* Eds. Betsy Erkkila and Jay Grossman. New York: Oxford UP, 1996. 23–29.

Moore, George. *Confessions of a Young Man.* Ed. Susan Dick. Montreal: McGill-Queen's UP, 1972.

Morris, Mitchell. "Tristan's Wounds: On Homosexual Wagnerians at the fin de siècle." ACCUTE Conference. Brock University, St. Catharines, ON. 23 May 1996.

Mort, Frank. "Sexuality: Regulation and Contestation." *Homosexuality: Power and Politics.* Ed. Gay Left Collective. London: Allison and Busby, 1980. 38–51.

Muir, Edwin. Rev. of *A Passage to India.* By E. M. Forster. *Nation* 8 Oct. 1924. Rpt. in Gardner, 379–80.

Munich, Adrienne. *Queen Victoria's Secrets.* New York: Columbia UP, 1996.

Nattiez, Jean-Jacques. *Wagner Androgyne.* Trans. Stewart Spencer. Princeton: Princeton UP, 1993.

Nietzsche, Friederich. *The Genealogy of Morals.* 1887. Trans. Francis Golffing. New York: Anchor-Doubleday, 1956.

Ozick, Cynthia. "Forster as Homosexual." *Commentary* 52.6 (1971): 81–5.

Page, Norman. *E. M. Forster's Posthumous Fiction.* ELS Monograph Series 10. Victoria, BC: U of Victoria: 1977.

Parker, Andrew, et al., eds. *Nationalisms and Sexualities.* New York: Routledge, 1992.

Parry, Benita. "*A Passage to India:* Epitaph or Manifesto?" In Das and Beer 129–41.

———. "The Politics of Representation in *A Passage to India.*" In J. Beer, *Passage,* 27–43.

Partridge, Frances. *Memories.* London: Victor Gollancz, 1981.

Piggford, George. " 'Who's That Girl?': Annie Lennox, Woolf's *Orlando,* and Camp Androgyny." *Mosaic* 30.3 (1997).

Plant, Richard. *The Pink Triangle: The Nazi War Against Homosexuals.* New York: Holt, 1986.

Plato. *The Dialogues of Plato*. 4 Vols. Trans. Benjamin Jowett. London: Oxford UP, 1892.

———. *The Republic*. Trans. Benjamin Jowett. New York: Heritage, 1944.

Poole, Roger. "Passage to the Lighthouse." *Charleston Newsletter* 16 (1986): 16–32.

Potter, Nicholas. "*A Passage to India*: The Crisis of 'Reasonable Form.'" *Durham University Journal* 83 (1991): 209–13.

Pound, Ezra. *Literary Essays of Ezra Pound*. New York: New Directions, 1968.

———. *Selected Poems*. New York: New Directions, 1957.

Pratt, Mary Louise. *Imperial Eyes: Travel Writing and Transculturation*. New York: Routledge, 1992.

Ragland-Sullivan, Ellie. "Plato's *Symposium* and the Lacanian Theory of Transference: Or, What Is Love?" *South Atlantic Quarterly* 88 (1989): 725–55.

Rahman, Tariq. "The Significance of Oriental Poetry in E. M. Forster's *A Passage to India*." *Durham University Journal*. 81 (1988). 101–110

———. "The Homosexual Aspect of *A Passage to India*." *Studies in English Literature* (1984): 37–54.

Raitt, Suzanne. *Vita and Virginia: The Work and Friendship of V. Sackville-West and Virginia Woolf*. Oxford: Clarendon, 1993.

Ratti, Rakesh, ed. *A Lotus of Another Color*. Boston: Alyson, 1993.

Reed, Christopher. "Bloomsbury Bashing: Homophobia and the Politics of Criticism in the Eighties." *Genders* 11 (1991): 58–80.

———. "Imminent Domain: Queer Space in the Built Environment." *Art Journal* 55.4 (1996).

———. "Making History: The Bloomsbury Group's Construction of Aesthetic and Sexual Identity." *Gay and Lesbian Studies in Art History*. Ed. Whitney Davis. New York: Haworth, 1994. Simultaneously released as *Journal of Homosexuality* 27. 1–2 (1994): 189–224.

———. Review of *The Women of Bloomsbury: Virginia, Vanessa, and Carrington*, by Mary Anne Caws. *Charleston Magazine* 4 (1991–92): 49–52.

"Report from Bay Windows." Reprinted under "National Briefs." *Philadelphia Gay News* (3 May 1996): 3–9.

Restuccia, Frances L. "'A Cave of My Own': E. M. Forster and Sexual Politics." *Raritan* 9.2 (1989): 110–28.

Richards, I. A. "A Passage to E. M. Forster: Reflections on a Novelist." *Forum* 88 (1927): 914–20. Rpt. in Bradbury 15–20.

Rose, Phyllis. "Love in Bloomsbury." *New York Times Book Review* 22 July 1990: 11–12.

———. *Woman of Letters: A Life of Virginia Woolf*. New York: Oxford UP, 1978.

Rosecrance, Barbara. *Forster's Narrative Vision*. Ithaca: Cornell UP, 1982.

Rosenbaum, S. P., ed. *The Bloomsbury Group: A Collection of Memoirs and Commentary*. Revised Ed. Toronto: U of Toronto P, 1995.

————. *Edwardian Bloomsbury: The Early Literary History of the Bloomsbury Group*. London: Macmillan, 1994.

————. "*The Longest Journey*: E. M. Forster's Refutation of Idealism." In Das and Beer 32–54.

————. *Victorian Bloomsbury: The Early Literary History of the Bloomsbury Group*. New York: St. Martin's, 1987.

Ross, Andrew. "Uses of Camp." In Bergman, *Camp Grounds* 54–77.

Rowbotham, Sheila. "Edward Carpenter: Prophet of the New Life." *Socialism and the New Life: The Personal and Sexual Politics of Edward Carpenter and Havelock Ellis*. Sheila Rowbotham and Jeffrey Weeks. London: Pluto, 1977. 25–138.

Rushdie, Salman. "Outside the Whale." *American Film* 10.4 (1985): 70.

Said, Edward. *Orientalism*. New York: Vintage, 1978.

Salter, Donald. "That Is My Ticket: The Homosexual Writings of E. M. Forster." *London Magazine* 14.6 (1975): 5–33.

Schleiner, Winfried. "*Divina virago*: Queen Elizabeth as an Amazon." *Studies in Philology* 75.2 (1978): 163–80.

Schumpeter, Joseph A. *Ten Great Economists*. New York: Oxford UP, 1951.

Scott, Bonnie Kime. *Refiguring Modernism*. Vol. 1: *The Women of 1928*. Bloomington: Indiana UP, 1995.

Sedgwick, Eve Kosofsky. *Between Men*. New York: Columbia UP, 1986.

————. *The Epistemology of the Closet*. Berkeley: U of California P, 1990.

————. "Queer Performativity." *Pop Out: Queer Warhol*. Eds. Jennifer Doyle, Jonathan Flatley, and José Esteban Muñoz. Durham: Duke UP, 1996.

————. *Tendencies*. New York: Routledge, 1993.

Sessa, Anne Dzamba. *Richard Wagner and the English*. Rutherford, NJ: Fairleigh Dickinson UP, 1979.

Sharpe, Jenny. "Figures of Colonial Resistance." *Modern Fiction Studies* 3 (1989): 137–55.

Sherbo, Arthur. "Jamesiana: Assessments of James and His Work by Marianne Moore, Beerbohm, Forster, Madox Ford, and George Stonier." *Henry James Review* 15 (1994): 199–218.

Showalter, Elaine. *A Literature of Their Own: British Women Novelists from Brontë to Lessing*. Princeton: Princeton UP, 1977.

————. *Sexual Anarchy*. New York: Viking, 1990.

Sicker, Philip. *Love and the Quest for Identity in the Fiction of Henry James*. Princeton: Princeton UP, 1980.

Silver, Brenda. "Periphrasis, Power and Rape in *A Passage to India*." *Novel* 22 (1988): 86–105.

Silverman, Kaja. *Male Subjectivity at the Margins*. New York: Routledge, 1992.

Sinfield, Alan. *Literature, Politics and Culture in Postwar Britain*. Oxford: Basil Blackwell, 1989.

Skidelsky, Robert. *John Maynard Keynes: Hopes Betrayed.* New York: Viking, 1983.

Sontag, Susan. "Notes on Camp." *Partisan Review* 1964. Rpt. in *Against Interpretation.* 1966. New York: Anchor-Doubleday, 1990. 275–92.

Spurr, Barry. "Camp Mandarin: The Prose Style of Lytton Strachey." *ELT* 33 (1990): 31–45.

Stallybrass, Oliver, ed. *Aspects of E. M. Forster.* London: Edward Arnold, 1969.

Stape, J. H. "Leonard's 'Fatal Forgotten Umbrella': Sex and the Manuscript Revisions of *Howards End.*" *Journal of Modern Literature* 9 (1981–82): 123–32.

Steiner, George. "Under the Greenwood Tree." *New Yorker* 9 Oct. 1971: 158–69. Rpt. in Gardner 475–82.

Stevens, Wallace. "Men Made Out of Words." *The Palm at the End of the Mind.* Ed. Holly Stevens. New York: Vintage, 1972. 281–2.

Stone, Wilfred. *The Cave and the Mountain: A Study of E. M. Forster.* Stanford: Stanford UP, 1966.

———. " 'Overleaping Class': Forster's Problem in Connection." *MLQ* 39 (1978): 386–404.

Strachey, Lytton. *Biographical Essays.* San Diego: Harcourt, n.d.

———. *Eminent Victorians.* London: Penguin, 1971.

———. *Literary Essays.* San Diego: Harcourt, n.d.

———. *Queen Victoria.* San Diego: Harcourt, 1978.

Suleri, Sara. *The Rhetoric of English India.* Chicago: U of Chicago P, 1992.

Summers, Claude J. *E. M. Forster.* New York: Ungar, 1983.

———. *Gay Fictions: Wilde to Stonewall: Studies in a Male Homosexual Literary Tradition.* New York: Ungar, 1990.

Sussman, Herbert. *Victorian Masculinities: Manhood and Masculine Poetics in Early Victorian Literature and Art.* Cambridge: Cambridge UP, 1995.

Syberberg, Hans Jurgen, dir. *Parsifal* (film, West Germany). 1982.

Symons, Arthur. *Plays, Acting, and Music.* New York: Dutton, 1909.

Thomson, George H. "Cambridge Humor." In AE 37–43.

Thwaite, Ann. *Edmund Gosse: A Literary Landscape, 1849–1928.* Chicago: U of Chicago P, 1984.

Trilling, Lionel. *E. M. Forster.* New York: Harcourt, 1964.

———. *Freud and the Crisis of Our Culture.* Boston: Beacon, 1955.

———. *The Liberal Imagination.* New York: Viking, 1950.

The Upanisads. Trans. F. Max. Müller. 2 vols. Oxford: Clarendon, 1879 and 1884. Rpt. New York: Dover, 1962.

Vlastos, Gregory. *Platonic Studies.* Princeton: Princeton UP, 1973.

Wagner, Cosima. *Diaries.* Eds. M. Gregor-Dellin and D. Mack. Trans. G. Skelton. New York: Harcourt, 1976.

Wagner, Richard. *Parsifal* (libretto) in reissue of Bayreuth 1951. Cond. Hans Knappertsbusch. Teldec Classics International GMBH, 1993.

Warner, Michael. *Fear of a Queer Planet.* Minneapolis: U of Minnesota P, 1993.

Watney, Simon. "Critics and Cults." *Charleston Newsletter* 17 (1986): 25–29.

Watt, Donald. "Mohammed el Adl and *A Passage to India.*" *Journal of Modern Literature* 10 (1983): 311–26.

Weeks, Jeffrey. *Coming Out: Homosexual Politics in Britain, From the Nineteenth Century to the Present.* London: Quartet, 1977.

Weiner, Marc A. *Richard Wagner and the Anti-Semitic Imagination.* Lincoln: U of Nebraska P, 1994.

Wells, H. G. *Boon, The Mind of the Race, The Wild Asses of the Devil, and The Last Trump.* New York: Doran, 1915.

Wharton, Edith. *The Letters of Edith Wharton.* Eds. R. W. B. Lewis and Nancy Lewis. New York: Collier/Macmillan, 1988.

White, Gertrude. "*A Passage to India:* Analysis and Reevalution." *PMLA* 68 (1953): 641–57.

Whitman, Walt. *Complete Poetry and Selected Prose.* Ed. James E. Miller, Jr. Boston: Houghton Mifflin, 1959.

Widdowson, Peter. *E. M. Forster's Howards End: Fiction as History.* London: Sussex UP, 1977.

Wilde, Alan. "Desire and Consciousness: The 'Anironic' Forster." *Novel* 9 (1976): 114–29.

———. "The Naturalization of Eden." In Das and Beer 196–207.

Wilde, Oscar. *The Picture of Dorian Gray.* New York: Tudor, 1930.

Wilson, Angus. "A Conversation with E. M. Forster," *Encounter* 9 (1957): 52–57.

The Wolfenden Report. 1957. New York: Stein and Day, 1963.

Woolf, Virginia. *Between the Acts.* London: Hogarth 1941.

———. *The Diary of Virginia Woolf.* 5 vols. Eds. Anne Olivier Bell and Andrew McNeillie. New York: Harcourt, 1977–1984.

———. *Flush.* 1933. San Diego: Harcourt, 1983.

———. *Jacob's Room.* 1922. New York: Harcourt, 1960.

———. *The Letters of Virginia Woolf.* 6 vols. Eds. Nigel Nicolson and Joanne Trautmann. New York: Harcourt, 1975–1981.

———. *Moments of Being.* Ed. Jeanne Schulkind. New York: Harcourt, 1985.

———. "Old Bloomsbury." In Rosenbaum, *Bloomsbury* 40–59.

———. *Orlando.* 1928. San Diego: Harcourt, 1956.

———. *Roger Fry.* 1938. London: Hogarth, 1940.

———. *A Room of One's Own.* 1929. New York: Harcourt, 1940.

———. *Three Guineas.* 1940. London: Hogarth 1938.

———. *A Writer's Diary: Being Extracts from the Diary of Virginia Woolf.* Ed. Leonard Woolf. London: Hogarth, 1953.

Yingling, Thomas E. *Hart Crane and the Homosexual Text: New Thresholds, New Anatomies.* Chicago: U Chicago P, 1990.

Contributors

GREGORY W. BREDBECK, associate professor of English at the University of California, Riverside, is the author of *Sodomy and Interpretation* (Cornell, 1991). He has written essays on desire and sexuality that have appeared in many journals and anthologies, including *The Politics and Poetics of Camp* (Routledge, 1994) and *Between Men and Feminism* (Routledge, 1992).

JOSEPH BRISTOW has published extensively on the subject of homosexuality and literature and is the author of a large number of critical essays and book-length studies, including *Effeminate England: Homoerotic Writing after 1885* (Columbia, 1995). He is editor of collections including *Activating Theory: Lesbian, Gay, and Bisexual Politics* (co-editor, Lawrence and Wishart, 1993) and *Sexual Sameness* (Routledge, 1992). He is professor of English at the University of California, Los Angeles. He was previously senior lecturer in English at the University of York, England.

TAMERA DORLAND is a Ph.D. candidate in the English Department of the University of California, Los Angeles. Her essay in this volume was originally published in *Style*.

ERIC HARALSON, assistant professor of English at the State University of New York at Stony Brook, is writing a book on Henry James and masculinity, portions of which have appeared in *American Literature, Arizona Quarterly,* and *The Henry James Review*. He is also editor of *The Garland Encyclopedia of American Nineteenth-Century Poets*.

JUDITH SCHERER HERZ is professor of English at Concordia University, Montreal. Her major areas of research are seventeenth-century poetry, Bloomsbury, and narratology. Her publications include articles on E. M. Forster, literary biography, Chaucer, Shakespeare, Milton, Donne, and Aemilia Lanyer. She is the author of *A Passage to India: Nation and Narration* (Twayne, 1992); *The Short Narratives of E. M. Forster* (Macmillan, 1988); and, with Robert Martin, co-editor of *E. M. Forster: Centenary Revaluations* (Toronto, 1982).

CHRISTOPHER LANE is associate professor of English and Comparative Literature at the University of Wisconsin, Milwaukee. He is the author of *The Ruling Passion: British Colonial Allegory and the Paradox of Homosexual Desire* (Duke, 1995) and editor of *The Psychoanalysis of Race* (Columbia, 1998). He is currently completing *From Man to Man: Psychoanalysis and Victorian Masculinity* (Chicago, 1998).

CHARU MALIK, assistant professor in the English Department at Cardinal Stritch College, Milwaukee, teaches Third World and postcolonial women's literature. She is currently working on the representation of women and sexuality in the modern short story in Hindi and Urdu.

ROBERT K. MARTIN has written widely on gay studies, beginning with *The Homosexual Tradition in American Poetry* (Texas, 1979). He is the author of *Hero, Captain, and Stranger: Male Friendship, Social Critique, and Literary Form in the Sea Novels of Herman Melville* (North Carolina, 1986), editor of *The Continuing Presence of Walt Whitman: The Life after the Life* (Iowa, 1992), and co-editor, with Judith Herz, of *E. M. Forster: Centenary Revaluations* (Toronto, 1982). He is professor of English Studies at the Université de Montréal.

GEORGE PIGGFORD is assistant professor of English at Tufts University. His essay in this volume is part of a larger study of Bloomsbury and modernism; other essays have appeared in *Modern Drama* and *Mosaic*.

DEBRAH RASCHKE is teaching on a visiting appointment in the English Department at the College of William and Mary. She has published essays on modern and contemporary literature, and on poststructuralist theory and film, and she has recently completed a book on British modernism.

CHRISTOPHER REED is assistant professor of art history at Lake Forest College. His two edited volumes, *A Roger Fry Reader* (Chicago) and *Not at Home: The Suppression of Domesticity in Modern Art and Architecture* (Thames and Hudson), were published in 1996.

YONATAN TOUVAL is a Ph.D. candidate in the Department of English at Rutgers University.

Index of Forster's Works

General Index